DB2 Certification Guide

for Common Servers

Grant Hutchison
and
Calene Janacek

To join a Prentice Hall PTR internet mailing list, point to
http://www.prenhall.com/register

International Technical Support Organization
San Jose, California 95120

Prentice Hall PTR
Upper Saddle River, New Jersey 07458
http://www.prenhall.com

Note to U.S. Government Users--Documentation related to restricted rights--Use, duplication, or disclosure is subject to restrictions set forth in GSA ADP Schedule Contract with IBM Corp. More information about IBM, DB2, and the ITSO:

> http://www.ibm.com/services
> http://www.software.ibm.com/data/db2
> http://www.redbooks.ibm.com/redbooks

Editorial/production supervision: *Nicholas Radhuber*
Cover design: *Julie Santilli,* IBM
Cover design director: *Jerry Votta*
Manufacturing manager: *Alexis Heydt*
Acquisitions editor: *Mike Meehan*
Marketing Manager: *Stephen Solomon*
Editorial Assistant: *Kate Hargett*

Published by Prentice Hall PTR
Prentice-Hall, Inc.
A Simon & Schuster Company
Upper Saddle River, New Jersey 07458

The Publisher offers discounts on this book when ordered in bulk quantities.
For more information, contact: Corporate Sales Department, Prentice Hall PTR, 1 Lake St., Upper Saddle River, NJ 07458 Phone: 800-382-3419 Fax: 201-236-7141 ;E-mail:dan_rush@ prenhall.com.

The following terms are trademarks or registered trademarks of the IBM Corporation in the United States and/or other countries: ADSTAR, Distributed Database Connection Services, DRDA, DATABASE 2, DB2, Distributed Relational Database Architecture, AIX, AS/400, OS/400, VSE/ESA, OS/2, SQL/DS, MVS/ESA, IBM, VM/ESA.

The following terms are trademarks of other companies as follows:

HP-UX	Hewlett-Packard Company
Lotus, 1-2-3	Lotus Development Corporation
Microsoft, Windows, Windows 95	Microsoft Corporation
Windows NT, Open Database	Microsoft Corporation
Connectivity	Microsoft Corporation
PostScript	Adobe Systems, Incorporated
IPX/SPX, NetWare, Novell	Novell, Inc.
Solaris	SUN Microsystems Inc.
UNIX, X/Open	X/Open Company Limited

UNIX is a registered trademark in the U.S. and other countries licensed exclusively through X/Open Company Limited. DB2 Information on the Internet--http://www.software.ibm.com/data/db2

Printed in the United States of America
10 9 8 7 6 5 4 3 2 1

ISBN 0-13-727413-0
Prentice-Hall International (UK) Limited, *London*
Prentice-Hall of Australia Pty. Limited, *Sydney*
Prentice-Hall Canada Inc., *Toronto*
Prentice-Hall Hispanoamericana, S.A., *Mexico*
Prentice-Hall of India Private Limited, *New Delhi*
Prentice-Hall of Japan, Inc., *Tokyo*
Simon & Schuster Asia Pte. Ltd., *Singapore*
Editora Prentice-Hall do Brasil, Ltda., *Rio de Janeiro*

Table of Contents

*C*hapter 8 - Database Monitoring and Tuning 377

Foreword

Relastional database technology was invented at IBM Research over two decades ago and IBM delivered its first commercially available relational database products for mainframe and mid-range systems in the early 1980s. The power and promise of relational technology was the ability to represent data in simple tabular form and through the powerful SQL query language and put it in the hands of business analysts and other decision makers. Over the last fifteen years, many businesses have realized that promise. The presence of DB2 has grown incredibly as the DB2 family of products has expanded to include all of the popular UNIX and PC platforms. Today tens of thousands of businesses, large and small, in all corners of the world, rely on DB2 databases to store their key corporate data assets, and thousands of dedicated database professionals are charged with keeping these systems up and running 24 hours a day, 7 days a week, 365 days a year. But what we have seen over the last decade is only a small fraction of what is to come.

Data has become the addiction of the 1990s as businesses attempt to leverage it to improve the productivity of their people, provide better service and support to customers, improve overall efficiency, and reduce time to market with new products and services. All of these elements are driving the requirements for not only more business data, but also for database management systems that can store and search new data types such as text, image, time series, and spatial data. Key to achieving this will be the ability to store, organize, and search vast amounts of data -- and the advent of networked computing with the Internet and intranets has accelerated the requirement for these data types while it opens up enterprise databases to a whole new class of end users. All of these requirements are placing a tremendous amount of stress on existing database professionals. There is a shortage of qualified skills and there is an increasing demand to keep up with the latest advances in database technology.

The *DB2 Certification Guide for Common Servers* was developed to meet the needs of database professionals throughout enterprises of all sizes. Its purpose is to guide you through the fundamentals of administering and developing applications for IBM's latest database technology, DB2 Common Server. Because it is a self–study guide, you have the flexibility to proceed at your own pace. Upon completion of the exercises and sample tests, you should be able to pass the formal certification exams for the DB2 Database Administrator role and the DB2 Application Developer role. This is a very cost–effective way for database professionals to obtain a high level of competency with DB2 as well as an effective way for enterprises to ensure that they have the right skills on board.

The next millenium will bring tremendous opportunity and challenge to database professionals charged with the task of database adminstration or database application development. There will be an increasing demand for skilled professionals who can deal with the complexity of administering these very large, complex data stores and a corresponding pressure within organizations to reduce training costs. Increasingly the trend will be the responsibility of the individual to keep their technical skills current. This guide is a start. It was developed with the future in mind.

Janet Perna
Director of Database Technology
IBM Software Solutions Division

Preface

*T*his book is a complete guide to IBM's relational database servers, known as DB2 Version 2 for common servers. DB2 Version 2 is available on many operating systems, and the book has been written with this in mind. Any significant differences in the implementation of DB2 on various operating systems are highlighted. If you are planning to become certified, or you would simply like to understand the powerful new DB2 database servers from IBM, then read on. Those interested in becoming an IBM Certified Professional will want to review the sample questions at the end of each chapter. There are exercises provided at the end of many of the chapters to provide hands-on use of DB2.

The book is divided into 3 main sections:

- DB2 Fundamentals (Chapters 1–5)
  Installing and configuring DB2 servers and clients are covered in Chapters 1, 2, and 3. The Structured Query Language (SQL) is discussed in Chapter 4 and database conurrency is discussed in Chapter 5.
- DB2 Database Administration (Chapters 6–8)
  Creating a DB2 database and its related table spaces is covered in Chapter 6. The common administration tasks are discussed in Chapter 7, database monitoring and performance considerations are discussed in Chapter 8.
- DB2 Application Development (Chapters 9–10)
  Developing a static embedded SQL application is covered in Chapter 9. Alternate DB2 programming interfaces, including Call Level Interface (CLI) and dynamic embedded SQL, are discussed in Chapters 9 and 10.

Exercises are provided at the end of most of the chapters. The exercises make references to files which can be found on the companion CD-ROM. The exercises are provided to help confirm that the concepts discussed in the chapter are understood. Any DB2 operating environment can be used to perform the exercises.

This book can be used as a self-study guide to prepare for the DB2 certification exams or as a complete guide to DB2 Version 2.

The **path** to certification involves successfully completing two exams:

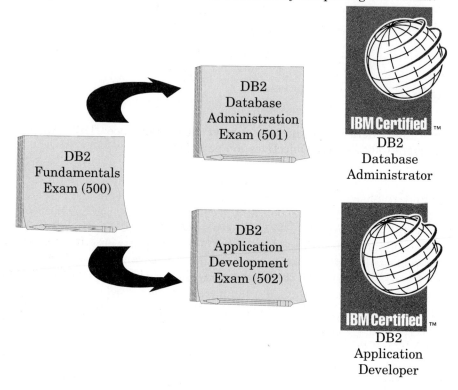

The test objectives are provided in Appendixes A, B, and C. These should be used as a guide to ensure that you are fully prepared to take the DB2 exams.

The DB2 Fundamentals Exam (500) covers these skills:

- Understanding DB2 products and components
- Creating database objects
- Understanding various DB2 data types
- Using SQL to manipulate database objects
- Describing DB2 concurrency

For more details on the contents of this exam, see "DB2 Fundamentals (500) — Test Objectives" on page 538.

The DB2 Database Administration Exam(501) covers these skills:

- Managing DB2 instances
- Creating and maintaining database objects
- Managing table spaces
- Using utilities: IMPORT, LOAD, REORG, RUNSTATS
- Managing recovery procedures (BACKUP/RESTORE)
- Analyzing resource problems

For more details on the contents of this exam, see "DB2 Database Administration (501) — Test Objectives" on page 542.

The DB2 Application Development exam (502) covers these skills:

- Developing static embedded SQL programs
- Developing dynamic embedded SQL programs
- Using host variables, parameter markers, and cursors
- Understanding dynamic SQL (Call Level Interface)

For more details on the contents of this exam, see "DB2 Application Development (502) — Test Objectives" on page 546.

Conventions

Many examples of SQL statements, DB2 commands, and operating system commands are included throughout the book. SQL statements are usually displayed within a shaded box and any of the mandatory sections of the statements are shown in uppercase. An example of an SQL statement is shown:

```
SELECT lname, fname
FROM candidate
WHERE          lname = 'HUTCHISON' OR
               lname = 'JANACEK'
```

SQL is not a case-sensitive language, so the above query would provide the same result regardless of the case of the SQL keywords, or the database object (table names or column names). Of course the data stored in the database is stored **exactly** as it was entered (including case). Therefore, the above query would only find the candidates with the last name of 'HUTCHISON' or 'JANACEK'. If the data were stored as 'Hutchison', it would not be part of the result table.

If SQL keywords are referred to in the text portion of the book, they will be shown as a bold mono-spaced font. For example, the **SELECT** statement is used to retrieve data from a DB2 database.

DB2 commands will be shown using the same method as SQL keywords. For example, the **CREATE DATABASE** command allows you to define the initial location of database objects. DB2 commands are issued from the Command Line Processor (CLP) utility. This utility will accept the commands in upper and lowercase. The CLP program itself is an executable called db2. In some operating systems, such as AIX, the program names are case sensitive. Therefore, be careful to enter the program name using the proper case.

There are a few operating system specific commands in this book. If the commands must be in lowercase they will be shown as such. For example, the UNIX command to create a user is the **mkuser** command.

Occasionally, notes are provided to highlight a particular point.

✍   A note may be used to explain a minor operating system difference
     or it may be used to summarize a concept.

There are a few syntax diagrams shown in the book. We recommend that the
Command Line Processor be used to verify the syntax of DB2 commands. Some
of the commands are shown with the complete syntax as shown in the Command
Line Processor. The following is an example of complete syntax of the DB2
BACKUP DATABASE command.

```
BACKUP DATABASE database-alias [USER username
[[USING password]] [TABLESPACE tbspace-name
[{,tblspace-name} ... ]] [ONLINE] [USE ADSM
[OPEN num-sess SESSIONS]] [TO dir/dev
[{, dir/dev} ...] | LOAD lib-name
[OPEN num-sess SESSIONS]] [WITH num-buff BUFFERS]
[BUFFER buffer-size] [WITHOUT PROMPTIMG]
```

A syntax diagram shows how the command should be entered using the
Command Line Processor. The diagram should be followed from left to right, and
from top to bottom. Parameters are regarded as keywords or variables. A
parameter can be a combination of a keyword and a variable.

- **Keywords** represent constants in the command. They are shown in
  uppercase in the syntax diagram. For example, **BACKUP DATABASE** is a
  keyword. A keyword may be entered in upper–, lower–, or mixed case.
- **Variables** are values that are user supplied. They are indicated in the
  command syntax using lowercase. At the command prompt, they may be
  entered in either upper–, lower–, or mixed case, unless case restrictions are
  explicitly stated. Some of the user-supplied variables are required, such as
  database-alias in the **BACKUP DATABASE** command.

The vertical bar "|" means that the keyword following is required. Optional
parameters are indicated in the syntax with square brackets "[" . An optional
parameter may have a possible list of user-supplied input values. This is
indicated with the combination of "[{" and three periods "...". For example, a
user may back up multiple tablespaces using a single **BACKUP DATABASE**
command. The *DB2 SQL Reference* should be used to verify the syntax of SQL
statements. To emphasize a term or concept, the term is shown in **bold** type or
emphasized with *italics*. If a user–defined column or table is being referenced it
will be shown in *italics*.

How this Book was Created

This book was a joint effort between the IBM Toronto Lab and the Austin ITSO (International Technical Support Organization). The ITSO is a group within IBM whose mission is to provide skill transfer on new products and technology worldwide. We provide direct feedback to the IBM software labs as we gather input from various groups of DB2 users, including IBM support personnel, customers and business partners.

The ITSO provides a working environment for interested individuals to work with new IBM software products. These individuals may include IBM employees and customers. The team develops a workshop or book, known as a redbook.

✐   ITSO redbooks — http://www.redbooks.ibm.com/redbooks

For the *DB2 Certification Guide for Common Servers*, three people came to IBM Austin, Texas for eight weeks. They brought with them different skills and knowledge, including customer experiences with DB2 common server. They were:

- Gabriel Banuelos
  Gabriel works for Infomedia, a database consulting firm in Mexico. He has been a database specialist working with DB2 since 1991. Today, he works primarily with DB2 for AIX, DDCS and other related products. Gabriel has also participated in DSS and data warehousing benchmarks and pilot projects for the financial industry in Mexico.
- Volker Gosch
  Volker is an I/T specialist at IBM Germany. He has been engaged in several projects as a DB2 specialist for OS/2 and AIX in the German Software Development Lab. He has been involved in helping many customers install and implement the Distributed Database Connection Service (DDCS) product as part of client/server solutions.
- Greta Mantesso
  Greta Mantesso is from Milan, Italy. She has worked for IBM since 1990. Greta works in the AIX Support Center supporting DB2 customers directly. She installs and customizes DB2 at a growing number of customer sites in Italy.

About the Authors

Grant Hutchison

Grant is a Staff Development Analyst at the IBM Toronto Lab. Since joining IBM in 1991, he has been working in the DB2 service and development team. He was part of the DB2 Version 2 development team and developed the DB2 Certification Program. Currently, Grant is a member of the DB2 customer service team in Toronto and is responsible for the DB2 education and skills development for the DB2 common server products. Grant has been a speaker at IDUG (International DB2 Users Group) and occasionally teaches DB2 courses.

Calene Janacek

Calene is the DB2 Project Leader for the International Technical Support Organization (ITSO) in Austin, Texas. She has been with IBM since 1989, working for the ITSO since 1993. Calene is responsible for producing technical manuals called "redbooks" that are used worldwide by support personnel and customers. She also develops workshops for new releases of DB2 that she teaches worldwide. She has presented at DB2 and AIX technical conferences.

Acknowledgments

We would like to thank the following people for assisting in the creation of this book. First off, we would like to thank the ITSO assignees and fellow authors of this book: Greta, Volker and Gabriel. Without their effort and cooperation the book would not have been completed.

There are many people in the IBM Toronto Lab we would like to thank for reviewing chapters and providing some sample exercises. They include: Enzo Cialini, Kim Glover, Paul Zikopoulos, Laurie Francisco, Bob Harbus, Kevin Hoang, Tanya Morley, Murray Chislett, Jim LeBlanc and Aleem Rajpar. In Austin, Frank Rusconi of the ITSO provided technical expertise.

We would like to especially thank Andrea Ward, as it was her initial idea to develop a self–study guide for DB2. Thanks also to one of the best DB2 instructors, Melanie Stopfer.

Thanks to the team at Prentice Hall PTR. Who were great to work with and very patient as we completed this book. Calene would like to thank Peter Coldicott for his support and understanding. Grant would like to thank Maria Morianou for her patience during the summer weekends of writing this book.

Products and Components

*I*n this chapter, you will be introduced to the DB2 family of products for the workstation environment. A description of each of the DB2 products will be provided, along with implementation scenarios for various clients and servers. The DB2 database server is available for many operating systems.

The DB2 database products are collectively known as the **DB2 Family**. The DB2 Family can be divided into two main groups:

- DB2 for midrange and large systems
  This group includes   DB2 for OS/400
                                 DB2 for VM
                                 DB2 for VSE
                                 DB2 for MVS
- DB2 for workstation environments (common servers)
  This group includes   DB2 for OS/2
                                 DB2 for Windows NT
                                 DB2 for AIX
                                 DB2 for Unix (various versions)

The DB2 products described in this chapter are all part of the DB2 common server section of the DB2 Family. The DB2 common server products include:

- DB2 Server
- DB2 Single-User
- DB2 Software Developer's Kit (SDK)
- Distributed Database Connection Services (DDCS)

DB2 provides seamless database connectivity using popular network communications protocols, including: NetBIOS, TCP/IP, IPX/SPX and APPC. The communications infrastructure for DB2 database clients and DB2 database servers is provided by DB2.

The installation of DB2 products and the licensing considerations are also discussed in this chapter.

DB2 Family

In Fig. 1–1, all of the DB2 database servers are shown. The database servers located above the dotted line are collectively known as **DB2 common servers**. This group of database servers and the related products are the main subject of this book. The other members of the DB2 Family are very similar to DB2 common servers, but due to operating system differences, their features and implementations differ.

✍️ For simplicity, we will refer to the DB2 common server family of products as DB2.

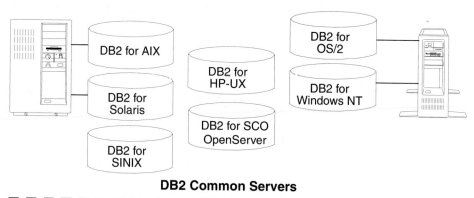

Fig. 1–1 DB2 Family of Database Servers

Every database application utilizes DB2 resources, known as databases. These databases can reside locally (on the same computer) or on a remote DB2 database server.

The database application can have been created to execute on any of the following platforms: AIX, OS/2, Windows, Macintosh, DOS or various UNIX operating environments. The operating environment of the client application is independent of the operating environment of the DB2 database server. Therefore, a single application can access one or more of the DB2 database servers shown in Fig. 1–1.

DB2 Components

Each DB2 product includes a number of components. These components provide a variety of functions. Most of the components are optionally installed; some are for database administration, and others are used for application development.

The DB2 folder is a full graphical user interface that is created on the desktop for environments such as, OS/2 and Windows NT. This DB2 folder is the most commonly used method to invoke the graphical tools provided with DB2. Fig. 1–2 shows some of the components of the DB2 product as they are displayed in the DB2 folder. A component usually relates to an executable application or utility. Therefore, simply double-clicking the DB2 icon will invoke the utility.

The DB2 components are packaged together within DB2 products. For example, the user-interface tool known as the Command Line Processor (CLP) is a component provided with **all** DB2 (common server) products.

✍🏻   DB2 components are provided within each of the DB2 products.

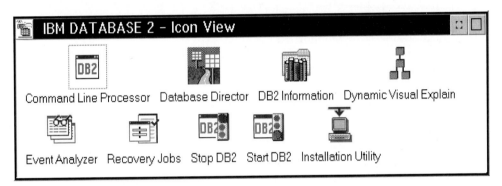

Fig. 1–2 DB2 Folder

Some of the available DB2 components are

- Client Application Enabler (CAE)
- Command Line Processor (CLP)
- Database Director
- Visual Explain
- Performance Monitor

The relationship between DB2 products and components is shown in Fig. 1–3. The functionality of the DB2 components can be slightly different across DB2 products. For example, the DB2 Command Line Processor (CLP) is a tool used to issue DB2 commands and SQL statements. The CLP component provided with the DB2 Software Developer's Kit (SDK) will provide the commands necessary for application development tasks. The CLP component provided with the CAE component does not include support for the application development commands.

Product / Component	DB2 Server	DB2 Single-User	DB2 SDK	DDCS Single-User	DDCS Multi-User
Client Application Enabler (CAE)	✓	✓	✓	✓	✓
Command Line Processor	✓	✓	✓	✓	✓
Database Director	✓	✓	✓	✓	✓
Visual Explain	✓	✓	✓		
Performance Monitor	✓				

Administrator's Toolkit { Database Director, Visual Explain, Performance Monitor }

Fig. 1–3 DB2 Products and Components

The **DB2 Client Application Enabler (CAE)** is a component common to **all** DB2 products. Once a DB2 application has been developed, the DB2 CAE component must be installed on each workstation executing the application. Fig. 1–4 shows the relationship between the application, CAE and the database server. If the application and database are installed on the same workstation, the application is known as a **local client**. If the application is installed on a different workstation than the DB2 server, the application is known as a **remote client**.

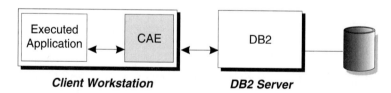

Client Workstation   *DB2 Server*

Fig. 1–4 Remote Client Accessing DB2 Server Using CAE

There are no licensing requirements to install the Client Application Enabler (CAE) component. Licensing is controlled at the DB2 database server.

The CAE installation depends on the operating system environment. For example, if you have a database application developed for AIX, you will need to install the Client Application Enabler for AIX.

There is a different CAE for each supported DB2 client operating system. Therefore, the CAE component should be installed on all end-user workstations.

A complete set of CAEs is provided with the DB2 Server and the DDCS Multi-Gateway products. This set of CAEs is provided on a CD-ROM and it is referred to as the *CAE Client Pack*.

DB2 Command Line Processor (CLP)

The Command Line Processor (CLP) is a component common to **all** DB2 products. It is a text-based application commonly used to execute SQL statements and DB2 commands. For example, you can create a database, catalog a database and issue dynamic SQL statements.

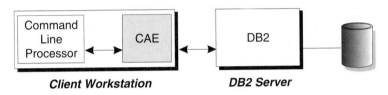

Fig. 1–5 Command Line Processor

Fig. 1–5 shows the Command Line Processor as an application that uses the CAE to communicate with the DB2 database server. The Command Line Processor can be used to issue interactive SQL statements or DB2 commands. The statements and commands can be placed in a file and executed in a batch environment or they can be entered from an interactive mode.

✍️   The DB2 Command Line Processor (CLP) is provided with the CAE component and the SDK, Single-User, Server and DDCS products.

All SQL statements issued from the Command Line Processor are dynamically prepared and executed on the database server. The output, or result, of the SQL query is displayed on the screen by default.

Many operations, such as making backup images of the database, are performed using DB2 commands. These commands can be issued from the CLP interface.

✍️   All of the DB2 commands are documented in the *DB2 Command Reference*.

DB2 Administrator's Toolkit

The DB2 Administrator's Toolkit contains a collection of tools that help manage and administer databases. You can optionally install the DB2 Administrator's Toolkit on any supported client or server workstation. The administration of the database can then be performed either locally at the server, or remotely from a client.

The DB2 Administrator's Toolkit consists of the following components:

- **Database Director**
- **Visual Explain**
- **Performance Monitor**

Database Director

The Database Director provides a graphical interface to perform many DB2 administrative tasks. These tasks are accomplished by manipulating the database objects within the database director (each database object is represented as an icon).

To invoke the Database Director either:

- type **DB2DD** at an operating system command line
- double-click on the Database Director icon from the DB2 folder (the folder is shown in Fig. 1–6)

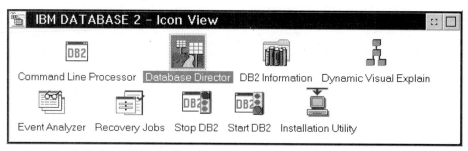

Fig. 1–6 Accessing the Database Director from the DB2 Folder

Each icon (DB2 object) is manipulated by using the **menu bar** or the **pop-up menu**. A single click of the mouse button will display the pop-up menu. Fig. 1–7 shows the Database Director interface. Many of the commands which can be issued from the DB2 Command Line Processor (CLP) can be performed using the Database Director interface.

In Fig. 1–7, the Database Director utility displays three database managers (known as DB2 instances): *DB2, INSTB,* and *SERV1.* DB2 databases are created within a DB2 **instance**. We can see in Fig. 1–7 that there is a database called *DB2CERT* created within the DB2 instance called *DB2.*

Let's compare the CLP interface and the Database Director interface. The Command Line Processor is a text interface used to issue DB2 commands and SQL statements. The Database Director is a graphical interface used to isssue DB2 commands only.

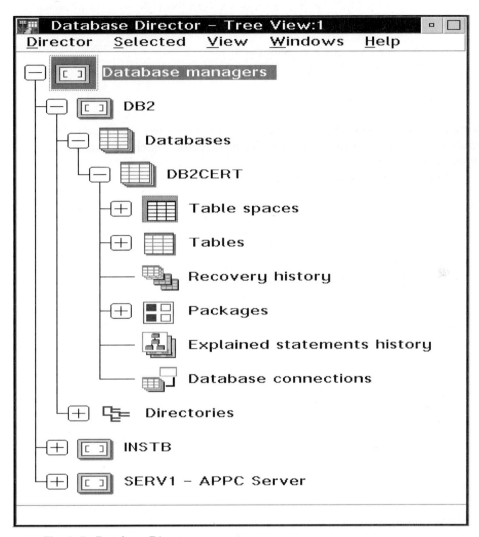

Fig. 1–7 Database Director

The Database Director can be used to perform the following tasks:

- Configure databases
- Configure instances
- Perform administrative tasks (back up and recover databases)
- Manage DB2 objects (table spaces, tables)

The Database Director, by default, displays the database objects as a tree view. You can decide to change the view representation into a list view. Using the mouse, you can highlight an object and then open the object to perform various actions. These actions are different for each database object.

A pop-up menu will be displayed when an object has been clicked once. You can perform various operations from the object's pop-up menu. For example, to configure a database, simply click on the database you wish to configure and select **Configure** from the pop-up menu.

You can notice in Fig. 1–7 that there is an icon called **Explained statements history**. This icon provides a method of invoking another graphical tool known as **Visual Explain**.

Visual Explain

The Visual Explain is a graphical utility that provides a visual representation of the access plans that the DB2 server used to obtain the data for an SQL statement.

Visual Explain can be invoked from the Database Director or by double-clicking on the Visual Explain icon in the DB2 folder. It also can be invoked by entering the command **DB2VEXP** from an operating system window. Fig. 1–8 shows an example of the type of information that is displayed. In this example the table being accessed is called *userid.test* and an index is being used. An approximation of the cost of the query is also provided in the Visual Explain output. The query in Fig. 1–8 has a cost of 537.46. These costs are only an approximation and they represent the complexity and resource usage expected for a given SQL query. More details on the usage of Visual Explain are provided in Chapter 8.

Performance Monitor

The Performance Monitor is a graphical utility available on most of the DB2 operating systems. There are two basic monitoring facilities:

- **Snapshot Monitor**
- **Event Monitor**

The **Snapshot Monitor** captures database information at specific intervals. The interval time and the data represented in the performance graph are configurable. Fig. 1–9 is an example of output from the Snapshot Monitor that displays the amount of logical reads and logical writes that occurred in the buffer pool. The example shows the buffer pool hit ratio. A buffer pool hit ratio of 100% means that the data for a query was retrieved from memory (buffer pool) and disk I/O (Input/Output) was not required. This is known as a high hit ratio and it is usually desirable for database queries. This tool can help to analyze performance problems, tune SQL statements and identify exception conditions based on limits or thresholds.

The **Event Monitor** captures database activity as defined by the monitor definition. The event monitor records are usually stored on disk and then analyzed after the data has been captured. There is a graphical tool called the **Event Analyzer** provided with DB2 to help analyze the captured data. More details on the usage of the DB2 monitors are provided in Chapter 8.

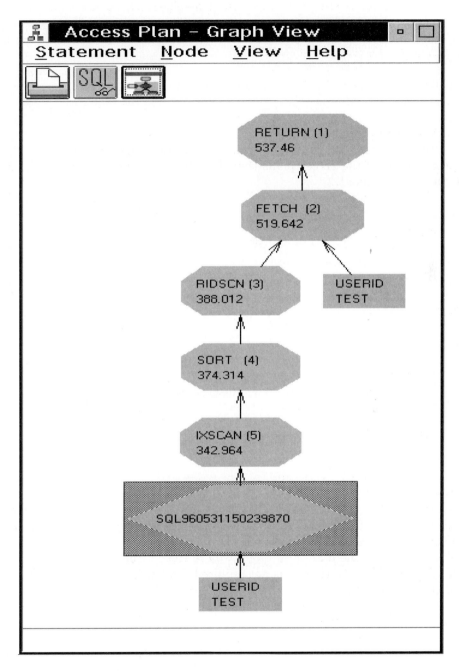

Fig. 1–8 Visual Explain Snapshot

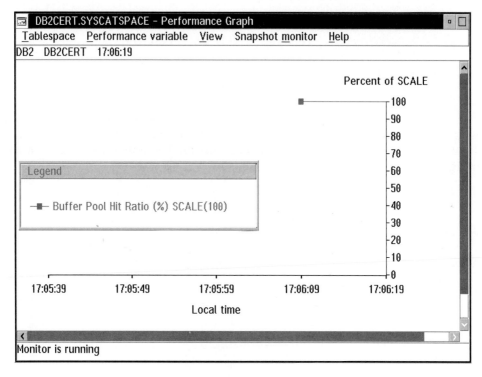

Fig. 1–9 Performance Monitor Sample Output

DB2 Products

The DB2 common server family consists of a number of DB2 products and components. We have discussed the installable DB2 components. Now let's examine the DB2 products. All DB2 products requires licensing. There are three main DB2 products, including:

- **Distributed Database Connection Services (DDCS)** — provides the necessary communication facilities to access DB2 for MVS and other 'host-based' databases
- **DB2 Software Developer's Kit (SDK)** — provides the necessary tools and utilities to develop DB2 applications
- **DB2 Server** — provides a relational database engine which allows incoming client requests for database information.

There are two DB2 products which provide a Relational Database Management System (RDBMS):

- **DB2 Single-User**
  An RDBMS engine which **will not** accept incoming database requests
- **DB2 Server**
  An RDBMS engine which **will** accept incoming database requests

The database engine is available in a standalone version called **DB2 Single-User** and a multi-user version called **DB2 Server**. The functionality of the database engine in both products is identical. The only difference is in the ability to accept incoming database requests.

DB2 Single-User

DB2 Single-User provides the same base–level engine functions found in DB2 Server. However, DB2 Single-User also includes the full DB2 application development environment found in the Software Developer's Kit.

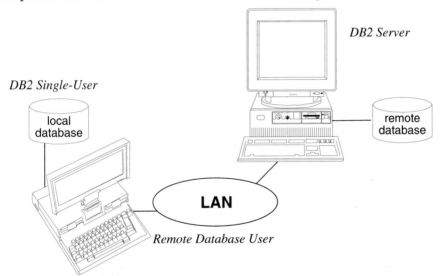

Fig. 1–10 DB2 Single-User

As the product name suggests, DB2 Single-User allows one person to create databases on the workstation where it was installed. DB2 Single-User contains the CAE component. Therefore, once the DB2 Single-User product has been installed, you can use this workstation as a remote client connecting to a DB2 Server on a Local Area Network (LAN).

The DB2 Single-User product is appropriate for the following users:

- DB2 developers creating applications which access local databases
- DB2 end users requiring access to local and remote databases

Fig. 1–10 shows an example of DB2 Single-User installation. In this example, the user can access a local database on their mobile workstation (laptop) and they can access remote databases found on the database server.

DB2 Single-User contains the Database Director, Visual Explain, Command Line Processor (CLP) and the Software Developer's Kit.

DB2 Server

DB2 Server contains all DB2 Single-User functions except the application development environment. For this functionality, you need to install the Software Developer's Kit (SDK) product on the same workstation. In Fig. 1–10 the DB2 Single-User workstation is shown as a mobile user which is occasionally connect to a LAN. This mobile user can access any of the databases on the DB2 Server workstation.

The DB2 Server is designed for use in a LAN environment. It provides support for both remote and local clients. A workstation with DB2 Server installed can be connected to a network and participate in a client/server environment as shown in Fig. 1–11.

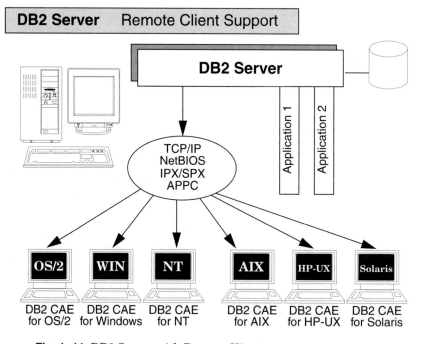

Fig. 1–11 DB2 Server with Remote Clients

In Fig. 1–11, *application 1* and *application 2* are local database applications. Remote clients can also execute *application 1* and *application 2*, if the proper client/server setup has been performed. A DB2 application does not contain any specific information regarding the physical location of the database. DB2 client applications communicate with the DB2 Server using a client/server–supported protocol via the DB2 CAE. Depending on the client and server operating system involved, the DB2 Server can support the following protocols: TCP/IP, NetBIOS, IPX/SPX and APPC.

DB2 Server includes the Database Director, Visual Explain and Performance Monitor.

Distributed Database Connection Services (DDCS)

The Distributed Database Connection Services product allows clients access to data stored on database servers which implement the Distributed Relational Database Architecture (DRDA). The target datbase server for a DDCS installation is known as a **DRDA Application Server**. In Fig. 1–12, the flow of database requests through DDCS is shown.

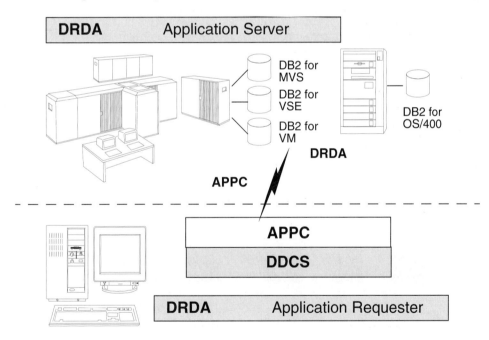

Fig. 1–12 DRDA Application Flow

✍ The most commonly accessed DRDA application server is DB2 for MVS. It is not recommended to connect from DDCS to a DB2 Common Server database, because CAE should be used instead.

DDCS currently requires the APPC communication protocol to provide the communications support between DRDA Application Servers and DRDA Application Requestors. Any of the supported network protocols can be used for the DB2 client (CAE) to establish a connection via the DDCS gateway.

The database application must request the data from a DRDA Application Server via a DRDA Application Requestor. The DB2 CAE component is not a DRDA Application Requestor.

✍️   The DDCS product provides the **DRDA Application Requestor** functionality.

The DRDA Application Server could be any of the following DB2 Servers:

- DB2 for MVS
- DB2 for OS/400
- DB2 for VM
- DB2 for VSE
- DB2 for common server (DB2 Server, on supported platforms)

In Fig. 1–12, the DB2 CAE component is not shown because the DB2 CAE component can only access DB2 common servers directly. The data flow from a DB2 CAE and a DB2 Server is a private database protocol. This protocol can only be used to communicate with DB2 common servers.

DDCS Single-User

DDCS Single-User is available on OS/2 and Windows NT operating systems. It provides access to host databases from the workstation where it is installed. It includes the Database Director and the Command Line Processor (CLP). Fig. 1–13 shows the DRDA flow between the Application Requester and the Application Server using the DDCS Single-User product.

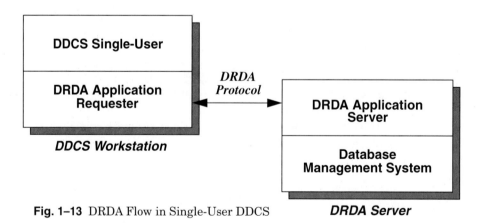

Fig. 1–13 DRDA Flow in Single-User DDCS

DDCS Multi-User Gateway

The DDCS Multi-User Gateway product provides the ability for multiple clients to access host data. A DDCS gateway routes each database request from the DB2 clients to the appropriate DRDA Application Server database. Fig. 1–13 shows the addition of a remote client. The remote client communicates with the DDCS workstation using any of the supported communication protocols.

The DDCS Multi-User product is acting as a DRDA Application Requestor, and it is also acting as a DB2 Server (in relation to the remote client connection). The DDCS product includes the Database Director and the Command Line Processor.

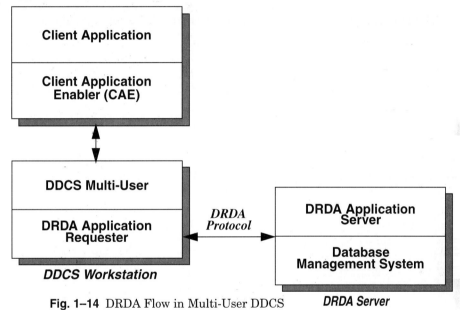

Fig. 1–14 DRDA Flow in Multi-User DDCS   *DRDA Server*

DB2 Software Developer's Kit (SDK)

The DB2 Software Developer's Kit (SDK) is a separate product that can be installed on either the DB2 server or on a DB2 client. It provides all of the necessary data access tools for developing embedded SQL applications and callable SQL applications, as shown in Fig. 1–15.

The application development environment provided with the SDK allows application developers to write programs using the following methods:

- Embedded SQL
- Callable SQL interface (compatible with the Microsoft ODBC standard)
- DB2 Application Programming Interfaces (APIs)

The programming environment also includes the necessary programming libraries, header files, code samples and precompilers for the supported programming languages. Several programming languages including COBOL, FORTRAN, REXX, C and C++ are supported by DB2.

An application developed with DB2 SDK can be executed on any workstation which has the DB2 CAE component installed. If the application development platform is different from the client platform where the application is executed, the application must be recompiled before executing on that client machine.

The Software Developer's Kit includes the Visual Explain Tool, the Database Director and the Command Line Processor (CLP).

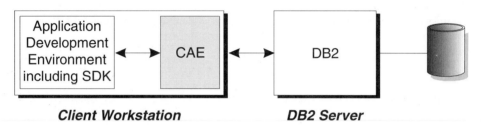

Fig. 1–15 Software Developer's Kit

Documentation

Depending on the DB2 product purchased, a set of operating system specific manuals are supplied. The entire DB2 library is available, but it is not supplied with the product. Table 1–1 contains a list of the available DB2 common server documentation.

✍ DB2 manuals which are referenced will be shown in *italics*.

All of the manuals shown in Table 1–1 are provided on-line with DB2. The format of the on-line manuals differs depending on the operating system.

Some of the DB2 manuals are to be used as references (*SQL Reference*, *API Reference*, *CLI Guide and Reference*, and *Command Reference*). Other DB2 manuals are to be used as tutorials or guides. A guide includes conceptual information and suggestions. The *DB2 Administration Guide* describes important aspects of administrating DB2. This includes database concurrency, configuration, and recovery scenarios. The *DB2 Application Programming Guide* describes important aspects of developing DB2 applications. This includes application programming methods, techniques and programming language considerations for COBOL, C, REXX, and FORTRAN. The *DDCS User's Guide* explains the DDCS environment and concepts.

There are operating system specific books for planning, installation, and application development purposes. Table 1–2 contains a list of these books.

Table 1–1 DB2 Library

Title	Description
Information and Concepts Guide	General information and concepts about the DB2 products and components.
Administration Guide	Information about how to use and administer the DB2 relational database management system (RDBMS) products.
Database Monitor Guide and Reference	Explains the methods of database monitoring and how to use the DB2 provided monitor facilities.
Application Programming Guide	Information on designing, writing and testing DB2 application programs.
Command Reference	Information about the DB2 commands which can be issued using the Command Line Processor.
API Reference	Information about using the DB2 specific application programming interfaces (APIs).
SQL Reference	Reference manual for information on relational database concepts, language elements, functions. The complete syntax of the supported SQL statements is provided.
Call Level Interface Guide and Reference	How to write applications using DB2 Call Level Interface (CLI) to access DB2 database servers.
DDCS User's Guide	General information about the DDCS product.
Problem Determination Guide	Guide to assist with identifying problems or errors and how to solve them. Also describes diagnostic tools.
Messages Reference	Detailed information about the SQL error conditions.
Master Index	The master index for the DB2 library.

Licensing

The DB2 products utilize a licensing mechanism to control the usage of DB2 software. A program license key is provided with all of the DB2 products. This product license key is provided as a label on the product media (usually CD-ROM).

As part of the installation and setup of a DB2 database server, the product license key must be entered into a special license file known as the **nodelock file**.

Table 1–2 Operating System Specific DB2 Books

Title	Description
Planning Guide	Information regarding the amount of memory and disk resources required for DB2
Installation and Operation Guide	Explains the initial product installation and setup for the DB2 product
Installing and Using Client	Explains the installation of DB2 clients.
SDK Building Your Applications	Describes the compile and link requirements for the development of applications
DDCS Installation and Configuration Guide	Provides communications setup information for the DDCS product. Each operating environment has different communications environments

The DB2 Single-User product does not accept incoming connections and, therefore, does need extra user **entitlements** (licenses).

The DB2 Server product provides a base license of five concurrent users, but many more users can access the database functions if additional user licenses are purchased. The user licenses are also known as entitlements. The DB2 Server and DDCS Multi-User products both allow five concurrent users, but there are additional entitlements available in multiples of 1, 5, 10 or 50.

    Entitlement keys are required for additional users.

DB2 Client/Server Environment

This section examines the supported communication protocols used by the DB2 products in various client/server configurations. Also covered are memory considerations for the DB2 Server and DDCS Multi-User Gateway products.

Supported Communication Protocols

The DB2 database engine (DB2 Server and DB2 Single-User) can be installed on various operating systems, including OS/2, AIX, SINIX, SCO OpenServer, HP-UX, Solaris and Windows NT. The DB2 Server is responsible to 'listen' for any DB2 requests from DB2 clients.

✎   The DB2 engine is available as a stand-alone database engine (Single-User) or as a remotely accessible database engine (Server).

A DB2 client can be configured to establish communications with a DB2 Server using various communication protocols. The supported protocols vary according to operating system. DB2 supports many popular communication protocols depending on the operating environment. Some the more popular DB2 implementations use the following communications protocols:

TCP/IP   Common protocol used in UNIX environments.

NetBIOS   Common protocol used in OS/2 and Windows environments.

APPC   Common protocol used in IBM operating environments.

IPX/SPX   Common protocol used in Novell NetWare environments.

✎   The *DB2 Planning and Installation Guide* provides operating system specific requirements for implementing DB2 Client/Server.

DB2 Resource Usage

In every computer system, there exist two resources:

- Temporary Storage (Memory)
- Permanent Storage (Disks)

The amount of memory on the database server is a very important element because it will determine the size of the database cache known as the buffer pool and also the number of concurrent users of the database. The amount of permanent storage (disk space) is crucial because the entire database must be stored on a single workstation.

The hardware and operating system requirements vary according to the operating system platform. The *DB2 Planning Guide* for each platform provides the base memory and disk requirements for product installation.

An important aspect of most database server environments is the number of concurrent users that can be supported. The *DB2 Planning Guide* also provides information regarding the amount of memory required on the DB2 server for each concurrent user. Each local and remote client requires additional memory on the database server. Also, consider how many DB2 instances will be used on the DB2 server, because each instance will consume a significant amount of memory resources.

DB2 Client/Server Scenarios

The next section gives some examples of client/server scenarios using the DB2 products. This should give you some guidelines in calculating licenses and user entitlements for a particular environment.

Scenario One

This scenario shows the requirements for an OS/2 application developer. As shown in Fig. 1–16, DB2 Single-User allows the user to develop and test applications with local databases. DB2 Single-User also can be a remote client to a DB2 Server.

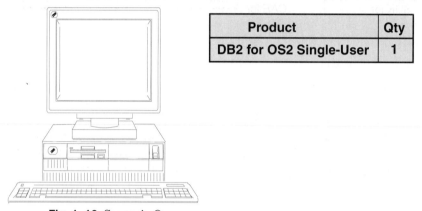

Product	Qty
DB2 for OS2 Single-User	1

Fig. 1–16 Scenario One

Scenario Two

In this example, there will be an OS/2 database server. A total of 15 remote clients, eight OS/2 end-users and the seven OS/2 application developers need to access both a host DB2 database on an MVS system and the OS/2 database server (Fig. 1–17).

The CAE Client Pack is shipped with both the DB2 Server and the DDCS products. You will need to install the CAE on each of the OS/2 end-user workstations. The seven application developers will install the SDK product. The SDK product contains the CAE component.

You do not need a separate CAE installation on the workstation in which the SDK product was installed. However, you need a separate SDK license on each of the seven workstations that will be doing application development. Each SDK client also counts as one user accessing the DB2 database server. To allow for a possible seven SDK users and eight end-users at any one time on the database server, you will need a base DB2 Server license and one entitlement for 10 users.

You also will need a base DDCS Multi-User Gateway license plus an entitlement for 10 additional users to provide access to a database on DB2 for MVS.

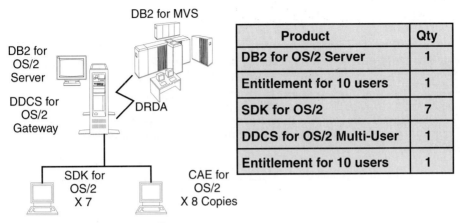

Product	Qty
DB2 for OS/2 Server	1
Entitlement for 10 users	1
SDK for OS/2	7
DDCS for OS/2 Multi-User	1
Entitlement for 10 users	1

Fig. 1–17 Scenario Two

Scenario Three

In this scenario (Fig. 1–18) there are two departments. One department uses OS/2 and the other department uses AIX. There will be one developer on an OS/2 workstation developing an application which accesses a DB2 for OS/2 database server. There will be 17 AIX clients accessing the AIX database server. Also, there will be five OS/2 clients using the database servers in both departments.

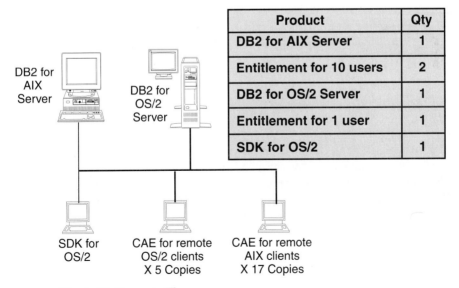

Product	Qty
DB2 for AIX Server	1
Entitlement for 10 users	2
DB2 for OS/2 Server	1
Entitlement for 1 user	1
SDK for OS/2	1

Fig. 1–18 Scenario Three

You will need to install CAE on the remote AIX and OS/2 client workstations. The OS/2 developer needs to install the SDK product. To allow for all possible remote users (1 OS/2 developer + 5 OS/2 remote clients + 17 AIX remote clients = 23 possible concurrent users) at any time on the AIX database server, you could purchase a base server license with two additional entitlements for 10 users. This would provide a possible 25 users access to the database on the AIX server. To allow for a possible six remote clients to the OS/2 database server, you would need a base server license and one additional entitlement for one user. Note that applications developed with the SDK on the OS/2 platform would have to be recompiled to run on AIX.

Summary

This chapter discussed the concept of products and components specific to DB2. DB2 products consist of components. These components provide many of the basic administration functions, but they differ slightly depending on the DB2 product.

The DB2 Command Line Processor and the DB2 CAE component are provided in each of the DB2 products. The capabilities of the Command Line Processor (CLP) vary across DB2 products. For example, the DDCS product contains a subset of the commands available when using the CLP provided with the DB2 Server product.

We discussed various DB2 products, including

- DB2 Server
- DB2 Single-User
- Distributed Database Connection Services (DDCS)
- Software Developer's Kit (SDK)

There are many operating environments for DB2 databases and even more for DB2 database applications. The underlying communications between the database application and the DB2 server is handled by DB2, not by the application.

Licensing is based on the number of users accesssing the DB2 Server or DDCS workstation. A product key, provided with the product, must be entered into a special file called a nodelock file. If more concurrent users require access to the DB2 Server or DDCS gateway, additional user entitlements can be added to the licensing system, and the nodelock file must be updated on the server.

Questions

1. Which is a DB2 component and NOT a DB2 product?

    ○   A. DB2 Server

    ○   B. DB2 CAE

    ○   C. DB2 SDK

    ○   D. DDCS

2. From which DB2 component could you invoke Visual Explain?

    ○   A. Event Monitor

    ○   B. Performance Monitor

    ○   C. Command Line Processor

    ○   D. Database Director

3. Which is the main function of the DDCS product?

    ○   A. DRDA Application Requester

    ○   B. RDBMS Engine

    ○   C. DRDA Application Server

    ○   D. DB2 Application Run-Time Environment

4. Which product contains a database engine and an application development environment?

    ○   A. DDCS

    ○   B. DB2 Single-User

    ○   C. DB2 SDK

5. Which communication protocol could you use to access a DB2 common server database?

    ○   A. X.25

    ○   B. AppleTalk

    ○   C. TCP/IP

6. What product is required to access a DB2 for MVS database from a DB2 CAE workstation?

    ○   A. DB2 SDK

    ○   B. DB2 Server

    ○   C. DDCS

    ○   D. DB2 Single-User

7. Which communication protocol is required between a DRDA Application Requester (e.g. DDCS) and a DRDA Application Server (e.g. DB2 for MVS)?

    ○   A. TCP/IP

    ○   B. NetBIOS

    ○   C. X.25

    ○   D. APPC

Answers

1. (B)

   The DB2 Client Application Enabler is an installable component and it is contained in all DB2 products to provide remote database access.

2. (D)

   Visual Explain can be invoked from the Database Director.

3. (A)

   The DRDA Application requester is part of DDCS Single– and Multi–User Gateway products.

4. (B)

   The DB2 Single-User product contains the relational database engine and the DB2 Software Developer's Kit (SDK) environment.

5. (C)

   The supported protocols vary across DB2 servers, but from the list only TCP/IP would be supported.

6. (C)

   The DDCS product is required to act as a DRDA Application Requester. The DB2 CAE cannot establish communication with a DRDA Application Server (e.g. DB2 for MVS). It must be cataloged through a DDCS Multi-User Gateway or the DDCS Single-User product needs to be installed on the CAE workstation.

7. (D)

   Currently only the APPC communication protocol can be used as the protocol to implement a DRDA Application Requester to DRDA Application Server environment.

Getting Started and Connected

Let's get started with setting up a DB2 database server. There are few steps required before we can create a DB2 database and access the database using SQL. First, we will examine the installation process for various operating environments. Specifically, we will discuss installation of DB2 servers and DB2 clients on AIX, OS/2 and Windows NT. We will also examine some of the unique client environments including setting up an ODBC (Open Database Connectivity) application, such as Lotus Approach. An ODBC driver is provided with DB2 and must be installed on each client workstation using an ODBC application.

Once the DB2 products have been installed, we will examine the required steps to create a DB2 database. Depending on your operating environment, you can need to create a DB2 server instance. Multiple instances will be discussed and various instance administration commands will also be examined. DB2 databases are created within an instance on a database server.

We will examine the DB2 interface tools which allow you to enter DB2 commands and SQL statements. A text-based interface called the Command Line Processor (CLP) and a graphical interface known as the Database Director are components provided with DB2. These tools will be described and used in this chapter and the rest of the book. We will demonstrate placing commands in a file and executing the commands from the file using the Command Line Processor.

Finally, we will use the Command Line Processor (CLP) to create the DB2 sample database, establish a connection to the database and issue SQL statements.

Product Installation

We will discuss the installation steps for DB2 on various platforms. In particular, we will examine the steps for AIX, OS/2 and Windows NT. There are some differences between the various environments, but once DB2 has been installed the administration is very similar within the DB2 common server family of database servers.

AIX Considerations

The DB2 products are distributed as **Licensed Program Products** (LPPs) in AIX. (See Fig. 2–1) An LPP is packaged as selectable components which allows you to select portions of the product to install. The DB2 products can be installed using the **installp** AIX command or the System Management Interface Tool (SMIT). SMIT is a user-friendly interface that allows you to execute various AIX commands. It is the preferred method of installing DB2 for AIX.

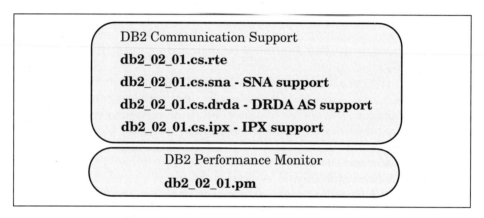

Fig. 2–1 Installation Options for DB2 Server for AIX

When you start the installation process of DB2 for AIX products SMIT will display the selectable options available. Figure 2-1 shows the selectable options for a DB2 Server for AIX installation. Each of the selectable options are described in the *DB2 for AIX Installation Guide*. For example, if you want to install the Command Line Processor component, you can select **db2_02_01.clp**. Alternatively, you can select all of the options. Selecting all of the options will install the complete product (see Fig. 2–2 for the installable options for DB2 for AIX Single-User).

There are two reasons why you might not wish to install all of the components of a DB2 product. First, you can not require specific components and wish to save disk space by not installing the option. For example, the SDK product contains various language options, such as C, FORTRAN and COBOL. If you do not program in one of these languages, you can not want to install the files. Second, you can not have the required software to install one of the options. AIX will verify any required software during installation and prevent installation if the required software is not present. For example, if your system is limited in disk space, you might want to install only those facilities that you intend to use.

The documentation is provided in a printable and viewable format. Fig. 2–2 shows the DB2 Single-User for AIX LPP. The %L shown in Fig. 2–2 indicates the language specific components (e.g. En_US for United States English). The AIX LPP consists of the database engine, CAE for AIX, the Command Line Processor, product documentation, the Database Director, the Software Developer's Kit and Visual Explain.

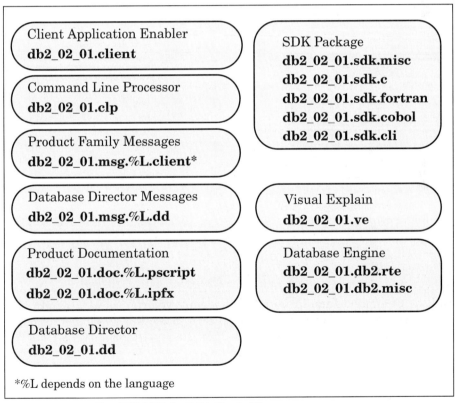

Fig. 2–2 The AIX LPP for DB2 Single-User

The DB2 Server AIX LPP provides the same basic installation options as those found in the DB2 Single-User LPP. DB2 Server provides communications support to allow remote applications to access the DB2 database. The Performance Monitor is also provided with the DB2 Server.

✍️ The AIX operating system level required for the installation of DB2 products is Version 3.2.5 or higher.

Fig. 2–1 shows the additional install options with DB2 for AIX. If the required communications software has not been previously installed, you can decide to only select the communications support that you will be using. It is important to understand that AIX will check all of the prerequisite software, by default, and this can prevent installation of DB2.

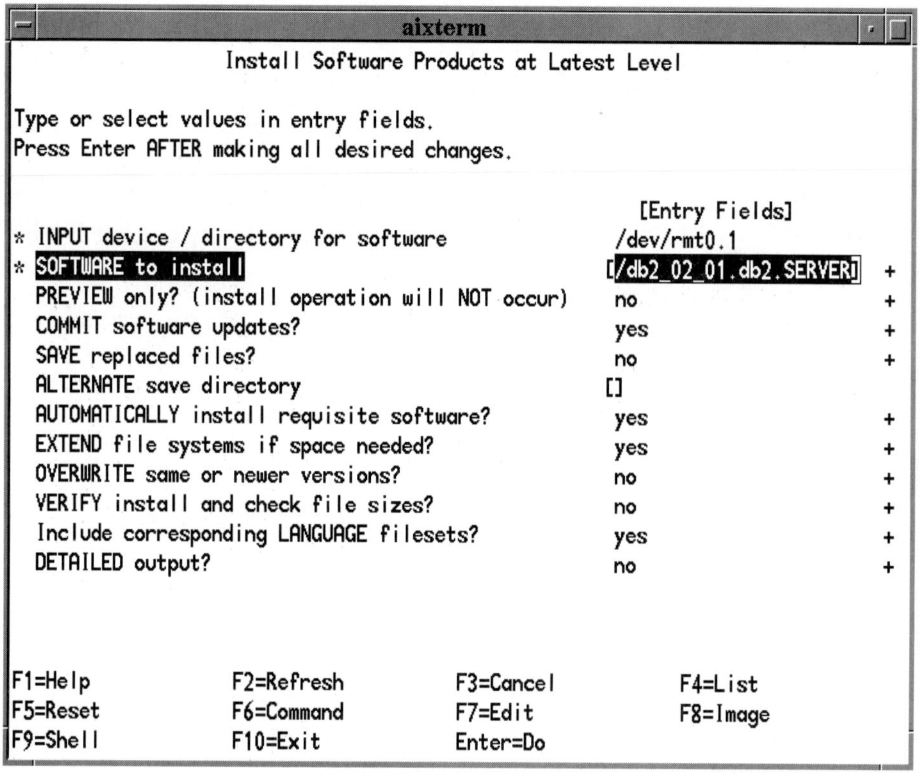

```
─                              aixterm                                  · □
                   Install Software Products at Latest Level

Type or select values in entry fields.
Press Enter AFTER making all desired changes.


                                                       [Entry Fields]
 * INPUT device / directory for software               /dev/rmt0.1
 * SOFTWARE to install                                 [/db2_02_01.db2.SERVER]  +
   PREVIEW only? (install operation will NOT occur)    no                       +
   COMMIT software updates?                            yes                      +
   SAVE replaced files?                                no                       +
   ALTERNATE save directory                            []
   AUTOMATICALLY install requisite software?           yes                      +
   EXTEND file systems if space needed?                yes                      +
   OVERWRITE same or newer versions?                   no                       +
   VERIFY install and check file sizes?                no                       +
   Include corresponding LANGUAGE filesets?            yes                      +
   DETAILED output?                                    no                       +




 F1=Help          F2=Refresh        F3=Cancel         F4=List
 F5=Reset         F6=Command        F7=Edit           F8=Image
 F9=Shell         F10=Exit          Enter=Do
```

Fig. 2–3 SMIT Installation Menu

The example SMIT screen in Fig. 2–3 is the installation of the DB2 Server for AIX products. Note that the file system will be automatically increased and requisite software is automatically installed (the requisite software must be on the input device). Instead of using the SMIT interface to install DB2, you can use the AIX command `installp`.

The following command is equivalent to the SMIT screen shown in Fig. 2–3 (input device is tape):

```
installp -ag -d /dev/rmt0.1 db2_02_01.db2.SERVER
```

✐   You require root authority to install DB2 products on AIX.

The DB2 products will be installed in the /usr/lpp/db2_vv_rr directory where **vv** represents the version of DB2 for AIX and **rr** represents the release. The directory structure created under /usr/lpp/db2_02_01 will be similar to the installation directories shown in Fig. 2–4.

/adm	- System administrator and executable files
/adsm	- ADSTAR Distributed Storage Manager Files
/bin	- Binary executable files
/bnd	- Bind files
/cfg	- Default system configuration files
/conv	- Code page conversion files
/dba	- Database Director
/deinstl	- Files to reject applied software
/doc/%L	- PostScript and On-line books INF format
/function	- User defined functions
/include	- C and Fortran include files
/include/cobol_m	- COBOL COPY files for MicroFocus COBOL
/include/cobol_a	- COBOL COPY files for ANSI COBOL
/instance	- Instance scripts
/lib	- Libraries
/map	- Map files for DDCS for AIX
/misc	- Utilities and examples
/msg/%l	- Message catalogs
/netls	- iFOR/LS files
/odbclib	- ODBC Driver Manager
/Readme/%L	- README files
/samples/c	- C sample programs
/samples/cli	- DB2 CLI examples
/samples/clp	- Command Line Processor examples
/samples/cobol	- COBOL samples programs
/samples/fortran	- Fortran sample programs
/samples/mon	- Performance Monitor samples
/samples/rexx	- DB2 REXX samples

Fig. 2–4 DB2 for AIX File and Directory Structure

Depending on the products you are installing, some of these directories can not exist. Symbolic links are created in the home directory of the DB2 instance owner. These links point to the installed DB2 code in the /usr/lpp location.

After the product has been installed, the license information that is shipped with the product must be entered into a nodelock file. In AIX, this file must be placed in the /usr/lib/netls/conf directory. The nodelock file must be owned by **root.system** and have permission bits set to 644.

It is possible to install different versions of DB2 products on the same AIX workstation as the product files will be installed in a different path under the **usr/lpp** directory. Following a successful installation of the product files, we will configure the DB2 environment. For details on configuring the DB2 environment, see "AIX Considerations" on page 39.

OS/2 Considerations

Both Single-User and Server versions of the DB2 product for OS/2 contain a series of components that you can selectively install. The products are available either on CD-ROM or diskette. To install, execute the following command from an OS/2 window:

```
X:\<LANGUAGE>\INSTALL for CD-ROM
X:\INSTALL for Diskettes
```

You will then be prompted to select the components that you would like to install as shown in Fig. 2–5 .

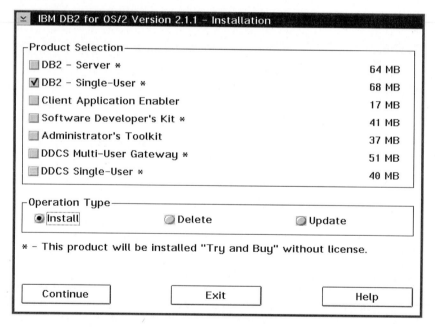

Fig. 2–5 DB2 for OS/2 Installation Menu Window

Click on the components you wish to install and then select **Continue**. The next window asks you if you want to update the *CONFIG.SYS* file; click on **OK**. You can choose where you want to install the products. The default location is C:\SQLLIB. This can be changed to a directory of your choice.

✍ When installing DB2 Single-User for OS/2, if you select **Windows Support**, you will be installing the DB2 SDK for Windows.

When the installation begins, you will be prompted to enter the product license key. You can also decide to enter the product license key at the end of the installation. If a license key is not entered the product is in "Try and Buy" mode and it can be used for 60 days.

The installation process will automatically set the DB2 environment variables in the *CONFIG.SYS* file and create an instance called **DB2**.

✍ The OS/2 operating system level required for DB2 is Version 2.1.1 or higher.

It is useful to understand where the DB2 components are installed. In Fig. 2–6 the installation directory structure is shown. These directories will be created under the directory called **SQLLIB** on the installation drive (e.g. C:\SQLLIB). Do not attempt to delete or modify any of these files.

```
\sqllib          -    DBM configuration file (db2systm),
                      nodelock file, ReadMe files

\sqllib\bin      -    Executables
       \bnd      -    Bind files for utilities
       \book     -    On-line manuals
       \cfg      -    Default DB and DBM configuration files
       \db2      -    Default instance directory
       \db2\sqldbdir-System database director (DB2 instance)
       \db2\sqlgwdir-Gateway (DCS) directory
       \db2\sqlnodir-Node directory
       \db2\tmp  -    Temporary files for (DB2 instance)
       \dcslib   -    DDCS files
       \dll      -    Dynamic Load Libraries for DB2
       \function -    Default location for User-Defined Functions
       \function\unfenced-Default location for unfenced UDFs
       \help     -    On-line help files
       \include  -    Development header files (C and Fortran)
       \install  -    Installation program
       \lib      -    Libraries for application development
       \map      -    Mapping file used by DDCS
       \misc     -    DB2 tools and utilities (Appendix D)
       \msg\prime-    Message files
       \samples  -    Sample code (all programming languages)
       \win      -    Windows development and run-time
```

Avoid directly modifying any of the files located under the SQLLIB directory.

Fig. 2–6 DB2 for OS/2 Directory Structure

Windows NT Considerations

DB2 Single-User and DB2 Server are also available for the Windows NT operating system. The DB2 products for NT are available on CD-ROM only, but diskettes can be created from the CD-ROM. The DB2 for Windows NT installed file structure is very similar to DB2 for OS/2, shown in Fig. 2–6.

✍️   To install DB2 for Windows NT products, you must have Windows
      NT administrator authority.

To install the DB2 for Windows NT product, simply run the **setup.exe,**
located on the CD-ROM or the first diskette. As with other Windows software,
the **File Manager Program** should be used to execute the installation program.
The installation program will prompt you for the DB2 products you wish to
install. After all of the files have been installed the workstation will need to be
shutdown and restarted.

DB2 will add **System Environment Variables** to the Windows NT
system configuration. The Windows NT System Environment variables are
similar to the *CONFIG.SYS* file in OS/2. The current settings can be verified by
double-clicking on the **System** icon within the Windows NT **Control Panel**
program group. For more information on setting up Windows NT, see "DB2 for
Windows NT - System Environment Variables" on page 42.

The install program also creates two program groups on the Windows NT
desktop. There is a program group which contains all of the DB2 on-line
documentation and there is a program group with the DB2 programs and
utilities, including:

- **Command Line Processor** - Clicking on it invokes a window from which
  the Command Line Processor (CLP) is started.
- **DB2 Command Window** - Click on it to initialize a window from which
  commands and statements can be issued.
- **ODBC Installer** - Click to install or set up the DB2 ODBC driver.
- **Uninstall DB2 Products** - Click to remove all DB2 products.
- **Database Director** - Clicking on it starts the Database Director.

Windows 95 Considerations

DB2 for Windows 95 products include the DB2 Software Developer's Kit (SDK)
and a DB2 Single-User. The installation process involves the following steps:

1. From the Start/Settings menu, open the Control Panel
2. Click on Add/Remove programs
3. Click on Install
4. Execute the **setup.exe** from the installation media
5. Select the components you wish to install.
6. Select the finish button

DB2 Client Installation

So far we have discussed the installation of the DB2 Single-User and Server versions (including AIX, OS/2 and Windows NT). We'll briefly look at other installation considerations, namely those for the Software Developer's Kit, the Client Application Enabler and the DB2 Open Database Connectivity (ODBC) Driver.

✍   ODBC Driver Managers are available on many platforms. It provides a standard interface to access various data sources.

Installing the DB2 SDK

The Software Developer's Kit is a separate product that can be installed independently or with other DB2 products. The Single-User version of DB2 includes the functionality of the SDK.

The SDK product requires a product license key. The base product is licensed for a single developer, but you can acquire additional user licenses. The installation of the SDK product is the same as that of the DB2 Server or Single-User products described for each platform.

✍   For the UNIX environments, like AIX, you can choose the language-specific portions of the SDK to save disk space.

Installing the CAE

The DB2 Client Application Enabler (CAE) provides a runtime environment which is required for all DB2 applications to access database resources. The CAE contains the communications infrastructure to communicate with remote database servers. You can also bind packages, use data manipulation utilities (Import/Export) and catalog remote nodes and databases. Most of the database administrator tasks can be performed from a DB2 client. SQL statements cannot be issued from the CLP provided with the DB2 CAE.

End user workstations will often use ODBC enabled applications to access DB2 databases residing on a DB2 server. Each of these end-user workstations simply requires the DB2 CAE component and the ODBC driver to be installed and configured. Remember, licensing is controlled on the DB2 Server or the DDCS Multi-User Gateway and not on each of the client workstations. Each operating environment is slightly different, so we will discuss setup and configuration of DB2 clients on each of the platforms.

CAE for AIX Installation

The SMIT interface or the **installp** command can be used to install the DB2 CAE for AIX. A DB2 for AIX client must also have the proper DB2 environment setup. Every DB2 Client requires that the proper links to the DB2 product files have been created (see "Creating an Instance" on page 38). A DB2 CAE instance cannot contain local databases as a DB2 Server instance can. In Fig. 2–7, a sample SMIT screen is shown for the installation of the DB2 Client Application Enabler.

✎ There is no need to update the licensing file on the DB2 CAE workstation as the licensing is controlled at the DB2 Server.

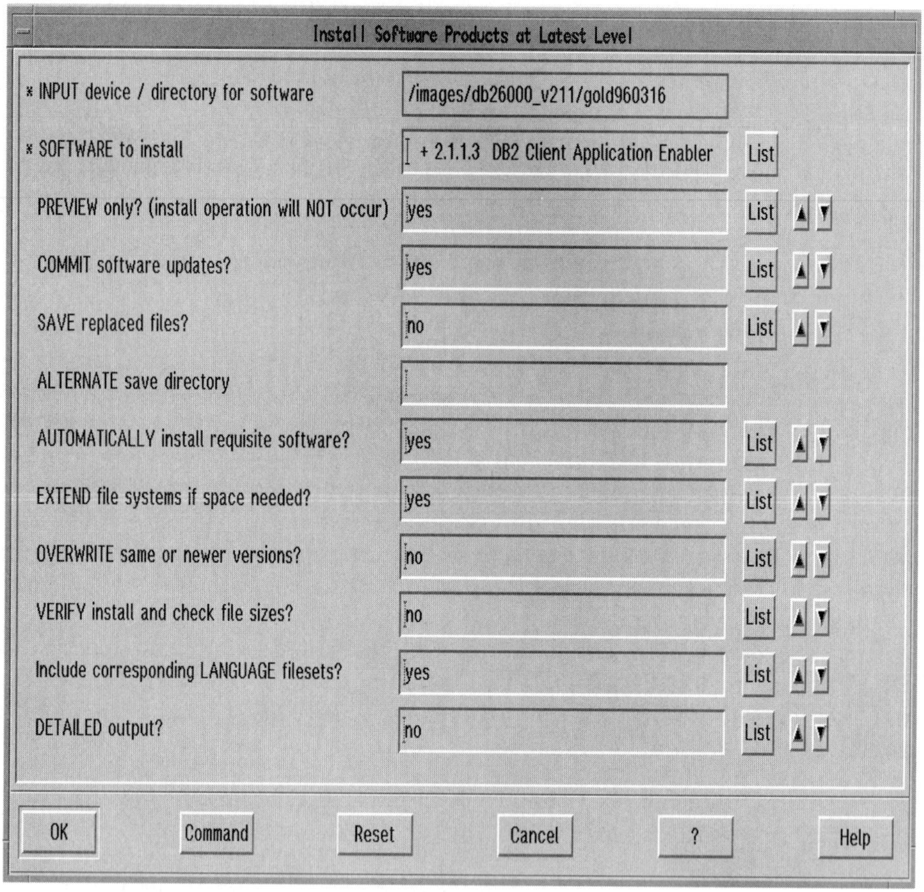

Fig. 2–7 Installing CAE on an AIX Client

CAE for OS/2 Installation

The DB2 Client Application Enabler for OS/2 is an installable component. The DB2 CAE is provided on the same media as the DB2 product. The DB2 Client Pak (CD-ROM) contains all of the various version of the DB2 CAE. To install DB2 for OS/2, perform the following steps:

1. Type: **x:\install** (where X is the installation drive)
2. In the window that appears, click on **OK**.
3. Read the README file.
4. Click on **Install.**
5. Click on **Files.**
6. You can decide to save your CONFIG.SYS or allow it to be updated.
7. Chose the components to install from the Install Directories window.
8. Click on **OK**, the installation status menu appears.
9. At the end of the installation when a window displays a successful installation message, click on **OK**.
10. Reboot the system. This is required to ensure that the proper DLLs are accessed by DB2.

✍   When the system is restarted, a DB2 tutorial will start.

Following the DB2 for OS/2 installation you should notice that the OS/2 configuration file (*CONFIG.SYS*) has been updated. One of the most important environment variables used by DB2 is the **DB2PATH** variable. It is used to locate the DB2 product executables. The **DB2PATH** variable should be set to the **SQLLIB** directory of the installation drive.

Installing the ODBC Driver

There is a ODBC driver provided with DB2. If you want to use applications like Lotus Approach, you should install and configure the ODBC driver. The driver should be installed on the DB2 client workstation.

To install the DB2 ODBC driver for Windows, either select the **Program Manager** and execute the program **x:\sqllib\win\bin\db2odbc**, where **x** is the drive where DB2 CAE for Windows is installed or use the ODBC Administration Tool located in the DB2 folder.

✍   It is recommended that the ODBC administration tool be used to install the ODBC driver.

The ODBC driver should be configured for the databases, known as data sources. There are a number of configuration parameters which can be set in a special file called the *db2cli.ini* file. To enable ODBC applications properly, the README file should be examined as many popular software programs have specific ODBC settings which must be adhered to in the configuration.

Setting Up the DB2 Environment

We will examine some of the remaining steps necessary to set up the DB2 environment. After the DB2 products have been installed and the license information entered, you need to either use the default instance or create a DB2 instance. An **instance** in DB2 can be defined as a logical database server environment. DB2 databases are created within a DB2 instance on the database server.

Creating an Instance

An **instance** is a unique database server environment. The creation of multiple instances on the same physical server provides a unique database server environment for each instance. For example, you can maintain a test environment and a production environment with the same databases. Depending on the platform, multiple instances and different versions of the product can coexist.

Each instance has an administrative group associated with it. This administrative group must be defined in the instance configuration file, known as the **database manager configuration file**. Creating user ids and user groups is different for each operating environment (see "Controlling Data Access" on page 59).

The DB2 command to create a DB2 instance is **DB2ICRT**.

DB2ICRT <instance_name>

The **<instance_name>** is supplied by the database administrator and it must be unique on the workstation. After the instance has been created, the operating system environment must be configured to use the instance.

Customizing the operating system environment for DB2, as you can guess, is different on each platform. Let's first examine some of the common environment variables defined by DB2 across all platforms. The following environment variables are defined on every DB2 Server workstation:

- **DB2INSTANCE** — Specifies the active DB2 instance.
- **DB2PATH** — Specifies the path for the DB2 executables.
- **DB2DBDFT** (optional) — This is the database alias name of the database that will be implicitly connected to when applications are started. The default is the sample database.
- **DB2COMM** — Specifies which communication protocols will be enabled when the instance is started.

A summary of the location of these DB2 environment variables is shown in Table 2–1. Before we can create a DB2 instance and set up the DB2 environment, there are some operating system specific tasks that need to be addressed.

Table 2–1 DB2 Environment Setup

Operating System	Location of DB2 Environment Variables
OS/2	CONFIG.SYS file used by OS/2 located on the OS/2 installation drive
Windows NT	System environment variables, specified for the system within the System icon from the Control Panel
UNIX Environments (AIX, Solaris, HP-UX, etc.)	Within a script file called db2profile (Bourne or Korn shell) or db2cshrc (C shell), usually incorporated with the user's initialization file (.profile or.login)

AIX Considerations

Before executing the command to create an instance on the AIX platform (**db2icrt**), an instance group and an instance owner must be created within AIX.

   In UNIX systems, like AIX, the group and user must exist before you create the instance. There is **no** default instance created during installation.

To create the user, group and instance in AIX, you must be the AIX system administrator (root authority). The steps to create the group, user and instance are as follows:

1. Create a **system administration group** which must be the primary group of the instance owner. For example, to create a group named *db2adm*, the command is

mkgroup db2adm

2. Create a user who will be a member of the system administration group created in step 1.

mkuser -a pgrp=db2adm groups=db2adm db2v2

3. Execute the DB2 command to create the instance:

db2icrt db2v2

   All of these steps must be performed by the AIX system administrator (**root**). Steps 1 and 2 can be performed using SMIT but the third step must be executed from the */usr/lpp/db2_02_01/INSTANCE* directory.

When an instance is created, links are established to the executables located in the */usr/lpp* directory. These links are created in the instance owner's home directory.

✍️ Remember all commands are case sensitive in UNIX environments.

One of the files placed in the instance owner's home directory, under the *sqllib* sub-directory, is a DB2 setup (profile) file. Depending on the UNIX shell you are using, the file will be called **db2profile** (Bourne or Korn shell) or **db2cshrc** (C shell). This profile must be executed prior to using the DB2 instance. It is usually added to the user's login profile to ensure that it has been executed.

If you have installed the DB2 documentation and want to view the manuals on-line, you must remember to set a special environment variable. To enable the IPF viewer, the **BOOKSHELF** variable should be set in your user profile environment according to the language you are using. This example is for US English (En_US):

```
BOOKSHELF=/usr/lpp/db2_02_01/doc/En_US
export BOOKSHELF
```

Once the environment has been customized and updated, you can invoke the on-line documentation by executing the following command from an AIX window:

```
db2help
```

✍️ UNIX environment variables need to be exported before they become effective.

To verify any DB2 environment variables, issue the **echo** command. For example, to verify the current active DB2 instance, issue:

```
echo $DB2INSTANCE
```

This would return the current DB2 instance which is defined in your environment. If nothing is displayed, then you have probably not executed the **db2profile** or **db2cshrc** script.

If you will be using the DB2 programming libraries, you can decide to create links from the */usr/lib* and */usr/include* directories to the DB2 application development files. This can be accomplished by executing the **db2ln** command.

✍️ Other UNIX systems, like HP-UX and Solaris, do not require that DB2 be installed in the */usr/lpp* location.

OS/2 Considerations

There is a default instance created during the installation of DB2 for OS/2 products. The instance is called **DB2**. The DB2 environment variables are set within the *CONFIG.SYS* file. If you decide that you would like a multiple instance environment, you can create the additional instances using the DB2 command **DB2ICRT**. The instance name does not directly correspond to a user id as it did in UNIX environments.

✍ DB2 for OS/2 sets the environment variable DB2INSTANCE=DB2
    in the *CONFIG.SYS* file during installation.

The executables are placed in a directory called **SQLLIB** on the installation drive. The values of the **DB2INSTANCE** or the **DB2PATH** environment variable can be verified at any time by opening an OS/2 window. For example, to identify the current active DB2 instance, type

```
ECHO %DB2INSTANCE%
```

If multiple DB2 instances are being used on a DB2 server, it is recommended to catalog each of the instances as local nodes.

Windows NT Considerations

Installing DB2 for Windows NT is similar to an OS/2 installation with a few exceptions. As in OS/2, there is a default instance created called **DB2**. However, the DB2 instance is defined to be a **Windows NT service**. Therefore, the DB2 instance name must adhere to any naming rules for NT services. There is also another service created during installation called the **DB2 for Windows NT Security Service**. The security service is required for DB2 to authenticate users accessing the database.

The DB2 Security service must be started along with the DB2 instance service. You can configure these services to start automatically. Click the **Services** icon located in the Windows NT **Control Panel** to verify the existence and status of these services.

The environment variables are set during installation. To verify these environment variables examine the **System** program group under the Main program group of the Program Manager Control Panel. The system setup window is shown in Fig. 2–8.

✍ DB2 for Windows NT sets the DB2 environment variables in the
    Windows NT **System Environment Setup**.

You can create multiple instances in a DB2 for Windows NT environment. Each instance is created using the command **DB2ICRT**.

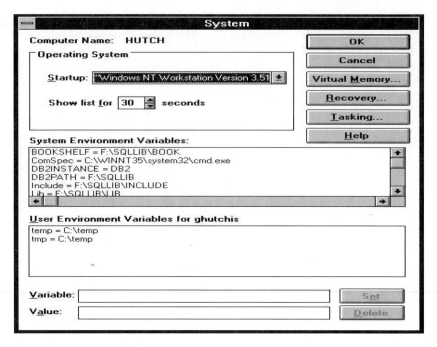

Fig. 2–8 DB2 for Windows NT — System Environment Variables

Starting the DB2 Instance

We have created a DB2 instance. The next step is to initialize or start the instance. The process of starting an instance is similar to starting a network file server; until the instance is started the clients will not be able to access the databases on the server.

The command to start a DB2 instance is called **DB2START**. This command will allocate all of the required DB2 resources on the same workstation. These resources include memory and communications support.

✍ DB2 for Windows NT has an optional method of starting a DB2 instance, since the instance is defined as a Windows NT service.

Fig. 2–9 shows the Control Panel for NT Services. The instance can be started from this control panel or from an operating system window using the command **NET START DB2**. The DB2 NT Security service will also need to be started with the command **NET START DB2NTSECSERVER**.

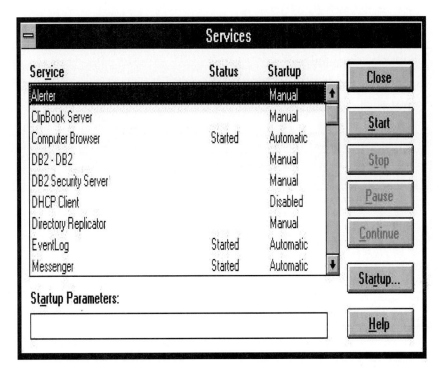

Fig. 2–9 DB2 for Windows NT - Services

This **DB2START** command can be issued from the system command line or from the CLP. If the instance is successfully started, the databases can be accessed locally and, depending on the communications setup, by remote DB2 clients. Let's start the DB2 instance using the **DB2START** command:

```
DB2START
SQL1063N DB2START processing was successful.
```

The SQL1063N message informs us that the instance was started without error. If an error occurs, the first thing to verify is the user setup, namely the **DB2INSTANCE** environment variable.

In UNIX systems, verify that the proper profile script has been executed. To start a DB2 instance you can require a special authority (called *SYSADM*) which we will discuss later (see "Controlling Data Access" on page 59).

Stopping the DB2 Instance

The command to stop the current database manager instance is **DB2STOP**. Messages are sent to the standard output device indicating the success or failure of the **DB2STOP** command.

   Stopping a DB2 instance in a Windows NT environment should be accomplished using the Windows NT services interface.

```
DB2STOP
SQL1064N DB2STOP processing was successful.
```

Managing Instances

You can decide to remove an instance or list the instances which have been previously created. The following instance administration commands are provided:

- **DB2ILIST** — returns a list of all instances that exist on the workstation
- **DB2IDROP <instance_name>** — removes an instance definition. This will remove the DBM configuration file and all DB2 directory entries. Therefore any cataloged databases will no longer be accessible.

DB2 Interfaces

A relational database is a collection of tables in which data is logically arranged in columns and rows. Each database includes a set of system catalog tables which describe the structure of the data. There is also a configuration file containing parameters whose values can be adjusted according to the database environment.

DB2 databases are always created within an instance. We'll create the sample database which is provided with the DB2 product. The tools we will use are the Command Line Processor (CLP) and the Database Director. Fig. 2–10 shows the two interfaces we will be using, and some of the basic differences between them. It is important to note that SQL statements can be issued using the Command Line Processor and not the Database Director.

   The Lotus Approach software product is being provided with DB2 as a query tool, but we do not discuss the use of Approach in this book.

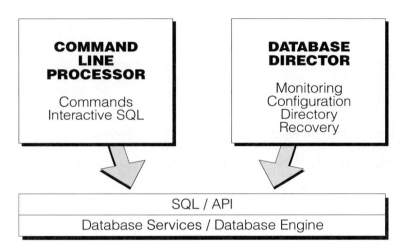

Fig. 2–10 DB2 Interfaces

Using the Command Line Processor

The Command Line Processor is installed with **all** DB2 products. Using the CLP, you can manage a database environment by entering DB2 commands and SQL statements in an interactive mode or from command files. All of the available DB2 commands are shown in Fig. 2–11 .

These commands can be issued from the CLP. You can also issue dynamic SQL statements from the CLP. You must preface all DB2 commands or SQL statements that are entered from the command line with **DB2** followed by the command or the SQL statement.

An alternative method is to issue the DB2 commands or SQL statements from an interactive CLP session. To enter the interactive CLP mode, issue the command **DB2** by itself or open a DB2 CLP window from the DB2 folder.

✎   The commands available within the Command Line Processor vary between the DB2 products (e.g. the **PRECOMPILE** command is not available unless the SDK product has been installed).

When using the Command Line Processor, be careful that the operating system does not mistake SQL statements for operating system commands. If you enclose any SQL statements or DB2 commands within quotation marks, it will ensure that they are not interpreted as operating system commands. From within the Command Line Processor(CLP) you can issue operating system commands by prefacing them with an explanation mark !, for example:

    !<operating-system-command>

```
ACTIVATE DATABASE              LIST APPLICATIONS
ATTACH                         LIST BACKUP/HISTORY
ATTACH TO                      LIST COMMAND OPTIONS
BACKUP DATABASE                LIST DATABASE DIRECTORY
BIND                           LIST DCS APPLICATIONS
CATALOG APPC NODE              LIST DCS DIRECTORY
CATALOG DATABASE               LIST INDOUBT TRANSACTIONS
CATALOG DCS DATABASE           LIST NODE DIRECTORY
CATALOG GLOBAL DATABASE        LIST PACKAGES/TABLES
CATALOG IPXSPX NODE            LIST TABLESPACE CONTAINERS
CATALOG LOCAL NODE             LIST TABLESPACES
CATALOG NETBIOS NODE           LOAD
CATALOG TCPIP NODE             LOAD QUERY
CHANGE DATABASE COMMENT        PREP/PRECOMPILE
CHANGE SQLISL                  PRUNE HISTORY
CONNECT                        QUERY CLIENT
CONNECT RESET                  QUIESCE TABLESPACES
CONNECT TO                     QUIT
CREATE DATABASE                REBIND
DB2START/DB2STOP               REGISTER
DEACTIVATE DATABASE            RELEASE
DEREGISTER                     REORG TABLE
DETACH                         REORGCHK
DISCONNECT                     RESET MONITOR
DROP DATABASE                  RESTART DATABASE
ECHO                           RESTORE DATABASE
EXPORT                         ROLLFORWARD DATABASE
FORCE APPLICATION              RUNSTATS
GET AUTHORIZATIONS             SET CLIENT
GET CONNECTION STATE           SET CONNECTION
GET INSTANCE                   TERMINATE
GET MONITOR SWITCHES           UNCATALOG DATABASE
GET SNAPSHOT                   UNCATALOG DCS DATABASE
GET/RESET/UPDATE DB CFG        UNCATALOG NODE
GET/RESET/UPDATE DBM CFG       UPDATE COMMAND OPTIONS
HELP                           UPDATE HISTORY
IMPORT                         UPDATE MONITOR SWITCHES
INVOKE
```

Fig. 2–11 DB2 Commands available from CLP

If the command exceeds the limit allowed by the operating system, use a backslash / as the line continuation character. The complete syntax and explanation of all SQL statements are documented in the *DB2 SQL Reference*. You can obtain syntax and information for all of the DB2 commands from the Command Line Processor (as listed in Fig. 2–11):

- `DB2 ?`   list of all DB2 commands
- `DB2 ? command`   on about a specific command
- `DB2 ? SQLnnnn`   information about a specific SQLCODE
- `DB2 ? DB2nnnn`   information about an error

To examine the current CLP settings issue the following command:

```
                        DB2 LIST COMMAND OPTIONS
```

Fig. 2–12 shows the default settings. These settings can be updated for each CLP session or globally using the **DB2OPTIONS** environment variable.

```
        Command Line Processor Option Settings

Backend process wait time (seconds)          (DB2BQTIME) = 1
No. of retries to connect to backend          (DB2BQTRY) = 60
Request queue wait time (seconds)            (DB2RQTIME) = 5
Input queue wait time (seconds)              (DB2IQTIME) = 5
Command options                              (DB2OPTIONS) =

Option Description                                   Current Setting
------  ----------------------------------------    -------------

  -a    Display SQLCA                                  OFF
  -c    Auto-Commit                                    ON
  -e    Display SQLCODE/SQLSTATE                       OFF
  -f    Read from input file                           OFF
  -l    Log commands in history file                  OFF
  -o    Display output                                 ON
  -p    Display interactive input prompt               ON
  -r    Save output to report file                     OFF
  -s    Stop execution on command error               OFF
  -t    Set statement termination character           OFF
  -v    Echo current command                          OFF
  -w    Display FETCH/SELECT warning messages          ON
  -z    Save all output to output file                 OFF
```

Fig. 2–12 Command Line Processor Option Settings

- **DB2 ? UPDATE COMMAND OPTIONS** — displays all the available options, the possible values for each option and the usage of the update command options command
- **DB2 UPDATE COMMAND OPTIONS USING <options...>** — changes the value of one or more options for a CLP session.

The Command Line Processor has two parts: a front-end process and a back-end process. The front-end process is called **DB2** and the back-end is **DB2BP**. The back-end process will maintain a connection to the database. To release this connection to the database, use the **TERMINATE** command. To end an interactive CLP session, issue the **QUIT** command (this does not release the database connection).

You can also create a file with SQL statements and DB2 commands that you wish to execute using the CLP. Suppose you create a file called *file.clp* as shown in Fig. 2–13. Every DB2 command or SQL statement in the file is terminated with a semicolon (;) (the default termination character). You can change the default terminating character if you wish using the -t option.

To execute the CLP input file in Fig. 2–13, type **DB2 -TVF file.clp**.

```
CONNECT TO SAMPLE;
CREATE TABLE tab1 (c1 CHAR (30));

SELECT * FROM tab1;
COMMIT WORK;
CONNECT RESET;
```

DB2 for Windows NT CLP Considerations

DB2 for Windows NT does not allow the Command Line Processor to be used in every operating system window. A DB2 command window must be used to issue any CLP statements. A command window can be created by either clicking on the CLP command window icon (located in the DB2 folder on Windows NT) or by entering the command **db2cmd**.

Using the Database Director

The Database Director is a graphical database administration tool. You can invoke it by typing **db2dd** from the operating system command prompt or double clicking on the Database Director icon in the DB2 folder (OS/2 and Windows NT).

Fig. 2–14 shows the main **Database Director** window. The database objects are displayed in a tree view. You can also obtain a list view of the same objects. There are two instances displayed: *DB2* and *DB2AIX*. These are the instances that are cataloged on the workstation. The instances can be remote or local. The DB2 instance contains two databases: *DB2CERT* and *SAMPLE*. Clicking on one of the database icons will also initiate an attempt to connect to the database. Once connected to the database, there are many types of administrative tasks that can be performed.

Using the Database Director, you can perform the following tasks:

- **Configuration** — You can display and alter the settings of the resources allocated to your database. You can set the size of the buffer pool, the log files and the sort buffer. You can specify the number of concurrent application programs that can connect to each database. You can also enable a database for roll forward recovery.

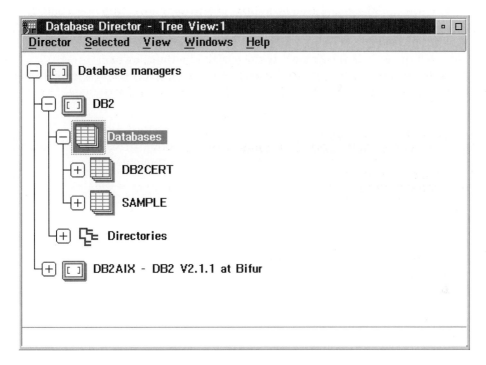

Fig. 2–14 Tree View of the Database Director

- **Recovery** — You can back up, restore, or roll forward a database or a table space.
- **Directory** — You can manage directories for accessing local and remote databases, create a database, catalog or uncatalog a local or remote node or database, and drop a database and list information contained in the node, database and dcs directories.
- **Managing Media** — You can create, drop or change table spaces. You can modify the storage assigned to table spaces.

Creating the Sample Database

You can execute a command to create a database named *sample*. The command is **db2sampl**. This will create a database named sample with eight user tables (see Fig. 2–15). If you are working in a UNIX environment, the syntax is:

```
db2sampl <path>
```

The initial database files are created in the defined **<path>** location. If you don't specify a path, the sample database will be created in the path specified by the **DFTDBPATH** environment variable in the database manager configuration file. By default, this is the home directory of the instance owner.

If you are using DB2 for OS/2 or Windows NT environment, the syntax is:

DB2SAMPL <drive>

The initial database files are created in the defined **<drive>** location. If you don't specify the drive, it will be created in the same drive where DB2 was installed, as defined by the **DFTDBPATH** environment variable.

```
db2 => CONNECT TO sample

   Database Connection Information

   Database product       = DB2/6000 2.1.1
   SQL authorization ID   = DB2
   Local database alias   = SAMPLE

db2 => LIST TABLES

Name              Creator Type CTIME
----------------------------- ----------------------
DEPARTMENT        DB2      T   1996-03-12-11.07.55.000003
EMP_ACT           DB2      T   1996-03-12-11.07.57.000905
EMP_PHOTO         DB2      T   1996-03-12-11.08.01.000503
EMP_RESUME        DB2      T   1996-03-12-11.08.06.000514
EMPLOYEE          DB2      T   1996-03-12-11.07.55.000618
ORG               DB2      T   1996-03-12-11.07.52.000052
PROJECT           DB2      T   1996-03-12-11.08.00.000598
STAFF             DB2      T   1996-03-12-11.07.53.000545


   8 record(s) selected.

db2 => SELECT * FROM org

DEPTNUMB DEPTNAME       MANAGER  DIVISION   LOCATION
-------- ------------   -------- ---------- -----------
    10   Head Office       160   Corporate  New York
    15   New England        50   Eastern    Boston
    20   Mid Atlantic       10   Eastern    Washington
    38   South Atlantic     30   Eastern    Atlanta
    42   Great Lakes       100   Midwest    Chicago
    51   Plains            140   Midwest    Dallas
    66   Pacific           270   Western    San Francisco
    84   Mountain          290   Western    Denver
```

Fig. 2–15 Connecting to the Sample Database

To access the sample database we must first establish a connection to the database. The **LIST TABLES** command can be issued after connecting to a database to show the tables which are defined for the database. In Fig. 2–15 we also retrieved all of the data stored in the table called *DB2.ORG*.

Summary

In this chapter we have discussed DB2 product installation on various platforms: AIX, OS/2 and Windows NT. We looked at sample installation screens for these platforms. After the product installation was completed we created a DB2 instance.

A DB2 instance can be defined as a logical database server environment. For each environment, we discussed the instance creation process, including any special user id and group setup required.

The DB2 environment had to be configured. Some DB2 platforms performed this setup during installation (Windows NT and OS/2) and other platforms required the definition of an instance owner. DB2 environment variables are defined on every DB2 workstation, including **DB2INSTANCE**, **DB2PATH**, **DB2DBDFT**, and **DB2COMM**. The location of the definition of the DB2 environment variables is different for OS/2, AIX and Windows NT.

Throughout this chapter, we used two common interfaces: the Command Line Processor and the Database Director. We used some of the commands available in the Command Line Processor. The Command Line Processor has default settings that can be modified for each session or changed globally using the **DB2OPTIONS** environment variable. We also discussed how to place DB2 commands and SQL statements in a file that can be executed from the CLP.

We discussed instance management, including starting and stopping the DB2 instance. It was discovered that DB2 for Windows NT is integrated with the Windows NT services environment and each DB2 instance is a Windows NT service. The commands used to start and stop the instance are **DB2START** and **DB2STOP**. Finally, we created a sample database, connected to the database, and retrieved a list of the tables in the sample database.

Questions

1. Which command would you use to list all of the DB2 instances on a DB2 server?

   ◯   A. db2inst

   ◯   B. db2ilist

   ◯   C. db2 list instances

   ◯   D. db2 display instances

2. Which environment variable is used to identify the active instance?

   ◯   A. DB2START

   ◯   B. DB2ACTIVE

   ◯   C. DB2DFTDB

   ◯   D. DB2INSTANCE

3. How can you invoke the Interactive Command Line Processor?

   ◯   A. typing DB2

   ◯   B. typing DB2CLP

   ◯   C. typing DB2ICRT

   ◯   D. typing DB2START

4. Which is the command to start the instance?

   ◯   A. db2begin

   ◯   B. startdb2

   ◯   C. db2start

   ◯   D. db2 start instance

Answers

1. (B)
   The command is db2ilist. It will list all the instances on the workstation.
2. (D)
   DB2INSTANCE is the variable that identifies the active instance.
3. (A)
   To enter the Command Line Processor, type db2 from the command prompt.
4. (C)
   The command to start the DB2 instance is db2start.

Exercises

> Notes:
> These exercises use the default instance (db2). In **UNIX** systems you will have to create the instance, use the **DB2ICRT** command.
> In Windows environments you will need to issue CLP commands from a DB2 CLP Window (use db2cmd to start CLP window).
> Ensure your **DB2PATH** and **DB2INSTANCE** variables are set properly.

1. Install the DB2 product in "Try and Buy" mode from the CD-ROM (see page 587 for installation instructions).

2. Make sure that you have an instance named **db2** on your system. For non-UNIX environments there should be a default instance called **db2** created. Issue the command:
   db2ilist

   If there are no entries, then follow the steps required for your operating system to create an instance called db2. You will need to use the command **db2icrt** to create the instance. If you receive the error "DB21061E Command Line environment not initialized." and you are using a DB2 for Windows NT or 95 installation, enter **DB2CMD** to start a CLP window.

3. Issue the command to start the instance from the command line:
   db2start

   When you start the instance you may need to specify a user id and password. For UNIX environments the user id should be called db2 and it should be part of the **SYSADM_GROUP** as specified during instance creation. Non-UNIX operating environments a valid operating system user id should be used. For Windows NT the user id must be a local **administrator** and the instance should be started using the **NET START DB2** command and not the **DB2START**. We will discuss the **SYSADM_GROUP** in more detail in the next chapter. Before proceeding to step 4, ensure the instance started successfully.

4. Type **db2 list database directory**.
   The output of this command is the system database directory for the instance. All databases must be recorded in this location. It should be empty as we have not created any databases yet.

5. Edit the **cr8db.ddl** file in \exercise\chapter2\parta and specify the location where you would like to create the database.
   For UNIX environments the location should be an operating system path and for Non-UNIX environments a drive letter is exepected.

6. Now you will execute the CLP file to create a database. The **CREATE DATABASE** command is used in the file.
    From the command line, type **db2 -tvf cr8db.ddl**

7. Let's make sure that you have created the database successfully.
    Type the following command:
    db2 list database directory

    There should be an entry for a database called *DB2CERT*. The amount of disk space required for the database is between 8MB and 20MB.

8. Now we will create tables in the database. View the contents of the file **db2cert.ddl**. This file contains the SQL statements for creating tables. It also creates some other items that will be used later. From the command line, type the following:
    db2 -tvf db2cert.ddl

    This command should have given you errors as we have not connected to the database. You must be connected to a database before you can create or access any of its objects.

9. Type the command to connect to the database:
    db2 connect to db2cert

    For now, the user id and password is not required during connect as the current user id will be used and since we just created the database we automatically have **CONNECT** authority.

10. Now you should create the tables.
    Type the command **db2 -tvf db2cert.ddl**

11. Let's look at the tables that were created.
    Type the command **db2 list tables**
    There should be 4 tables listed. These tables are called **user tables** as they are created by the user or database administrator.

12. Type the command **db2 list tables for system**
    There should be 29 tables listed. These tables are called **system tables**. They were created in step 6 and they are usually **not** directly modified.

13. To view the contents of the a DB2 table you must issue an SQL statement.
    Enter the following SQL statement:
    db2 SELECT * FROM test_taken WHERE DECIMAL(score) > 70

14. Was any data returned on the screen? Probably not. The SQL statement was not enclosed with quotation marks and therefore the operating system interpreted the statement instead. In this case there was probably a file called **70** created in the current directory.
When entering commands from CLP you should remember to protect special characters from the operating system. For example, the asterisk (*) and inequality operators (<,>) have another meaning in most operating systems.
Type the command that will disconnect you from the database:
db2 connect reset

15. Let's enter some of the same commands using the interactive Command Line Processor. Open an interactive DB2 (CLP) Command Window (Windows NT or Windows 95) or enter the command **db2**.

16. You should now be in the interactive Command Line Processor. Notice that your prompt has changed. List all the possible DB2 commands.
Enter the a question mark: **?**

17. The question mark (?) from within CLP will display the commands that can be issued. Let's examine the syntax of the **CONNECT** command.
? connect

18. Connect to the *DB2CERT* database.
CONNECT TO DB2CERT

19. Issue the SQL statement:
SELECT * FROM test_taken WHERE DECIMAL(score) > 70
Note that in from the interactive CLP the quotation marks are not necessary.

20. What happens if you enter the **TERMINATE** command from the CLP?
The interactive mode and the database connection is terminated.

21. Issue the command:
db2 list applications
SQL1611W No data was returned by Database System Monitor.

This means that no there are no connections to the database. When you issue the **TERMINATE** command from CLP, it disconnects you from the database and terminates the CLP interactive session.

22. Let's use the Database Director. Either double-click on the Database Director icon in the DB2 folder or type the following command:
db2dd

23. Double click on the instance icon labelled **DB2**.

24. Double click on the **Databases** icon. You should see the *DB2CERT* database
    as an object within the DB2 instance.

25. Double click on the **DB2CERT** icon. You should see various database objects.
    Double click on the **TABLES** icon to display the tables contained in the
    DB2CERT database. This is similar to the **LIST TABLES** command that was
    used in the CLP. The tables are grouped as **user** and **system** tables. The
    schema name (qualifer) for the system tables is called **SYSIBM**.

26. Double click on the **<USER-ID>.Tables** icon for user tables (where USER-
    ID is your current user id. You should see 4 tables.

27. Try to select rows from one of the tables using the Database Director. Did
    you succeed? Probably not, as there is currently no SQL interface provided
    with the Database Director. Close the Database Director.

28. Enter the command that will stop the instance:
    db2stop

    Remember that in Windows NT the DB2 instances should be started and
    stopped as Windows NT services.

CHAPTER 3

Controlling Data Access

Security is an important consideration whenever data is stored electronically in a relational database management system. In this chapter, we will implement controlled data access using many different methods. Access to data within DB2 is controlled at many levels, including instance, database, database object and application packages. DB2 utilizes the operating system's security as much as possible. The topics of authentication of userids and passwords will be discussed. We will configure groups of typical database users like data administrators, system administrators, transactional processing personnel and decision support users. Each of these database user-types can require different access privileges.

The first step in enabling a database server to be accessed in a networked environment is to start a DB2 instance which has been configured to allocate the proper communication resources. These resources could involve one or more network protocols, including NetBIOS, APPC, TCP/IP, and IPX/SPX. If your environment includes DB2 host databases, DB2 for MVS for example, an additional product known as Distributed Database Connection Services (DDCS) is required. Once the communication resources have been successfully allocated on the DB2 server, you must then perform cataloging steps on each of the DB2 clients.

DB2 client configuration steps include cataloging the DB2 server node and the associated databases residing on the server. More advanced DB2 database administrators can wish to modify server resources as well as access databases.

Security

When storing data in a relational database management system, the access to that data needs to be controlled. There are three factors to consider when controlling access to data in a database.

- Who will access the data? Users of the database will be able to access the data stored in the database at varying levels.
- What will be accessed? Data stored in the database are called database objects. There are many types of database objects that users can access.
- What type of access is allowed? These are the actions that a user is permitted to perform on database objects, such as reading, updating or deleting items.

Overview of Security

There are three levels of security that control access in a database system. The first level controls the access to the instance. The second level controls the access to the database. The last level relates to the access of objects within the database.

- Access to the instance is managed by the operating system functions. These functions allow the system to make sure that the user really is who he or she claims to be. It also controls access to objects like files and programs. The concept of users and groups is the basis of this mechanism.
- Access within a database is controlled at the instance level by the DB2 database manager. The concepts of administrative authorities and user privileges are the basis of this mechanism.

The database administrator must ensure that sensitive information is not accessed by those without a "need to know". A database security plan for database access should be developed by defining your objectives. For example, who should have the ability to start and stop DB2 instances.

Authentication

The first step in managing security is to verify the user's identity. This is called **authentication**. Authentication is the operation of verifying whether a user is who he or she claims to be based on user name and password. DB2 checks authentication at the instance level for each database user and verifies the user with the operating system.

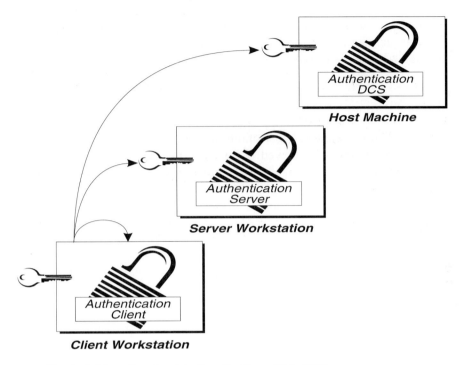

Fig. 3–1 Three Levels of Authentication within DB2

Every time a user tries to connect to a local or remote database, he or she is authenticated. DB2 uses the operating system's security mechanisms to perform this authentication. There are three levels of authentication within DB2. Fig. 3–1 shows the process of authentication as being a key that opens a lock to the DB2 instance. Once a user enters a user name and password, either at login time or with a DB2 command, it is like a key that can either open or not open the door to DB2. Where the lock is verified depends on the type of authentication defined for the instance. The authentication can occur in any of the following three places:

- **DCS** (Data Connection Services) — When the DDCS product is **not** installed, the behavior of **DCS** authentication is the same as that of **SERVER**. If the DDCS product is installed and the authentication is **DCS**, the user is authenticated at a host database machine. If authentication is **SERVER** and the DDCS product is installed, authentication is performed by DDCS.
- **SERVER** — This is the default setting. The user is authenticated at the database server machine. For a remote client, the user name and password flow from the remote client to the database server in ASCII format.
- **CLIENT** — The user is authenticated locally at the client machine. The password will not flow across the network but will be checked at the client machine where the user has logged on.

Authentication and Instances

Authentication is specified at the instance level. All databases within the instance must have the same authentication level. If you want different authentication levels, you must create separate instances on the database server. Fig. 3–2 shows some of the contents of an instance.

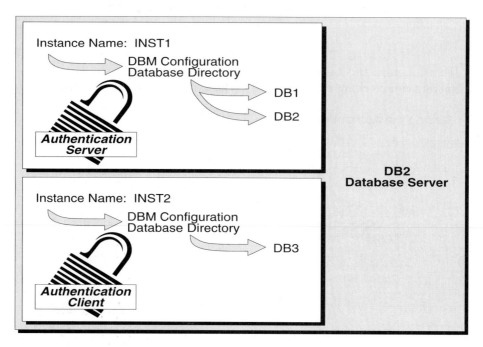

Fig. 3–2 Multiple DB2 Instances within a Server

Each instance is a unique database manager environment. An instance is a link to the installed DB2 product files (executables). This allows each database manager (instance) to maintain separate environments with different authentication types and configuration parameters.

Fig. 3–2 shows two instances, one with authentication **SERVER**, the other with authentication **CLIENT**. One possible reason for doing this is to allow for a production environment and a test environment. Instances are executed independently of one another. Each DB2 instance must be started with a separate **DB2START** command.

By maintaining separate instances, you can configure the DB2 resources separately. DB2 configuration files contain parameter values that define the resources allocated to DB2 and individual databases. There are two types of configuration files: the instance (DBM configuration) and the database (DB configuration).

Figure 3-2 shows two instances, *INST1* and *INST2* on the same database server. *INST1* has an authentication type of **SERVER**. There are two databases in *INST1* called *DB1* and *DB2*. There is an instance-level or database manager configuration file and two database-level configuration files for *INST1*. *INST2* has a database manager configuration file and one database configuration file for database *DB3*. *INST2* has the authentication type of **CLIENT**.

The database manager configuration file is created when an instance of DB2 is created; it affects the system resources allocated for each instance. A database configuration file is created at the same time the database is created. These parameters affect each application that uses the database. Many of these parameters can be changed to improve performance or increase capacity.

Setting the Authentication Level

The authentication level must be the same for all databases contained in that instance. The authentication type can be changed by updating the database configuration parameter. You can check the authentication level with the following command:

```
GET DATABASE MANAGER CONFIGURATION
```

The parameter is called **AUTHENTICATION** in the database manager configuration file. The default setting for **AUTHENTICATION** is **SERVER**. To change it, issue the following command:

```
UPDATE DBM CFG USING AUTHENTICATION CLIENT
DB2STOP
DB2START
```

Notice how we have used a shorthand method of the command within the CLP. Database manager can be abbreviated to **dbm**, configuration to **cfg**.

✍ The changes to the instance will take effect when the instance is stopped and then restarted.

You must be a member of the instance administrative group to make changes to the parameters in the database manager configuration file. This is for security reasons.

Authorization Levels

The first step in accessing data within a DB2 database is called authentication. Authentication is the process of verifying that potential users are who they claim to be. This occurs outside of the database manager and is dependent on the operating system.

✍️   DB2 users must be defined within the operating system. If **SERVER** authentication is used, the users are defined on the DB2 Server.

After a successful connection to the database, access control to the database objects is controlled by DB2 itself. This involves verifying that the user has the proper database authorities and object privileges. Different levels of authority are available and they are defined in the DBM configuration file.

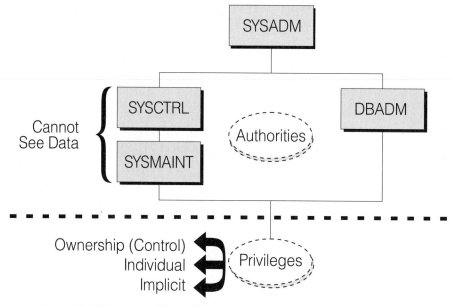

Fig. 3–3 DB2 Access Control Hierarchy

There are different levels of authority in DB2:

SYSADM	System Administration Authority
SYSCTRL	System Control Authority
SYSMAINT	System Maintenance Authority
DBADM	Database Administration Authority

Authorization levels in DB2 provide a hierarchy for administration capabilities, as shown in Fig. 3–3. An authority is a set of privileges covering a set of databases or database objects. These authorities are assigned to a group of users. Each member of the group has the same DB2 authority, unless they are explicitly removed.

At the top of this hierarchy is the **DB2 System Administrator** or **SYSADM**. This is referred to as the instance owner in UNIX environments. Any member of the SYSADM user group is able to perform any of the DB2 administration operations as well as access all database objects. SYSADM members are the only users that are allowed to configure the DB2 instance.

✍ Membership to the DB2 SYSADM user group should be controlled by the DB2 administrator.

System control (SYSCTRL) provides the ability to perform almost any administration command. A member of the **SYSCTRL** user group does not have authority to access database objects or modify the instance configuration file (DBM configuration). SYSCTRL offers almost complete control of database objects defined in the DB2 instance, but **cannot** access user data directly, unless explicitly granted the privilege to do so. A user with this authority, or higher, can perform the following functions:

- Update the database, node and DCS directory entries
- Update database configuration parameters
- Create or drop a database
- Force applications
- Quiesce the DB2 instance or database
- Run the `RESTORE/BACKUP/ROLLFORWARD` commands
- Create or drop a tablespace

SYSMAINT, or **System Maintenance** authority, allows the execution of maintenance activities but cannot access user data. Only users with this level of authority or higher (SYSADM or SYSCTRL) can do the following tasks:

- Update database configuration files
- Back up databases and tablespaces
- Restore an existing database
- Restore table spaces
- Start and stop the DB2 instance
- Run the database monitor
- Start and stop traces

At the database administration level, there is the **DBADM** authority. The creator of a database will automatically have DBADM authority for the new database. Other users can be **granted** DBADM authority using the `GRANT` statement. It is possible to hold DBADM authority for multiple database. DBADM provides some common administration tasks, such as loading data, create any database objects, and monitor database activity.

A **privilege** is the right of a particular user or group to create or access a resource. There are three types of privileges: **Ownership**, **Individual**, and **Implicit**.

1. Ownership or control privileges — For most objects, the user or group who creates the object has full access to that object. **CONTROL** privilege is automatically granted to the creator of an object. There are some database objects, such as views, that are exceptions to this statement. Having control privilege is like having ownership of the object. You have the right to access the object and give access to others. Privileges are controlled by users with ownership or administrative authority, they provide other users with access using the **GRANT** SQL statement.

2. Individual privileges — These are privileges that allow you to perform a specific function, sometimes on a specific object. These privileges include **SELECT**, **DELETE** and **INSERT**.

3. Implicit privileges — As an example, a user who can execute a package where that package involves other privileges obtains those privileges while executing the package. This is known as the **EXECUTE** privilege.

Table 3–1 shows the valid commands for the various DB2 authority levels.

Table 3–1 Database Authorities

Function	SYSADM	SYSCTRL	SYSMAINT	DBADM
CATALOG/UNCATALOG DATABASE	YES			
CATALOG/UNCATALOG NODE	YES			
CATALOG/UNCATALOG DCS	YES			
UPDATE DBM CFG	YES			
GRANT/REVOKE DBADM	YES			
GRANT/REVOKE SYSCTRL	YES			
GRANT/REVOKE SYSMAINT	YES			
FORCE USERS	YES	YES		
CREATE/DROP DATABASE	YES	YES		
QUIESCE DATABASE	YES	YES		

Table 3–1 Database Authorities

Function	SYSADM	SYSCTRL	SYSMAINT	DBADM
CREATE/DROP/ALTER TABLESPACE	YES	YES		
RESTORE TO NEW DATABASE	YES	YES		
UPDATE DB CFG	YES	YES	YES	
BACK UP DATABASE/ TABLESPACE	YES	YES	YES	
RESTORE TO EXISTING DATABASE	YES	YES	YES	
PERFORM ROLL FOR- WARD RECOVERY	YES	YES	YES	
START/STOP INSTANCE	YES	YES	YES	
RESTORE TABLESPACE	YES	YES	YES	
RUN TRACE	YES	YES	YES	
OBTAIN MONITOR SNAPSHOTS	YES	YES	YES	
QUERY TABLESPACE STATE	YES	YES	YES	YES
UPDATE LOG HISTORY FILES	YES	YES	YES	YES
QUIESCE TABLESPACE	YES	YES	YES	YES
LOAD TABLES	YES			YES
SET/UNSET CHECK PENDING STATUS	YES	YES		YES
READ LOG FILES	YES	YES		YES
CREATE/ACTIVATE/DROP EVENT MONITORS	YES	YES		YES
RUN LOAD UTILITY	YES	YES		YES

Security Considerations

The authority levels SYSADM, SYSCTRL and SYSMAINT are **NOT** established using the **GRANT** statement. These three authority levels are associated with groups and are specified at the instance level. As such, they must be set or changed in the database manager configuration file. Fig. 3–4 shows a portion of the database manager configuration file with the parameters for SYSADM_GROUP, SYSCTRL_GROUP and SYSMAINT_GROUP. There are no default values for SYSADM, SYSCTRL and SYSMAINT.

A member of the administrative group (SYSADM) can either modify these authorities for the instance. For example, to change the SYSCTRL group to *db2cntrl*, the following commands would be issued:

```
UPDATE DBM CFG USING SYSCTRL_GROUP db2cntrl
DB2STOP
DB2START
```

The **UPDATE DATABASE MANAGER CONFIGURATION** command uses the **USING** option with the field to be updated followed by the value. For any changes to take effect, the instance must be stopped and restarted. For the instance to be successfully stopped, all database connections must be released. The new values in the DBM configuration file are shown in Fig. 3–4.

```
SYSADM group name  (SYSADM_GROUP)  = DB2CERT
SYSCTRL group name (SYSCTRL_GROUP) = DB2CNTRL
SYSMAINT group name(SYSMAINT_GROUP)=
```

Fig. 3–4 Updating the Authorities for the DB2 Instance

The user groups *db2cert* and *db2cntrl* that are shown in Fig. 3–4 should match an existing operating system group of users. DB2 does not verify that the operating system user groups exist during the modification of the DBM configuration file. Therefore, the database administrator must ensure that the operating system user ids and groups are set properly.

The group authorities are also related to the security mechanisms of the operating system. For example, an UNIX user who is placed in the *db2cntrl* group, has their access controlled within DB2 according to the SYSCTRL authority. But the same user can have special access to their UNIX file system also. For example, an OS/2 user who is in the *db2cert* group (as defined in User Profile Management — UPM) will inherit SYSADM DB2 instance authority.

✍   The creation of users and group assignments should be strictly controlled on any DB2 server.

DB2 Privileges (Data Control Language)

A **privilege** is the right to create or access a database resource. Both DB2
authorities and privileges on database objects are hierarchical in nature. Fig. 3–
5 shows the hierarchy of authorities and privileges within DB2.

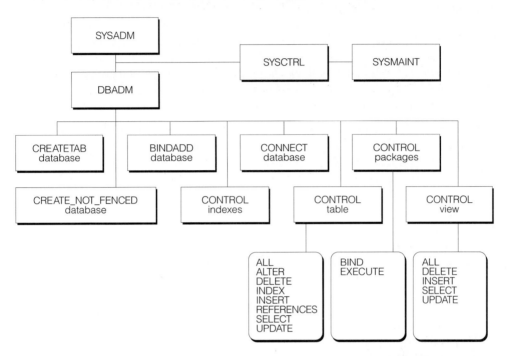

Fig. 3–5 Hierarchy of Authorizations and Privileges on Database Objects

Database Object Privileges

For each DB2 object, a specific authority or privilege is required in order to
create it, and a specific authority or privilege is needed in order to have control
over it. The following list describes the privileges on various objects within the
database.

- **Database authorities** — These include the ability to create and access a
  database. Any creator of a database automatically receives DBADM authority. The DBADM can issue any SQL statement against the database. The
  DBADM can grant connect privilege, the ability to create tables or new
  packages in the database.

- **Table privileges** — Control privilege on a table or view can only be granted by a user who has SYSADM or DBADM authority. To have control privileges on a table allows you to add columns to it, create a primary key, delete, retrieve, update or insert rows in the table, create an index, create referential constraints on the table, use the **EXPORT** utility and perform maintenance such as reorganizing or updating statistics on the table.
- **View privileges** — To create a view, you must be able to issue the SQL **SELECT** statement or have control privilege on every table or view that is referenced. You need to have control privilege on the view to grant delete, insert, select and update privileges on the view, unless the view is defined as a read-only view.
- **Index privileges** — The user that creates the index receives control privileges on the index. This means that user can drop an index. The table level index privilege allows a user to create a new index on a table.
- **Package privileges** — The creator of a package automatically receives control privilege on the package. That user can grant other users the ability to bind, rebind or execute the package. However, the person that binds a package must have the necessary privileges to access the objects referenced in the embedded static SQL statements. Control privilege on a package also allows you to drop the package. Any user who has execute privilege on the package can execute the statements within the scope of that package.

✍ To bind a new package to the database you must have **BINDADD** database authority or you must be in the SYSADM or DBADM user group.

There are two SQL statements used to administer database privileges:

- The **GRANT** statement gives privileges to a user.
- The **REVOKE** statement takes privileges away from the user.

For example, suppose you want user Frank to be able to drop the candidate table in the *db2cert* database. The statement would be as follows:

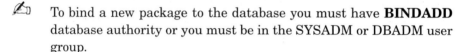

```
GRANT CONTROL ON TABLE candidate TO USER Frank
```

The **CONTROL** option of the **GRANT** statement gives *Frank* the ability to drop the *candidate* table or view. *Frank* cannot give another user the same privileges on the *candidate* table, unless *Frank* has created the table. The privileges and authorities combine to control access to database objects. If a user is given access to a database (**CONNECT** authority), by default they are **not** given access to any of the database objects. The database administrator must assign the access privileges to the users of the database.

To grant privileges on database objects, a user must have SYSADM authority, DBADM authority, or **CONTROL** privilege on the object. A user can grant privileges only on existing database objects. A user must have SYSADM or DBADM to grant **CONTROL** privilege to another user. To grant DBADM authority, a user must have SYSADM authority. Fig. 3–6 summarizes the privileges required for database objects within DB2 to perform the following:

- Create a resource (database, table, view, index or package)
- Control a resource

RESOURCE	NEEDED TO CREATE	NEEDED TO CONTROL	OTHER AUTHORITIES AND PRIVILEGES
Database	SYSADM	DBADM	CONNECT BINDADD CREATETAB CREATE_NOT_FENCED
Package	BINDADD	CONTROL	BIND EXECUTE
Table or View	To create a table CREATETAB. To create a view CONTROL or SELECT on the base tables.	CONTROL	SELECT INSERT DELETE UPDATE ALTER (Tables) INDEX (Tables) REFERENCES (Tables)
Index	INDEX on Table	CONTROL	none
Alias	If schema differs from current authid, requires DBADM.	CONTROL	none
Distinct Type (UDT)	If schema differs from current authid, requires DBADM.	CONTROL	none
User Defined Function	If schema differs from current authid, requires DBADM.	CONTROL	none

Fig. 3–6 Privileges Required for Database Objects within DB2

There are other situations that require special privileges. When creating DB2 applications or using DB2 applications there are additional securtiy considerations.

Application Development Privileges

There are certain privileges that apply only to application developers. Each step of the development process requires certain privileges on database objects. Let's examine the application development steps and the required privileges.

Table 3–2 summarizes the authorities and privileges needed do the following:

- Precompile a source program and create a bind (.bnd) file.
- Create a new package (**BINDADD**).
- Modify an existing package (**BIND**).
- Re-create an existing package (**REBIND**).
- Execute or run a package (**EXECUTE**).
- Drop a package (**CONTROL**)

Table 3–2 Privileges Required for Programming

Action	Privileges Required
Precompile to bindfile	**CONNECT** on database
Create a new package	**CONNECT** on database **BINDADD** on database Privileges needed to execute each static SQL statement
Modify an existing package	**CONNECT** on database **BIND** on package Privileges needed to execute each static SQL statement
Re-create an existing package	**CONNECT** on database **BIND** on package
Execute a package	**CONNECT** on database **EXECUTE** on package
Drop a package	**CONNECT** on database **CONTROL** on package or creator of package

An embedded SQL program must have the SQL statements prepared and bound as a package in the DB2 database. The static embedded SQL program preparation step does not required the proper privileges for the database objects. Warnings will be generated if the individual does not have the proper database access rights or the objects do not exist. The objects **must** exist during the bind phase of development as the existence and privileges of the objects are verified.

If the program contains dynamic embedded SQL statements, the statements are prepared and executed at runtime. There are no special requirements to create a package for dynamic embedded SQL statements as there are no database objects referenced.

To create a new package for any embedded SQL application you need **CONNECT** and **BINDADD** authority on the database. Since the access plans for static embedded SQL statements are created during the bind phase, you may wish to update the plan using the **REBIND** command or **BIND** the package using the bind file as the input. You only require **BIND** privilege on the package to update its contents. To execute a package, you need **EXECUTE** privilege on the package.

Let's look at a sample scenario and determine, according to the function that a user will be performing, the necessary authorities and privileges on the database objects. In our scenario, we will have a database where one of the applications called *app1* is used to manipulate names and addresses.

Volker wants to execute this program. He also wants to be able have his own table called *Volker.personal* to keep store other data. Therefore, we will provide Volker with **EXECUTE** privilege for the *app1* package. Volker also requires **CONNECT** authority to the database. We granted Volker the **CONTROL** privilege for the *Volker.personal* table. We could have given him **CREATETAB** authority for the database and let him create the table, but this would allow him the ability to create many tables. Remember, the *app1* package must exist in the database before we could grant Volker **EXECUTE** privilege.

Greta is the application developer who is writing the *app1* program. She needs to have **SELECT**, **INSERT**, **UPDATE**, and **DELETE** access to the various tables in the database. We would need to **GRANT** the required priviliges to Greta. She needs to be able to add the new package in the database and execute the application to test it, therefore we will give her **BINDADD** authority.

Gabriel needs to be able to load data using the **LOAD** command into various tables, but he will never execute the application. He needs DBADM authority. He could be given SYSADM authority instead, but for security reasons, we will have only one user with SYSADM authority.

Calene will be given SYSADM authority for the DB2 instance. Therefore, only Calene can create the database and modify the DBM configuration file for the instance.

✍ Remember — SYSADM, SYSCTRL and SYSMAINT cannot be granted in the same way as DBADM. They must be defined in the database manager configuration file.

Let's examine Fig. 3–7 to understand the required authorities and privileges for the scenario we have just discussed.

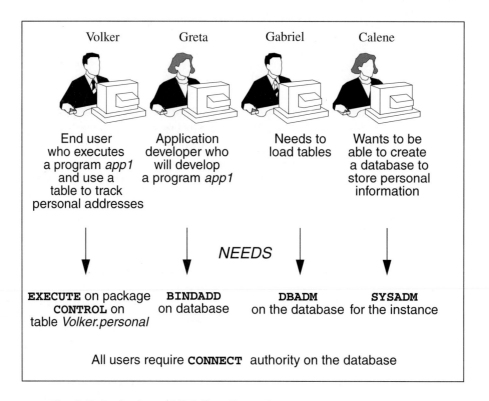

Fig. 3–7 Authority and Privilege Scenario

Other Authorizations

There are other security considerations within DB2. Privileges can be assigned to groups, individual users, or assigned to all users be specifying the **PUBLIC** group. An individual user can be given the privilege to access DB2 database objects. The user must be a valid operating system user as DB2 will verify existence of the user id. A user group consists of one or more individual users as defined in the operating system. Every member of the user group will have the same access rights on database objects unless they have been granted higher privileges individually.

A database privilege may be assign to **PUBLIC**. This special group is not defined within the operating system, only within DB2. All users with **CONNECT** authority to the database are automatically members of the PUBLIC group. Granting a privilege to PUBLIC provides all users with the privilege. There are certain privileges granted to PUBLIC by default. For example, all database users have **SELECT** privilege on the system catalog tables. You may decide to remove the privilege using the **REVOKE** statement after creating a database.

Explicit and Implicit Authorizations

Privileges and authorities within DB2 can be obtained either implicitly or explicitly. As a database administrator, you should be aware of the ways that users can obtain access to objects in your databases. This section examines the various ways that privileges and authorities can be obtained or revoked.

If a user who has SYSADM or SYSCTRL authority creates a database, that user is implicitly granted DBADM authority for the database. If that user has SYSADM or SYSCTRL authority removed, they maintain DBADM authority for each database they created. To remove their DBADM authority they must be removed explicitly for each database using the **REVOKE** statement.

When a user is granted DBADM authority on a database, the user is also implicitly granted **CONNECT, CREATETAB, BINDADD** and **CREATE_NOT_FENCED** authorities. If the DBADM authority is later removed, the other privileges remain in effect unless they are separately revoked.

When a user is granted **CONTROL** privilege on a table, the user is implicitly granted all other table privileges. If the **CONTROL** privilege is removed, the other privileges remain, unless they are separately revoked. All remaining privileges for the table can be explicitly removed using the **REVOKE ALL** statement.

```
REVOKE ALL ON tablename FROM username
```

 The privileges granted to the creator of a view can never exceed those belonging to the creator of the base table.

Determining Authorizations

Information about authorizations is maintained in four system catalog views:

- SYSCAT.DBAUTH — Contains database authorities
- SYSCAT.TABAUTH — Contains table and view privileges
- SYSCAT.PACKAGEAUTH — Contains package privileges
- SYSCAT.INDEXAUTH — Contains index privileges

Remember that the members of the SYSADM, SYSMAINT and SYSCTRL groups must be created within the operating system and simply referenced by DB2. To examine the groups specified for SYSADM, SYSMAINT and SYSCTRL view the database manager (DBM) configuration. For all other authorities and privileges, examine the system catalog views listed above to determine the users and groups that have access rights.

Group and User Support (UNIX)

Some operating systems will allow the same name for a user and a group. This can cause confusion for authorization and privilege checking within DB2.

 OS/2 and Windows NT does not permit a group and user with same name.

Let's look at how DB2 handles the different scenarios regarding groups and users. Suppose we have a user named Cal. We want to give this user the ability to perform a **SELECT** on the *candidate* table.

```
GRANT SELECT ON candidate TO cal
GRANT SELECT ON candidate TO USER cal
```

Both of these statements give **SELECT** privilege on the *candidate* table to the user. Suppose we have a group named Cal.

```
GRANT SELECT ON candidate TO cal
GRANT SELECT ON candidate TO GROUP cal
```

If there is no user named Cal defined in the operating system then the members of the group named Cal would be given the **SELECT** privilege. It is best to specify if the name is an individual user or a group of users. Therefore, the following statements specify that both the group and the user should be given **SELECT** privilege.

```
GRANT SELECT ON candidate TO USER cal
GRANT SELECT ON candidate TO GROUP cal
```

This will give both user Cal and group Cal the privilege on the *candidate* table. The **GRANT** and **REVOKE** statements can include either the **USER** or **GROUP** option to indicate the level of privilege that should be provided.

Establishing a DB2 Client/Server Connection

The remaining sections of this chapter deal with connecting to DB2 databases both locally and remotely. The information that DB2 uses to determine which database to connect to is stored in the client DB2 directories. Actually, we'll discuss more than simply connecting to databases. The concept is called attaching, and essentially it allows you to connect to the DB2 instance. Let's discuss how we establish database connections.

Configuring a DB2 Server

This section discusses the steps necessary to configure a DB2 server to receive incoming database requests. There are a number of communication protocols supported by DB2: APPC, NetBIOS, TCP/IP and IPX/SPX. Not all these protocols are supported on all DB2 server platforms.

✍️ The underlying communication support (software) needs to be installed prior to enabling communication with DB2.

The steps to configure the DB2 server are essentially the same.

1. Update the necessary environment variables.
2. Update the database manager (DBM) configuration file.
3. Stop and start the instance to listen for incoming connections.

Setting the Server Environment Variable

There is one communication environment variable that must be set for all protocols. The environment variable is called **DB2COMM**. The actual setting of this variable is operating system dependent. If more than one protocol is used, the protocols are separated using a comma. For example, to enable TCP/IP and IPX/SPX communications on an DB2 Server for AIX, you would need to set the **DB2COMM** environment variable with the following UNIX command:

```
export DB2COMM=TCPIP,IPXSPX
```

To enable NetBIOS and APPC on an DB2 for OS/2 or DB2 for Windows NT server the following command should be used:

```
SET DB2COMM=NetBIOS,APPC
```

The **DB2COMM** variable should be updated in the DB2 environment so that it is enabled when the instance is started. For example, in UNIX the **db2profile** script should be updated, in OS/2 the *CONFIG.SYS* file should be updated, and in Windows NT the system environment should be updated.

There are several other communication variables that can be changed depending on the remote clients you are supporting and the communication protocol. For example, **DB2SERVICETPINSTANCE** is a communications variable used with APPC to support down-level remote clients. NetBIOS has a number of other parameters that can be set for performance reasons.

Updating the DBM Configuration Parameters

When updating the database manager configuration, you'll need to be a member of the instance administration group (SYSADM). We'll examine the required information using four scenarios.

The **UPDATE DBM CONFIG USING** <option> <value> should be used to modify any of the DBM configuration parameters.

TCP/IP — DB2 Server Configuration

For TCP/IP, you'll need the service name defined in the **services** file on the database server.

 The update of the services file must be performed on the DB2 server and the DB2 clients. The services file is updated using an editor and cannot be updated from DB2.

The parameter in the database manager configuration file is called **SVCENAME**. The service name is assigned as the main connection port name for the instance and defined in the services file. For example, if the name defined in the services file is **db2tcp**, the command would be the following:

```
UPDATE DATABASE MANAGER CONFIGURATION USING SVCENAME db2tcp
```

After updating the DBM configuration. The DBM configuration should be similar to the one shown in Fig. 3–8.

```
              Database Manager Configuration

    Node type = Database Server with local and remote clients

Database manager configuration release level            = 0x6000


Service name                                  (SVCENAME) = db2tcp
  ...
```

Fig. 3–8 TCP/IP Database Manager Configuration Parameter

NetBIOS — DB2 Server Configuration

To enable the NetBIOS protocol the DB2 server must have the **DB2COMM** environment variable set to NETBIOS. The workstation name (**NNAME**) on both the client and server must be set. This name must be unique within the network. A NetBIOS error will occur if the workstation name is not unique.

For example, if the **NNAME** is **db200**, the command would be

```
UPDATE DATABASE MANAGER CONFIGURATION USING NNAME db200
```

After updating the DBM configuration. The DBM configuration should be similar to the one shown in Fig. 3–9.

Database Manager Configuration

Node type = Database Server with local and remote clients

Database manager configuration release level   = 0x6000

...

Workstation name   **(NNAME) = db200**

Service name   (SVCENAME) = db2tcp

Fig. 3–9 NetBIOS Database Manager Configuration Parameter

IPX/SPX — DB2 Server Configuration

To enable IPX/SPX clients you must ensure that the IPX/SPX interface has been enabled on the DB2 server. Set the **DB2COMM** environment variable to include IPXSPX. There are two methods of enabling the DB2 server to accept IPX/SPX clients on a network: **file server addressing** or **direct addressing**.

A DB2 client locates the DB2 server via the NetWare file server when file server addressing is used. Direct addressing avoids this step, as the DB2 client communicates directly with the DB2 server, and therefore bypasses the NetWare file server.

To enable file server addressing you must place the IPX/SPX fileserver name (**FILESERVER**) in the database manager configuration as shown in Fig. 3–9. The **FILESERVER** is the name of the NetWare file server where the database server is registered. When file server addressing is used DB2 must be registered at the NetWare file server. During the register process, the NetWare Workgroup or Supervisor id must be specified. The DB2 server can be registered using the following command:

```
REGISTER DB2 SERVER IN NWBINDERY
USER user1 PASSWORD pass1
```

When direct addressing is used, the **FILESERVER** and **OBJECTNAME** should be set to *. The **db2ipxad** utility should be executed on the server to determine the NetWare internetwork address for the server workstation. This internetwork address is used at each DB2 client to locate the DB2 server. The internetwork address is specified as the server name during the **CATALOG NODE** command.

The IPX/SPX socket number used for communications is defined by the DBM configuration parameter **IPX_SOCKET**. The **OBJECTNAME** represents the DB2 server on the network. It must be unique for all DB2 instances registered at the same NetWare fileserver. Usually, it is best to use the same name as the instance to avoid confusion.

The **IPX_SOCKET** is required for setting up the server only. You select a hex number representing the connection endpoint identifier that must be unique for each DB2 server instance and unique among all IPX/SPX applications running on one DB2 server. If you have more than one instance on the server, select unique socket values for each instance in the range of 879E (default setting) to 87A2.

An example of configuring the DB2 server using the file server addressing technique follows:

```
UPDATE DBM CFG USING FILESERVER ipxfs OBJECTNAME db2o
```

The updated database manager configuration file would then resemble the one shown in Fig. 3–10.

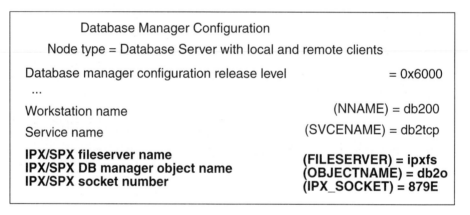

Fig. 3–10 IPX/SPX Database Manager Configuration Parameters

APPC — DB2 Server Configuration

For APPC, you'll need to know the transaction program name (**TPNAME**) that DB2 will be using. For example, if the **TPNAME** on the server were **db2tp00**, the **UPDATE** command would be:

```
UPDATE DATABASE CONFIGURATION USING TPNAME db2tp00
```

The updated information in the database manager configuration file would then resemble the one shown in Fig. 3–11.

✍ The instance must be stopped and restarted when any changes are made in the database manager configuration file.

```
        Database Manager Configuration

   Node type = Database Server with local and remote clients

Database manager configuration release level              = 0x6000
   ...

Workstation name                                (NNAME) = db200
Service name                                    (SVCENAME) = db2tcp
Transaction program name                        (TPNAME) = db2tp00

IPX/SPX fileserver name                         (FILESERVER) = ipxfs
IPX/SPX DB manager object name                  (OBJECTNAME) = db2o
IPX/SPX socket number                           (IPX_SOCKET) = 879E
```

Fig. 3–11 APPC Database Manager Configuration Parameter

DB2 Directories

Access to both local and remote databases is performed using DB2 directories. The directories hide the requirement for the user to know where a database actually resides. Users are able to connect to local databases, remote databases and DRDA (Application Server) databases simply by specifying a database name. The directories that make this possible are:

- System Database Directory
- Local Database Directory
- Node Directory
- Database Connection Services (DCS) Directory

System Database Directory

The **system database directory** resides in the sqldbdir subdirectory of the instance. This directory is used to access both local and remote databases. The directory contains the database name, alias, type and node where the database resides. If the database is local, a pointer to the local database directory is located in the system database directory. If the database is remote, there is a point to the node directory.

Local Database Directory

The **local database directory** resides in every subdirectory that contains a database. It is used to access local databases in that subdirectory. Each entry in the directory contains the database name, alias, type and storage information about the database. Let's look at two workstations, a database server and a remote client to see how directories are used.

Node Directory

Each database client maintains a **node directory**. The node directory contains entries for all instances that a client will access. The node directory is used to contain communication information about the network connection to the instance. If multiple instances exist on a remote machine, then each instance must be known as a separate node before you will be able to access any information contained within the instance.

DCS Directory

The connection information for DRDA host databases is different from the information for LAN-connected databases. A separate directory maintains this host information. The directory used is the **Database Connection Services** (DCS) directory. This directory will only exist if the DDCS product has been installed on your system. The DCS directory stores information used by the database manager to access databases on a DRDA Application Server.

Examining DB2 Directories

From the database server, we'll issue the command to list the contents of the system database directory

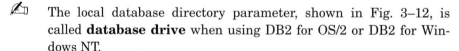

Fig. 3–12 shows the partial contents of the output of the **LIST DB DIRECTORY** command. There are four databases cataloged on the server. The first database is the *DB2CERT* database.

✍ The local database directory parameter, shown in Fig. 3–12, is called **database drive** when using DB2 for OS/2 or DB2 for Windows NT.

In Fig. 3–12 the local database directory is shown to exist in the path / home/db2. If we wanted to examine more details of the database we could examine the **local database directory** at the location using the command: **LIST DB DIRECTORY ON** */home/db2*. This would provide more detail information regarding the location of some of the database files.

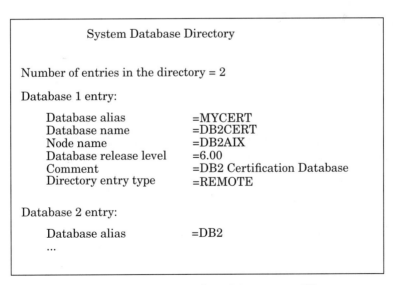

Fig. 3–12 Contents of System Database Directory on Server

Next, we'll examine the contents of two directories on the client workstation: the **system database directory** and the **node directory**. A client will not have a local database directory as it cannot have local databases. The command to examine the system database directory is the same on the client as it was on the server.

```
                    System Database Directory


Number of entries in the directory = 2

Database 1 entry:

        Database alias          =MYCERT
        Database name           =DB2CERT
        Node name               =DB2AIX
        Database release level  =6.00
        Comment                 =DB2 Certification Database
        Directory entry type    =REMOTE

Database 2 entry:

        Database alias          =DB2
        ...
```

Fig. 3–13 Contents of System Database Directory on Client

Fig. 3–13 shows the system database directory on the client. The database alias name of the database on the client is called *mycert*, this name corresponds to the actual database name on the server called *db2cert*. You should note that the directory entry type is **INDIRECT** on the server (Fig. 3–12) for the *DB2CERT* database and the type is **REMOTE** on the client (Fig. 3–13).

✍ When a database is **created** an entry automatically placed in the system database directory and the local database directory.

When cataloging the remote database on the client, the database name on the client must match the database alias on the server. The database alias specified on the client workstation is used in the **CONNECT** statement. Therefore, the name used to **CONNECT** to the *db2cert* database as shown in Fig. 3–13 would be *mycert*.

There is always an associated **node name** with a **client** system database directory entry. The node name defines the location of the DB2 server on the network, in Fig. 3–13 the node name is *db2aix*.

To discover more information about the location of the database server we should examine the *db2aix* node entry in the node directory using the command.

LIST NODE DIRECTORY

The contents of the node directory on the client are displayed in Fig. 3–14. The *db2aix* node name corresponds to a TCP/IP connection. The host name for the DB2 server is *db2aix* and the service name is *db2tcp1*. The information in the client's node directory must match with the information in the server's DBM configuration file.

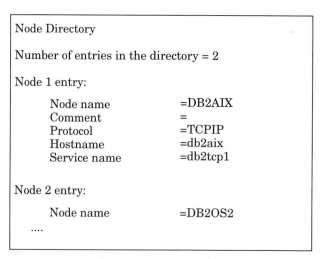

```
Node Directory

Number of entries in the directory = 2

Node 1 entry:

        Node name              =DB2AIX
        Comment                =
        Protocol               =TCPIP
        Hostname               =db2aix
        Service name           =db2tcp1

Node 2 entry:

        Node name              =DB2OS2
    ....
```

Fig. 3–14 Contents of Node Directory on Client

Configuring DB2 Clients

Remote database access is accomplished by making entries into the DB2 directories. This process is called cataloging. A DB2 database server can support both local and remote clients concurrently. We will examine the **CATALOG** commands which must be performed on each of the DB2 clients.

Cataloging a Database from a Client

Before cataloging, the client machine must be able to communicate with the DB2 server. The administrator of the client system sets up the system to communicate with the DB2 server. This setup will depend on the operating system and the communication protocol that the DB2 server is using for the instance. The supported protocols are:

- TCP/IP
- NetBIOS
- IPX/SPX
- APPC

After the communication setup has been completed, the remote client must perform the following steps:

1. Catalog the remote node
2. Catalog the remote database

Cataloging a TCP/IP Client

When cataloging a TCP/IP client to communicate with a DB2 database server, the client must know the main connection port number used for the instance on the database server that is being accessed. The hosts file on the client workstation must be updated to include the address of the server. An alternative to using a hosts file is to have a Domain Name Server for the network, or to explicitly indicate the host IP address when cataloging the client node. We'll use the information found in Fig. 3–12 as the server we want to access. The node directory information found in Fig. 3–14 shows the updated information:

```
CATALOG TCIP NODE db2aix REMOTE db2aix SERVER db2tcp1
```

The node name *db2aix* must be unique in the client node directory. This node name will be used in the **CATALOG DATABASE** command. The host name, *db2aix*, specified on the **REMOTE** parameter must match the host name specified in the client's hosts file. This host name is used as an alias for the IP address of the server.

The service name specified with the **SERVER** parameter must match the port name found in the services file on the client workstation. The port number points to the DB2 server instance that will be accessed during the **CONNECT**.

Once the node has been cataloged the remote database can be cataloged.

```
CATALOG DATABASE db2cert AS mycert AT NODE db2aix
```

If we issue a **LIST DATABASE DIRECTORY** command, we'll see the output shown in Fig. 3–13. The database name on the client, *db2cert*, must match the system database directory alias on the server machine. The alias in the **CATALOG DATABASE** command is the name that the client workstation will use when connecting to the remote database, here *mycert*. The node name in the client's system database directory must match the node name in the client's node directory *(db2aix)*.

Cataloging a NetBIOS Client

When configuring a client to use NetBIOS, the workstation name (**NNAME**) of the client must be defined in the client's DBM configuration file. The DB2 server's workstation name (**NNAME**) is used during the node catalog command.

```
CATALOG NETBIOS NODE ninst00 REMOTE db200 adapter 0
```

The server nname parameter, *db200*, matches the nname found in the database manager configuration in Fig. 3–9. The node name, *ninst00*, is unique in the client node directory.

To catalog a database whose alias is *mypay* on the DB2 server, the command would be similar to the following:

```
CATALOG DB payroll AS mypay AT NODE ninst00
```

The database name on the client matches the alias defined in the system database directory on the server. The client uses the alias name, *mypay,* when connecting to the database server. The node name, *ninst00*, matches the entry in the client's node directory.

Cataloging an IPX/SPX Client

When cataloging the client node directory, the server's IPX/SPX fileserver name and IPX/SPX object name must be specified as parameters of the **CATALOG** command. This information can be found in the server's database manager configuration file (see Fig. 3–10). The command would be similar to the following if file server addressing were being used:

```
CATALOG IPXSPX NODE iinst00 REMOTE ipxfs SERVER db2o
```

The fileserver specified in the **CATALOG IPXSPX NODE** command on the client matches that found in the IPX/SPX fileserver name in the DBM configuration on the DB2 server. The object name specified on the **SERVER** parameter must match the IPX/SPX object name specified in the server's database manager configuration file.

If direct addressing is used by all clients connecting to the server using IPX/SPX, then a value of * can be used in the server's database manager configuration file and in the client's **CATALOG IPXSPX NODE** command. If direct addressing is being used by all clients, then the object name is specified as the DB2 server's NetWare internetwork address. A NetWare internetwork address has the following form:

`<8 byte net id>.<12 byte node id>.<4 byte socket number>`

The DB2 server's NetWare internetwork address can be found by executing the **DB2IPXAD** utility at the DB2 server.

The **CATALOG DATABASE** command would be similar to the following:

```
CATALOG DB employee AS myemp AT NODE iinst00
```

Cataloging an APPC Client

When cataloging the client node directory, you need to know the symbolic destination name in the CPI-C Side Information profile that points to your server. This is called the Partner LU (logical unit). The profile name is specified following the **REMOTE** parameter. The **CATALOG APPC NODE** command would be similar to the following:

```
CATALOG APPC NODE ainst00 REMOTE db2cpi00 SECURITY SAME
```

Verifying the Connection

To connect to either a local or remote database you use the **CONNECT TO <dbname>** command, where <dbname> maps to the alias name specified in the system database directory. After the connect is issued, all SQL requests are executed against the database to which you are connected.

If the connection is a Remote Unit of Work (RUOW, CONNECT = 1), **CONNECT RESET** terminates the connection, and a subsequent SQL statement will cause a connection to the default database, if it is defined. The default database is defined in the environment variable **DB2DBDFT**.

If the connection is a Distributed Unit of Work (DUOW, CONNECT=2), **CONNECT RESET** puts the current connection in a dormant state and establishes a connection with the default database if it is defined. From within the Command Line Processor (CLP), **TERMINATE** issues a disconnect and also terminates the CLP back-end process. The **QUIT** command ends the input mode and returns the user to the command prompt but does not terminate the CLP nor disconnect the connection to the database.

The authentication level of the instance will affect the client, either local or remote, when connecting to a database. The other consideration is the type of client machine attempting access to the DB2 database server.

AIX Client

When an AIX client connects to a DB2 database server, there are two forms of the **CONNECT** statement to consider. One specifies the user name and password, and one does not.

When connecting to a DB2 server with authentication **SERVER**, the following behavior results from the **CONNECT** statement:

```
CONNECT TO <database> USER <user id> USING <password>
```

The user name and password combination is sent to the AIX DB2 server for authentication. This information is checked against what is contained in the server machine for user authorization to the system. The system authorization will depend on the hardware platform and operating system. For AIX, the user name/password is found in the /etc/passwd file.

The following format of the **CONNECT** statement is not allowed from an AIX client where the authentication type is **SERVER** on the database server:

```
CONNECT TO <database>
```

Authentication CLIENT means that the AIX client user is validated at the local workstation. When using authentication **CLIENT** on the database server, there are two forms of the **CONNECT** statement that are valid:

```
CONNECT TO <database> USER <user id> USING <password>
CONNECT TO <database>
```

OS/2 Client

When an OS/2 client connects to a database server, there are two forms of the **CONNECT** statement to consider with an authentication type of **SERVER**.

```
CONNECT TO <database> USER <user id> USING <password>
```

If the OS/2 client is accessing an AIX DB2 server, the user id/password is sent to an AIX server for authentication. The /etc/passwd file on the AIX server is checked for the user name and password. The user name and password are passed as it is typed on the command line. The AIX DB2 server is case sensitive therefore there must be a user id and password matching on AIX.

The other form of the **CONNECT** statement to consider with authentication **SERVER** is:

```
CONNECT TO <database>
```

Here, the current user id and password is sent to the DB2 server for validation. It is recommeded to specify the user id and password when establishing the database connection to avoid using an invalid user id and password. The password in the **CONNECT** statement is always converted to uppercase. If the OS/2 client is accessing an AIX DB2 server the password would need to be defined in uppercase. This is also be true for DB2 for Windows NT servers as the passwords are case-sensitive in Windows NT.

When the DB2 server has its authentication type set to **CLIENT**. The user id and password are verified locally and only the the user id is passed to the server.

Windows NT Clients

In a Windows NT environment user's are usually created within an NT Domain. A user either logs on locally to a Windows NT workstation or they log into the Windows NT Domain. To simplify user id administration in a DB2 for Windows NT environment it is recommended to set up the DB2 server as a *Backup Domain Controller* and use **SERVER** authentication.

A *Backup Domain Controller* is associated with a *Primary Domain Controller* and the domain user id is used for verification purposes. This is referred to as *Domain Database Access*. In Windows NT you may decide to set up a *Trusted Domain* in which two domains share the same name space. Remember, that you must always specify a user id and password if **SERVER** authentication is used.

If **CLIENT** authentication is specified then only *trusted* DB2 clients are allowed to access the DB2 server. A trusted client is a client that runs on an operating system that has a native security system. For example, OS/2 clients are considered trusted, but a DOS or Windows 95 client is considered untrusted. Any untrusted clients must explicitly logon to the database server (specify user id and password).

Binding Utilities

When a remote client wants access to a database server where the operating system of the database server is different from that on the client system, another step must be taken. The database utilities must be bound on the server for the client to use. The database utilities that a remote client must bind to the DB2 server include:

- Ad hoc SQL functions in the Command Line Processor (CLP)
- DB2 Call Level Interface (CLI)
- The binder program
- **IMPORT/EXPORT** functions
- The **REORG** command

If you create a new database on the server, packages for the database utilities must also be created in the system catalog tables. All of the client packages are contained in a file called *db2ubind.lst*. These packages can be created by executing the bind command from the client workstation. Before executing this command, you must first connect to the server database and then execute the **BIND** command. For example, to bind all the DB2 utilities from a DB2 client:

```
CONNECT TO <database> USER <user> USING <pwd>
BIND <path> @db2ubind.lst BLOCKING ALL

<database>    is the database alias specified
              during the CATALOG DATABASE command.

<path>        is the complete path to the file
              containing the list of bind files.
```

✍ The symbol @ is used to identify to the binder that the file db2ubind.lst is a list of bind files and not a bind file itself.

The **BIND** command must be run separately for each database that you wish to access. Once a package has been successfully bound to the database all DB2 clients can access it. If you have different types of clients on your network, you must bind the utilities from each type of client.

Let's look at an example where we are binding from an OS/2 client to the *DB2CERT* database which is on an AIX server. We'll issue the following commands:

```
CONNECT TO db2cert
BIND @db2ubind.lst BLOCKING ALL GRANT PUBLIC
```

The output from the **BIND** command can be sent to a file using the **MESSAGES** parameter. By default, the information is displayed to the screen. When a bind is performed you should ensure that there were no errors encountered. If errors are encountered the package will not be created in the database. Common errors include the non-existence of database objects. All of the objects must exist during the bind process.

We used the **GRANT PUBLIC** option in the **BIND** command, this option is used to provide **EXECUTE** and **BIND** privileges to all users that can access the database. Also note that there are different **BIND** command options for DRDA (host) databases, like DB2 for MVS (see the *DB2 Command Reference* for details). The output of a successful **BIND** command is shown in Fig. 3–15.

✍ Remember you must have BINDADD authority to create a new package in a DB2 database. If the package exists then BIND privilege for the package is the only requirement to update the package.

LINE	MESSAGES FOR db2ubind.list
	SQL0061W The binder is in progress.

LINE	MESSAGES FOR db2ubind.list
	SQL0091N Binding was ended with "0" errors and "0" warnings.

Fig. 3–15 Messages from the **BIND** Command

The utilities that are bound include **IMPORT, EXPORT, LOAD, CLP, BACKUP, RESTORE,** and **REORG.** The *db2ubind.lst* file contains the list of bind (.BND) files that are required to create the packages for these utilities. The files that comprised the *db2ubind.lst* are shown in Fig. 3–16.

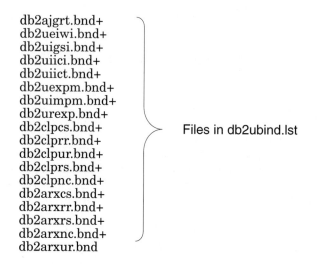

db2ajgrt.bnd+
db2ueiwi.bnd+
db2uigsi.bnd+
db2uiici.bnd+
db2uiict.bnd+
db2uexpm.bnd+
db2uimpm.bnd+
db2urexp.bnd+
db2clpcs.bnd+   Files in db2ubind.lst
db2clprr.bnd+
db2clpur.bnd+
db2clprs.bnd+
db2clpnc.bnd+
db2arxcs.bnd+
db2arxrr.bnd+
db2arxrs.bnd+
db2arxnc.bnd+
db2arxur.bnd

Fig. 3–16 List of Files in db2ubind.lst

Instance Administration (ATTACH Command)

Certain tasks in DB2 can only be performed at the instance level, such as creating a database, forcing users off of databases, monitoring a database or updating the database manager configuration. Other tasks require a database connection, such as issuing SQL Data Manipulation Language (DML) statements, using the **LOAD** utility or using the **BIND** command.

DB2 provides the ability for remote instance administration of a server node. By attaching to an instance, you are able to perform functions such as the following:

- Create/drop databases
- Get/update/reset database manager configuration
- Get/update/reset database configuration
- Monitor a database
- Back up/restore a database
- Roll forward a database
- Force applications — terminate applications using the database

To attach to an instance, you would use the **ATTACH** command. The syntax of the **ATTACH** command is shown here.

```
ATTACH [TO nodename] [USER username [USING password]]
```

If the **ATTACH** command is specified without any arguments, the current attachment status is returned. Otherwise if you attempt to attach to an instance while already attached to a instance, the current instance will be detached and the new attachment is attempted. In other words, you can only attach to one instance at time. If an instance level function is specified without being preceded by the **ATTACH** command, the instance name contained in the **DB2INSTANCE** environment variable is used.

✏️   The currently active instance can be identified using the **GET INSTANCE** command or checking the **DB2INSTANCE** variable.

Database connections are independent of instance attachments. A single application can maintain several database connections at the same time it has an instance attachment, but it can only maintain a single instance attachment at any one time. The database connection can be implicit or explicit. An implicit database connection will connect to the database specified in the environment variable, **DB2DBDFT**. An explicit database connection can be made using the **CONNECT TO DATABASE** command.

When attached to another instance, you will still be using the directory services of the local instance. This is determined by the value contained in the **DB2INSTANCE** variable. Because of this, you will not be able to perform catalog changes or list, update or reset commands on database, node or DCS directories.

If you create a new database, the database will be created at the attached instance and a catalog entry will be created in the local and system database directories on the instance workstation.

Local Instance Administration

After the DB2 server has been installed and an instance exists on the server, a user can become a local client. There are several ways that a local user can access the instance.

1. Set the **DB2INSTANCE** environment variable for the user. Make sure that the **DB2PATH** environment variable is also set to the location of the DB2 executables. This is known as an implicit attachment.
2. Catalog a local instance and issue the **ATTACH** command. This is known as an explicit attachment.

User Attach Scenario

In this section, we've talked about connections and attachments. We'll show a user scenario where a local user wants to access two instances on the same database server without changing his environment when he logs into the system.

The two local instances are called *db2test* and *db2*. They are located on an AIX database server. The user, Grant, is a local user on the database server. Grant has set the **DB2INSTANCE** and **DB2PATH** variables to allow access to the *db2test* instance. In AIX, Grant would edit his profile to include the following entry:

```
.  /home/db2test/sqllib/db2profile
```

There is another instance that Grant wants to access on the same server. Grant will catalog the other instance, *db2*, as a local node and then catalog the local database. An example of the **CATALOG LOCAL NODE** command is provided:

```
CATALOG LOCAL NODE mydb2 INSTANCE db2


LOCAL identifies that this is a local instance
mydb2 is the instance name that is particular to
      the local client user
db2   is the local instance name as it is defined
      on the server
```

The contents of the node directory for the local user are shown in Fig. 3–17.

```
Node Directory

Number of entries in the directory = 1

Node 1 entry:

        Node name              = MYDB2
        Comment                =
        Protocol               = LOCAL
        Instance name          = db2
```

Fig. 3–17 Contents of the Node Directory — Local Node

Next, Grant will catalog the local database. The syntax of the **CATALOG DATABASE** command is:

```
CATALOG DATABASE db2cert AS mycert AT NODE mydb2

db2cert    is the name of the database as it exists
           in the instance on the database server

mycert     is the alias that user Grant will use
           when connecting

mydb2      is the reference name given to the local
           instance by Grant in the CATALOG NODE
           command
```

If Grant were to issue the **LIST DATABASE DIRECTORY** command, the output would be similar to Fig. 3–18.

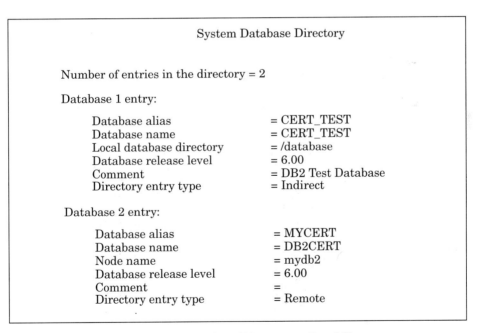

System Database Directory

Number of entries in the directory = 2

Database 1 entry:

Database alias	= CERT_TEST
Database name	= CERT_TEST
Local database directory	= /database
Database release level	= 6.00
Comment	= DB2 Test Database
Directory entry type	= Indirect

Database 2 entry:

Database alias	= MYCERT
Database name	= DB2CERT
Node name	= mydb2
Database release level	= 6.00
Comment	=
Directory entry type	= Remote

Fig. 3–18 Contents of the Database Directory — Local User

Notice that there are two entries in the database directory (Fig. 3–18). The first one is the database *CERT_TEST*. This database is located within the *db2test* instance. The entry is an **INDIRECT** and therefore created locally within the current the DB2 instance. The second entry is a **REMOTE** entry type. The database has been cataloged via the *mydb2* node. It turns out that this node is a local node on the same workstation. A local node is actually another DB2 instance. In this case the instance is called *db2* as shown in Fig. 3–17.

Summary

This chapter discussed a number of topics relating to accessing data, both locally and remotely. We discussed security, first to the database and then within DB2. We talked about authentication, the process of verifying who a user claims to be based on a user id and password combination. There are three different methods of authentication: **SERVER**, **CLIENT** and **DCS**. Depending on the DB2 products installed, authentication tells where the user is validated. The authentication can be set or changed in the database manager configuration. Authentication is set at the instance level. All databases within the instance will have the same authentication.

Next, we talked about several of the authorization levels within DB2: SYSADM, SYSCTRL, SYSMAINT and DBADM. SYSADM has system administrative authority over the instance. SYSADM is able to perform any administration operations as well as access any information from any database that exists within that instance. SYSCTRL does not have the authority to access the database (unless explicitly granted) nor can SYSCTRL modify the database manager configuration. SYSMAINT also cannot access user data. SYSMAINT allows you to perform functions such as backup or restore databases and tablespaces, start and stop the instance, and use the database monitor. At the database level, DBADM has complete authority over the database objects. This authority includes creating or dropping tables, performing a query and setting privileges for other users of the database. We also examined the granting and revoking of database object privileges using the **GRANT** and **REVOKE** SQL statements.

The next section dealt with accessing a database, both remotely and locally. We talked about the steps that a database server must perform to communicate with a remote client using one of the supported protocols. Remember that the database server must set the **DB2COMM** environment variable and update the database manager configuration. We then looked at how the remote client prepares to connect to the database server. The remote client catalogs the database server and the database within directories. The concept of directories within DB2 was discussed as well as how the information contained in the directories is used to access databases, both locally and remotely. Finally, we looked at the **ATTACH** command that allows both local and remote users to access an instance to perform tasks such as creating or monitoring a database.

Questions

1. Given the following users:
    USER1 needs to be able to backup databases
    USER2 needs to be able to monitor database activity

    If USER1 and USER2 belong to GROUPA, which task is required to setup
    these users?

    O   A. Add their userids to the SYSADM group, as specified in the DBM
             configuration

    O   B. Add their userids to the DBADM group, as specified in the DBM
             configuration

    O   C. GRANT SYSADM authority to GROUPA

    O   D. GRANT DBADM authority to GROUPA

2. Given that the statement:
    "CONNECT TO sample USER user1 USING mypwd:
    returns:
    SQL1403N The username and/or password supplied is incorrect. SQL-
    STATE=08004
    Which task can correct this problem?

    O   A. Update the DBM configuration

    O   B. Update the database configuration

    O   C. Update the node directory

    O   D. Update the user's password

3. Which authority or privilege is specified in the DBM configuration?

○ A DBADM

○ B DBCTRL

○ C CONTROL

○ D CONNECT

○ E SYSADM

○ F SYSCAT

4. If a user has ALTER privilege for a table, which task can they perform?

○ A DROP the table definition

○ B CREATE a view on the table

○ C SELECT data from the table

○ D DROP a primary key definition

5. Which steps are required to enable a DB2 server for clients to connect to a database, residing on the server, using TCP/IP? (select 2)

○ A. Set the DB2COMM environment variable on the client.

○ B. Set the DB2COMM environment variable on the server.

○ C. Update the DBM configuration on the server.

○ D. Update the DB configuration on the server.

6. What is the relationship between DB2 instances and databases?

○ A. A single database can span instances.

○ B. You can have only one database for each instance.

○ C. The instance name and the database name must match.

○ D. The authentication for the database and its instance must match.

7. If the DBM configuration is updated when do the changes take effect?

    ○   A. During the "CONNECT TO dbname" statement.

    ○   B. After the "FORCE APPLICATIONS ALL" command.

    ○   C. When the instance is stopped using the "DB2STOP" command.

    ○   D. When the instance is restarted using the "DB2START" command.

8. Where would you look to determine which users had the ability to create a table?

    ○   A. SYSSTAT.PRIVILEGES

    ○   B. SYSTEM.TABLES

    ○   C. SYSIBM.TABAUTH

    ○   D. SYSCAT.DBAUTH

Answers

1. (A)
   USER1 and USER2 would need their user id added to the SYSADM group, as specified in the DBM configuration. This is performed within the user management facilities of the operating system, not within DB2 itself.
2. (D)
   Update the user's password
3. (E)
   SYSADM authority is specified in the database manager configuration.
4. (D)
   Drop a primary key definition.
5. (B and C)
   Set the **DB2COMM** environment variable on the server and update the DBM configuration on the server with the TCP/IP service name.
6. (D)
   The authentication for a database and its instance must match.
7. (D)
   The changes in the database manager configuration take effect on the next **DB2START**.
8. (D)
   The ability to create a table is defined at the database level as the **CREATETAB** authority. The *SYSCAT.DBAUTH* view can be examined to determine which users or user groups can create new tables.

Exercises

Part A — Creating Multiple DB2 Instances

1. Create another instance on your system called **db2a**. This instance should be separate from the (db2) instance you have previously created. You will also need to create a new user group and user id within the operating system. These new users need to be created prior to executing the db2icrt command in UNIX environments. We will be creating a database called sample in this chapter, but we will be creating the database within the new instance called **db2a**.

    The command to create a new instance is **db2icrt**.
    AIX only : The db2icrt command must be executed as **root** and you need to specify the instance name. The instance name (AIX) must be a user id defined in AIX. Therefore, create a user id called **db2a** and a group called **grpdb2a** and make db2a a member of the group grpdb2a.

    Windows/OS/2 only : Create a user called **db2a** and a group called **grpdb2a** in UPM on OS/2 or User Manager in Windows. In Windows NT make db2a a member of the local administrator group (The user db2a can be removed from the local administrator group later.) Once the instance was created issue the following commands:
    `SET DB2INSTANCE=db2a`
    `db2 UPDATE DBM CONFIGURATION USING SYSADM_GROUP grpdb2a`

2. Set the environment for the new instance (db2a):
    db2profile (UNIX) or
    CONFIG.SYS (OS/2) or
    System Environment Variables (Windows NT) or
    AUTOEXEC.BAT (Windows 95)

    db2start
    Windows NT - NET START db2a (Set the db2a service to auto start)

3. Type the command that lists the instances that are on your system:
    `db2ilist`
    `db2 get instance`
    You should see the db2a instance listed (probably see db2 instance also). The second command should return db2a as the current instance.

4. To create the sample database, issue the following command (as user db2a):
    `db2sampl <path/drive>` - path/drive is the location for the database.

5. Check the system database directory (for the new instance - db2a) to find the entry for the sample database.

Type:
db2 LIST DATABASE DIRECTORY
There should be an entry shown for the sample database.

6. Type the following command:
db2 LIST DATABASE DIRECTORY ON path/drive
where path/drive is where the sample database has been created. This command lists the contents of the local database directory. It contains the initial directory location for the SAMPLE database.

7. Verify the amount of disk space allocated during the create database command in step 4. This can be performed by examining the amount of allocated storage under the directory/path where the SAMPLE database was placed.

Part B — Setting Authorities and Privileges

1. Create a user, **deb**, on your system. You may require special operating system privileges to create users (UNIX - root, Windows NT - administrator). Place the user **deb** in the group named **dbgrp** and make her password **db2**. Creating user ids and user groups is different in each operating system, refer to the details in this chapter for the appropriate method of creating user ids. In AIX, Windows NT and OS/2 make deb a *regular* user.

2. Ensure that the **db2a** instance is still active.
The command **GET INSTANCE** will determine the current instance.
Once you are sure that the instance has been started, have **deb** login using the password **db2**.

Have **deb** set up her environment properly (as in part A, step 4). The environment variable **DB2INSTANCE** must be set to the instance name for a local user. Therefore, in this case ensure that **DB2INSTANCE** is set to **db2a**.

3. Connect to the sample database as user deb.
db2 CONNECT TO sample USER deb USING db2

Note: In Windows NT if you receive any authentication errors, set the DB2 Security Service to automatically start as an NT service.

4. Determine the current database authorizations that all users possess against the sample database with the following SQL statement:
SELECT *
FROM SYSCAT.DBAUTH
WHERE GRANTEE = 'PUBLIC'

The DB2 group called **PUBLIC** does not correspond to a user group defined in the operating system. Any user that has **CONNECT** authority for the database can perform any of the privileges provided to **PUBLIC**.

Therefore they have **CONNECT** authority to the database, **CREATE TABLE** authority for the database and they can add new application packages to the database. Some of these authorities you should probably like to **REVOKE**, as most users will not need to **CREATE TABLES** and **BIND** new packages.

5. Issue the SQL statement:
    ```
    db2 SELECT *
        FROM SYSCAT.PACKAGEAUTH
        WHERE GRANTEE = 'PUBLIC'
    ```

    The output of this statement shows that a number of application packages have been bound and **PUBLIC** has been given **BIND** and **EXECUTE** privilege for these packages. These packages are the DB2 utilities like the Command Line Processor (the bind files are in db2ubind.lst).

6. Issue the SQL statement:
    ```
    CREATE TABLE mydeb (part1 INTEGER, part2 INTEGER)
    ```

    Were you successful? This command should have worked. As part of the default authorities, **deb** should be able to create tables in the database. However, a member of the **SYSADM** or **DBADM** user groups (as defined in DB2) can revoke the **CREATETAB** authority from PUBLIC.

    This needs to be done explicitly. In order to begin securing the environment, **REVOKE** the **CREATETAB** authority from the group PUBLIC, this must be performed as a member of the **DBADM** or **SYSADM** group.

    Let's examine the privileges the deb has for her newly created table, issue :
    ```
    db2 SELECT *
        FROM syscat.tabauth
        WHERE tabname = 'MYDEB'
    ```
    Notice that deb is given full privileges for the table as she was the creator.

7. In the directory \exercise\partb\<platform>\src you will find two programs: called **constat.sqc** and **condyn.sqc**.
    <platform> corresponds to WIN/OS2/AIX

    Examine the programs. They are quite similar as they both connect to the sample database and select all the rows from the staff table. The difference is that **constat** uses only static embedded SQL, while **condyn** uses some dynamic embedded SQL.

    You will need to **PRECOMPILE** the programs and **BIND** the package. Issue prepit from an operating system window. Once you have successfully precompiled the two programs you should BIND the packages using a user id with

SYSADM authority for the instance. While connect as a SYSADM user execute **db2 BIND constat MESSAGES 1.1; BIND condyn MESSAGES 2.2**.

You can create these C programs if you have the supported compiler.
Windows NT & 95 using Microsoft Visual C++ (run: vcvars32 x86
OS/2 using IBM compiler (run: csetenv.cmd)
To build both Windows and OS/2 versions of the application run: **nmake all**

If you do not wish to create the application simply use the executables in the directory \exercise\partb\<platform>\bin.

AIX Note: From the directory containing the source code, simply type **make**. If you are receiving errors during the execution of the Makefile, ensure that the DB2 libraries are linked properly. As root, execute the command /usr/lpp/db2_02_01/cfg/db2ln. This will create the links to the DB2 libraries. Of course you must have a C compiler installed also.

8. As the user **deb** execute the program **constat** and connect to the sample database. But you'll notice that there is no output from the staff table.

9. The user **deb** needs to obtain execute privilege on the package. Check who can execute the package with the following command:
   db2 "SELECT * FROM SYSCAT.PACKAGEAUTH
       WHERE PKNAME = 'CONSTAT'"

10. As db2a, issue the command:
    db2 GRANT EXECUTE ON PACKAGE CONSTAT TO USER deb

11. As deb, run the **constat** program and you should see the results of the select from the staff table.

12. As deb execute the **condyn** program. You should recieve privilege errors as you do not have the select privilege for the table.

13. As deb, try to execute the **condyn** program. The output from the table should still not be displayed. Check the privileges that deb has on the staff table with the following command:
    SELECT * FROM SYSCAT.TABAUTH WHERE GRANTEE = 'DEB'

    The reason that no rows are displayed is that deb does not have select privilege on the staff table. Remember that if the application uses dynamic SQL, the end user requires all database object privileges.
    As db2a, issue As db2a, issue the command:
    db2 GRANT SELECT ON TABLE db2a.staff TO USER DEB

14. Suppose you also want the user deb to be able to do administrative tasks on the DB2CERT database. As db2a, examine the currently define DB2 system authority groups. Issue **GET DBM CFG**

    Note the values of SYSADM_GROUP, SYSMAINT_GROUP and SYSCTRL GROUP.

15. You would like deb to be able to start/stop the instance and be able to force users off. Which group would you place deb in? If the user deb is placed in the SYSCTRL_GROUP, she could perform these instance administration duties. Enter the command that would do this.
    UPDATE DBM CFG USING SYSCTRL_GROUP dbgrp

16. Remember that to make deb part of the SYSCTRL group, the change must be made in the database manager configuration file. You must specify a defined operating system group. Any user that is placed in the dbgrp or has dbgrp as part of their group set, will inherit SYSCTRL privileges.

    When DBM configuration parameters are updated you must perform a **DB2STOP** and a **DB2START** before the changes are activate.

17. The user deb needs to be able to access both instances. Now that deb is part of the **SYSCTRL_GROUP** for the db2a instance, she can do administrative functions. But she wants to be able to access the other instance (db2) to access the database resources within the instance.
    She could switch between environments locally by changing her environment variable, but the better method is to catalog the other instance as a node.

    Then deb can **ATTACH** to the db2 instance and perform administrative duties. Check the environment variable in deb's environment that tells which instance she is currently using.
    (AIX) echo $DB2INSTANCE
    (Windows / OS/2) echo %DB2INSTANCE%
    This is operating system dependent. You can also use **db2 GET INSTANCE**.

18. Next, catalog the db2 instance as a local node.
    CATALOG LOCAL NODE debdb2 INSTANCE db2
    Remember that debdb2 is a user-defined nodename.

19. As deb, enter the command to access the db2 instance.
    ATTACH TO debdb2
    The **ATTACH** command cause the current instance to change from the db2a instance to the db2 instance (in this example).

20. Have deb check the contents of the database manager configuration file for the db2 instance.
GET DATABASE MANAGER CONFIGURATION

21. Next, have deb update the authentication for the instance changing it from server to client.
db2 UPDATE DBM CFG USING AUTHENTICATION CLIENT
Did this work? It should not have, Deb does not have any special authority within the db2 instance, only the db2a instance.

Even if Deb was define in the **SYSCTRL_GROUP** for the db2 instance she could not update the DBM configuration as only **SYSADM_GROUP** members can change the DBM configuration. Let's say that deb want to change one of the logging parameters, **LOGFILSIZ**, from the default of 1000 4KB to 1024 4KB for the DB2CERT database. Here's the command:
UPDATE DB CFG FOR db2cert USING LOGFILESIZE 1024
Did this work? Only if Deb was a member of the DBADM group for the DB2CERT database. You can try this out by adding Deb as a member of the DBADM group for the DB2CERT database.

CHAPTER 4

Using SQL

*T*he standard language of relational database access is the Structured Query Language (SQL). SQL is not a programming language. It was designed for the single purpose of accessing structured data. Every Relational Database Management System (RDBMS) implements a slightly different level of SQL.

In this chapter we will examine the DB2 implementation of the SQL language. If you are familiar with other RDBMS products, then many of the aspects of the DB2 implementation of SQL will already be understood, thanks to the industry acceptance of SQL standards.

We will first examine the DB2 database objects that can be referenced from an SQL statement, and then we will examine the SQL language elements. A database object, for the purpose of this book, is any component of a DB2 database, such as table spaces, tables, columns, views, indexes, packages, logs, locks and transactions. It is important to note that some of these database objects cannot be directly referenced using the SQL language.

Many of these objects can be directly referenced from an SQL statement; thus, it is important to understand their purpose.

SQL is divided into three major categories:

- DDL — Data Definition Language
  Used to create/modify/drop database objects.
- DML — Data Manipulation Language
  Used to select/insert/update/delete database data (records).
- DCL — Data Control Language
  Used to provide database object access control.

As SQL has evolved, many new statements have been added to provide a more complete set of data access methods. We will explore some of these new features, including constraints, triggers, large object data access and common table expressions.

Understanding Database Objects

A **database** is an organized collection of related objects. Each database has its own catalog, log files, security and tuning parameters.

The Structure Query Language (SQL) is used throughout the database industry as a common method of issuing database queries. SQL is considered a database access language, the language is comprised of SQL **statement**. An SQL statement is used to access database objects using *relational* operations. The SQL language is comprised of **statements**, **functions**, and **data types**. Before we examine the SQL language we need to understand some DB2 terminology. We will be referring to the basic components or objects which are defined for each DB2 database. These objects include:

- Data types
- Columns
- Tables
- Table spaces
- Views
- Indexes
- Packages
- Log files
- Transactions
- Locks

Data Types

There are two major categories of data types in DB2. The data types are either defined by DB2 or defined by the user. Fig. 4–1 shows the database architect using the DB2 built-in data types to design User-Defined Data Types (UDTs).

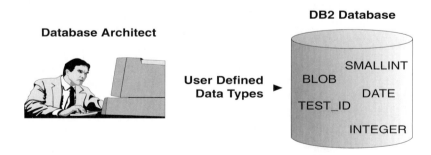

Fig. 4–1 Data Types

DB2-Supplied Data Types

The built-in data types are defined by DB2. When the database design is being implemented, any of these data types can be used. Data is stored in DB2 tables which are comprised of columns and rows. Every DB2 table is defined using columns. These columns must be one of the built-in DB2 data types or a user-defined data type. The valid built-in DB2 data types are shown in Fig. 4–2.

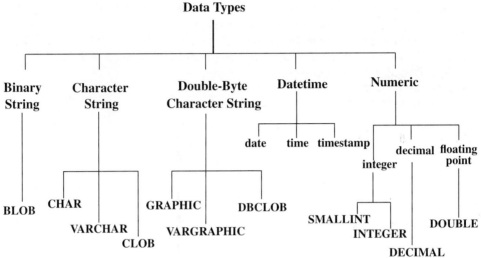

Fig. 4–2 DB2 Data Types

There are three major categories of DB2 data types shown in Fig. 4–2.

1. **String** (Binary, Character, Double-Byte)
2. **Datetime**
3. **Numeric**

String Data Types
Binary Large Object (BLOB)

Binary large objects are varying-length binary strings. The data is stored in a binary format in the database. There are restrictions when using this data type including the inability to sort using this type of column. The **BLOB** data type is useful for storing non-traditional relational database information as shown in Fig. 4–3.

The maximum size of each **BLOB** column is 2 GB (gigabytes). Since this data type is of varying-length, the amount of disk space allocated is determined by the amount of data in each record, not the defined maximum size of the column in the table definition.

The **FOR BIT DATA** clause can be used at the end of a character string definition. This clause can be used to store binary information in a DB2 table but its maximum size is 32 KB (kilobytes).

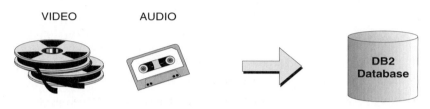

Binary Data (Variable length - up to 2 GB/column)

Fig. 4–3 Binary Strings (BLOBs)

Character Large Object (CLOB)

Character large objects are varying-length character strings (stored in the database using a single byte to represent each character). There is a code page associated with each **CLOB**. For more details regarding a DB2 code page, see "Code Page Considerations" on page 123. The code page for each **CLOB** column must be the same for the entire database. **CLOB** columns are used for large amounts (> 32 KB) of text data as shown in Fig. 4–4.

The maximum size for each **CLOB** column is 2 GB (gigabytes). Since this data type is of varying-length, the amount of disk space allocated is determined by the amount of data in each record. Therefore, you should create the column specifying the length of the longest string.

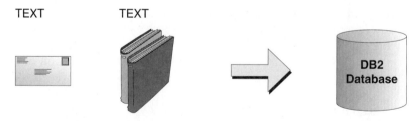

Character Data (Variable length - up to 2 GB/column)

Fig. 4–4 Character Strings (CLOBs)

Double-Byte Character Large Objects (DBCLOBS)

Double-byte character large objects are varying-length character strings (stored in the database using two bytes to represent each character). There is a code page associated with each column. **DBCLOB** columns are used for large amounts (>32KB) of double-byte text data such as Japanese text.

The maximum size for each **DBCLOB** column is 1 GB of text data for a total of 2 GB of database storage. The maximum length should be specified during the column definition as each data record will be varying in length.

The **GRAPHIC** data-type is similar to the **DBCLOB** data type as they are both used to represent a single character using two-bytes of storage. The **GRAPHIC** data types include:

GRAPHIC (fixed length — maximum 127)

VARGRAPHIC (varying-length — maximum 2000 characters)

LONG VARGRAPHIC (varying-length — maximum 16350 characters).

Fixed-Length Character String (CHAR)

Fixed-length character strings are stored in the database using the entire defined amount of storage. If the data being stored always has the same length then a **CHAR** data type should be used. In Fig. 4–5, the Candidate ID field is defined as a fixed-length character string of 8 characters.

Using fixed-length character fields can potentially waste disk space within the database if the data is not using the defined amount of storage. However, there is overhead involved in storing varying-length character strings and if a varying-length character string is updated, it could possibly be split onto two pages of storage in the database. The term **CHARACTER** can be used as a synonym for **CHAR**.

The length of a fixed-length string must be between 1 and 254 characters. If you do not supply a value for the length, a value of 1 is assumed.

✍ Character strings are stored in the database without a terminating character. Depending on the development environment a null-terminator can or can not be appended to the end of a character string when the data is stored or retrieved.

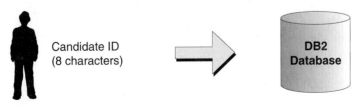

Character Data (Fixed length - up to 254 bytes/column)

Fig. 4–5 Fixed-Length Character Strings (CHARs)

varying-Length Character String (VARCHAR)

Varying-length character strings are stored in the database using only the amount of space required to store the data. The individual names are stored as varying-length strings (**VARCHAR**) as each person has a different length (up to a maximum length of 30 character) for their name as shown in Fig. 4–6. The term **CHAR VARYING** or **CHARACTER VARYING** can be used as a synonym for **VARCHAR**.

If a varying-length character string is updated and the resulting value is larger than the original, the data can span multiple database pages on disk. These data records are known as *tombstone* records or pointer records. Too many of these records can cause significant performance degradation as multiple pages are required to return a single data record. The maximum length of a **VARCHAR** column is 4,000 bytes.

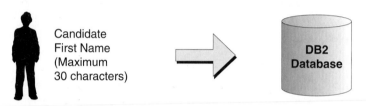

Character Data (Variable length - up to 4000 bytes/column)

Fig. 4–6 Varying-Length Character Strings (VARCHARs)

Varying-Length Long Character Strings (LONG VARCHAR)

Varying-length long character strings are stored in the database using only the amount of space required to store the data (not the maximum amount defined). This data type is used to store character data which has a maximum length greater than 4,000 bytes. The maximum length of a **LONG VARCHAR** column is 32,700.

   LONG VARCHAR data types are similar to **CLOB** data types (both types have usage restrictions).

Numeric Data Types

The four DB2 data types that can be used to store numeric data are:

- **SMALLINT**
- **INTEGER**
- **DOUBLE**
- **DECIMAL**

These data types are used to store different numeric types and precisions. The precision of a number is the number of digits used to represent its value. The data is stored in the DB2 database using a fixed amount of storage for all numeric data types. The amount of storage required increases as the precision of the number increases.

You must also be aware of the range limits of the data types and the corresponding application programming language when you are manipulating these numeric fields.

Some data values are of type integer by nature, such as the number of test candidates. It is impossible to have a number representing people which contains fractional data (numbers to the right of the decimal). On the other hand, some values require decimal places to accurately reflect their value, such as the test score. These two examples should use different DB2 data types to store their values (**SMALLINT** and **DECIMAL**).

Numeric values should not be enclosed in quotation marks. If they are, then the value is treated as a character string instead.   Even if a field contains numbers in its representation, a DB2 numeric data type should be used to represent the data, only if arithmetic operations should be allowed. In our example database, we will represent test numbers as characters because there is no arithmetic significance to the test number.

Small Integer (SMALLINT)

A small integer uses the least amount of storage in the database for each value. An integer does not allow any digits to the right of the decimal.

The data value range for a **SMALLINT** is -32768 to 32767.The precision for a **SMALLINT** is 5 digits (to the left of the decimal). Two bytes of database storage used for each **SMALLINT** column.

Integer (INTEGER)

An integer takes twice as much storage as a **SMALLINT**, but it has a much greater range of possible values.

The range for an **INTEGER** is -2,147,483,648 to 2,147,483,647. The precision for a **INTEGER** is 10 digits to the left of the decimal. Four bytes of database storage are used for each **INTEGER** column.

Decimal (DECIMAL/NUMERIC)

A decimal or numeric data type is used for numbers with fractional and whole parts. A good example of decimal data is currency. The decimal data is stored in a packed format known as Binary Coded Decimal (BCD) notation.

The precision and scale must be provided when a decimal data type is used. The precision is the total number of digits (range from 1 to 31) and the scale is the number of digits in the fractional part of the number. For example, a decimal data type to store currency values of up to $1 million would require a definition of **DECIMAL (9,2)**. The terms **NUMERIC, NUM, DECIMAL**, and **DEC** can all be used to declare a decimal/numeric column. If a decimal data type is to be manipulated in a C program the host variable must be declared as a double.

If the precision and scale values are not supplied for a **DECIMAL** column definition, a default value (5,0) is used.

Double-Precision Floating-Point (DOUBLE/FLOAT)

A **DOUBLE** or **FLOAT** data-type is an approximation of a number. The approximation is always represented using 64 bits or 8 bytes of storage.

The range for a **DOUBLE/FLOAT** is -1.79769E+308 or +1.79769E+308 (maximum negative and maximum positive). The smallest positive value is +2.225E-307, and the largest negative value is -2.225E-307 (closest to zero is considered the largest negative).

   Exponential notation is used to represent **DOUBLE/FLOAT** data values.

Datetime Data Types

There are three DB2 data types specifically used to represent dates and times:

- **DATE** — Stored internally as a (packed) string of 4 bytes. Externally, the string has a length of 10 bytes (MM-DD-YYYY varies).
- **TIME** — Stored internally as a (packed) string of 3 bytes. Externally, the string has a length of 8 bytes (HH-MM-SS).
- **TIMESTAMP** — Stored internally as a (packed) string of 10 bytes. Externally, the string has a length of 26 bytes (YYYY-MM-DD-HH-MM-SS-NNNNNN).

From the user perspective, these data types can be treated as character or string data types. Every time you need to use a datetime attribute, you will need to enclose it using quotation marks. However, datetime data types are **NOT** stored in the database as fixed-length character strings.

DB2 provides special functions that allow you to manipulate these data types. These functions allow you to extract the month, hour or year of a datetime column.

The date and time formats correspond to the country code of the application (as the representation of dates and times varies in different countries). Therefore, the string that represents a date value will change depending on the country code of the application. In some countries, the date format is DD/MM/YYYY, while in other countries, it is YYYY-MM-DD. You should be aware of the country code used by your application in order to use the correct date string format. If an incorrect date format is used an SQL error will be reported.

As a general recommendation, if you are interested in a single element of a date string, let's say month or year, always use the SQL functions provided by DB2 to interpret the column value. By using the SQL functions, your application will be more portable.

TIMESTAMP fields use the most storage, but they contain the most accurate time as they include microseconds.

We stated that all datetime data types have an external and internal format. The external format is *always* a character string. Let's examine the various datetime data types available in DB2.

Date Strings (DATE)

There are a number of valid methods of representing a *date* as a string.

Table 4–1 Valid Date Formats

Format Name	Abbreviation	Date Format
International Standards Organization	ISO	YYYY-MM-DD
IBM USA Standard	USA	MM/DD/YYYY
IBM European Standard	EUR	DD.MM.YYYY
Japanese Industrial Standard	JIS	YYYY-MM-DD
Database code page	LOC	Depends

Any of the string formats shown in Table 4–1 can be used to store dates in a DB2 database. When the data is retrieved (using a **SELECT**), the output string will be in one of these formats. There is a **BIND** option, called **DATETIME**, which allows you to define the external format of the date and time values. The **abbreviation** column in Table 4–1 contains the possible values for the **DATETIME** **BIND** option. Each **DATE** column requires four bytes of storage (internally).

Time String (TIME)

There are a number of valid methods of representing a *time* as a string.

Table 4–2 Valid Time Formats

Format Name	Abbreviation	Date Format
International Standards Organization	ISO	HH.MM.SS
IBM USA Standard	USA	HH:MM AM or PM
IBM European Standard	EUR	HH.MM.SS
Japanese Industrial Standard	JIS	HH:MM:SS
Database Code Page	LOC	Depends

Any of the string formats in Table 4–2 can be used to store times in a DB2 database. When data is retrieved the external format of the time will be one of the formats shown in Table 4–2.

There is a **BIND** option, called **DATETIME**, which allows you to define the external format of the date and time values. The **abbreviation** column in Table 4–2 contains the possible values for the **DATETIME BIND** option. Each **TIME** column requires three bytes of storage (internally).

     TIME data types are always stored the same internally. Their external representation can be changed using a different **BIND** option.

Timestamp Strings (TIMESTAMP)

Timestamps data types have a single external format. Therefore, the **DATETIME** bind option does not affect the external format of timestamps. Timestamps have an external representation as YYYY-MM-DD-HH.MM.SS.NNNNNN (Year-Month-Day-Hour-Minute-Seconds-Microseconds). Every **TIMESTAMP** column requires ten bytes of storage (internally).

Large Object Considerations

Traditionally large unstructured data was stored somewhere outside the database. Therefore, the data could not be accessed using SQL. Besides the traditional database data types, DB2 implements data types that will store large amounts of unstructured data. These data types are known as **Large Objects** (LOBS). Multiple LOB columns can be defined for a single table.

     The maximum amount of LOB data for a single data record is 24 GB (gigabytes).

DB2 also provides special considerations for handling these large objects. You can elect to not log the large object portion of a transaction. You can decide not to log the LOB values to avoid exhausting the transaction log files. There is a **NOT LOGGED** option which can be specified during the **CREATE TABLE** statement to avoid logging any modifications to LOB columns.

There is also a **COMPACT** option which can be specified during the **CREATE TABLE** statement. This option is used to avoid allocating extra disk space when storing these large data objects.

In our DB2 certification database, we can decide to store a bitmap of each test candidate's picture. We would use a **BLOB** data type to store the photograph.

If you would like to manipulate textual data which is greater than 32 KB in length, then you would use **CLOB** or character large object data type. For example, if each test candidate were required to submit their resume, then the resume could be stored in a **CLOB** column along with the rest of the candidate's information. There are many SQL functions which can be used to manipulate large character data columns.

User-Defined Data Types

User-Defined Data Types (UDTs) are created by the database administrator based on the data types provided by DB2. They are used to further define the type of data being represented in the database. If columns are defined using different UDTs based on the same base data type, these UDTs cannot be directly compared. This is known as *strong typing*. DB2 provides this strong data typing to avoid end user mistakes during the assignment or comparison of different types of real-world data.

✍ User-Defined Data Types (UDTs) must be based on built-in DB2 data types.

Let's say we have a table that will be used to store different measures of weight such as pounds and kilograms. We should use a numeric data type for these columns as arithmetic operations are appropriate. We will use the **INTEGER** data type as the base DB2 data type for the UDTs, **KILOGRAM** and **POUND**. The values represent different units and therefore should not be directly compared.

✍ The term **distinct type** can be used instead of UDT.

Let's define two new data types: **KILOGRAM** and **POUND**. These data types will be based on the integer (**INTEGER**) data type. Once the KILOGRAM and POUND UDTs have been defined, they can be referenced in the **CREATE TABLE** statement.

When the UDTs are defined, system-generated SQL functions are created. These functions are known as **casting functions**. The casting functions serve two purposes:

- To convert between the base data type and the user-defined data type (UDT)
- To allow comparisons of columns defined using the same UDT

In the real world, you cannot directly compare pounds and kilograms without converting one of the values. In DB2, this conversion is provided by the system-generated casting functions.

Creating User-Defined Data Types (UDTs)

Let's create the user-defined data types for POUND and KILOGRAM.

```
CREATE DISTINCT TYPE pound
                AS INTEGER WITH COMPARISONS
CREATE DISTINCT TYPE kilogram
                AS INTEGER WITH COMPARISONS
```

Fig. 4–7 Creating User-Defined Data Types

In the example shown in Fig. 4–7, we are creating the new data types known as POUND and KILOGRAM. You may have decided to use the **DECIMAL** data type to allow for fractional values (for example, **DECIMAL (7,2)** can be more appropriate for a measure of weight, depending on how heavy the objects are).

The keyword **DISTINCT** is mandatory for all user-defined data types. The **WITH COMPARISONS** clause is also a mandatory clause (except for LOB data types). Let's create a table using the pound and kilogram data type.

```
CREATE TABLE person
              (f_name      VARCHAR(30),
               weight_p    POUND
               weight_k    KILOGRAM)
```

Fig. 4–8 Using the UDTs in a Table Definition

As we can see in Fig. 4–8, the new data types are used in the table definition just like the built-in data types. DB2 will not allow you to compare or perform arithmetic operations on the POUND and KILOGRAM columns directly. A casting function would need to be used to perform arithmetic operations using these columns. In other words, you could not use the average function (**AVG**) for a column defined as POUND or KILOGRAM, unless you create a user-defined function called **AVG.**

The SQL statement in Fig. 4–9 would result in an error. The data type for the constant value of 30 is of type **INTEGER**. It cannot be directly compared with the POUND data type.

```
SELECT f_name, weight_p
           FROM person
           WHERE weight_p > 30
```

Fig. 4–9 Selecting Data Involving UDTs (in expressions)

To resolve the error in Fig. 4–9, a simple cast of the constant value of 30 is required. By casting, the value of 30 is treated as an **INTEGER** data type. In Fig. 4–10, the **POUND(INTEGER)** casting function is being used to convert the value of 30 to the POUND data type.

Let's look at another example of a UDT involving telephone numbers. You always compare phone numbers with other phone numbers; you don't compare them with street numbers or department numbers. This means that a column representing telephone numbers would be an ideal candidate to be defined using a distinct type or UDT.

```
SELECT f_name, weight_p
            FROM person
            WHERE weight_p > POUND(30)
```

Fig. 4–10 Selecting Data Involving UDTs Using a Casting Function

Should telephone numbers be stored as numeric or string data? Does it make sense to perform arithmetic operations on a telephone number? No, a telephone number has no significant mathematical properties (for example, adding one to your telephone number is not a useful operation). Therefore, we should base the new data type on a **CHARACTER** or **CHAR** column. A varying-length character string or **VARCHAR** is not required as the length of telephone numbers is consistent.

Let's create a user-defined data type for the telephone numbers. This will ensure that all the columns containing telephone numbers share the same data type.

✍ The valid data values for a user-defined data type cannot be specified. Therefore, any valid value for the base data type is allowed.

The SQL statement to create the distinct type *phone* is shown:

```
CREATE DISTINCT TYPE phone
            AS CHAR(10) WITH COMPARISONS
```

The creation of this user-defined data type will result in the creation of the following casting functions:

- **CHAR(<PHONE>)**, which translates data values from the **PHONE** data type to the base data type **CHAR**.
- **PHONE(<CHAR>)**, which translates data values from the base data type **CHAR** to the **PHONE** data type.

In fact, DB2 will create two **PHONE** casting functions: one that converts fixed **CHAR** strings and another that works with **VARCHAR** columns. The number of casting functions created will vary according to the base data type being used.

Let's say that we have two columns which represent phone numbers: **HPHONE** (home phone number) and **WPHONE** (work phone number). Both of these columns should be defined using the same data type **PHONE**.

Examples of using these columns in expressions:

- An expression involving the same data type (**PHONE**).
  phone = hphone   or hphone <> wphone
- An expression using the casting function **HPONE(CHAR)**.
  hphone = PHONE('5555551234')
- A similar expression using the casting function **CHAR(PHONE)**.
  `CHAR(hphone) = '5555551234'`

Removing a User-Defined Data type

User-defined data types (UDTs) are only defined for a single database. They can be created and removed from a database by the database administrator. If tables have been defined using a UDT, you will not be allowed to drop the UDT. The table would need to be dropped before the UDT could be dropped.

Assuming there is no table defined using the pound data type, you could remove the definition of the *pound* data type using the following statement:

```
DROP DISTINCT TYPE pound
```

The **DROP DISTINCT TYPE** statement will delete the pound data type and all of its related casting functions.

✍ Remember that if you don't qualify a DB2 object, the current user id will be used as the qualifier (schema name). For example, if your user id is volker then the above statement would attempt to drop the data type *volker.pound*.

NULL Values

A null value represents an unknown state. Therefore, when columns containing null values are used in calculations, the result is unknown. All of the data types discussed in the previous section support the presence of null values. During the table definition you can decide that a value **must** be provided. This is accomplished by adding a phrase to the end of a column definition. The **CREATE TABLE** statement can contain the phrase **NOT NULL** following the definition of each column. This will ensure that the column contains a real data value.

Special considerations are required to properly handle null values when coding a DB2 application. For more information on handling null values within an application, see "Indicator Variables" on page 464. DB2 treats a null value differently than any other data values.

✍ Relational databases allow null values and it is important to remember that they can be appropriate for your database design.

The result of logical operations involving null values are shown in Tables 4–3 and 4–4.

Table 4–3 Logical AND operations

AND	True	False	Null
True	true	false	null
False	false	false	false
Null	null	false	null

Table 4–4 Logical OR operations

OR	True	False	Null
True	true	true	true
False	true	false	null
Null	true	null	null

To define a column to not accept null values, add the phrase **NOT NULL** to the end of the column definition, for example:

```
CREATE TABLE t1 (c1 CHAR(3) NOT NULL)
```

From the example, DB2 will not allow any null values to be stored in the *c1* column. In general, avoid using nullable columns unless they are required to implement the database design.

Code Page Considerations

A character code page is associated with all DB2 character data types (**CHAR**, **VARCHAR**, **CLOB**, **DBCLOB**). This code page is set at the database level during the **CREATE DATABASE** command.

A code page can be considered a reference table which is used to convert alphanumeric data to binary data, which is stored in the database. A DB2 database can only use a single code page. The code page is established during the **CREATE DATABASE** command using the options **CODESET** and **TERRITORY**. The code page can use a single byte to represent an alphanumeric (a single byte can represent 256 unique elements) or multiple bytes.

Languages like English contain relatively few unique characters; therefore a single byte code page is sufficient to store data. Languages like Japanese require more than 256 elements to represent all of the unique characters; therefore, a multi-byte code page (usually a double-byte code page) is required.

A code point is the unique value used to locate the character within the code page. DB2 will attempt to perform code page conversion if the application and the database have not been defined using the same code page.

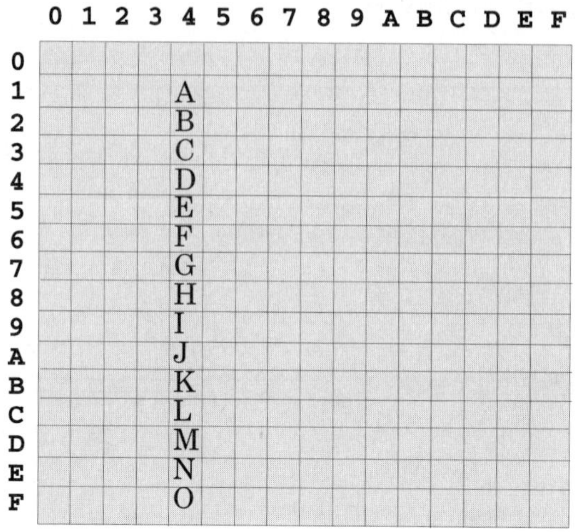

```
     0 1 2 3 4 5 6 7 8 9 A B C D E F
0
1                 A
2                 B
3                 C
4                 D
5                 E
6                 F
7                 G
8                 H
9                 I
A                 J
B                 K
C                 L
D                 M
E                 N
F                 O
```

CODE PAGE (code points 0-255)

Fig. 4–11 Code Page

In Fig. 4–11, an example code page is shown. This example represents a portion of the ASCII character set (as hexadecimal code point 41 represents the character A).

✍ Binary strings, such as **FOR BIT DATA** and **BLOB** columns, are not associated with the database code page.

When a DB2 application is bound to a DB2 database, the application and database code page are compared. If the code pages are not equal, then code page conversion will be attempted for each SQL statement. If you will be using applications with different code pages than the database, then it is important to ensure that the code pages are compatible.

✍ You cannot have different code pages used for data within the same DB2 database.

The **collating sequence** is defined according to the code page if the **CREATE DATABASE** command specifies the option **COLLATE USING SYSTEM**. If the **SYSTEM** collating sequence is specified, then the data values are compared based on the **TERRITORY** specified for the system. If the option **COLLATE USING IDEN-TITY** is used, then all values are compared using their binary representation.

When you need to store data in its native (binary) format, avoid using data types with code pages. It is generally advantageous to have the application and the database code page the same to avoid the code page conversion process.

Selecting the Correct Data Type

Knowledge of the possible data values and their usage is required to be able to select the correct data type. Specifying an inappropriate data type when defining the tables can result in:

- wasted disk space
- improper expression evaluation
- code page inconsistencies

A small checklist for data type selection is shown in Table 4–5.

Table 4–5 Data Type Checklist

	Question	Data Type
✓	Is the data variable in length?	VARCHAR
✓	If the data is variable in length, what is the maximum length?	VARCHAR
✓	Do you need to sort (order) the data?	CHAR, VARCHAR, CLOB, DBCLOB
✓	Is the data going to be used in arithmetic operations?	DECIMAL, DOUBLE, INTEGER, SMALLINT
✓	Does the data element contain decimals?	DECIMAL, DOUBLE
✓	Is the data fixed length?	CHAR
✓	Does the data have a specific meaning (beyond DB2 base datatypes)?	USER DEFINED TYPE

DB2 Certification Database Design and Implementation

The best way to understand data type selection is to design a database and implement the design using DB2. We will create a database which could be used to schedule and track the results of a certification program. This database will be used to illustrate many aspects of the SQL language and features of DB2.

Problem Domain

Defining the problem domain is the first step in database design. This database will be used to schedule test candidates to take exams, and following the completion of the test, it will contain the candidates' test scores. Based on the test scores, the candidate can become a **IBM Certified DB2 Database Administrator** and/or a **IBM Certified DB2 Application Developer**.

The database and its application will need to perform the following tasks:

1. Insert-update-delete testing center information
2. Insert-update-delete test information
3. Insert-update-delete test candidate information
4. Schedule a candidate to take a test
5. Update candidate test scores once they have completed the exams
6. Determine which candidates qualify for certification
7. Generate various reports on the candidates and tests

The database will be named **DB2CERT**. The data to be stored in the **DB2CERT** database can easily be grouped into three reference tables and a fourth table used to relate the other tables. The primary relationship can be defined as "a test **candidate** takes a specific **test** at a **test center**."

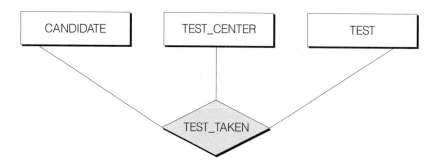

Fig. 4–12 Tables for the DB2CERT Database

Fig. 4–12 shows the relationships within the problem domain. The rectangles represent the base tables: **candidate**, **test_center** and **test**. The fourth table is a relationship table called **test_taken**.

DB2CERT Database Table Descriptions

Let's examine the type of records that will be stored in each of the tables:

• The **CANDIDATE** table stores information about each test candidate for the DB2 Certification Program. Data such as candidate name, address and phone number will be stored in this table.

  A data record represents a single test candidate (person).

- The **TEST_CENTER** table stores information about the test centers where a candidate can take a DB2 Certification exam. Data such as the test center name, address, number of seats at the test center and its phone number will be stored in this table.
  A data record represents a single test center location.

- The **TEST** table stores information about each of the DB2 Certification exams. Data such as the test name, type, cut score (passing percentage) and the length of each test will be stored in this table.
  A data record represents a single test. For example, there are currently three tests in the DB2 Certification Program; therefore, there are only three data records in this table.

- The **TEST_TAKEN** table associates the records from the other three tables.   It serves a dual purpose to schedule tests and to track each test result. Data such as the candidates' test scores, date_taken, start time and seat number will be stored in this table.
  This will be the **most active** of the four tables, as multiple exams are required to be taken by each candidate to become certified and each test taken will have a corresponding data record in this table.

Once you have defined the tables and their relationships, the following should be considered:

1. Define any user-defined data types.
2. Define columns or attributes for the tables.
3. Define any primary key (PK) for the tables.
4. (Optional) Define foreign keys (Referential Constraints) for the tables.
5. (Optional) Define any table check constraints for the tables.
6. (Optional) Define any triggers for the database.

In Fig. 4–13 the database design is shown. The rectangles represent the entities or tables. The columns or attributes are shown as ellipses. Note, some of the columns are *derived* columns. A derived column is a column which represents a concept and not a physical attribute about an object. The derived columns are included in the model as their values will be populated by the database using a constraint mechanism.

We must map the attributes shown in Fig. 4–13 to DB2 as supported data types or user-defined data types. To demonstrate some of the powerful features of DB2, we have decided to create distinct types for many of the attributes.

It is beneficial to have a primary key defined for each of the tables as this will ensure uniqueness of the data records. The attributes which are underlined will be used as primary keys.

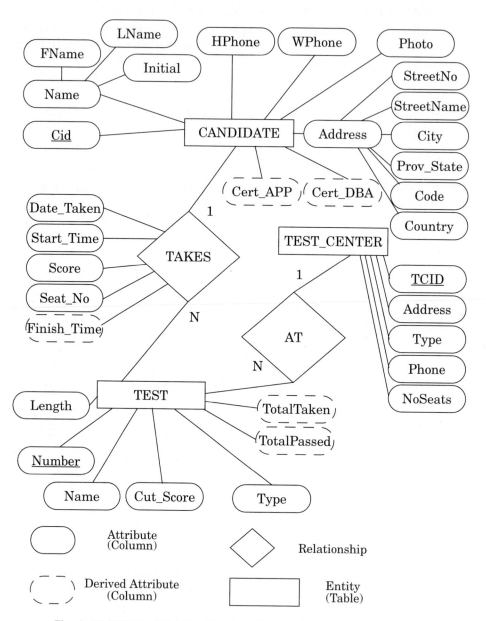

Fig. 4–13 DB2 Certification Database Entity-Relationship Diagram

In the previous section we mentioned that there will be four tables in the *DB2CERT* database but, the design shown in Fig. 4–13 has only three tables defined. There is an implied table defined in the relationship "candidate takes a test". A table is required to store each time a candidate takes a certification test.

We will impose a restriction on the candidates: they can **ONLY** take the test once on any given day. A candidate can take different tests on the same day, but not the same test. With this restriction in place, we will define a primary key for the *test_taken* table as a compound key including tcid (test center id), cid (candidate id), date_taken (date the test is being taken). By defining the primary key as a combination of these three values, we can enforce this constraint.

The diamond shapes are used to describe the relationships between the tables including the parent-child relationship. For example, there is a one-to-many relationship between the candidate and the *test_taken* table as a single candidate can take many tests. This relationship is shown by denoting the values of 1 and N (many) on the appropriate side of the diamond.

The database design shown in Fig. 4–13 is just one type of diagramming technique. A logical database design could be represented many ways but, it should not dictate the physical implementation of the database. We have included it here as it will be used throughout the rest of the book in many of the SQL statements.

Define User-Defined Data Types

If you wish to utilize user-defined data types, they must exist (in your database) before they can be referenced in a **CREATE TABLE** statement.

We have decided to create a number of user-defined data types as shown in Fig. 4–14. The **candidate_id**, **test_id**, **center_id** and **phone** data types are all based on the fixed-length character (CHAR) data type. These attributes were chosen to be user defined as they have meaning in their structure and they should not be used in expressions with other character data types. For example, a telephone number data type could be defined and then a user-defined function could be created to extract the area code. The function would only be used for phone data types.

We also decided to create some numeric user-defined data types including the data types **score** and **minutes**. There is also a user-defined data type called **bitmap** which is used to store the candidate's photograph. The bitmap data type was defined using as a binary large object (BLOB) with a maximum size of 2 GB (gigabytes).

Defining Columns

Designing a database involves many considerations. We will only examine some of these considerations in this book. If we use the database design in Fig. 4–13 as a starting point, we can start creating database objects.

The first step in creating a database is to issue the **CREATE DATABASE** command. This command is **not** part of the SQL language as each database product has a different syntax for the creation of a database. The most important consideration during the creation of the database (from a design point of view) is the specification of the **CODESET** and **TERRITORY**. For more information code pages, see "Code Page Considerations" on page 123.

```
CREATE DISTINCT TYPE candidate_id AS CHAR(8)
                WITH COMPARISONS
CREATE DISTINCT TYPE test_id AS CHAR(6)
                WITH COMPARISONS
CREATE DISTINCT TYPE center_id AS CHAR(4)
                WITH COMPARISONS
CREATE DISTINCT TYPE phone AS CHAR(10)
                WITH COMPARISONS
CREATE DISTINCT TYPE score AS DECIMAL(6,2)
                WITH COMPARISONS
CREATE DISTINCT TYPE minutes AS SMALLINT
                WITH COMPARISONS
CREATE DISTINCT TYPE bitmap AS BLOB(1M)
```

Fig. 4–14 Defining the User-Defined Data Types

Once the database has been created, we can start creating objects. We have already created distinct (user-defined) data types as shown in Fig. 4–14. Let's start creating tables. The database design had a number of attributes shown. Each of these attributes will be a column in the table definitions.

✍ To avoid confusion the term **SCHEMA** refers to a "qualifier" for database objects as defined in the SQL standards. It does not refer to the database design.

Every DB2 table contains one or more columns. The tables and their corresponding columns are given names. In the previous section, we discussed all of the data types that can be used for column definitions.

Data is placed in a DB2 table using the SQL statement **INSERT** or **UPDATE**. (The DB2 **LOAD** utility is another option.) Usually, it is desirable for each column, or data value, to have a value. Sometimes, there is no value provided for a column during the **INSERT** statement. If the column is defined as **NOT NULL,** the **INSERT** statement will fail. Otherwise, a default value will be stored.

Each column is given a name as in Fig. 4–15. The table shown is called *db2.candidate* and it contains 15 columns. This is sometimes referred to as the **degree** of a table.

Each column is assigned a data type. There are 3 user-defined data types being used in this table. Theses data types are **candidate_id**, **phone**, and **bitmap**. There are also constraints defined for the valid values for some of the columns. For example, the null constraint is specified for all of the columns except *HPhone, WPhone, Initial,* and *Photo*.

```
CREATE TABLE     db2.candidate (
                 Cid          candidate_id    NOT NULL,
                 LName        VARCHAR(30)     NOT NULL,
                 FName        VARCHAR(30)     NOT NULL,
                 Initial      CHAR(1),
                 HPhone       phone,
                 WPhone       phone,
                 StreetNo     VARCHAR(8)      NOT NULL,
                 StreetName   VARCHAR(20)     NOT NULL,
                 City         VARCHAR(30)     NOT NULL,
                 Prov_State   VARCHAR(30)     NOT NULL,
                 Code         CHAR(6)         NOT NULL,
                 Country      VARCHAR(20))    NOT NULL,
                 Cert_DBA     CHAR(1)         NOT NULL
                              WITH DEFAULT 'N',
                 Cert_APP     CHAR(1)         NOT NULL
                              WITH DEFAULT 'N',
                 Photo        bitmap,
                 CONSTRAINT   Unique_Candidate
                              PRIMARY KEY (Cid))
```

Fig. 4–15 Creating the candidate Table

Defining Primary Keys

It is usually beneficial to define a **primary key** for each of your DB2 tables, as this will guarantee the uniqueness of a column value or group of column values (composite key). In Fig. 4–15, the primary key is defined as the column *cid* (candidate id). By specifying this column as a primary key, DB2 will create a unique index to maintain the uniqueness of the data values.

✍ A unique index is always created to enforce primary key constraints.

Let's look at the other tables representing the tests and the test centers. In Fig. 4–16, the test and test center tables are shown. These tables each have a primary key defined.

✍ The primary key constraint was given a name (*unique_test* and *unique_center*) for referencing purposes. If a name is not provided, DB2 will assign a name to the constraint. The primary key constraint is enforced using a unique index. This index is given the name (**SQL<timestamp>**) by default and **cannot** be modified.

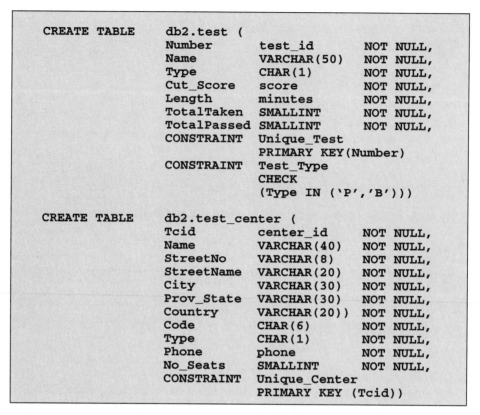

```
CREATE TABLE       db2.test (
                   Number        test_id        NOT NULL,
                   Name          VARCHAR(50)    NOT NULL,
                   Type          CHAR(1)        NOT NULL,
                   Cut_Score     score          NOT NULL,
                   Length        minutes        NOT NULL,
                   TotalTaken    SMALLINT       NOT NULL,
                   TotalPassed   SMALLINT       NOT NULL,
                   CONSTRAINT    Unique_Test
                                 PRIMARY KEY(Number)
                   CONSTRAINT    Test_Type
                                 CHECK
                                 (Type IN ('P','B')))

CREATE TABLE       db2.test_center (
                   Tcid          center_id      NOT NULL,
                   Name          VARCHAR(40)    NOT NULL,
                   StreetNo      VARCHAR(8)     NOT NULL,
                   StreetName    VARCHAR(20)    NOT NULL,
                   City          VARCHAR(30)    NOT NULL,
                   Prov_State    VARCHAR(30)    NOT NULL,
                   Country       VARCHAR(20))   NOT NULL,
                   Code          CHAR(6)        NOT NULL,
                   Type          CHAR(1)        NOT NULL,
                   Phone         phone          NOT NULL,
                   No_Seats      SMALLINT       NOT NULL,
                   CONSTRAINT    Unique_Center
                                 PRIMARY KEY (Tcid))
```

Fig. 4–16 Defining the test and test_center Tables

Defining Foreign Keys

A **foreign key** is a reference to the data values in another table. There are different types of foreign key constraints. Let's look at the remaining table in the DB2 Certification database and in particular its foreign key constraints. In Fig. 4–17 there is a single compound primary key defined and three foreign key constraints.

The primary key is defined as the columns *cid*, *tcid*, and *number*. The foreign key constraints will perform the following:

- If a record in the candidate table is deleted, all of the matching records in the *test_taken* table will be deleted (**DELETE CASCADE**).
- If a test center in the test_center table is deleted, all of the matching records in the *test_taken* table will be deleted (**DELETE CASCADE**).
- If a test in the test table is deleted and there are matching records in the *test_taken* table, the **DELETE** statement will result in an error (same for an **UPDATE** of the test number) (**RESTRICT**).

✎ A foreign key constraint always relates to the primary key of the table in the references clause of the **CREATE TABLE**.

```
CREATE TABLE     db2.test_taken (
                 Cid          candidate_id    NOT NULL,
                 Tcid         center_id       NOT NULL,
                 Number       test_id         NOT NULL,
                 Date_Taken   date            NOT NULL
                                              WITH DEFAULT,
                 Start_Time   TIME            NOT NULL,
                 Finish_Time  TIME            NOT NULL,
                 Score        score,
                 Seat_No      CHAR(2)         NOT NULL,
                 CONSTRAINT   number_const
                 PRIMARY KEY (Cid,Tcid,Number),
                 FOREIGN KEY (Cid)
                 REFERENCES db2.candidate
                              ON DELETE CASCADE,
                 FOREIGN KEY (Tcid)
                 REFERENCES db2.test_center
                              ON DELETE CASCADE,
                 FOREIGN KEY (Number)
                 REFERENCES db2.test
                              ON DELETE RESTRICT
                              ON UPDATE RESTRICT)
```

Fig. 4–17 Defining the *test_taken* Table Definition

Defining parent-child relationships between tables is known as **declarative referential integrity** as the child table *refers* to the parent table. These constraints are defined during table creation. DB2 will enforce the constraints for all **INSERT**, **UPDATE**, and **DELETE** activity.

Tables

A table is an unordered set of data records. In the previous section, we have shown the SQL statements used to create the tables for the DB2 Certification database. Tables, once created and populated with data, are referenced in the **FROM** clause of the SQL statements. There are two types of tables:

- Permanent Tables
- Temporary (Derived) Tables

We have only discussed permanent tables (otherwise known as base tables). These tables are created using the **CREATE TABLE** statement. The table represents a physical representation of the data stored on disk. We will discuss the temporary tables later in this chapter.

In DB2, there are two types of permanent tables:

- **SYSTEM CATALOG TABLES** are created automatically when you create a DB2 database. They will store data used by DB2 to manage the database and the database objects. The system catalog tables will contain all of the information regarding the design of the database, including table definitions and database object privileges. You cannot directly **INSERT** or **DELETE** entries from these tables. You can update the statistical information contained in the system catalog tables using the updatable views defined in the **SYSSTAT** schema.
- **USER TABLES** are created by the database administrator using the **CREATE TABLE** statement. The data in these tables can be directly updated using the **INSERT, UPDATE** or **DELETE** statements (if the user has the required authority).

System Catalog Tables

There are special tables used by DB2 which contain *meta* information about the database objects. These tables are called system catalog tables and they are examined by DB2 during query processing. Some of the information contained in the system catalog tables includes:

- Column data types
- Defined constraints
- Object dependencies
- Object privileges

SQL Data Definition Language (DDL) statements will update the system catalog tables. The system catalog tables are automatically created during the processing of the **CREATE DATABASE** command. There are 29 base system tables in a DB2 common server database and they always reside in a special table space called *SYSCATSPACE*.

✍ To display the names of the system catalog tables and their creation time enter the command **LIST TABLES FOR SYSTEM**.

The system catalog tables **cannot** be modified using an **INSERT** or **DELETE** statement. However, some of the data can be modified. For example, the **COMMENT ON** statement and **ALTER** statement will update information stored in the system catalog tables. For more details on the use of the **ALTER** statement, see "The ALTER Statement" on page 143.

The system tables also contain statistical information about the structure of the database. For example, the number of pages allocated for each table is stored in the system catalog tables. The statistical information is updated by the **RUNSTATS** command.

Database object privileges (such as **INSERT**, **SELECT**, and **CONTROL**) are also maintained within the system catalog tables. The privileges are established using special SQL statements known as **Data Control Language** (DCL). The main DCL statements are **GRANT** and **REVOKE**. These statements were discussed in the chapter 3.

As a database administrator, you can need to query the system tables to gain a better understanding of the database structure. Usually, the database administrator creates all of the database objects.

Only a subset of the system catalog tables is **updatable**. There is a special set of views defined on the base tables which are to be used to update database statistics. These views are defined using the *SYSSTAT* schema.

✍ Use the **RUNSTATS** command to update the statistics and only update the *SYSSTAT* views directly for detailed performance purposes.

There is also a set of read-only views defined for the system catalog base tables. To determine information about a DB2 database, the most common method is to issue **SELECT** statements against the system catalog tables. There are views defined for this purpose and they have the schema name *SYSCAT*.

The system catalog base tables are defined using the *SYSIBM* schema. You can query the *SYSIBM* tables, but they are not documented in the DB2 publications. The *SYSCAT* views are documented and their view names and column definitions are much easier to remember.

✍ System table data can also be obtained using ODBC (Open Database Connectivity) or CLI (Call Level Interface) APIs.

In general, there is at least one system catalog table for each of the database object types. Table 4–6 lists some of the system catalog views.

Table 4–6 System Tables and Views

Database Object	SYSIBM System Catalog Tables	SYSCAT System Catalog Views	SYSSTAT Updatable Views
Table Spaces	SYSTABLESPACES	TABLESPACES	-
Tables	SYSTABLES	TABLES	TABLES
Views	SYSVIEWS	VIEWS	-
Columns	SYSCOLUMNS	COLUMNS	COLUMNS
Indexes	SYSINDEXES	INDEXES	INDEXES
Packages	SYSPLANS	PACKAGES	-
Triggers	SYSTRIGGERS	TRIGGERS	-

Table 4–6 System Tables and Views

Database Object	SYSIBM System Catalog Tables	SYSCAT System Catalog Views	SYSSTAT Updatable Views
Data Types	SYSDATATYPES	DATA TYPES	-
Constraints	SYSCHECKS	CHECKS	-
Referential Integrity	SYSRELS	REFERENCES	-
Functions	SYSFUNCTIONS	FUNCTIONS	FUNCTIONS

There are 27 views defined within the *SYSCAT* schema and only 5 views defined within the *SYSSTAT* schema. Remember, the *SYSSTAT* schema views are to be used for updating statistical information for the database, an attempt to update any non-statistical value is rejected by DB2. The system catalog views use a common naming convention for database objects. In Table 4–7 the database objects and their corresponding column names are shown. Columns, table spaces, and event monitors **do not** have an associated schema name.

Table 4–7 Column Names Used in the SYSCAT Views

Database Object	Column Name in the System Catalog Views
Table	TABSCHEMA, TABNAME
View	VIEWSCHEMA, VIEWNAME
Index	INDSCHEMA, INDNAME
Constraint	CONSTSCHEMA, CONSTNAME
Trigger	TRIGSCHEMA, TRIGNAME
Package	PKGSCHEMA, PKGNAME
User-Defined Data Type (UDT)	TYPESCHEMA, TYPENAME, TYPEID
User-Defined Function (UDF)	FUNCSCHEMA, FUNCNAME, FUNCID
Column	COLNAME
Table Space	TBSPACE
Event Monitor	EVMONNAME

User Tables

When the user tables are created, the column definitions, their size and data type are specified. Once the table is defined, the column names and data types *cannot* be modified. However, new columns can be added to the table (be careful adding new columns as default data values will be used).

These user tables are always created within a table space. The user data is stored in the database using one of these methods:

- **INSERT** statement
- **IMPORT** command
- **LOAD** command

 The terms *utility* and *command* are used interchangeably throughout the book. All of the DB2 utilities are documented in the *DB2 Command Reference*, but they can also be issued from an application using an API defined in the *DB2 API Reference*.

There are many options which can be used when creating a user table, some of these options are:

- Define if a column should accept **NULL** values
- Define a **DEFAULT** value for a column
- Define a primary key
- Define foreign keys
- Define table check constraints
- Define the table space(s) to be used
- Define data capture options (used for replication)
- Define logging options for LOB columns

Views are defined using one or more base (permanent) tables. The data contained in a view is physically located in one or more base tables. Views provide the database administrator with an alternate form of representing the base tables to the end users.

Views can be used to provide a simple interface to a complex table relationship and/or used to implement a security mechanism to allow end user access to portions of a table (at a column or row restriction).

Table Spaces

Table spaces are used to define physical storage (disk/device) which can be used by DB2. Tables are created within these table spaces. This allows the database tables to span devices. If more devices are added to a database server, DB2 can be configured to use the new devices.

When the table is being defined using the **CREATE TABLE** statement, explicitly state in which table space the table data should reside. Table spaces provide the database administrator with the ability to control the location of the database objects (tables). You can define any number of table spaces within a single database.

   If the database query needs to access index and base table data, the query performance can be greatly improved by storing the index keys in a different table space (on a physically different device) than the base table data.

Schemas

Schemas are used in DB2 to logically group a set of database objects. Most of the database objects are named using a two-part naming convention (**<schema_name>.<object_name>**).

The first part of the name is referred to as the schema (otherwise known as a qualifier for the database object). A specific schema can be used to prefix the names of all the objects that are used for a payroll application. For example, these tables could be named:

- PAYROLL.EMPLOYEE
- PAYROLL.SALARIES

Schema names are associated with tables, views, user-defined data types, user-defined functions, packages and triggers. There is **no** schema name associated with the name of a DB2 database.

When you create an object and don't specify a schema, the object will be implicitly qualified using the your user id. When an object is being referenced in an SQL statement, it is also implicitly qualified with user id of the issuer (dynamic SQL) if no schema name is specified in the SQL statement. Static SQL statements are qualified with the user id of the person binding the application (by default). For example, if user *adri* created a table called *tasks*, the complete name of the table as stored in the database would be *adri.tasks*.

   DB2 database objects are stored in *uppercase*.

As a rule of thumb, you are only allowed to create objects within your schema (your authid), unless you have special authority, such as **SYSADM** or **DBADM**.

In DB2, there are four predefined schemas:

- **SYSCAT**, system catalog views.
- **SYSSTAT**, updatable system catalog views.
- **SYSIBM**, system catalog tables.
- **SYSFUN**, user-defined functions provided by DB2.

Resolving Function Name Schemas

We have not yet discussed the creation of user-defined functions (UDFs) within a DB2 database. If there is a reference to an SQL function, such as average **AVG**(), the function could be a built-in function or it could be a user-defined function.

Each SQL function, just like other DB2 objects, has a schema name (two part name). Therefore, if the function is referenced in a SQL statement without the schema name, the schema name must be implicitly assigned.

A **special register** is a memory area on the DB2 server which contains information used by DB2 for the processing of an SQL statement. One of these special registers is called **CURRENT FUNCTION PATH**. It contains an ordered list of schemas which will be used to locate the proper SQL function. To view this list of schemas, examine the contents of the **CURRENT FUNCTION PATH** special register.

The **VALUES()** function is used to return the current settings of any special register. The following is an example of obtaining the current value of the **CURRENT FUNCTION PATH**:

```
VALUES(CURRENT FUNCTION PATH)
```

The default setting for **CURRENT FUNCTION PATH** is **SYSIBM, SYSFUN, USER**. The USER schema represents the currently active user id. For static SQL statements the function path is resolved using the **FUNCPATH BIND** option.

For example, to set the value of the special register (to include the *DB2* schema during function resolution), issue the following statement:

```
SET CURRENT FUNCTION PATH
              SYSIBM,SYSFUN,USER,DB2
```

Indexes

Indexes are physical objects that are associated with a single table. Any permanent table (user table or system table) can have indexes defined on them. You **cannot** define an index on a view. You can define multiple indexes for a single table. Indexes are used for two primary reasons:

- Ensure uniqueness of a data values
- Improve SQL query performance

Indexes can be used to access data in a sorted order more quickly and avoid the time-consuming task of sorting the data using temporary storage. The index will be maintained automatically by DB2 as data is inserted, updated and deleted.

  The maintenance overhead of indexes will negatively impact the performance of **INSERT**, **UPDATE** and **DELETE** statements.

Indexes can be defined in ascending or descending order (ordering is dependent on the code page). They can be defined as unique or non-unique, and they could involve a single column's data values or multiple columns' data values. The **Visual Explain** utility will provide index usage information for every explainable SQL statement (if the explain data is gathered).

Packages

Packages are database objects which contain executable forms of SQL statements. These packages contain statements which are referenced from a DB2 application. A package corresponds to a program source module.

  Only the corresponding program source module can invoke the contents of the package.

Packages are stored in the database system catalog tables. The packages contain the DB2 access plan which was selected by DB2 during the **BIND** process. This type of **BIND** is known as static binding, as it is performed prior to the execution of the SQL statement. Packages cannot be directly referenced in an SQL data manipulation (DML) statement.

Most applications that access a DB2 database will have a package or group of packages stored (bound) in the system catalog tables.

Log Files

A number of log files are associated with each DB2 database. As transactions are processed, they are tracked within the log files. DB2 will track all of the SQL statements that are issued for a database within its database log files.

DB2 uses a *write-ahead* logging method which ensures that the changes to the database will be applied (even during a crash recovery scenario). The changes are first written to the log files, and at a later time, these changes are applied to the physical database tables.

If there is a crash (fatal error) during the processing of an SQL statement, the log files are used to return the database to a consistent state.

Every DB2 database has its own set of log files. The number and the size of these files are configurable when setting up the database.

Transactions

Transactions are a set of one or more SQL statements which execute as a single operation. The term *unit of work* is synonymous with the term *transaction*. There is no physical representation of a transaction as it is a series of instructions (SQL statements). You can think of transactions as activity in the database which is tracked using the database log files.

A transaction is treated as a single operation; it either *succeeds* or *fails*. A transaction is started implicitly with the first executable SQL statement in a program. The transaction is completed when either an explicit **COMMIT** or a **ROLLBACK** statement is encountered. An implicit **COMMIT** or **ROLLBACK** can occur when a DB2 application terminates.

 It is best to explicitly **COMMIT** or **ROLLBACK** any outstanding SQL transactions prior to terminating a DB2 application. Otherwise the result of any outstanding transactions during application termination varies on different operating environments.

Locks

DB2 is a multi-user database server and as users request data, the DB2 locking mechanism attempts to avoid resource conflicts and still provide full data integrity. As SQL statements are processed, the transactions will obtain locks. The locks are released when the resource is no longer required at the end of the transaction. The locks are stored in memory on the database server (known as the *locklist*).

The locking strategy used by DB2 during transaction processing is specified using an *isolation level* as defined when binding the application. CLI applications set the isolation level in the *db2cli.ini* file.

Using SQL Data Definition Language (DDL)

Let's create some database objects using SQL statements. At the beginning of this chapter, we divided SQL into three parts:

- **DDL**   Data Definition Language
- **DCL**   Data Control Language
- **DML**   Data Manipulation Language

The group of SQL statements which allow us to define and modify database objects is known as DDL or Data Definition Language.

The Data Definition Language contains three main SQL statements:

- **CREATE**
- **ALTER**
- **DROP**

The CREATE Statement

```
CREATE <database object>....
```

The **CREATE** statement is used to initially define database objects. The <**database object**> being created can be any of the following:

- Table
- View
- Alias
- User-Defined Function (FUNCTION)
- Trigger
- Event Monitor
- Index
- User-Defined Data Type (DISTINCT TYPE)
- Table Space

The creation of any database object using DDL will result in an update of the system catalog tables. Special database authorities or privileges can be required to create the database objects.

Database objects are used for different purposes. Some are used to define a condition or relationship (index, event monitor, trigger) and others simply define the location for user data (table, table space).

The DROP Statement

```
DROP <database object> ....
```

The **DROP** statement is used to remove constraints or definitions within the system catalog tables. Since the system catalog tables cannot be directly deleted, the **DROP** statement is used to remove data records from these tables. Since database objects can be dependent on other database objects the act of dropping an object can result in a related object being rendered invalid.

The <**database object**> being dropped can be any of the following:

- Table
- View
- Alias
- User-defined Function
- Trigger
- Event Monitor
- Index

- User-defined Data Type (DISTINCT TYPE)
- Table Space

The ALTER Statement

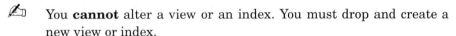

```
ALTER <database object> ....
```

The **ALTER** statement allows you to change some of the database object information (the database object must already exist in the database). You can alter a table or a table space. The **<database object>** being altered can be any of the following:

1. **Table**
2. **Table Space**

 You **cannot** alter a view or an index. You must drop and create a new view or index.

Every time you issue a DDL statement, the system catalog tables will be updated. The update will include a creation or modification timestamp and the authid of the creator (modifier).

 It is useful to store all of the DDL statements for the database in a Command Line Processor (CLP) input file to allow for easier creation of the database objects.

Creating a DB2 Database

A DB2 database must exist before any of the database objects can be created. The database must be given a name. (There is no schema associated with the database.) Once the database has been created, the next logical step is to create the table spaces.

 The **CREATE DATABASE** command is not an SQL statement The database name can be 1 to 8 characters in length.

Table Space Types

In DB2 there are two types of table spaces:
- System Managed Storage (SMS) table spaces
- Database Managed Storage (DMS) table spaces

System Managed Table Spaces (SMS)

In a System Managed Storage (**SMS**) table space, the operating system's file system is utilized to store the database objects. The disk space for the database objects will be allocated *only* when it is required.

Database Managed Table Spaces (DMS)

In a Database Managed Storage (**DMS**) table space, DB2 uses its own storage mechanism to store and locate database objects. The disk space for the table space is allocated during the **CREATE TABLESPACE** command.

   You will need to calculate the expected disk space for the tables if DMS table spaces are used.

Default Table Spaces

DB2 will create three table spaces by default when a database is created. These table spaces are SMS table spaces.   They are

SYSCATSPACE — Contains the system catalogs

TEMPSPACE1 — Holds temporary tables

USERSPACE1 — Contains all the user data

Views

Views are logical tables which are created using the **CREATE VIEW** statement. Once a view is defined, it can be accessed using DML statements (**SELECT, INSERT, UPDATE, DELETE**) as if it was a base table. A view is a *temporary* table and the data in the view is only available during query processing.

Let's create a view for the DB2 Certification database based on a single table called *test_taken*. This table is used to store all test candidate ids, test numbers, and test center numbers where a candidate has taken the DB2 certification exam.

For security reasons, a testing location should only be able to schedule candidates to take tests at their location. Instead of creating a separate **table** for each test center, you could create a **view** for each test center which references a single table. If we created a separate table for each test center and you wanted a report on all test centers, a large number of tables would need to be joined.

After the view has been created the access privileges can be specified. This provides data security as a **restricted** view of the base table is accessible. A view can contain a **WHERE** clause to restrict access to certain rows or a view can contain a portion of the columns to restrict access to certain columns of data.

In our example the view needs to restrict access to rows of the *test_taken* table. Fig. 4–18 shows the definition of the *db2.test_taken_tx01* view which is used to restrict the rows to contain only tests taken at test center *tx01*.

```
     CREATE VIEW db2.test_taken_tx01
                                 (tcid,
                                  cid,
                                  number,
                                  date_taken,
                                  start_time,
                                  finish_time,
                                  score,
                                  seat_no)
     AS
       SELECT
                                  tcid,
                                  cid,
                                  number,
                                  date_taken,
                                  start_time,
                                  finish_time,
                                  score,
                                  seat_no
     FROM db2.test_taken
                     WHERE CHAR(tcid)='TX01'
```

Fig. 4–18 Defining the *Test_Taken_Tx01* View

As shown in Fig. 4–18, we are selecting all of the columns from *test_taken*, but, we are restricting on the column *tcid*. This definition will only show the information of those candidates who have applied for the test in the test center *tx01*. The **CREATE VIEW** statement is used to define the view name and its columns. The view is always defined using a **SELECT** statement for one or more tables.

✍ A view is always defined using a **SELECT** statement.

The column names in the view do not have to match the column names of the base table. The table name has an associated schema, as does the view name. The schema name for both the base table and the view in Fig. 4–18 is *db2*.

Once the view has been defined, it can be used in DML statements like **SELECT, INSERT, UPDATE**, and **DELETE** (with restrictions). The database administrator can decide to provide a group of users with a higher-level privilege on the view than the base table. In our example, a test center coordinator can have update privileges for the view *db2.test_taken_tx01* and not have update privilege for the table *db2.test_taken*.

If the view *db2.test_taken_tx01* were used as the target table of an update operation, the **WHERE** condition would not be verified. Therefore, the view as defined in Fig. 4–18 does **not** ensure that any **INSERT** or **UPDATE** operations will not affect other testing centers data.

The predicates (**WHERE** clause) in a view definition are not enforced for **UPDATE** by default.

Views with Check Option (Symmetric Views)

If the view definition includes conditions (such as a **WHERE** clause) and the intent is to ensure that any **INSERT** or **UPDATE** statement referencing the view will have the **WHERE** clause applied, then the view must be defined using the **WITH CHECK OPTION** also known as a *symmetric view*. This option can ensure the integrity of the data being modified in the database. An SQL error will be returned if the condition is violated during an **INSERT** or **UPDATE** operation.

Fig. 4–19 is an example of a view definition using the **WITH CHECK OPTION**. Let's say that for the test center TX01 there are only two seats available. You want to restrict the values in the table to ensure that the seat number is 1 or 2. The **WITH CHECK OPTION** is required to ensure that the condition is always checked.

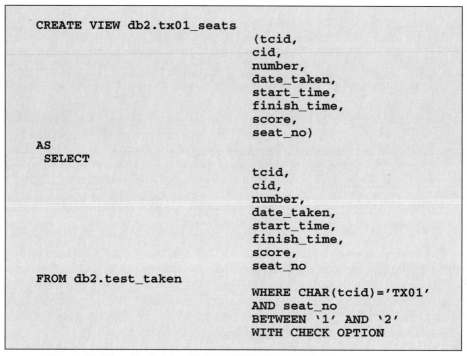

```
CREATE VIEW db2.tx01_seats
                              (tcid,
                              cid,
                              number,
                              date_taken,
                              start_time,
                              finish_time,
                              score,
                              seat_no)
AS
  SELECT
                              tcid,
                              cid,
                              number,
                              date_taken,
                              start_time,
                              finish_time,
                              score,
                              seat_no
FROM db2.test_taken
                              WHERE CHAR(tcid)='TX01'
                              AND seat_no
                              BETWEEN '1' AND '2'
                              WITH CHECK OPTION
```

Fig. 4–19 View Definition Using WITH CHECK OPTION

The view in Fig. 4–19 contains the **WITH CHECK** option. This will restrict the **input** values for the *seat_no* columns. When a view is used to insert a new value, the **WITH CHECK OPTION** is always enforced.

If the view in Fig. 4–19 were used in an **INSERT** statement the row would be rejected if the *seat_no* column was not the value 1 or 2. It is important to remember that there is no data validation during modification if the **WITH CHECK OPTION** is **not** specified.

If a view in Fig. 4–19 were used in a **SELECT** statement, the condition (**WHERE** clause) would be invoked and the result table would only contain the matching rows of data. In other words the with **CHECK OPTION** does not affect the result of a **SELECT** statement.

There are some administration issues that need to be addressed with the view as it is defined in Fig. 4–19. The **BETWEEN** clause needs to be changed if the testing center *tx01* adds more seats to its testing facility. We could create a slightly different view which would avoid this problem by adding a sub-query which has a single-value result as shown in Fig. 4–20.

```
CREATE VIEW db2.tx01_seats
                              (tcid,
                              cid,
                              number,
                              date_taken,
                              start_time,
                              finish_time,
                              score,
                              seat_no)
       AS
         SELECT
                              tcid,
                              cid,
                              number,
                              date_taken,
                              start_time,
                              finish_time,
                              score,
                              seat_no
       FROM db2.test_taken
                    WHERE        CHAR(tcid)='TX01'
                    AND          SMALLINT(seat_no)
                                 BETWEEN 1 AND
       (SELECT no_seats FROM db2.test_center
                    WHERE CHAR(tcid) = 'TX01')
                                 WITH CHECK OPTION
```

Fig. 4–20 View with Sub-query in Predicate

In Fig. 4–20, the view is defined using the value of the table *db2.test_center* to check the validity of the seat number when the view is used to insert new values. The second **SELECT** statement is guaranteed to return no more than 1 value because the tcid column is a primary key.

Nested View Definitions

If a view is based on another view, then the amount of predicate checking is based on a used of the phrase **WITH CHECK OPTION**.

If a view **V2** is based on view **V1** and the check option for **V2** is **WITH CAS-CADED CHECK OPTION**, the predicates for both views are evaluated during **INSERT** and **UPDATE** activity using the view **V2**.

If a view **V2** is based on view **V1** and the check option for **V2** is **WITH LOCAL CHECK OPTION**, then only the predicate for the view **V2** will be evaluated during **INSERT** and **UPDATE** activity using the view **V2**.

   The **WITH CHECK OPTION** does not effect the result set of a read-only view.

Modifying a View

Views are temporary table definitions. The view definition is stored in the system catalog tables. Therefore, if a backup of the database is performed, the view definition is contained in the backup image. The data contained in the view is only available when the view is being referenced in an SQL statement.

Unlike other DB2 objects, a view cannot be altered using the **ALTER** statement. If a view needs to be changed in any way, the original view must be dropped and re-created. A view can become **inoperative** if any of the referenced database objects are dropped from the database. These view dependencies are stored in the system table called **SYSCAT.VIEWDEP**.

The system catalog table **SYSCAT.VIEWS** contains a column called **VALID** which will contain the character X if the view has become inoperative. If we were to drop the table *db2.test_taken,* then the view *db2.test_taken* and the view *db2.tx01_seats* would become inoperative as shown in Fig. 4–21.

```
SELECT VIEWNAME,VIEWCHECK,READONLY, VALID
       FROM SYSCAT.VIEWS
       WHERE VIEWSCHEMA ='DB2'
```

VIEWNAME	VIEWCHECK	READONLY	VALID
TEST_TAKEN_TX01	N	N	X
TX01_SEATS	C	N	X

Fig. 4–21 Inoperative Views

Two inoperative views are shown in Fig. 4–21, as the *valid* column contains the value X (value of Y means that the view is valid). The query in Fig. 4–21 does not show the contents of the text column,. This column contains the original **CREATE VIEW** statement text. The column *viewcheck* corresponds to the **WITH CHECK OPTION** in the **CREATE VIEW** statement. A value of N means that **no** check option was specified, L means that a **local** check option was specified, and C means that a **cascaded** check option was specified.

✍ A view will **always** enforce the base table constraints. These constraints could include primary key, foreign key, table-check or not-null constraints.

Deletable Views

Depending on the view definition, it can or can not be used in a **DELETE** statement. In Fig. 4–21 the column read-only is used to determine if the view can only be used in a **SELECT** statement. The views that we have defined are considered updatable, insertable, and deletable as the *read-only* column contains the value N. A view can be used in a **DELETE** statement if its definition adheres to all of the following rules:

- Each **FROM** clause of the outer fullselect identifies only one base table, deletable view, deletable nested table expression, or deletable common table expression.
- The outer fullselect does not contain a **VALUES** clause.
- The outer fullselect does not contain a **GROUP BY** or **HAVING** clause.
- The outer fullselect does not contain column functions in the select list.
- The outer fullselect does not use set operations (**UNION, EXCEPT,** or **INTERSECT**) with the exception of **UNION ALL.**
- When using a **UNION ALL,** all the operands must be deletable and cannot be the same table.
- The select of the outer fullselect does not contain **DISTINCT.**

Updatable Views

A view is considered updatable if it meets all of the requirements of a deletable view and the following conditions:

- The column being updated must resolve to a column in the base table. It cannot be a derived column.
- All of the columns in a view based on a **UNION ALL** must have matching data types and default values.

Insertable Views

A view is considered insertable if **all** of the columns of the view are updatable and the fullselect of the view does not include **UNION ALL**.

Indexes

Indexes represent a duplication of data within a database. The index is maintained in a specified order (ascending or descending) as data is inserted, updated or deleted.

This duplication of data requires extra physical storage. The index is defined by the database administrator for two main reasons:

- To ensure uniqueness of values.
- To improve query performance.

The uniqueness of the data values can be guaranteed if a UNIQUE index has been defined for the column(s). The unique index can be used during query selection to perform faster retrieval of data.

A NON-UNIQUE index can also improve query performance by maintaining a sorted order for the data.

If a unique index is defined for a table, then DB2 will not allow any duplicate key values. The index keys are generated by DB2 based on the index definition (**CREATE INDEX** statement.). An index key can consist of one or multiple column.

  Data records are stored in the database in no defined order. However, the index keys are stored in order defined by the **CREATE INDEX** statement.

The index contains key values which correspond to a row of data in the base table. Multiple indexes can be defined for a table, but remember that each index must be maintained by DB2 (possible increase in the update, delete, insert time).

Therefore, if three indexes exist for a table and the table contains 100 rows of data, then there will be 300 index key values generated.

The indexes contain a pointer, known as a **record id** (**RID**), to the physical location of the rows in the table.

Let's create a unique index on the *db2.candidate* table using the columns *lname*, *fname*, and *initial*.

```
CREATE UNIQUE INDEX db2.icandidate_by_lname
            ON db2.candidate
            (lname,
            fname,
            initial)
```

Fig. 4–22 Index Creation Example

The *db2.icandidate_by_lname* index will store RIDs sorted in ascending order according to the key columns (*lname, fname, initial*).

✍ The default index sort order is **ascending**.

Let's issue the following SQL statement:.

```
SELECT lname, fname, initial
            FROM db2.candidate
            ORDER BY lname
```

The index *db2.icandidate_by_lname* would likely be used to retrieve the results because all of the data that is being requested resides in the index and it is already in the proper order (ascending). There would be no need to sort a temporary table to order the data. If the SQL statement stated a descending order result table, then the index in Fig. 4–22 would not likely be used to resolve the query.

DB2 indexes cannot be traversed in both directions (ascending and descending). Therefore, you can want to have two indexes defined on the same key columns where one is in ascending order and the other is in descending order.

To create a descending ordered index, use the keyword **DESC** following the column names.

```
CREATE UNIQUE INDEX db2.icandidate_by_lname
            ON db2.candidate
            (lname DESC,
            fname,
            initial)
```

Fig. 4–23 A Descending Order Index

The index defined in Fig. 4–23 shows an example of a descending index column specification. To create a non-unique index, omit the **UNIQUE** key word in the **CREATE INDEX** statement. In Fig. 4–23, the index should probably have been defined as a non-unique index as there can exist duplicate test candidates with the same last name, first name and initial.

Unique indexes are used by DB2 to implement declarative referential constraints. When we created the tables for the certification database (Fig. 4–15), we declared a primary key constraint. By specifying the primary key constraint DB2 generated a unique index. This index is used to ensure the uniqueness of each data record and it cannot be dropped using the **DROP INDEX** command.

General Indexing Guidelines

Indexes consume disk space. The amount of disk space will vary depending on the length of the key columns. The size of the index will increase as more data is inserted into the base table. Therefore, consider the disk space required for indexes when planning the size of the database. Some of indexing considerations include:

- Primary key constraints will **always** create a unique index.
- It is usually beneficial to create indexes on foreign key constraint columns.
- Select key columns with the highest *cardinality* (different values).

Altering Indexes

You cannot change index attributes without re-creating the index definition. For example, you cannot add a column to the list of key columns without dropping the previous definition and creating a new index. You can decide to add a comment, to describe the purpose of the index, using the **COMMENT ON** statement.

  There is no **ALTER INDEX** statement.

Referential Integrity and Indexes

We have discussed how defining a primary key will ensure the uniqueness of column values and the primary key is maintained using an index. This index is known as the primary index of the table. These indexes are given the name **SYSIBM.SQL**<timestamp>. For an example system generated index, see "Visual Explain Snapshot" on page 9.

To remove a primary index, use the **ALTER TABLE** statement with the **DROP PRIMARY KEY CONSTRAINT** option.

  DB2 uses unique indexes and the **NOT NULL** option to maintain the primary key constraint.

When you define a foreign key on a table, a system-defined index will **not** be created. It can be beneficial, for performance reasons, to create an index on the foreign key column.

Null Values and Indexes

It is important to understand the difference between a primary key constraint and a unique index. DB2 uses two elements to implement the relational database concept of primary keys: unique indexes and the **NOT NULL** option. Therefore, a unique index does not enforce the primary key constraint as null values must also not be allowed in the table.

A non-unique index can be created using nullable columns. An example of such a table is shown in Table 4–8. The table consists of three columns: first name, initial, last name. A non-unique index is defined using the three columns and the *initial* column is defined to allow null values.

Null values are unknown, but, when it comes to indexing, a null value is treated as equal to all other null values. In our example, the second record would result in an error during the **INSERT** statement as it violates the uniqueness rule for the index.

   Avoid using nullable columns within a unique index definition.

Table 4–8 Using Null Values with a Index

First name	Initial	Last name
Anna	NULL	Padilla
Anna	NULL	Padilla

Data Manipulation Language (DML)

In the previous section, we discussed the creation or definition of various database objects using the Data Definition (DDL) section of the SQL language. In this section, we will start to manipulate the database objects using the portion of SQL known as Data Manipulation Language (DML).

We will be populating (inserting) data into the database and retrieving the data using many powerful methods. Depending on the sophistication of the database users, they can use SQL to query the database. The majority of the SQL statements within a DB2 application involve DML statements. Therefore, application developers must understand the various methods of inserting, updating and retrieving data from the database.

We will start with simple retrieval statements and gradually introduce more complex methods of data manipulation. The DB2 certification database will be used for most of the examples. There are four main DML SQL statements:

- **SELECT**
- **INSERT**
- **UPDATE**
- **DELETE**

Data Retrieval (SELECT)

The SQL language is based on mathematical principles, specifically set theory and relational algebra. The data is stored in the database as unordered sets of data records.

The SQL language is a set-oriented language and many of its language elements are directly related to relational algebraic terms like *PERMUTATION, PROJECTION, RESTRICTION* and *JOIN*.

A set of data is represented in a DB2 database as a table or view. Therefore, the data is stored in a DB2 table without regard to order. To retrieve data in a particular order, an **ORDER BY** phrase must be added to the statement. Similarly, if the data is to be grouped, then a **GROUP BY** phrase must be added to the statement.

Now, let's review the *DB2CERT* database design and manipulate data using various SQL statements. There are three main tables: CANDIDATE, TEST and TEST_CENTER. Each of these tables represents a set of records which correspond to a test candidate (person), a test, and a test center (location). There is an associative table, known as the *test_taken* table, which is used to reflect the relationships among the three main tables. The *test_taken* table is used to schedule the test candidates and also to maintain their test scores.

   Remember that in order to execute any operation, you must have the necessary privileges.

Retrieving the Entire Table

Let's start with a simple data retrieval operation. We want to retrieve all of the candidates who have taken a DB2 certification test. The information requested is contained in the table *test_taken*.

SQL is a data access language which consists of language statements and clauses. An SQL statement must have a complete syntax. There are many optional clauses which can be used to modify the output. The output of a **SELECT** statement is known as a result set or result table. Fig. 4–25 displays the result set for the query in Fig. 4–24.

```
SELECT * FROM db2.test_taken
```

Fig. 4–24 Simple SELECT Statement

```
CID        TCID NUMBER DATE_TAKEN START_TIME FINISH_TIME SCORE    PASS_FAIL SEAT_NO
---------  ---- ------ ---------- ---------- ----------- -------- --------- -------
111111111  TR01 500    03/05/1996 15:02:36   15:02:36    98.00 P  1
111111111  TR01 501    03/10/1996 15:02:38   15:02:38    98.00 P  1
111111111  TR01 502    04/13/1996 15:02:39   15:02:39    98.00 P  1
222222222  TR01 500    04/15/1996 15:02:40   15:02:40    98.00 P  1
222222222  TR01 502    03/02/1996 10:00:00   -           87.00 P  1
222222222  TR01 502    01/02/1996 10:00:00   -           23.00 F  1
333333333  TR01 500    01/02/1996 10:00:00   -           80.00 P  1
333333333  TR01 501    01/03/1996 10:00:00   -           80.00 P  1
333333333  TR01 502    01/04/1996 10:00:00   -           80.00 P  1
```

Fig. 4–25 Query Result from Simple SELECT Statement

In SQL, the asterisk or star character (*) is used to indicate that all columns of a table are being referenced. In Fig. 4–24, the SQL statement refers to all of the columns defined for the table *db2.test_taken*.

If the table is altered and a new column is added to the table definition, then the result table would contain the new column.

✍   Adding a new column to an existing table will result in default values being populated for the existing rows.

Since the output of this SQL statement varies according to the table definition, it is recommended that you specify all of the column names in the **SELECT** statement.

We could have obtained the same result as in Fig. 4–25 with the following SQL statement:

```
SELECT          cid, tcid, number,
                date_taken,start_time,finish_time,
                score,pass_fail,seat_no
FROM

                db2.test_taken
```

This SQL statement will provide the same result table even if new columns are added to the table definition.

✍   The asterisk (*) character is used to refer to all of the columns defined for a table. The order of the columns in the result table is the same order as specified in the **CREATE TABLE** or **CREATE VIEW** statement.

The **FROM** clause is required for the DML SQL statement, as it describes the location (table or view) of the data. Our example references a single table called *db2.test_taken*. The **SELECT** and the **FROM** clauses are required in all data retrieval statements. The list of columns following the **SELECT** keyword is referred to as the *select list*.

Projecting Columns from a Table

Projection is a relational operation that allows you to retrieve a subset of the defined columns from a table. Let's say that we only want the test center, test candidate id and test number attributes from the table.

```
SELECT cid,tcid,number
              FROM db2.test_taken
```

Fig. 4–26 Example of the Projection Operation

The **SELECT** statement in Fig. 4–26 contains a select list of three columns. Notice that all of the rows from the table will be in the result table. Therefore, the number of data rows which will be in the result list is not known; even if the number of rows is known, it is not possible to specify the number of rows in an SQL statement.

The output of the **SELECT** statement is shown in Fig. 4–27. The order of the columns in the result table will always match the order in the select list. The order of the columns as they were defined in the **CREATE TABLE** or **CREATE VIEW** statement is ignored when a select list is provided in the SQL statement. In this example, the order of the columns is similar to the order in the **CREATE TABLE** statement, as the CID column was defined prior to TCID and NUMBER columns.

```
CID        TCID NUMBER
---------- ---- ------
111111111 TR01 500
111111111 TR01 501
111111111 TR01 502
222222222 TR01 500
222222222 TR01 502
222222222 TR01 502
333333333 TR01 500
333333333 TR01 501
333333333 TR01 502
```

Fig. 4–27 Result Table of a Projection

Changing the Order of the Columns

Permutation is the relational operation that allows you to change the order of the columns in your result table. Permutation is used every time that you select your columns in an order different than the order defined in the **CREATE TABLE** statement. For example, let's say that you need the candidate ids to appear before the test center id and the test number.

```
SELECT cid,tcid,number
           FROM db2.test_taken
```

Fig. 4–28 Selecting a Subset of the Defined Columns

The **SELECT** statement shown in Fig. 4–28 specifies the select list in a different order than it was defined.

✍ We refer to the output of a **SELECT** statement as the result table because the output of all **SELECT** statements can be considered a relational table.

Restricting Rows from a Table

Restriction is a relational operation that will filter the resulting rows from a table. Restriction is accomplished through the use of predicates defined in an SQL **WHERE** clause.

✍️ A *predicate* is a condition placed on the data. The result of the condition is *true, false* or *unknown*.

Let's say that you are only interested in the candidates who have taken a DB2 certification test at the test center TR01. To restrict the result set, we need to add a **WHERE** clause to the SQL statement. The **WHERE** clause specifies conditions or predicates which must be evaluated by DB2 before the result table is returned to the end user. There are many valid types of predicates which can be used. In Fig. 4–29, the equality (=) predicate is being used.

```
SELECT tcid,cid
              FROM db2.test_taken
              WHERE CHAR(tcid) ='TR01'
```

Fig. 4–29 Example of the WHERE Clause

The query will just retrieve the information for those candidates who have taken the test at the TR01 test center. The **WHERE** clause also accepts other comparison operators, such as greater than (>), less than (<), greater or equal to (>=), less or equal to (<=) and not equal to (<>). The statement in Fig. 4–29 is an example of a *basic predicate*. A basic predicate compares two values.

Predicate Evaluation for UDTs

The column tcid was defined as a User-Defined Data Type (UDT). So we needed to *cast* our constant value in order to make the comparison in the **WHERE** clause (as shown in Fig. 4–30).

Predicate evaluation requires that the data types be compatible (same data type or a compatible data type). The *tcid* column needs to be converted to a character data type.

We can accomplish the data type conversion (cast) using one of two methods:

- Use the **CAST** expression
- Use a casting function

In the example shown in Fig. 4–30, we are using the **CAST** expression in order to perform a comparison using the same data types. The **CAST** expression requires that you specify the input data value and the output data type. In our example, the input data value is TX09 and the output data type is *db2.center_id* (the full two-part name of the UDT).

```
SELECT tcid,cid
            FROM db2.test_taken
            WHERE tcid=
            CAST('TX09' AS db2.center_id)
```

Fig. 4–30 Using the CAST Expression

The other method of converting UDTs involves the use of a system-gener-ated SQL function known as a *cast function*. When we created the user-defined data type called *db2.center_id,* a number of SQL functions were automatically created. DB2 will create these casting functions for data type conversion pur-poses.

```
SELECT tcid,cid
            FROM db2.test_taken
            WHERE tcid=db2.center_id('TX09')
```

Fig. 4–31 Using the TEST_CENTER Casting Function

In Fig. 4–31, the casting function being used is called *db2.center_id*. It is easy to remember the name of the casting function, as it is the same as the UDT itself. It is also possible to cast the left-side argument using the CHAR() casting function as shown in Fig. 4–32.

```
SELECT tcid,cid
            FROM db2.test_taken
            WHERE CHAR(tcid)='TX09'
```

Fig. 4–32 Using the CHAR Casting Function

A quantified predicate is used to compare a value with a collection of val-ues. In Fig. 4–33, the syntax diagram for a quantified predicate is shown. The left side of the expression is a fullselect.

A *fullselect* statement is a **SELECT** statement without any **ORDER BY** or **FOR UPDATE** clause or several **SELECT** statements combined using a set operator like **UNION, INTERSECT**, or **EXCEPT.**

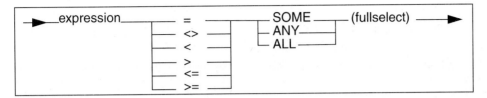

Fig. 4–33 Quantified Predicates

Let's examine the use of a quantified predicate in a **SELECT** statement.

```
SELECT cid, lname, fname FROM db2.candidate
```

CID	LNAME	FNAME
111111111	Hutchison	Grant
222222222	Janacek	Calene
333333333	Banelos	Gabriel
444444444	Smith	Fred
555555555	User	George
666666666	Mantesso	Greta
777777777	User	Joe
888888888	Gosch	Volker

```
SELECT cid FROM db2.test_taken
```

CID
111111111
111111111
222222222
222222222
333333333
111111111
111111111
222222222
333333333
333333333
333333333

```
SELECT cid, lname, fname FROM db2.candidate a
            WHERE cid = SOME
            (SELECT cid FROM db2.test_taken
                        WHERE a.cid = cid)
```

CID	LNAME	FNAME
111111111	Hutchison	Grant
222222222	Janacek	Calene
333333333	Banelos	Gabriel

Fig. 4–34 Using a Quantified Predicate in a SELECT Statement

A *quantified predicate* is used in Fig. 4–34 to find the test candidates who have taken or are scheduled to take a test. When **SOME** or **ANY** is specified for the fullselect statement, the predicate is true if the relationship is true for at least one value returned by the fullselect. The phrase **ALL** would result in all of the test candidate names being returned as the specified relationship is true for every value returned by the fullselect. The relationship cid = fullselect is true for ALL values returned by the fullselect because of the referential integrity constraints. It is impossible to have a cid value in the *test_taken* table which does not have a corresponding value in the candidate table.

Restricting Rows Using Multiple Conditions

It is possible to combine multiple conditions (predicates) in a single SQL statement. The predicates can be combined using boolean operators like the **AND** operator. These operators allow you to combine multiple conditions in a single SQL statement. DB2 will decide the order of predicate evaluation. The order of the predicate evaluation will not affect the result set (known as set closure). The optimizer will decide the order in which the conditions are applied to maximize query performance.

Let's say that you want to retrieve the records for the test candidates who took a test at test center 'TR01' and achieved a score greater than 65. The rows which satisfy the predicates are known as the *qualifying rows*.

```
SELECT tcid,cid,score
FROM db2.test_taken
                WHERE tcid=db2.test_center('TX09')
                AND score > db2.score(65)
```

Fig. 4–35 Example of Multiple Predicates

In Fig. 4–35, the order in which the two predicates are evaluated is not specified, as the DB2 optimizer will decide if the equality or the inequality predicate will be evaluated first. DB2 uses information from the system catalog tables, known as statistics, to decide which predicate should be evaluated first.

✍ DB2 determines the order of predicate evaluation based on the database statistics.

Selecting Columns from Multiple Tables

There are basically two operations that combine columns from multiple tables in a single SQL statement. These operations are:

- Cartesian Product
- Join

Cartesian Product

A **cartesian product** is a relational operation that will merge all the values from one set or table with all the values from another set of tables. This operation is not used frequently as the result table can be very large.

The number of rows in the result table is always equal to the product of the number of rows in the qualifying rows for each of the tables being accessed.

Let's examine an SQL statement which produces a cartesian product result table.

```
Q1  SELECT number,name
       FROM db2.test


NUMBER NAME
------ ------------------
500     DB2 Fundamentals
501     DB2 Administration
502     DB2 Application Dev
```

```
Q2  SELECT cid
       FROM db2.test_taken


CID
---------
111111111
222222222
333333333
```

```
Q3  SELECT db2.test_taken.number, cid
       FROM db2.test, db2.test_taken


NUMBER   CID
------   ---------
500      111111111
501      111111111
502      111111111
500      222222222
501      222222222
502      222222222
500      333333333
501      333333333
502      333333333
```

Fig. 4–36 Cartesian Product Query

There are three queries (Q1, Q2, Q3) shown in Fig. 4–36.

1. Query Q1 is a simple select of all test numbers from the test table.
2. Query Q2 is a simple select of all candidates from the *test_taken* table.
3. Query Q3 is an example of a cartesian product result table.

There are two tables referenced in the **FROM** clause of query Q3. The tables are separated by commas. There is no relationship expression in the **FROM** clause. This type of query results in a cartesian product.

The result table is a representation of all possible combinations of the input tables Q1 and Q2. Note the first column name in query Q3; it was necessary to fully qualify the column name by providing the table name with the column name. In this case, we needed to specify that the number column is to be retrieved from the *db2.test_taken* table and not the *db2.test table*.

The query Q3 represents all of the possible tests that could be taken for all of the registered test candidates.

```
SELECT db2.test.number, cid
            FROM db2.test, db2.test_taken
            WHERE CHAR(TCID) = 'TR01'
```

```
NUMBER        TCID
------        ------
500           TR01
501           TR01
502           TR01
```

Fig. 4–37 Cartesian Product with a Predicate

By adding a predicate to a cartesian product SQL query, the result table can represent a more useful representation of the data. In Fig. 4–37, the query represents all of the tests that were taken at the test center TR01.

Adding a **WHERE** clause to your query does not always provide the desired result. Let's say that we would like to find the "list all of the candidates who have taken the 500 exam and the test center location".

The query below uses a **WHERE** clause to filter out the candidates who took the 500 exam from the *test_taken* table, but there was no filter on the *test_center* table. Therefore, the result of the query would always be a multiple of the number of testing centers. If the same query were executed with a condition that was not satisfied (a test number of 504, for example), then the result table would be an *empty set*. Usually when multiple tables are referenced you should include a relationship predicate.

```
SELECT cid, test_center.name
            FROM test_center, test_taken
            WHERE
            CHAR(test_taken.number) = '500'
```

The SQL statement will still produce a cartesian product. A cross-table relationship must be established using a table merge or join method. We will examine table join methods in the next section. Sometimes a cartesian product is referred to as a cross-product table.

Join

To avoid data redundancy it is recommended that the database tables are *normalized*. Following the normalization process, a number of related tables will exist. To satisfy some of the required queries, the tables must be reconstructed. The tables are reconstructed temporarily using a table join strategy to produce a single result table.

The result tables in the previous examples usually provide candidate id numbers and not the complete name of the test candidates. The candidate ids are stored in the *test_taken* table, and the full names are stored in the *candidate* table. To obtain the name of a candidate, the data must be retrieved from the candidate table using a relationship or join strategy.

Let's consider an example that will list the name and phone numbers of candidates who are registered to take a DB2 Certification test before the end of the year. To accomplish this, we need to select data from two different tables:

- *db2.candidate*
- *db2.test_taken*

Let's retrieve a list of candidate names, phone numbers, and ids from the candidate table. The candidate names were stored in multiple columns to allow for easy retrieval by last name.

```
SELECT fname, initial, lname, hphone, cid
         FROM db2.candidate
```

Fig. 4–38 Retrieving Names of the Candidates

The output of example Fig. 4–38 is shown. Pay special attention to the values in the CID column.

FNAME	INITIAL	LNAME	HPHONE	CID
Greta	E	Mantesso	5542342343	111111111
Gabriel	F	Banuelos	5345353645	222222222
Volker	J	Gosh	5558978978	333333333
Grant	L	Hutchison	9128277391	444444444

Now, let's retrieve the id numbers of those candidates who are registered to take the test this year.

The output of Fig. 4–39 is displayed as follows. We will now compare the candidate id numbers for each of these result tables.

CID
111111111
222222222
333333333

```
SELECT cid

          FROM test_taken
          WHERE
          YEAR(date_taken) = 1996
```

Fig. 4–39 Retrieving the Candidate IDs

The candidate ids in the *test_taken* table **must** correspond to a candidate id in the candidate table due to the declarative referential integrity constraints. The *parent table* in the relationship is the candidate table and the *child table* (dependent table) is the *test_taken* table.

The result table from the second query does not include the test candidate 444444444 as that candidate does not have a test scheduled this year. We need to join the two result tables based on the candidate id values. This column is known as the *join column*.

✍️   Query performance can significantly improve if the join columns are appropriately indexed.

The single query that will satisfy the end user requirement is shown in Fig. 4–40.

```
SELECT fname, initial,lname, hphone
          FROM test_taken, candidate
          WHERE YEAR(date_taken) = 1996
          AND test_taken.cid = candidate.cid
```

Fig. 4–40 Joined Result Table

A table join query requires that there be a predicate which includes an expression based on columns from the tables referenced in the **FROM** clause. This is known as a *join predicate*. The **FROM** clause has not changed from the cartesian product examples. The only difference is in the second predicate (*test_taken.cid = candidate.cid*).

The table names needed to be explicitly stated as there is a column named cid in both of the referenced tables. When multiple tables are being accessed in a single query, you can have to qualify the column names with the table name as in Fig. 4–40.

✍️   An error will occur if the columns being referenced are ambiguous (not properly qualified).

There is no defined limit, except in storage, to the number of tables which can be referenced in a single SQL statement. However, there is a limit of 255 columns in the **SELECT** list of a query.

✍ There is a limit of 255 columns in a **SELECT** statement.

Using Correlation Names

If each of the columns needed to be fully qualified with the table name such as *tableschema.tablename.columnname*, the queries would become very large and cumbersome to work with. Fortunately, there is an easier way to qualify the ambiguous columns resulting from a multi-table **SELECT** statement.

The columns can be qualified using a *correlation name*. A correlation name is a temporary alias for the tables referenced in an SQL statement. We will rewrite the previous query using correlated names in Fig. 4–41.

```
SELECT fname, initial,lname, hphone
         FROM test_taken tt, candidate c
         WHERE YEAR(date_taken) = 1996
                   AND tt.cid = c.cid
```

Fig. 4–41 Joining Two Tables Using Correlation Names

The correlation name immediately follows the name of the table as stated in the **FROM** clause. In the example, the correlated name for the *test_taken* table is tt and the correlated name for the candidate table is *c*.

The correlated names are accessible within the SQL statement only. Following the execution of the SQL statement, the correlation name is no longer defined. Once you have defined a correlation name, you must reference it instead of the table name in the rest of the query. Also, remember that the correlation name must follow the table name in the **FROM** clause of the query.

✍ Use simple, easy to remember correlation names.

Sorting Your Output

We have been retrieving data from one or more tables. The order of the result table has not been included in any of the SQL statements. The data is retrieved in an undetermined order if there is no **ORDER BY** clause in the SQL statement.

List the test candidates alphabetically by last name who have taken a DB2 certification test at the TR01 test center.

The example in Fig. 4–41 contains a new clause, **ORDER BY**. After the **ORDER BY** clause, you can list the columns that will specify the sort order and the type of sort.

```
SELECT lname,initial, fname
            FROM candidate c,test_taken tt
            WHERE tcid='TR01'AND c.cid=tt.cid
            ORDER BY lname
```

Fig. 4–42 Sorting the Result Table

Let's say that you would like the order of the output changed to be in descending order by last name and a secondary order column on the first name in ascending order.

```
SELECT lname,fname,hphone
FROM candidate c, test_taken tt
            WHERE char(tcid)='TR01'
            AND     c.cid=tt.cid
            ORDER BY lname DESC, fname
```

Fig. 4–43 Sorting Output in Descending Order

The **DESC** keyword, as shown in Fig. 4–41, that follows the *lname* column indicates that the result table should be in descending order based on the last name. More than one record can have the same last name. This situation is quite common. There is a second column specified in the **ORDER BY** clause, fname. There is no keyword specifying the sort sequence based on the *fname* column. Therefore, the default ordering sequence (ascending) is used.

✍🏻   The default order sequence is ascending.

The column(s) specified in the **ORDER BY** clause must be part of the select list for the SQL statement. The select list in Fig. 4–44 contains three columns: lname, fname, and hphone. You can reference the column which should be used to sort the data using the column name or by specifying its position in the select list. Using the column position is very useful when the column in the select list are derived columns (calculated columns) and they have no explicit name.

```
SELECT lname,fname,hphone
FROM candidate c,test_taken tt
            WHERE CHAR(tcid)='TXR01'
                             AND c.cid=tt.cid
            ORDER BY 1 DESC, 2
```

Fig. 4–44 Sorting Output by Position

In Fig. 4–44, the sort order is specified using the column position. Therefore, the query is exactly the same as the query in Fig. 4–41.

You can also rename a column using an *alias*. The alias can then be referenced in the **ORDER BY** clause.

 The **ORDER BY** clause must be the last clause in your SQL statements

Derived Columns

There are cases when you will need to perform calculations on the data. The SQL language has some of the most basic mathematical and string functions. Mathematical operations include the standard: addition, subtraction, multiplication and division.

The calculation can be defined in the **WHERE** clause of the SQL statement or the **SELECT** list. Let's say that you need to calculate a passing rate for a DB2 test. The passing rate is defined as the percentage of candidates that pass the test (totalpassed/totaltaken).

```
SELECT number,totalpassed/totaltaken
            FROM test
            WHERE number='500'
```

Fig. 4–45 Using Calculated Columns

In Fig. 4–45, the second column of the output list is a calculated column. Remember that a calculated column, doesn't have a usable name for the **ORDER BY** clause.

Naming Derived/Calculated Columns

You can specify a column name for any expression. By providing the derived (calculated) column with a name, the **ORDER BY** clause can reference the derived name to allow for a more readable SQL statement.

Let's calculate again the rate of people that have passed the DB2 certification exams and order the output in descending order using the passing rate.

```
SELECT number,totalpassed/totaltaken AS PassedRate
            FROM test
            ORDER BY PassedRate DESC
```

Fig. 4–46 Naming Calculated Columns

The **AS** clause is used to rename the default name of an element in the select list. In the example shown in Fig. 4–46, we are giving the name of PassedRate to the result of the division of columns totalpassed by totaltaken. The named column is used in the query to specify the column which should be used for sorting of the output.

DB2 Functions

In DB2, there are two types of functions provided:

- **SCALAR** functions are also known as row functions. Scalar functions provide a result for each row of the table. A scalar function can be used any place an expression is allowed.
- **COLUMN** functions are also known as vector functions. This is because they work with a group of rows to provide a result. The groups are specified using a fullselect and optionally grouped using the **GROUP BY** clause.

In this section, we will introduce you to *some* of the SQL functions provided with DB2. SQL functions are categorized by their implementation type. Either the functions are built-in and specified in the SQL standards or they are extensions to the SQL standards and known as User-Defined Functions (UDFs).

- **Built-in Functions** are defined within the SQL standards, and they are provided by the database manager. Some of these built-in functions are scalar functions and others are column functions.
- **User-Defined Functions** (UDFs) are not defined within the SQL standards as they are extensions to the current SQL language. These functions can be developed by a DB2 administrator or application developer. Once the UDFs have been created, they can be invoked by any end user with the proper privileges. Some of the new functions provided in DB2 are UDFs. The functions with the schema name of SYSFUN are provided by DB2.

Scalar Functions

Scalar functions are applied for each row of data, and there is a per-row result provided. If we wanted to retrieve only the first three digits of telephone numbers for each candidate, we could using an SQL (scalar) function. The function which will be used is called **SUBSTR**. The arguments for this function include a string data type column, a beginning offset and a finishing offset. The output of the function is a string as defined by the offsets provided.

Let's retrieve the telephone area code for the column wphone.

```
SELECT lname, SUBSTR(wphone,1,3)
              FROM db2.candidate
```

Fig. 4–47 Example of Scalar Function SUBSTR

The **SUBSTR** function is a row or scalar function. In this example, **SUBSTR** returns a character string of three characters.

The result string corresponds to the first three characters of the wphone column. This function is known as a string function because it works with any string data type. If we wanted to provide the output column with a meaningful name, we could provide an **alias**, as was done for the calculated columns.

In the example shown in Fig. 4–47, the sub-string starts from the beginning of the string, because we indicate one (1) as the first parameter of the function. The length of the resulting string is indicated in the second argument. In our example, the length is three.

✍ A casting function can also be used inside a *scalar* or *column* function. For example, **SUBSTR(CHAR(wphone),1,3)** can be used to cast the phone column wphone to a character string.

Let's take a look at another scalar function. This time the function is a user-defined function, as it is defined in the **SYSFUN** schema and it is not part of the SQL specifications.

The query in Fig. 4–48 will provide the month when the exam was taken. The input for this function is a **DATE** string and the output is a character string.

```
SELECT fname, MONTHNAME(date_taken)
           FROM candidate c, test_taken tt
           WHERE c.cid=tt.cid
```

Fig. 4–48 Example of Scalar Function MONTHNAME

Column Functions

Column functions provide a single result for a group of qualifying rows for a specified table or view. Many common queries can be satisfied using column functions as they include common tasks like finding the smallest value, largest value and the average value for a group of data records.

Let's obtain the maximum length of any of the DB2 certification exams.

```
SELECT MAX(length)FROM test
```

Fig. 4–49 Example of the Vector Function MAX

The SQL statement shown in Fig. 4–49 will return the maximum length value stored in table *test*. If we added a **WHERE** clause, the maximum would represent the maximum length for the qualifying rows as the predicate is used to filter the data prior to the invocation of the maximum column function.

Let's calculate the average of the number of seats for all of the test centers.

```
SELECT AVG(noseats)FROM test_center
```

Grouping Values

Many queries involve the grouping data. As we have said before, SQL is a set-oriented language. Grouping values in a result table is accomplished by adding a **GROUP BY** clause to the end of the SQL statement.

Let's say that you wanted to obtain the average number of seats grouped by each country.

```
SELECT country,AVG(noseats)
           FROM test_center
           GROUP BY country
```

Fig. 4–50 Example of the GROUP BY Clause

The SQL statement in Fig. 4–50 needed to obtain the average number of seats per country. The **GROUP BY** clause tells DB2 to group the rows that have the same values in the columns indicated in the group by list. In our example, we are grouping the countries into subsets. Then DB2 calculates the average of each of those groups or subsets, in this case each country.

When you combine vector functions and other elements like column names, scalar functions or calculated columns, you **must** use the **GROUP BY** clause. In this case, you must include every element that is not a column function in the group by list. The only elements that can be omitted in the **GROUP BY** clause are constant values.

Let's obtain a list that includes the average cut score and minimum test length for the DB2 Certification exams. We will group this list by the type of exam in Fig. 4–51.

```
SELECT type,AVG(cut_score),MIN(length)
           FROM test
           GROUP BY type
```

Fig. 4–51 Using GROUP BY

It is possible to sort the output of the previous example using an **ORDER BY** statement. In this case, you can also use an **AS** clause to name the average column.

```
SELECT type, AVG(cut_score) as Average_Cut,
              MIN(length) AS Minimum_Length
       FROM test
       GROUP BY type
       ORDER BY Average_Cut
```

Fig. 4–52 Combining GROUP BY and ORDER BY

Remember that the **ORDER BY** clause is always the last clause in an SQL statement. In the example shown in Fig. 4–52, we are combining the **ORDER BY** and the **GROUP BY** clauses. The **ORDER BY** clause is used to sort the output and the **GROUP BY** clause is used to group the sets of data.

Restricting Using Sets of Data

Up to now, we have discussed how to restrict output based on row conditions. In SQL, it also is possible to restrict that output using vector functions and the **GROUP BY** clause.

Let's say that you want a list of all the test centers that have administered the DB2 certification exams to more than 10 candidates.

To make it easier to understand, let's first get the number of candidates who have taken the exams in each test_center.

```
SELECT tcid, count(*)
             FROM test_taken
```

Fig. 4–53 Using the COUNT Vector Function

We are using the **COUNT** vector function to get the number of candidates who have taken the test in each test center. When you use an asterisk (*) with the **COUNT** function, you are indicating that you want to count all the rows in a table. The **COUNT** function will only count the rows that meet the criteria established in the SQL statement.

In the example shown in Fig. 4–53, we are grouping by *tcid* because we have a number of occurrences for all the test centers in the *test_taken* table. The *test_taken* table has an entry for every candidate who applies for the DB2 Certification exams.

Now, let's restrict the output to only those test centers that have more than five candidates registered.

```
SELECT tcid
              FROM test_taken
              GROUP BY tcid
              HAVING COUNT(*) > 5
```

Fig. 4–54 Restricting Groups Using the HAVING Clause

The example in Fig. 4–54 introduces the **HAVING** clause. **HAVING** is the equivalent to the **WHERE** clause for groups and vector functions. The **HAVING** clause will restrict the resulting set to only the groups that meet the condition specified in it.

In our example, only the test centers that have more than five candidates will be displayed.

Eliminating Duplicates

The **JOIN** example, shown in Fig. 4–48, might produce duplicate names in the names list. The duplicate values will appear when a candidate has passed or taken more than one DB2 Certification exam.

The SQL language provide a special clause to remove the duplicate rows from your output.

Let's generate a list of names and phone numbers for all the candidates who have taken the test. In the example in Fig. 4–55, we will eliminate the duplicate rows from our output list.

```
SELECT DISTINCT fname,wphone,hphone
              FROM candidate c,test_taken tt
              WHERE c.cid=tt.cid
```

Fig. 4–55 Eliminating Duplicates from a List

The **DISTINCT** clause will eliminate the duplicate rows from the output. The **DISTINCT** clause can also be used with the **COUNT** function. When you use **DISTINCT**, the **COUNT** function will not count the duplicate entries for a particular column.

Let's say that you want to count how many different test centers have candidates registered.

```
SELECT COUNT(DISTINCT tcid)
              FROM test_taken
```

Fig. 4–56 Using DISTINCT in the COUNT Function

This example in Fig. 4–56 will provide the number of test centers that are registered in the test taken table. Remember that all the candidates who have applied for the DB2 Certification exam are stored in that table.

Make sure that you understand the difference between **COUNT(*)** and **COUNT(DISTINCT)**. They are very similar in syntax but differ in functionality.

Searching for String Patterns

SQL has a powerful predicate that allows you to search for patterns in the character strings columns. This predicate is the **LIKE** predicate. Let's say that you want to generate a list of the candidates whose names start with the letter A.

```
SELECT fname,lname,wphone,hphone
            FROM candidate
            WHERE fname LIKE'A%'
            ORDER BY lname,fname
```

Fig. 4–57 Using the LIKE Predicate

In the SQL statement shown in Fig. 4–57, we are using *wildcard characters* use with the **LIKE** predicate.

In this example, the percent sign character(%), is a substitute for one or many characters. So, the search string (A%) can be substituted with names like Adriana, Alan, Anna, Andre and so on, As the percent character can substitute zero or more characters, the search string can also be a single letter A.

The percent character can be used any place in the search string. It also can be used as many times as you need it. The percent sign is not case sensitive, so it can take the place of uppercase or lowercase letters. However, the constant characters included in your search string are case sensitive.

The other wildcard character used with the **LIKE** predicate is the underline character (_). This character substitutes one and only one single character. The underline character can take the place of any character. However, the underline character cannot be substituted with an empty character.

Let's say that we want a report that includes all the candidates names and the telephone numbers for those candidates whose name has a letter A as its second letter.

```
SELECT fname,lname,wphone,hphone
            FROM candidate
            WHERE fname LIKE '_A%'
            ORDER BY lname,fname
```

Fig. 4–58 Using the Underline Wildcard Character

The example presented in Fig. 4–58 uses two wildcard characters that work with the **LIKE** predicate. The search string, in this example, can include names like Calene, Gabriel or Natalie. All of them have a previous character, the letter A is the second character in the string and the string ends with any number of characters.

Searching for Data in Ranges

SQL offers us a range operator. This operator is used to restrict rows that are in a particular range of values.

Let's say that we want a list of those candidates whose scores in the DB2 Fundamentals Exam are between 90 and 95.

```
SELECT DISTINCT fname,lname,wphone,hphone
                FROM candidate c, test_taken tt
                WHERE c.cid=tt.cid
                AND score BETWEEN 90 AND 95
```

Fig. 4–59 Using the BETWEEN Predicate

The **BETWEEN** predicate includes the values that you specify for searching your data. An important fact about **BETWEEN** is that it can work with characters ranges as well.

Let's say that for those candidates selected in the example presented in Fig. 4–59, we are now only interested in those whose last names begins with a letter between B and G.

```
SELECT DISTINCT fname,lname,wphone,hphone
                FROM candidate c, test_taken tt
                WHERE c.cid=tt.cid
                AND score BETWEEN 90 AND 95
                AND lname BETWEEN 'B' AND 'GZ'
```

Fig. 4–60 Using BETWEEN with Character Columns

In the previous example, Fig. 4–60, the second **BETWEEN** predicate involves character values. We need to specify the GZ value to include all the possible names that start with the letter G. This was made assuming that the letter Z is the last possible value in the alphabet.

Searching for NULL values

NULL values represent an unknown value for a particular occurrence of an entity. We can use a **NULL** value in the cases where we don't know a particular value of a column.

Let's say that we want a list of all those candidates who don't have a seat number assigned yet. This condition is represented with a **NULL** value.

```
SELECT fname,lname,wphone,hphone
            FROM candidate c, test_taken tt
            WHERE c.cid=tt.cid
            AND seatno IS NULL
```

Fig. 4–61 Searching for NULL Values

The **IS** predicate is used to search for the **NULL** value in Fig. 4–61. Remember that the **NULL** value means unknown. Since it has no particular value, you can't compare it so, you can't use conditional operands, such as equal (=), with null values.

Searching for Negative Conditions

The **BETWEEN, IS** and **LIKE** predicates always look for the values that meet a particular condition. These predicates can also be used to look for the values that don't meet a particular criterion.

The **NOT** predicate can be used to look for the opposite condition, combined with the **LIKE, BETWEEN** and **IS** predicate, to accomplish negative searches as shown in Fig. 4–62.

Let's start with the **LIKE** predicate combined with **NOT**. We want a list of those candidates whose last names don't end with a letter S.

```
SELECT DISTINCT fname,lname,wphone,hphone
            FROM candidate
            WHERE lname NOT LIKE '%S'
            ORDER BY lname,fname
```

Fig. 4–62 Using the NOT LIKE Predicate

Now, let's combine the **NOT** predicate with the **BETWEEN** predicate in Fig. 4–63. Let's say that we want the list of those candidates whose score is not between the range of 90 to 95.

```
SELECT DISTINCT fname,lname,wphone,hphone
            FROM candidate c, test_taken tt
            WHERE c.cid=tt.cid
            AND score NOT BETWEEN 90 and 95
```

Fig. 4–63 Using the NOT BETWEEN Predicate

In Fig. 4–63, the **NOT** predicate will exclude all the values that are in the range of 90 to 95.

Finally, let's search for values that are not null. Let's say that we want a report that contains those candidates that have a seat number assigned. This is expressed with a **NOT NULL** value.

```
SELECT DISTINCT fname,lname,wphone,hphone
                FROM candidate c, test_taken tt
                WHERE c.cid=tt.cid
                AND seatno IS NOT NULL
```

Fig. 4–64 Searching for NOT NULL Values

The **NOT** predicate can be combined with the **LIKE**, **BETWEEN** and **IS** predicates as shown in Fig. 4–64. The **NOT** predicate can also be combined with the **IN** predicate.

Searching for a Set of values

In SQL, it is possible to establish a restriction condition based on a set of values. Suppose that you need a list of the test centers that have candidates registered for the DB2 Fundamentals test and for the DB2 Application Development exam.

```
SELECT DISTINCT name,phone
                FROM test_center tc, test_taken tt
                WHERE tc.tcid=tt.tcid
                AND number IN ('500','503')
```

Fig. 4–65 Searching a Set of Values

The **IN** clause is used to denote a set of values. In Fig. 4–65, we are using a constant set of values. In this particular case, the SQL statement can also be coded using the **OR** operator to restrict the test numbers.

You can also use the **NOT** predicate with the **IN** clause. In this case, the condition will be true when a value is not present in the set of values provided to the **IN** clause.

You can use as many values as you wish in the **IN** clause. However, there will be cases when the list of values is very long and it would be better to retrieve them using another SQL statement.

The **IN** predicate can also be used to define a set based upon conditions. In this case, the **IN** predicate also accepts a SQL statement that defines the set of values. When you define the set of values using a SQL statement, the SQL statement that defines that set is called a sub-query.

Sub-Queries

A sub-query is an SQL statement that is used inside another SQL statement. Sub-queries can be used with the **IN** clause to specify the search arguments for a SQL statement.

Let's say that you don't know the numbers of the DB2 certification program exams. You want to produce a report that includes all the test centers that have candidates registered for the DB2 Certification exams.

In the example, we'll use the word DB2 as the search string to find out the numbers of the DB2 Certification Program exams.

```
SELECT DISTINCT name,phone
               FROM test_center tc, test_taken tt
               WHERE tc.tcid=tt.tcid
               AND number IN
               (SELECT number
                        FROM test
                        WHERE name like 'DB2%')
```

Fig. 4–66 Using Sub-queries

In Fig. 4–66, the sub-query appears after the **IN** clause. In the sub-query, we are retrieving all the numbers from those tests that have the word DB2 in their name.

As you can see in Fig. 4–66, the sub-query is a standard SQL statement. The only difference here is that the sub-query is used as a restriction condition. You will never see its output. We are only using the sub-query to create a list of values that will be used later by the outer **SELECT** statement.

The sub-query used in Fig. 4–66, is known as an uncorrelated sub-query. An **uncorrelated sub-query** is one where the values retrieved by the sub-query are not directly related with the rows processed by the outer **SELECT** statement.

A **correlated sub-query** is a query in which the sub-query references values of the outer **SELECT**.

Let's say that you want to count how can candidates are registered in each test center. This time you want to display the name of the center near the number of candidates. Let's use a correlated sub-query to accomplish this.

Observe the **WHERE** clause in the sub-query in Fig. 4–67. It is making reference to a table that is listed in the outer **FROM** clause.

If you write this query as a uncorrelated sub-query, you will have different results. In this example, you need to use a correlated sub-query to be sure that all the rows of the test taken table are counted. When you use an uncorrelated sub-query, you will only count one occurrence of the test number for each test center. This is because the sub-query only returns non-duplicate values to the outer **SELECT**.

```
SELECT tc.name, count(*)
            FROM test_center tc,test out
            WHERE          tc.tcid IN
            (SELECT tcid
            FROM test_taken tt
            WHERE tt.number=out.number
            )
            GROUP BY TC.NAME
```

Fig. 4–67 Correlated Sub-Query to Count the Candidates for Each Test Center

Case Expressions

You can add some logic to your SQL output using **CASE** expressions. Let's say that you want to generate a list of those candidates who have passed the DB2 Fundamentals exam.

In the report, you want to print the score of the tests. But, instead of printing the numeric score, you want to print a message. If the score is below the cut_score, you want to print "Not Passed". If it is between the cut_score and 90, you want to print "Passed" and if the score is above 90, you want to print "Excellent".

```
SELECT fname,lname
            CASE
            WHEN SCORE < 65 THEN 'Not Passed'
            WHEN SCORE < 90 THEN 'Passed'
            ELSE
                            'Excellent'
            FROM candidate c, test_taken tt
            WHERE c.cid=tt.cid
                     AND number='500'
```

Fig. 4–68 Case Expressions

The SQL statement presented in Fig. 4–68 will print messages based on the conditions of the **CASE** expression. In this example, the score column features a numeric value, but we are using it to produce a character value.

The order of the conditions for the case expression is very important. DB2 will process the first condition first, the second later and so on. So, if you don't pay attention to the order in which the conditions are processed, you might be retrieving the same result for every row in your table. For example, if you coded the < 90 option before the < 65, all the data that is lower than 90, even 64 or 30, will display the message "Passed".

Nested Table Expressions

A nested table expression is a special kind of sub-query or sub-select. This sub-select is used in the **FROM** clause of an SQL statement. Nested table expressions will create local temporary tables that are only known in the SQL statement that defines them.

These sub-selects can be considered as temporary views. You can use nested table expressions to select from a grouped table or to obtain the same results that you can expect from a view.

Let's say that you want to obtain the maximum average score for the DB2 Certification Program exams. To gather this result, you must first obtain the averages and then you must select the maximum value from that list.

Let's use a nested table expression to accomplish this request.

```
SELECT MAX(avg_score)
              FROM (
              SELECT number as num,
               avg(score) as avg_score
              FROM test_taken
              GROUP BY number
) AS averages
```

Fig. 4–69 Using Table Expressions

In this example, Fig. 4–69, the sub-select will create a temporary table that will be used by the outer **SELECT** to obtain the maximum average score. This temporary table is called averages.

The number column is included in the sub-select to be able to gather the average for each one of the exams. After the sub-select is completed, the outer **SELECT** will be able to obtain the maximum value of the averages calculated in the nested table expression.

An advantage of using common table expressions over views is that common table expressions exist only during the execution of the query, so you don't have to worry about their maintenance. They also reduce contention over the system catalog tables because they don't use the catalog tables. They are also created at execution time, meaning you can define them using host variables.

Scalar Full-Select

Scalar full-selects are **SELECT** statements that return only one value. This type of select can be used in different parts of an SQL statement. It can be used in the select list or in the **WHERE** clause.

Scalar full-selects can be used to combine grouped information, such as averages or sums, with detailed information in a single query.

Let's say that you want a list that shows the candidate's id, score, the average score and the maximum score for the DB2 certification exams. This information cannot be gathered without the help of temporary tables or views. Let's see how the scalar full-select can be used to retrieve this data.

```
SELECT cid,number,score,
   (SELECT AVG(score)
              FROM test_taken
              ) AS AVG_Score,
   (SELECT MAX(score)
                           FROM test_taken
              )AS MAX_Score
              FROM            test_taken
```

Fig. 4–70 Combining Detailed and Aggregated Information

In the example shown in Fig. 4–70, we are using two scalar full-selects to retrieve the information about the aggregated data.

The first scalar full-select calculates the average score and the second one calculates the maximum score for the DB2 certification exams.

Observe how the SQL statements that produce the average and the maximum values are scalar full-selects. They are complete SQL statements that return only one value.

Now, let's say that you want to calculate the average and maximum scores for each one of the DB2 certification exams.

To accomplish this request you need to use a *correlated sub-select*. This is because you must ensure that the **SELECT** statement returns only one value at a time.

The correlated sub-select will let you generate the average and maximum scores for each one of the DB2 certification exams.

```
SELECT cid,number,score,
   (SELECT AVG(score)
     FROM test_taken tt1
              WHERE tt1.number=out.number
              ) AS AVG_Score,
   (SELECT MAX(score)
     FROM test_taken tt2
              WHERE tt2.number=out.number
              )AS MAX_Score
              FROM test_taken out
```

Fig. 4–71 Using a Correlated Scalar Full-Select

Examine the **WHERE** clauses in the Fig. 4–71 example. They both make reference to the table of the outer **SELECT** statement. The **WHERE** clauses are used to obtain a separate average and a maximum value for each one of the test numbers in the *test_taken* table.

Now, let's use a scalar full-select to create a list of those candidates who have a higher than average score for the DB2 Fundamentals exam.

```
SELECT fname,lname,score
            FROM candidate c, test_taken tt
            WHERE c.cid=tt.cid
            AND tt.score
            (SELECT AVG(score)
                        FROM test_taken
                        WHERE number='500')
```

Fig. 4–72 Using a Full-Select in the WHERE Clause

In Fig. 4–72, the scalar full-select is used in the **WHERE** clause. This scalar full- select calculates the average score for the DB2 Fundamentals exam.

The value returned from the scalar full-select is used to compare it against the score of the candidate. This way, we will retrieve those candidates whose score is higher than the average.

Common Table Expressions

A common table expression is a local temporary table that can be referenced many times in a SQL statement. However, this temporary table only exists in the SQL statements that define them.

Every time that you reference a common table expression, the result will be the same. This means that the SQL statement that generates it won't be reprocessed each time that you reference the common table expression.

Let's say that you need a list of the candidates who have earned the highest score for each of the DB2 Certification Program exams.

This will be accomplished using three common table expressions. Each of them corresponds to each one of the DB2 Certification Program exams. The common table expressions will be called *MAX500*, *MAX501* and *MAX502*. They will contain the maximum score value for each one of the DB2 Certification Program exams.

Then, after calculating the maximum score for each one of the tests, we will use those values to search for the candidates whose score is equal to the maximum score for a particular test. This will be accomplished by joining the score of each candidate with the maximum score of each one of the exams.

After the definition of a table expression, you can use it in an SQL statement just as another table. The example is shown in Fig. 4–73.

```
WITH MAX500 AS
                  (SELECT MAX(score) AS M500
                             FROM test_taken
                             WHERE number='500'),
           MAX501 AS
           (SELECT MAX(score) AS M501
                      FROM test_taken
                      WHERE number='501'),
           MAX502 AS
           (SELECT MAX(score) AS M502
                      FROM test_taken
                      WHERE number='502')
   SELECT fname, lname, wphone
             FROM max500,max501,max502,
             candidate c, test_taken tt
             WHERE c.cid=tt.cid
             AND ((score=m500 and number='500')
             OR (score=m501 and number='501')
             OR (score=m502 and number='502'))
```

Fig. 4–73 Using Common Table Expressions

The **WITH** clause is used to define a common table expression. The example shown in Fig. 4–73 defines three different common table expressions. These are *MAX500*, *MAX501* and **MAX502**. Observe the commas that are used to separate each one of the common table expression definitions.

The common table expressions are used in the SQL statement that follows their definition. These SQL statements treat the common table expressions as if they were normal tables.

You can use a common table expression as can times as you wish. You can even create a common table expression based on a previously created common table expression. However, you can only use them in the SQL statement that defined them.

Set Operators

SQL offers a group of operators that are used to implement the relational operations of **UNION, INTERSECTION** and **DIFFERENCE**.

We will only focus on the **UNION** operation. The **UNION** operation is the most used set operation in SQL. The **UNION** operation lets you combine the results of two or more different SQL statements into only one answer set.

You can combine many different tables or SQL statements using the **UNION** operator; the only restriction is that every table or SQL statement must have the same column structure. That is, the resulting sets from each SQL statement must have the same type, number and order of columns.

Let's say that you want to combine the minimum and maximum score for each of the DB2 Certification Program exams. You also want to add a string constant that indicates which value is the maximum and which one is the minimum.

```
SELECT number,'Minimum:', MIN(score)
              FROM test_taken
              GROUP BY number
UNION
SELECT number,'Maximum:', MAX(score)
              FROM test_taken
              GROUP BY number
ORDER BY number,2
```

Fig. 4–74 UNION Operator

The **UNION** operator shows you the results of two or more separate queries as a single one. In our example, the first query calculates the minimum score of the *test_taken* table. The the second query calculates the maximum score value. Both queries have the same type, order and number of columns.

In Fig. 4–74, the two SQL statements are very similar. However, you can combine quite different queries using the **UNION** operator. Just remember the restriction about the resulting rows. The **UNION** operator removes duplicate rows from the resulting set. However, there will be times when you'll need to list all the rows processed by your SQL statements.

SQL provides you with an operator that allows you to keep all the rows involved in a **UNION** operation. This is the **ALL** clause. Let's create a list of all the first names and last names in our candidate table. In this example, shown in Fig. 4–75, we want all the first names that start with a letter G and all the last names for the candidates who have taken the DB2 Administration Exam.

This example cannot be processed with an OR operator because we are not interested in the first names of those candidates who have taken the DB2 Administration Exam. Since there can be a first name that is the same as a last name, we will use a **UNION ALL** operator to show all the rows.

```
SELECT Fname
              FROM candidate
              WHERE fname like'G%'
UNION ALL
SELECT Lname
              FROM candidate c,test_taken tt
              WHERE c.cid=tt.cid
```

Fig. 4–75 An Example of UNION ALL

As a general rule, always try to code a **UNION ALL**. Only code a **UNION** when duplicates are not desired. The **UNION ALL** offers a better performance. However, you can't always substitute a **UNION** with a **UNION ALL**. The **UNION ALL** operator is needed to create recursive SQL statements.

Recursive SQL

A recursive SQL statement is used when an SQL statement repeatedly uses the resulting set to determine further results. This kind of SQL statements is built using common table expressions that make references to themselves.

Such statements are useful to solve queries such as hierarchal trees, routing airline flights or bill-of-material kinds of queries.

Let's say that we have a table that indicates the distances between two different cities. For this example, we are using the flights table. It contains information about the origin, destination and distance between cities.

You want to obtain a list with the distance and number of stops of all the destinations you can reach departing from Germany. We'll create a recursive SQL statement to retrieve this information.

Let's first explain why this kind of query is resolved using recursive SQL. The table contains information about destinations and origins. After reaching one specific destination, this destination can be treated itself as an origin. This is where the recursion appears; the destination becomes an origin, and the new destination itself can become a new origin and so on.

The way to resolve this query is by writing an SQL statement that given an origin will retrieve its destinations, then treat them as origins, obtain the new destinations and so on.

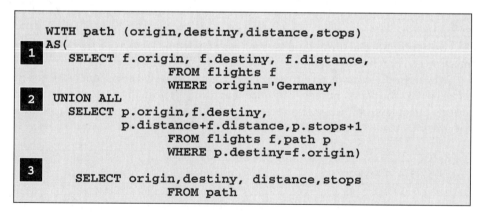

```
   WITH path (origin,destiny,distance,stops)
   AS(
1     SELECT f.origin, f.destiny, f.distance,
               FROM flights f
               WHERE origin='Germany'
2  UNION ALL
      SELECT p.origin,f.destiny,
               p.distance+f.distance,p.stops+1
               FROM flights f,path p
               WHERE p.destiny=f.origin)

3     SELECT origin,destiny, distance,stops
               FROM path
```

Fig. 4–76 Obtaining All the Destinations Departing from Germany

As we have said before, recursion is built upon table expressions. In the example shown in Fig. 4–76, the table expression is called path.

In **1** , we are obtaining the destinations that you can reach directly from Germany. In this case, the stops column is set to 0, because they are non-stop flights.

Then in **2** , we are referencing the recently created table expression path. In this part, we join the table expression with the base table to create the recursion. This is where the destination becomes a new origin. We are also incrementing the distance and the stops number. Observe that a **UNION ALL** clause is needed in the definition of a recursive query.

Finally in **3** , we are retrieving all the possible routes accessible from Germany, the distance and the number of stop flights. The output of the SQL statement is show in Fig. 4–77.

```
ORIGIN            DESTINY          DISTANCE     STOPS
---------------   ---------------- -----------  -----------
SQL0347W The recursive common table expression "DB2.PATH" can contain an
infinite loop. SQLSTATE=01605

Germany           New York            8000         0
Germany           Chicago             8700         0
Germany           Toronto             9000         1
Germany           Houston            10500         1
Germany           Chicago            10000         1
Germany           Toronto            10700         1
Germany           Austin             10000         1
Germany           Austin             10700         2
Germany           Toronto            12000         2
Germany           Austin             11300         2
```

Fig. 4–77 Destinations Reached from Germany

The SQL statement shown in Fig. 4–77 can run forever if there is a loop found in the *flights* table. When you are coding this kind of SQL statement, you must be aware of the possibility of infinite loops. To avoid an infinite loop, you can restrict the query using the number of stops.

Let's say that you are only interested in the routes that make less than five stops. You need to add the following restriction to the last SQL statement **WHERE** stops < 5.

Now, let's create a more complex example based on the same idea. We want to obtain a list of the possible flights from Germany to Austin. This time, we want to obtain the flight route, the distance and the number of stops.

As we can see from the output in Fig. 4–77, there are three different paths to reach Austin from Germany. Let's create the SQL statement that can tell us the complete path in each case.

```
     WITH detail_path
 1   (origin,destiny,route,distance,stops)
     AS(
        SELECT f.origin,f.destiny,
           VARCHAR(SUBSTR(f.origin,1,2),35),f.distance,0
                    FROM flights f
                    WHERE origin='Germany'
     UNION ALL
 2     SELECT p.origin,f.destiny,
              route||'>'||substr(p.destiny,1,2),
              p.distance+f.distance,p.stops+1
                   FROM flights f,detail_path p
                   WHERE p.destiny=f.origin)
 3   SELECT route||'>'||substr(destiny,1,2),
                  distance,stops
                  FROM detail_path
                  WHERE destiny='Austin'
                  ORDER BY distance
```

Fig. 4–78 Obtaining the Routes from Germany to Austin

The basics of the SQL statement in Fig. 4–78 are the same as in the previous example. The difference is that now we are creating the route column. This column is created by extracting the first two characters of each visited airport on the way from Germany to Austin. The || operator is used to concatenate each one of cities visited with each other.

In **1**, we are using the **VARCHAR** function to create a varchar column that will store all the cities visited in a specific path. This step will also add the origin city.

Then in **2**, we are concatenating the route with each one of the intermediary cities visited.

Finally in **3**, we concatenate the final destination to the path. Also in this step, we specify the desired destination.

```
1                                          DISTANCE     STOPS
----------------------------------------- ----------- -----------
SQL0347W The recursive common table expression "DB2.DETAIL_PATH" can contain an
infinite loop. SQLSTATE=01605

Ge>Ch>Au                                      10000          1
Ge>Ne>Ho>Au                                   10700          2
Ge>Ne>Ch>Au                                   11300          2
```

Fig. 4–79 Detailed Path from Germany to Austin

Fig. 4–79 shows that the shortest path is Germany-Chicago-Austin.

Data Modification (INSERT/UPDATE/DELETE)

Up to now, we have discussed basic and advanced **SELECT** statements. The **SELECT** statement allow you to retrieve data from your database. The **SELECT** statement assumes that data has been previously loaded into tables. This section will concentrate on getting data into the database tables. There are three main statements which can be used to change the data stored in a DB2 database. They are **INSERT, DELETE** and **UPDATE.**

To perform these operations, you must have the required privileges. Usually, these privileges are more strictly enforced, as they allow the end user to modify data records.

Inserting Data Records

To initially populate data for a DB2 table, usually the **INSERT** statement is used to store a single data record at a time. The statement can be targeted to insert data directly into a base table, or a view can be used instead. If a view is being used as the target, remember that it is the base table where the actual data is being stored.

Every row that is populated using the **INSERT** statement must adhere to table-check constraints, data type validation, dynamic (trigger) constraints and referential integrity constraints. An SQL error will be encountered if any of these conditions are violated during the **INSERT** statement

✍️   Remember that you must have the necessary view or table privileges to perform an **INSERT** statement.

Let's start with a simple **INSERT** statement. We will insert the data for the DB2 Fundamentals Exam into the test table.

```
INSERT INTO db2.test
(number,name,type,avg_score,cut_score,length,
 total_taken,total_passed)VALUES
('500','DB2 Fundamentals','p',NULL,65,90,0,0)
```

Fig. 4–80 Single Row Insert

In Fig. 4–80, we are specifying all the column names and their corresponding values for this data record. Following the **VALUES** portion of the statement, we include all of the data values for this record.

In the **VALUES** clause, the number and order of the inserted elements must match the number and order of the column names defined in the **INSERT** statement. However, the order of the columns doesn't have to match the order in which they are defined in the table.

✍️   The number of elements following the **VALUES** clause must match the number of names in the column list.

For those columns that don't require a value, you can indicate null or *default* values. In Fig. 4–80, we are using the null value for the *avg_score* column. Depending on your column definition, the default value can insert a system-defined default, a user-defined default or a null. Be aware that if the column doesn't accept nulls and it wasn't defined as **WITH DEFAULT**, you will receive an error message when using the default value. This error is because the *default value* for those columns that doesn't use the **WITH DEFAULT** option is the null value.

When you want to insert values into all the columns of a table, you can skip the column names in the **INSERT** statement. This example is shown in Fig. 4–81.

```
INSERT INTO db2.test VALUES
('500','DB2 Fundamentals','p',DEFAULT,65,90,79,11)
```

Fig. 4–81 Inserting Values into All the Columns of a Table

This method will only work if you specify a value for all the columns in a table. If you miss one of the columns of the table, DB2 will not allow you to insert the row into the table.

Inserting Data to Some Columns

There are times, when you need to add data to only certain columns. Every column that is not included in the **INSERT** statement will receive a null value.

This can be accomplished only if the omitted columns accept nulls or have a default definition. This means that you must specify a value for the columns defined as **NOT NULL**. This restriction excludes columns defined as **NOT NULL WITH DEFAULT**. If you define a column as **NOT NULL WITH DEFAULT**, you can omit it from the insert column list.

Let's insert a row into the *test_taken* table. In the example shown in Fig. 4–81, we will only insert data for the columns cid, tcid, number and seatno.

```
INSERT INTO db2.test_taken
              (CID,TCID,NUMBER,SEATNO)
VALUES('797979798','TC09','500','1')
```

Fig. 4–82 Inserting Values into Columns of a Table

Remember that the columns not listed in the **INSERT** statement will receive a null or a default value, if you have defined them as **WITH DEFAULT**.

Inserting Multiple Rows

You can insert multiple rows into a table using a single **INSERT** statement. Let's say that you want to schedule a candidate for the DB2 Certification exams. This candidate will take all the exams on three different days.

```
INSERT INTO db2.test_taken
(CID,TCID,NUMBER,DATE_TAKEN,SEATNO)VALUES
('797979798','TC09','500','1996-06-04','1'),
('797979798','TC09','501','1996-07-11','2'),
('797979798','TC09','502','1996-11-08','1')
```

Fig. 4–83 Multiple Row INSERT Statement

In Fig. 4–83, we separate the values for different rows with a comma. When inserting multiple rows in a single statement, you have to consider that all the rows must have the same number, type and order of columns. This means that you can't insert values to one column in the first row and values to five columns in the last row.

Inserting a Set of Values

Using SQL, you can insert the result of a **SELECT** statement into the same or a different table. The SQL statement that generates the resulting set must follow these rules:

- The number of columns from the **SELECT** must equal the number of columns
  in the insert column list.
- The data type of each of the columns in the select list must match the data type of those columns in the insert list.
- You can omit the column names from the insert list only if you insert values to all the columns in the table.
- Only columns defined to allow nulls or defined as **NOT NULL WITH DEFAULT** can be omitted from the insert list.

Let's say that you have created a copy of the *test_taken* table called *test_passed*. You will use this new table to extract the information about those candidates who have passed any of the DB2 Certification exams.

The select list used in the full-select in Fig. 4–84 can also be substituted by a select asterisk (*). This is possible because the *test_passed* table has the same column structure as the *test_taken* table. However, to keep this query isolated from future table modifications, it is recommended that you use the select list instead of the asterisk.

When you use a **SELECT** statement to load data into a table, you must enclose it between parentheses. You can also use a table expression to insert values into a table or view using the **INSERT** clause.

```
INSERT INTO db2.test_passed
  (cid,tcid,number,
  date_taken,start_time,finish_time,
  pass_fail,score,seat_no)

(SELECT cid,tcid,number,
        date_taken,start_time,finish_time,
        pass_fail,score,seat_no
FROM db2.test_taken
  WHERE pass_fail='P')
```

Fig. 4–84 Using a SELECT Statement to Insert Values

Inserting Large Amounts of Data

Using the **SELECT** statement to insert data into a table can be very useful. However, when you have large amounts of data, it is not recommended to load data into a table using the **INSERT** statement, as the transactional logging overhead can become unmanageable.

DB2 provides you with two utilities that are designed to insert large amounts of data into a table. These utilities are **IMPORT** and **LOAD**.

Removing Data

There are <many methods available to remove data from a DB2 database. To remove all of the data within a database, perform the **DROP DATABASE** command. This can remove more data than you intended, as the entire database including its configuration will be physically removed.

It is also possible to remove data using the **DROP TABLESPACE** or **DROP TABLE** commands. These commands are usually only issued by the SYSADM or DBADM, as they will remove large amounts of data. If you wish to remove all of the data records from a table, it is easier and quicker to perform the **DROP TABLE** command. If the table is dropped, it must be created again before any data can be populated.

To remove a single data record or a group or records within a table, the **DELETE** statement should be used. The syntax of the **DELETE** statement is different from the **SELECT** statement because columns can be selected but only rows can be deleted.

The **DELETE** statement can also be used with views. However, there are restrictions on the type of views which can be used within a **DELETE** statement.

🖎   Remember that you must have the necessary privileges over a table
   in order to perform the **DELETE** operation.

In general, there are two kinds of **DELETE** statements:

- **Searched Delete**. This **DELETE** statement is used to delete one or multiple rows from a table. It can use a **WHERE** clause to establish the delete condition.
- **Positioned Delete**. This kind of **DELETE** operation is always embedded into a program. It uses *cursors* to delete the row where the cursor is positioned.

In this section we will focus on the searched delete.

✍ The following examples are provided to show you how to use the **DELETE** statement. They are not designed to delete data from the tables. If you want to execute **DELETE** operations against the tables, turn OFF the auto-commit option of the CLP. To undo the changes, issue a **ROLLBACK** statement.

Let's say that you want to delete from the candidate table all those candidates who don't have a telephone number or photo loaded into the table. We will use a *searched delete* to accomplish this task.

```
DELETE FROM db2.candidate
    WHERE hphone IS NULL AND
                    wphone IS NULL AND
                    photo IS NULL
```

Fig. 4–85 Deleting Rows That Meet a Search Condition

The example shown in Fig. 4–81 uses a **WHERE** clause to delete the data that meets a specific criterion.

To verify the result of the **DELETE** statement, you can issue a **SELECT** statement with the same **WHERE** clause. It must return an empty set.

Now, let's say that you want to delete all the candidates who took the DB2 Certification exams in February.

```
DELETE FROM db2.candidate
    WHERE cid IN (SELECT cid
    FROM test_taken
    WHERE MONTH(date_taken)=2)
```

Fig. 4–86 Using a Sub-Select to Delete Values

In Fig. 4–86, we are using a sub-select to retrieve the cids of the candidates who took the DB2 Certification exams in the month of February. This list will be used to search for the candidates we want to delete.

Deleting All the Rows in a Table

You can delete all the rows in a table if you don't specify a search condition in your **DELETE** statement. You must be aware of the implications of this type of statement. However, this is not the only way to delete all the rows in a table. You can also delete all the rows in a table if all the rows meet the search condition.

However, deleting all the rows in a table using a **DELETE** statement can not be the most efficient way to do it. This kind of statement can consume a lot of log space when your tables are big.

Updating Data

We have examined the **INSERT** and **DELETE** statements. You can wish to update only a column with values for a group of data records. There is an **UPDATE** statement which can be used to specify the column and its new values. A table or a view can be referenced as the target for the **UPDATE** statement.

✍ Remember that you must have the correct privileges over a table in order to perform the **UPDATE** operation

The **UPDATE** statement is similar to the **DELETE** statement as it can be used in two forms:

- **Searched update**. This type of **UPDATE** statement is used to update one or more rows in a table. It requires a **WHERE** clause to establish the update condition.
- **Positioned update**. This kind of **UPDATE** statement is always embedded into a program. It uses *cursors* to update the row where the cursor is positioned. As the cursor is repositioned using the **FETCH** statement, the target row for the **UPDATE** statement changes.

We will focus on searched updates in this chapter. Similar to the **INSERT** statement, all of the database constraint mechanisms will be enforced during an **UPDATE** statement. There can be specific update constraint triggers and referential integrity constraints which could be different from the delete and insert constraints.

Let's say that the candidate id '110807112' has decided to change the day on which he or she takes the Certification Exam.

```
UPDATE test_taken
            SET date_taken=date_taken + 3 days
            WHERE cid ='110807112'
            AND number='500'
```

Fig. 4–87 Changing the Date for a Scheduled Test

In Fig. 4–98, we are using an operator, known as a *labeled duration*, to add three days to the original date. As with the delete operation, it is very important that you provide the proper **WHERE** clause to avoid updating incorrect data records. In Fig. 4–98, we needed to specify the predicate number='500' to avoid changing the date for any of the other tests that the candidate can be scheduled for.

✍️ Other DB2 labeled durations for date data types include **YEARS**, **MONTHS**, **DAYS**, **HOURS**, **MINUTES**, **SECONDS** and **MICROSECONDS**.

The **UPDATE** statement can also be used with full-selects. In this case, the full-select must return a row with exactly the same number and data types of the row that will be updated. Observe that this full-select must return only one row.

Let's update a row using a **SELECT** statement to set the new value. Candidate id '110807112' decides to take the DB2 Fundamentals test today in the test center located in Toronto, Canada.

```
UPDATE test_taken
            SET (date_taken,tcid)=
            (SELECT current day,tcid
                        FROM test_center
                        WHERE city='Toronto'
                        AND country='CANADA')
            WHERE CHAR(cid)= '110807112'
                        AND number='500'
```

Fig. 4–88 Using a Row Full-Select to Update Data

In Fig. 4–98, we are updating two different columns in the same operation. These columns are indicated in the parentheses following the **SET** clause.

After indicating which columns are going to be updated, we use a **SELECT** statement to retrieve the current day (today) and the test center id for the test center located in Toronto, Canada. Notice the last **WHERE** in the statement will restrict the rows that will be updated

✍️ If you forget the update **WHERE** clause in a searched update, all of the data in your table will be updated.

The SQL statement that will update the *date_taken* and *tcid* is known as *row full-select*. This name is given because it returns only one row. Observe that the scalar full-select can be considered a special case of a row full-select.

✍️ **CURRENT DATE** is a DB2 special register that gives the system date. There are others including: **CURRENT TIME**, **CURRENT TIMESTAMP** and **USER** (the authid).

Updating Large Amounts of Data

There are times when you need to update a large number of rows of a particular table. You can accomplish this by issuing an *searched update*. However, this also could allocate a large amount of transactional log space. You can accomplish updates using positioned updates, where you can easily control the commit frequency.

View Classification

Now that we have examined various SQL DML statements, let's take a closer look at views. We have discussed the creation or definition of views. Now, we will examine the different types of views.

The view type is established according to its update capabilities. Views can be deletable, updatable, insertable and read-only views. The classification indicates the kind of SQL operation that is allowed while using the view.

The referential and check constraints are treated independently. They don't affect the view classification.

For example, let's say that you cannot insert a value into a table because of a referential constraint. If you create a view using that table you also can't insert that value using the view. However, if the view satisfies all the rules to be an insertable view, it will still be considered an insertable view. This is because the insert restriction is located on the base table, not on the view definition.

When you try an illegal operation using a view, you can receive a message as shown in Fig. 4–89:

```
Delete from Read_only_view

SQL0150N The view in the INSERT, DELETE, or UPDATE statement is a view for
which the requested operation is not permitted. SQLSTATE=42807
```

Fig. 4–89 Illegal Operation Intended against a View

Deletable Views

Depending on how a view is defined, the view can be deletable. A deletable view is a view against which you can successfully issue a **DELETE** statement. There are a few rules that need to be followed for a view to be considered deletable.

- There is only one table referenced in each **FROM** statement of every outer full-select that defines the view. This means there are no joins or cartesian products in the outer full-select.
- The outer full-select doesn't use the **VALUES** clause.
- The outer full-select doesn't use the **GROUP BY** or **HAVING** clauses.
- The outer full-select doesn't include column functions in its select list.

- The outer full-select doesn't use set operands with the exception of **UNION ALL**.
- When using a **UNION ALL,** the SQL statements must be deletable and cannot be from the same table.
- The select definition doesn't include the **DISTINCT** clause.

A view must follow all the rules listed above to be considered a deletable view.

```
CREATE VIEW deletable_view
  (tcid,
    cid,
    number,
    date_taken,
    start_time,
    seat_no,
    score)
AS
  SELECT tcid,cid,number,date_takne,
         start_time,seat_no,score
              FROM db2.test_taken
              WHERE tcid='TC79'
```

Fig. 4–90 Example of Deletable View

The view shown in Fig. 4–90 is deletable. It follows successfully all the rules for a deletable view.

Updatable Views

An updatable view is a special case of deletable views. A deletable view becomes an updatable view when **at least one** of its columns is updatable.

A column of a view is updatable when all of the following rules are true:

- The view is deletable.
- The column corresponds to a base table column.
- When using a **UNION ALL** clause, all the columns of each SQL statement must be exactly of the same data type (length and precision) and have the same default values.

```
CREATE VIEW updatable_view
  (tcid,
    cid,
    number,
    current_date,
    current_time,
    seat_no,
    score)
AS
  SELECT tcid,cid,number,CURRENT DATE,
         CURRENT TIME,seat_no,score
  FROM db2.test_taken
    WHERE char(tcid)='TR01'
```

Fig. 4–91 Example of Updatable View

The view definition in Fig. 4–91 uses constant values which cannot be updated. However, the view is a deletable view and at least you can update one of its columns. Therefore, it is an updatable view.

Insertable Views

Insertable views will allow you to insert rows using the view definition. A view is insertable when:

- All of its columns are updatable.
- The view definition doesn't include **UNION ALL**.

```
CREATE VIEW insertable_view
(test_number,
 test_name,
 total_taken
)
AS
SELECT number,name,totaltaken
FROM test
```

Fig. 4–92 Example of an Insertable View

The view shown in Fig. 4–41, is an insertable view. However, an attempt to insert the view will fail. This is because there are columns in the base table that don't accept null values. Some of these columns are not present in the view definition. So, when you try to insert a value using the view, DB2 will try to insert a null into a not null column. This action is not permitted.

✍ Remember, the constraints defined on the base table are independent of the operations that can be performed using a view.

Read-Only Views

A read-only view is a non-deletable view. This is a view that doesn't comply with at least one of the rules for deletable views. A view can be read-only if:

- The **SELECT** statement contains more than one table (for example, join or cartesian product).
- The outer full-select contains a **GROUP BY** or **HAVING** clause.
- The outer full-select contains the **VALUES** or **DISTINCT** keywords.
- The outer full-select uses a column function.
- The definition of the view contains **EXCEPT, INTERSECT** or **UNION** operators. (A **UNION ALL** is acceptable.)

Let's examine a read-only view.

```
CREATE VIEW read_only_view
              (name,
              work_phone,
              home_phone)
AS
SELECT DISTINCT fname,wphone,hphone
              FROM candidate c,test_taken tt
              WHERE c.cid=tt.cid
```

Fig. 4–93 Example of a Read-Only View

The view shown in Fig. 4–93 contains at least two of the conditions listed above. It uses the **DISTINCT** clause, and the SQL statement involves more than one table.

Advanced SQL

We have discussed many different SQL statements in this chapter. DB2 provides many powerful SQL statements which we will discuss briefly as they are not required for all database implementations. DB2 includes very powerful SQL extensions including table-check constraints, recursive SQL and dynamic constraint mechanisms like database triggers.

User-Defined Defaults

You can remember that when you insert a row into a table and omit the value of one or more columns, that records will either be populated used a defined default or null. DB2 has a defined default value for each of the DB2 data types, but, you can elect to provide a user-defined default value for each of the columns. The user-defined default value is specified during the **CREATE TABLE** statement. By defining you own default value, you can ensure that the data value has been populate with a known value.

Let's say that the DB2 Certification Program has established a default cut-off (passing grade) score for all of its exams. In Fig. 4–98, we can see how the default cut-off score can be specified during table creation.

```
CREATE TABLE test
(test_id           NOT NULL,
 name              VARCHAR(50) NOT NULL,
 type              CHAR(1)     NOT NULL,
 avg_score         SCORE       NOT NULL,
 cut_score         DECIMAL(6,2)
                   NOT NULL WITH DEFAULT 65,
 length            MINUTES     NOT NULL,
 totaltaken        TOTAL       NOT NULL,
 totalpassed       TOTAL       NOT NULL)
```

Fig. 4–94 Defining User Default Values for Columns

Now, all the **INSERT** statements that omit the *cut_score* column will populate the column with the default value of 65. The *cut_score* column could also be defined as **NULL WITH DEFAULT**. In this case, you can choose, at insert time, between null values or default values.

Notice that we are defining the cut_score column with a built-in data type. If you use a user-defined data type (UDT), you must use a casting function with the constant. If that is the case, you must change the column definition to look like this:

```
CUT_SCORE SCORE NOT NULL WITH DEFAULT SCORE(65)
```

When you use defaults for UDT columns, don't forget to use the casting function. Besides constant values, you can use the datetime special registers and the user special register as user-defined column defaults.

The user special register as a default value can be useful in applications that need to track which user is issuing the SQL statement.

To ensure that the user-defined default value is being used during an **INSERT** operation, the keyword **DEFAULT** should be specified in the **VALUES** portion of the **INSERT** statement.

Check Constraints

Table-check constraints will enforce data integrity at the table level. Once a table-check constraint has been defined for a table, every **UPDATE** and **INSERT** statement will involve a checking of the restriction or constraint. If the constraint is violated, the data record will not be inserted/updated, and an SQL error will occur.

A table-check constraint can be defined at table creation time or later using the **ALTER TABLE** statement.

The table-check constraints can help implement specific data validation rules for the data values contained in the table. This can save the application developer time, as the validation of each data value can be performed by the database and not by each of the applications accessing the database.

Let's say that we would like to ensure that the cut-off score is never modified to be lower than 55 or higher than 70.

```
ALTER TABLE test
            ADD CONSTRAINT check_cut_score
            CHECK (cut_score BETWEEN 55 AND 70)
```

Fig. 4–95 Using Check Constraints

In Fig. 4–98, the check constraint is named *check_cut_score*. DB2 will use this name to inform us which constraint was violated if an **INSERT** or **UPDATE** statement fails. The CHECK clause is used to define a table-check constraint. An **ALTER TABLE** statement was used because the table had already been defined. If there are values in the test table which conflict with the constraint being defined, the **ALTER TABLE** statement will not complete.

✍   It is a good idea to label every constraint (triggers, table-check or referential integrity).

The constraint shown in Fig. 4–98 checks for valid entries in a single column. It is possible to define check constraints that validate the entries based on a multiple condition.

For example, you can say that for the tests that have a length greater than 100 minutes, the cut-off score cannot be greater than 65. Let's create this check constraint. This time we'll create the constraint in the table definition.

```
CREATE TABLE test
(number         TEST_ID      NOT NULL,
 name           VARCHAR(50)  NOT NULL,
 type           CHAR(1)      NOT NULL,
 avg_score      SCORE        NOT NULL,
 cut_score      DECIMAL(6,2)
                NOT NULL WITH DEFAULT 65,
 length         MINUTES      NOT NULL,
 totaltaken     TOTAL        NOT NULL,
 totalpassed    TOTAL        NOT NULL,
CONSTRAINT cut_length
CHECK (cut_score <=65 OR length<=100))
```

Fig. 4–96 Defining a Table Constraint

Notice in Fig. 4–98 the conditions used to define the check constraint. The requirement was to avoid a *cut_score* higher than 65 for tests with a *length* greater than 100.

The conditions used to define the check constraint are the negative form of those conditions you would use to retrieve the data you want to avoid.

For example, if you want to select those tests with a score higher than 65 and a length greater than 100, you will use a condition like this:

WHERE cut_score>65 AND length >100

When you want to avoid those rows in your table you must use the negative form of the conditions:

cut_score <= 65 OR length <= 100

This example was provided to explain how the conditions were established in the check constraint defined in Fig. 4–98.

Adding Check Constraints

When you add a check constraint to a previously loaded table, two things can happen:

- All the rows meet the check constraint
- Some or all the rows don't meet the check constraint

In the first case, all the rows meet the check constraint. The check constraint will be created successfully. Future attempts to insert or update data that doesn't meet the constraint will be rejected.

When there are some rows that don't meet the check constraint, the check constraint will not be created.

However, it is possible to turn off constraint checking just to let you add a new constraint. When you turn off the constraint checking for a table, it will be put in a **CHECK PENDING** state, and only limited access will be granted to it.

Modifying Check Constraints

As check constraints are used to implement business rules, you can need to change them. This will happen when the business rules change in your organization.

However, there is no special command used to change a check constraint. So, whenever a check constraint needs to be changed, you must drop it and create a new one. Check constraints can be dropped at any time. This has no affect in your table.

When you drop a check constraint, you must be aware that data validation, performed by the constraint, will no longer be in effect. The statement used to drop a constraint is the **ALTER TABLE** statement.

Let's say that the DB2 Certification program now allows a cut score higher than 70. Some of the exams have raise their cut score to 75.

So, let's modify the *check_cut_score* constraint to allow scores up to 75.

```
ALTER TABLE test DROP CONSTRAINT check_cut_score
```

After dropping the constraint, you have to create it with the new definition.

```
ALTER TABLE test
              ADD CONSTRAINT check_cut_score
              CHECK (cut_score BETWEEN 55 AND 75)
```

The check constraint's definition is stored in the system catalog tables. In our example, it is stored in the *SYSIBM.SYSCHECKS* table. By querying this table, you can "extract" the definition of all the check constraints defined in your database. You can also query the *system view SYSCAT.CHECKS* to retrieve their definition.

Triggers

A trigger is a set of actions that will be executed when a defined event occurs. The triggering events can be

- **INSERT**
- **UPDATE**
- **DELETE**

Triggers are defined for each table. Once a trigger has been defined, it is automatically active. A table can have multiple triggers defined for it. If multiple triggers for the same operation are defined for a given table, the order of operation is based on the trigger creation timestamp.

Trigger definitions are stored in the system catalog tables:

- *SYSCAT.TRIGGERS*
  Each trigger definition is stored in this table.
- *SYSCAT.TRIGDEP*
  Each trigger dependency is stored in this table.

Trigger Usage

A trigger is usually used for one of the following reasons:

- **Data Validation**
  Ensuring that a new data value is within the proper range. This is similar to table-check constraints, but it is a more flexible data validation mechanism.
- **Data Conditioning**
  Data conditioning is implemented using triggers that fire before data record modification. This allows the new data value to be modified or conditioned to a predefined value.
- **Data Integrity**
  This can be used to ensure that cross-table dependencies are maintained. The triggered action could involve updating data records in related tables. This is similar to referential integrity, but it is a more flexible alternative.

Trigger Activation

A trigger can be defined to be fired in one of two ways:

- **Before**
  A before trigger will fire before the triggering statement has completed. Therefore, the trigger body is seeing the new data values prior to their being inserted or updated into the table.
- **After**
  An after trigger will fire after the triggering statement has successfully completed. Therefore, the trigger body is seeing the table as being in a consistent state. (All transactions have been completed.)

Another important feature about triggers is that they can fire other triggers or other constraints such as a delete cascade referential integrity constraint. These are known as cascading triggers.

During the execution of a trigger, the new and old data values can be accessible depending on the nature of the trigger (before or after).

The best method of understanding the usage of triggers is to see some in action. The *DB2CERT* database contains many relationships that can be maintained using triggers. By using triggers, a large amount of application code will be avoided for the DB2 certification application.

Trigger Example (After)

In Fig. 4–98, a trigger is defined to set the value of the *pass_fail* column for each of the tests taken by a candidate. The trigger has been given the name *pass-fail* (no relationship with the column called *pass_fail*). Once the trigger has been created, it is active.

The *passfail* trigger is an **AFTER, INSERT, FOR EACH ROW** trigger. Every time there is a row inserted into the *test_taken* table, this trigger will fire. The trigger body section will perform an **UPDATE** statement to set the value of the *pass_fail* column for the newly inserted row. The column is populated with either the value 'P' (representing a passing grade) or the value 'F' (representing a failing grade).

✍ Remember that a trigger defined in one table can modify other tables in the trigger body.

```
CREATE TRIGGER PassFail AFTER INSERT ON test_taken
        REFERENCING NEW AS N
        FOR EACH ROW MODE DB2SQL
UPDATE test_taken
SET PASS_FAIL =
                CASE
                WHEN N.SCORE >=
                     (SELECT CUT_SCORE FROM TEST
                        WHERE NUMBER = N.NUMBER)
                              THEN 'P'

                WHEN N.SCORE <
                     (SELECT CUT_SCORE FROM TEST
                        WHERE NUMBER=N.NUMBER)
                END           THEN 'F'

                WHERE N.CID = CID
                     AND N.TCID = TCID
                     AND N.NUMBER = NUMBER
                     AND N.DATE_TAKEN = DATE_TAKEN
```

Fig. 4–97 Creating a Trigger

Trigger Example (Before)

A before trigger will be activated before the trigger operation has completed. The triggering operation can be an **INSERT, UPDATE** or **DELETE** statement. This type of trigger is very useful for two purposes: to condition data or provide default values or to enforce data value constraints dynamically.

There are three before trigger examples shown in Fig. 4–98 which are used in the DB2 certification application.

All three of these triggers have been implemented to avoid seat conflicts for test candidates. The triggers will fire during an **INSERT** of each new candidate for a test.

```
CREATE TRIGGER pre9 NO CASCADE BEFORE
INSERT ON test_taken
        REFERENCING NEW AS N
        FOR EACH ROW MODE DB2SQL
            WHEN (N.START_TIME <'09"00"00')
SIGNAL SQLSTATE '70003'
('Cannot assign Seat before 09:00:00!')


CREATE TRIGGER aft5 NO CASCADE BEFORE
INSERT ON test_taken
        REFERENCING NEW AS N
        FOR EACH ROW MODE DB2SQL
            WHEN (N.START_TIME +
        (SELECT SMALLINT(Length) FROM TEST
    WHERE NUMBER = N.NUMBER) MINUTES > '17:00:00')
SIGNAL SQLSTATE '70004'
('Cannot assign Seat after 17:00:00!')


CREATE TRIGGER start NO CASCADE BEFORE
INSERT ON test_taken
        REFERENCING NEW AS N
        FOR EACH ROW MODE DB2SQL
            WHEN (
            EXISTS (SELECT cid FROM test_taken
                WHERE SEAT_NO = N.SEAT_NO AND
                    TCID         = T.CID     AND
                    DATE_TAKEN = N.DATE_TAKEN AND
                    N.START_TIME BETWEEN
                        START_TIME AND FINISH_TIME))
SIGNAL SQLSTATE '70001'
('Start Time Conflict!')
```

Fig. 4–98 Before Trigger Examples

If the conditions are encountered, an SQL error will be flagged using the SQL function called **SIGNAL**. A different **SQLSTATE** value will be provided when the triggered conditions are encountered.

The *pre9* trigger shown in Fig. 4–98 is used to ensure that a test candidate is not scheduled to take a test before 9:00 am. The *aft5* trigger is used to ensure that a test candidate is not scheduled to take a test after 5:00 pm. The start trigger is used to avoid conflicts during a testing day.

Summary

In this chapter we have talked about two of the three groups of SQL. All the examples presented were created using DB2. The intention of the chapter is to provide you with the basic elements to use SQL. This is a very long chapter, but it is divided in different sections, so you can take from it what you consider more practical or important.

Some of the SQL features presented here are very powerful and will save you a lot of development and processing time.

We have talked about a lot of concepts, but they are all tied together. Understanding them will provide you with the elements to administer databases or develop SQL applications under DB2. Some of the chapter can also be useful for end-users who want to learn more about SQL and the features that DB2 offers.

The level of SQL and DB2 knowledge will vary depending on your main activity. If you are an end user executing a query, you may only need to understand the concepts presented in the beginning of the chapter. For a database administrator, SQL knowledge is always important. It is also important to known the relationship between the objects and the system catalog tables. You will need SQL to retrieve information from a given table or to make updates in order to simulate a different environment.

For an application developer, knowledge of SQL is fundamental as it is the mechanism of storing and retrieving data in a relational database. Many SQL features that DB2 provides can save programming effort. Such features include the case expressions, common table expressions, triggers and recursive SQL.

Questions

1. Which action will cause an index to be created?

   O   A. Define a table check constraint

   O   B. Define a user-defined data type

   O   C. Define a primary key constraint

   O   D. Define a foreign key constraint

2. What action can result in internal record deletes?

   O   A. table-check constraints

   O   B. user-defined data types

   O   C. referential integrity constraints

   O   D. primary key constraints

3. Which SQL statement changes a view definition?

   O   A. ALTER VIEW ...

   O   B. CREATE VIEW ...

   O   C. UPDATE VIEW ...

   O   D. RECREATE VIEW ...

4. Which statement defines table check constraints?

   O   A. CREATE INDEX

   O   B. CREATE TABLE

   O   C. CREATE CHECK CONSTRAINT

   O   D. SET CONSTRAINTS

5.Given the tables:

PC		EMPLOYEE	
serial_num	INT	employee_num	INT NOT NULL
model_num	INT		PRIMARY KEY
owner_id	INT		

Which action ensures that no rows can be inserted into the PC table unless the owner_id matches an employee_num value in the EMPLOYEE table?

○   A. Add a foreign key constraint to the EMPLOYEE table.

○   B. Add a primary key constraint to the PC table.

○   C. Add a foreign key constraint to the PC table.

○   D. Add a table check constraint to the EMPLOYEE table.

6.   Which statement modifies the system catalog tables?

○   A. INSERT

○   B. GRANT

○   C. DELETE

○   D. SELECT

Answers

1. (C)
   A primary key constraint will always create a system generated unique index. This index can only be dropped by altering the table definition and removing the primary key constraint.
2. (C)
   An internal record delete can occur when referential integrity constraints are defined.
3. (B)
   Views cannot be altered; they must be dropped and created using a different definition.
4. (B)
   A table-check constraint is defined when the table is being created, using the **CREATE TABLE** statement.
5. (C)
   A foreign key constraint can be used to ensure that the data record matches a corresponding value in the parent table.
6. (B)
   A **GRANT** statement will update data in the system catalogs as the database object privileges are maintained in the system catalogs.

Exercises

Part A — Creating the DB2CERT Database

1. Go to the directory \exercise\chapter4\parta

2. Issue: **db2start**
    Ensure that the database manager instance has been started successfully.
    Issue:
    db2 list database directory
    If you receive an error SQL1032N then the database instance was no started
    in step 2. If there is already a database called DB2CERT, remove it using the
    command **DROP DATABASE DB2CERT.**

3. Edit the file *cr8db.ddl* to specify the location(drive) where you would like to
    place the database.

4. Issue:
    db2 -tvf cr8db.ddl

5. Issue:
    db2 list database directory
    There should be an entry for the database: DB2CERT.

6. Issue:
    db2 list database directory on x
    Substitute x for the drive/location of the database as you specified in the
    cr8db.ddl file. This command lists the local database directory. It contains
    the initial directory location for the *DB2CERT* database.

7. Verify the amount of disk space allocated during the **CREATE DATABASE**
    command in step 5. This can be performed by examining the amount of allo-
    cated storage under the directory/path shown in the output of step 6.
    (Using OS/2, the amount of disk space is approximately 6MB)

Part B — Data Types and Case-Sensitivity

1. Go to the directory \exercise\chapter4\partb

2. Connect to the *DB2CERT* database. Issue **db2 connect to db2cert**

3. Issue:
    db2 -tvf datatyp1.ddl
    This file contains a single **CREATE TABLE** statement. Note that six columns
    have been defined for this table and the name of the table is "DATATYP1".

4. Let's verify the table, its columns and their data types.
    Issue:
    db2 -tvf listcols.dml

    This file contains a single table **SELECT** statement on the system catalog
    table SYSCAT.COLUMNS. The typename column is the built-in (DB2) data
    type. The length column is the defined size of the data type.
    If the data type is variable in length (**CLOB**, **VARCHAR**, for example), the
    value in the length column is the maximum size of each record.

    ✍   There is a column number associated with each column. This num-
         ber corresponds to the order in which they are specified in the cre-
         ate table statement.

5. Issue:
    db2 -tvf tabsize.dml

    This file contains a query to determine the maximum size of each record for
    the table "DB2.DATATYP1".

    ✍   The size of each record according to the query should be 36 Bytes.

6. Let's insert some data into the "DB2.DATATYP1" table.
    Issue:
    db2 -tvf insert.dml
    All of the **INSERT** statements should have been successful.

7. Perform the SQL statement:
    db2 "select * from db2.datatyp1"
    View the file containing the input data for the table:
    type insert.dml (In Unix use: **pg insert.dml**)
    Compare the output of the SELECT statement with the insert.dml file. The
    data values should appear different. The external and internal representa-
    tion of data is different form some DB2 data types.

    ✍   Quotation marks are required for character string input. Note that
         the double/float field stores data in exponential notation.

8. Let's obtain a more accurate record size using a different query:
    Issue:
    db2 -tvf tabsize2.dml

    The average record size according to the query should be 30 bytes.
    Why is there a difference in record sizes?
    If you examine the *tabsize2.dml* file you will note that the average length of
    the character data stored in **VARCHAR** columns is used and **not** the maximum

(defined) length as defined in the system catalog table. This is a more accurate calculation of the average record size for the table. Compare the query with the query in the *tabsize.dml* file.

9. Type the following:
    db2 INSERT INTO db2.datatyp1 VALUES
    **   ('1', '2', 3, 4, 1/3, 1000000000.375)**

    You should have received an error (SQL0413N) the last value (1000000000.375) is too large according to its definition **DECIMAL (10,2)**. The cause of this error can be verified using the command:
    db2 -tvf listcols.dml
    Note that the SCALE field is 2 and the LENGTH field is 10.

10. Upper and lowercase considerations are also important when using SQL.

    ✍   Keep all of the DB2 objects uppercase as they are stored in the system catalogs in uppercase.

    Edit *listcols.dml* and change:
    .... WHERE tabname = TRANSLATE('datatyp1')
    to
    .... WHERE tabname = 'datatyp1'

    Issue:
    db2 -tvf listcols.dml

    No data was retrieved! The information enclosed in quotes is always case-sensitive and the table name was stored in SYSCAT.COLUMNS in upper-case.

11. Edit *listcols.dml* file and change:
    .... WHERE tabname = 'DATATYP1'
    to
    .... WHERE TABNAME = 'DATATYP1'
    Issue the command:
    db2 -tvf listcols.dml
    The data is retrieved as before because the column name was automatically converted to uppercase by the Command Line Processor (CLP) and the data was located.

12. We will not be using the table *db2.datatyp1* table again so let's remove the table and all of its records using the command **db2 drop table db2.datatyp1**

Part C — Creating Database Objects (DDL)

1. Go to the directory \exercise\chapter4\partc.

2. Connect to the *DB2CERT* database
   The first DDL statements we will issue, will create new user-defined data types which can use in the **CREATE TABLE** statement. We are using UDTs to enforce *strong typing* and avoid inconsistent comparisons of data.
   To create these new data types, issue:
   db2 -tvf udt1.ddl

3. Let's ensure that the data types have been created and that the necessary **casting** functions have also been created.
   Issue:
   db2 -tvf chkudt1.dml

   The output shows the fully qualified distinct types and the meta-type column has a value of 'T'. The meta-type specifies if the data type is user-defined or provided by DB2. The DB2 data type source is also shown in the SOURCE-NAME column.

4. Issue:
   db2 -tvf chkudt2.dml

   The output of this query shows all of the valid DB2 data types.

   ✍ Do you notice a data type which was not mentioned in the text?
   The boolean data type cannot be used by user tables.

5. Casting functions are automatically generated by DB2 when a UDT is created. Let's examine the casting functions which were created in step 2.
   Issue:
   db2 -tvf chkcast1.dml

   There should be 19 records retrieved. The casting function names are provided in the first two columns. The third column is an internal function number used by DB2. The next column is 'S' as these functions are 'System-Generated'.
   We will need to use some of these casting functions in our SQL DML (**SELECT, INSERT, UPDATE, DELETE**) statements.

6. Finally, we will create the tables for the DB2 Certification Database.
   Issue:
   db2 -tvf cr8tab.ddl
   This command creates the four tables for the DB2 Certification database.

   ✍ Take a look at the *cr8tab.ddl* file and note that the current function path was set to locate the UDTs that were created in step 2.

   Let's examine the table definitions as stored in the system catalog views.

7. Each table that has been created needs to have a record in the
    SYSCAT.TABLES system catalog view.
    Issue:
    db2 SELECT tabname, tabschema FROM syscat.tables
    There should have been 65 records in the result report. Most of these tables
    are the system catalog tables. Let's examine the user tables.
    Issue:
    db2 SELECT tabname, tabschema
        FROM syscat.tables
        WHERE tabschema = 'DB2'

8. Have we created any indexes yet?
    Yes, we have indirectly created 4 indexes.
    Issue:
    db2 -tvf listinx.dml

    The output should show 4 indexes: one for each of the tables that were cre-
    ated in step 6.
    The indexes were automatically created to enforce the primary key con-
    straint. The *uniquerule* column contains the value 'P', which represents a
    primary key based index.

9. Which columns are use to defined for the index?
    This can be answered using two methods.
    The first one is to examine the **CREATE TABLE** statement in the file
    cr8tab.ddl, and the second is to issue:
    db2 -tvf listicol.dml

    The key columns are listed in the last column of the result table.

Part D — Using Views

1. Before we can perform **SELECT** statements against the *DB2CERT* database,
    we will have to populate the database with some data. There will be more
    exercises on data loading techniques in later chapters.
    Go to the \exercise\chapter4\partd directory and issue:
    db2 -tvf data.imp
    This command will insert data records into the previously created tables
    using the **IMPORT** command. Examine the *import.msg* file to check for any
    errors that may have occurred during the import. You may notice some warn-
    ings, but should not encounter any errors.

2. We will now create some view definitions. Issue:
    db2 -tvf view1.ddl
    A view called *db2.test_taken_tx01* was created. This view is based on a single
    table (*db2.test_taken*) and a single condition. It is important to realize that
    the condition will **always** be applied when the view is used to retrieve data.
    The condition may be ignored when the view is used to update/delete/insert,
    depending on the existence of a **WITH CHECK OPTION** clause.

3. Let's retrieve data using the newly created view. Issue:
    db2 SELECT *
    **   FROM db2.test_taken_tx01**
    There **WHERE CHAR(tcid) = 'TX01'** clause was applied to the result.

4. Now, we will attempt to use the same view to insert a new record.
    Issue:
    db2 INSERT INTO db2.test_taken_tx01 VALUES
    ** ('888888888','TR01','502','1996-04-05',**
    **   '9:00',NULL,NULL,'3')**
    The statement is successful even though the view definition had a **WHERE**
    clause that stated **TCID = 'TX01'**. The *TCID* column in the above insert
    statement was 'TR01'. If you want DB2 to enforce the **WHERE** condition for
    INSERT statements involving views, then you must include the phrase **WITH**
    CHECK OPTION at the end of the view definition.

5. Let's define a view using the **WITH CHECK OPTION**. Issue:
    db2 -tvf view2.ddl
    A view called *db2.tx01_seats* was created. This view is based on the
    db2.test_taken table, but there are two conditions and the phrase **WITH**
    CHECK OPTION. This clause will enforce all of the conditions when the view
    is used to update or insert data records.
    Attempt to insert the following data record, Issue:
    db2 INSERT INTO db2.tx01_seats
    **   VALUES ('888888888','TR01','502',**
    **   '1996-04-05','9:00',NULL,NULL,'3')**

    The insert is rejected by DB2 because the **BETWEEN** condition is not satisfied
    as the value of '3' is not between '1' and '2'. This examples shows that views
    defined using the **WITH CHECK** option can be used to valid user input.

6. If you examine the definition for the view *db2.tx01_seats* you can notice that the definition has a hard coded or predefined **BETWEEN** clause. If the test center TX01 has more than 2 seats and all **INSERT** statements were issued using the *db2.tx01_seats* view, then the seat assignments in seat 3 would always fail.

    Let's examine a different (easier to maintain) view definition. First, we should drop the existing view *db2.tx01_seats*. Issue:
    ```
    db2 drop view db2.tx01_seats
    ```

    Create the new view definition, Issue:
    ```
    db2 -tvf view3.ddl
    ```
    This view contains a sub-select to determine the number of available seats at the TX01 testing center. Therefore, if the record for the TX01 testing center is updated with new number of seats, then the view is still correct.

7. Let's create a non-updatable view involving the **UNION ALL** operator. This operator is used to append data from multiple **SELECT** statements.
    Issue : `db2 -tvf view4.ddl`
    Issue : `SELECT * FROM db2.test1`
    The result table is a **UNION ALL** of two **SELECT** statements. This type of view cannot be used in **INSERT, UPDATE** or **DELETE** statements.

PART E — Controlling Access (Data Control Language)

1. Data access controlled was discussed in the previous chapter, but we will examine the **GRANT** and **REVOKE** statements here also. Go to the \exercise\chapter4\parte directory.
    Issue : `db2 -tvf control.dcl`

    This will provide **CONTROL** privilege on the **DB2CERT** database tables to a user group called *FULLDB*. This user group must be defined in the operating system. **CONTROL** privileges allows the user to perform any DML and DCL statement for the table.
    To verify the new current privileges for the *TEST* table, issue :
    ```
    db2 -tvf auth1.dml
    ```

2. When can also provide individual user access to DB2 database objects.
    Issue : `db2 -tvf select1.dcl`
    This will provide **SELECT** only access to a user with the user id of *STUDENT*.

3. Let's remove the **CONTROL** privileges from the *FULLDB* group.
    Issue : `db2 -tvf revoke1.dcl`
    Let's check to see if this user group still has any privileges on the TEST table. Issue : `db2 -tvf auth1.dml`

Notice that the *FULLDB* group maintains all other privileges unless they are all removed using the **REVOKE** statement.

PART F — Using Set Operators

1. We will examine how a common set operator can be used in SQL statements. Go to the \exercise\chapter4\partf directory.
    Issue : **db2 -tvf inter.dml**

    If you examine this query, it is returning the candidate ids who are scheduled to take an exam at the TX01 test center. The **INTERSECT** operator was used to find the rows that qualify. The **INTERSECT** operator will produce a result set of matching rows for both of the SQL statements. The invocation is similar to the **UNION ALL** operator used in part D of the exercises.

2. Issue: **db2 -tvf inter2.dml**

    This query is using a join predicate to produce a similar result query. If you were to change the **SELECT a.cid** to **SELECT DISTINCT(a.cid)**, you would obtain the same output as the query in step 1.

    Bottom Line — there are many ways of describing the same query using different SQL statements.

CHAPTER 5

Database Concurrency

A database server acts as a central source of data access for a group of end users. The number of end users can vary from one to one thousand users. When many users access the same data source there must be *rules* established for the reading, inserting, deleting, and updating of the data records.

The rules for data access are set by each application connected to a DB2 database. These rules are established using two methods:

- Explicit control — Locking resources using an SQL statement or using a DB2 command.
- Implicit control — Locking resources by specifying an **isolation level**.

Some of the DB2 database resources can be explicitly controlled (for concurrency purposes). These resources include **databases**, **table spaces**, and **tables**. One of the main features of DB2 common server is its ability to lock database resources at the row or record level. This can provide greater concurrency and therefore, avoid resource conflicts. Record locking behavior is specified using an isolation level. We will examine the supported isolation levels and their locking semantics.

We will examine the types of DB2 locks and their behavior in an application environment. DB2 must also handle concurrency conflicts including **deadlocks** and resource contention. Some of the database configuration parameters affect the amount and type of locks acquired by DB2 applications. Monitoring for database concurrency problems is an important part of a database administrator's duties and we will examine some of the lock **monitoring** abilities.

We will examine concurrency problems that can occur in a multi-user environment. The concurrency examples will be based on the *db2cert* certification testing application.

Concurrency Considerations

Data integrity is a primary concern in any database environment. The database server must guarantee the integrity of the data as it is modified. Every executable SQL statement which is issued is considered to be part of a **transaction**.

A transaction will contain at least one SQL statement. Multiple SQL statements can be grouped together and executed as a single action. Any data that has been accessed or modified by the SQL statements will be tracked by DB2 and either permanently changed (committed), or the modifications returned to their original state (rolled back). This *all or nothing* behavior is known as **atomicity**. A transaction does not only guarantee atomicity, it also guarantees **persistency**.

Persistency is provided through transactional logging. The log files are used to ensure that all committed transactions are physically applied to the database.

A transaction is started implicitly during the processing of the first SQL statement. The transaction is completed when a **COMMIT** or **ROLLBACK** statement has been issued, either explicitly or implicitly.

✍️   The term *unit of work* is the same as *transaction*.

When the data has been permanently changed using the **COMMIT** or **ROLLBACK** statement, a point of consistency is established. A **point of consistency** is important as it is used during database crash recovery and rollforward recovery.

In the previous chapter we discussed data access control. The access control was based on using the **GRANT** and **REVOKE** statements to provide database users with the ability to access tables, views and packages. Once *access control* has been established, *resource control* must be considered. Concurrency problems can occur if resource control is **not** properly managed.

DB2 provides mechanisms to manage resource control. We will discuss these mechanisms or strategies. The accuracy of the data is based on the correctness of the input, and the control of the modification of the data. The correctness of the input data needs to be monitored by the database administrator. DB2 does provide some mechanisms to avoid incorrect data entry, including the use of triggers, table-check constraints and referential integrity.

We will discuss the control of data modification using transactions. Let's examine some of the possible concurrency problems and the strategies which can be used to avoid them. We will examine some concurrency issues which need to be addressed by the *db2cert* application.

Concurrency Problems

Database resource control involves the establishment of data modification rules. There are concurrency anomalies which we will consider using the *db2cert* database application they include

- Lost update
- Uncommitted read
- Nonrepeatable read
- Phantom read

Lost Update Problem

The **lost update** problem occurs when the same data is retrieved by different test coordinators, and they both change the data, and save their changes. The last successful change to the data will be the kept and the first change will be overwritten.

Let's look at an example. Suppose Grant is a DB2 certification test candidate, and he wants to take the first DB2 exam. Grant calls the testing center in Austin. The test coordinator, Mary, gets the call. She looks at the availability of seats at the Austin testing center for the date that Grant wants. Mary's application screen is shown in Fig. 5–1. Mary notes that seat number four is available.

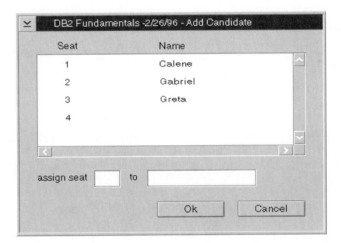

Fig. 5–1 Available Seats

Grant is not sure if he wants to take the test that day. Mary maintains her list of seats on the screen until Grant decides if he will take the test on that day.

Meanwhile, Richard calls the testing center. Andrea, another test coordinator, takes Richard's call. Richard wants to take the same DB2 Fundamental exam on the same day that Grant has requested. Andrea checks the seat availability and obtains the same list as Mary. Andrea's screen is shown in Fig. 5–1.

The other test candidate, Grant, decides to take the test and Mary clicks the OK button. The OK button on Mary's application issues an **UPDATE** statement, but it does not issue a **COMMIT**. The **COMMIT** statement was not coded in Mary's application (due to a programming error). Mary assigns seat four to Grant by clicking the OK button, as shown in Fig. 5–2.

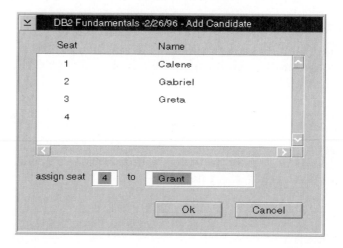

Fig. 5–2 Mary Clicks the OK Button (UPDATE with no COMMIT)

Andrea does not see that Mary has assigned seat four to Grant, so she assigns the seat to Richard. Remember, seat four was not permanently modified by Mary, because Mary's application did not commit the transaction. Andrea assigns the seat to Richard as shown in Fig. 5–3. Andrea's application was coded correctly as the OK button corresponds to a **COMMIT** statement. The commit operation was successful for Andrea as no resource conflict was encountered.

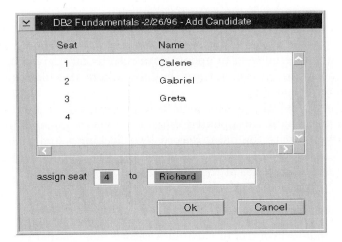

Fig. 5–3 Andrea Assigns Seat to Richard (commits the UPDATE)

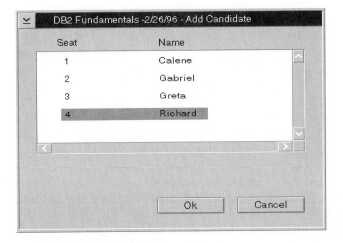

Fig. 5–4 A Refresh of the Seat Assignments

If the list of seats is refreshed (retrieved again) we see that seat four was assigned to Richard and the update made by Mary was overwritten. Fig. 5–4 shows the refreshed screen. On the day of the test, Grant and Richard arrive at the testing center and the database shows that Richard has a proper seat assignment. Grant walks away unhappy and has to reschedule to take the exam another day.

What was the problem? To maintain the accuracy of the data, control mechanisms need to be enforced. The goal of the application was to avoid these situations. In this case, the update was not committed by Mary.

This scenario can only occur if record level locking is being used. If only table level locking is used, then Mary's application would have controlled any update to the table. But, if Mary's application had update control for the table, then other test centers would not be able to assign seats. Should only one test center coordinator be allowed to update data records for a given day? For some applications this can be appropriate, but for others this does not provide a sufficient degree of concurrency.

The integrity of the database is not guaranteed in this example. An application has to **lock** the updated data to makes it impossible for another application to overwrite the data. Record level locking usually involves cursor processing. Cursor processing is discussed in the application development chapters and in the exercises at the end of this chapter.

Lost Update Solutions

To avoid lost updates, control of each data record must be maintained by DB2. The most strict control mechanism involves, obtaining update control of all of the matching records or possible matching records for the query. This is known as **repeatable read**. DB2 does not provide an SQL statement to lock all of the matching data records. See "Repeatable Read" on page 230, for more details on establishing a repeatable read concurrency strategy.

The only explicit SQL control mechanism provided by DB2 is the **LOCK TABLE** statement. According to the design of the *db2cert* database, there is a table which represents all of the tests being taken at all of the tests centers, known as *db2.test_taken*. If the application were to explicitly lock the table for update (known as **EXCLUSIVE** mode), then other test centers would not be allowed to update, or even read any of the data in the table. The less restrictive statement, **LOCK TABLE** <table-name> **IN SHARE MODE**, could be used. Simply stated, a **share** mode table lock allows others to read data but not update the data.

Mary's application could have obtained a share lock on the *test_taken* table. The share lock would have prevented Andrea from successfully performing an **UPDATE** of the table (assignment of seat four to Richard). The table lock would remain in effect until Mary's application released the lock using the **COMMIT** or **ROLLBACK** statement.

An alternative method could involve record or row level locking. If Mary's application acquired record locks for seat four, Andrea's update would have failed. You cannot explicitly acquire row level locks from an SQL statement. See "Cursor Stability" on page 229, for more details on row level locking.

Uncommitted Read

Mary's application locks the rows of unassigned seats and makes a temporary update to assign seat four to Grant. Until Mary has committed or rolled back this update, no one else can update the record for seat four. Fig. 5–5 shows the list retrieved by George. George has permission to read uncommitted changes, and therefore he can see Grant assigned to seat four instead of Richard.

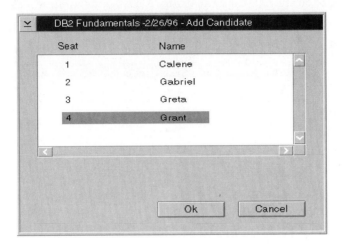

Fig. 5–5 George Retrieves Uncommitted Data

If George were to reissue his query after Andrea assigned seat four to Richard, he would obtain a different result. This is known as an **uncommitted read** (dirty read).

Let's look at another example. The test center secretary runs a report to determine how many people will be tested in February. The following query was issued

```
SELECT COUNT(*)
FROM test_taken
WHERE date_taken
BETWEEN ('1996-01-31') AND ('1996-03-01')
```

The result will include the temporary assigned seat. This is not correct because Mary can never commit the update. To avoid this behavior, the application should **NOT** be able to read uncommitted changes. It is usually **not** recommended to have applications reading uncommitted data.

Non-Repeatable Read

A non-repeatable read scenario involves obtaining a different result set within the same transaction. Uncommitted read applications do not guarantee this behavior.

Let's look at an example of a non-repeatable read scenario. Suppose Grant is going to take the certification exam. He asks Mary to check in which location (Austin or Houston) he can take the exam. Mary sends a request to the database and retrieves the list of available seats in Austin and Houston, as shown in Fig. 5–6.

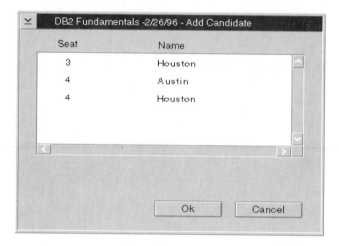

Fig. 5–6 List of Available Seats (first time)

In the meantime, Andrea has assigned and committed the last available seat in Austin to Richard. Grant would like to take the test in Austin, so Mary attempts to assign the seat in Austin. The update fails and when Mary refreshes her screen, the seat in Austin is no longer available. Mary's refreshed screen is shown in Fig. 5–7.

The scheduling application was performing row level locking because if a table lock (share mode) was acquired by Mary, then the update made by Andrea would have failed. The application was coded to only lock the rows of data being updated. In this case an exclusive lock was obtained by Andrea when the assignment of the seat to Richard was made. This did not conflict with the locks held by Mary because she did not have that row locked. We are assuming that the row is only locked when it is chosen for update by the administrator.

To avoid this type of non-repeatable read scenario, all of the retrieved data needs to be locked. If you would like to guarantee that none of the selected data is modified, then simply locking these rows is sufficient. This is known as **read stability** in DB2. If you would like to guarantee that none of the possible qualifying rows are modified, then the entire table can need to be locked. This is known as **repeatable read**.

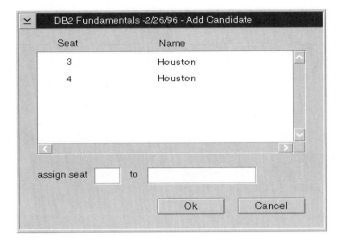

Fig. 5–7 Mary's Refreshed Screen

Phantom Read Problem

The **phantom read** phenomenon occurs if an application executes the same query twice; the second time the query is issued additional rows are returned. For many applications this is an acceptable scenario. For example, if the query involved finding all of the available seats at a concert, then reissuing the query and obtaining a better seat selection is a desirable feature.

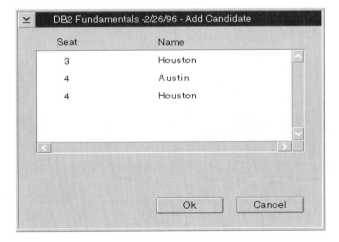

Fig. 5–8 Available Seats in Austin and Houston (first query)

Let's take a look at our application again. Grant wants to take the exam in Austin or in Houston. Mary requests the list of available seats for these locations, as shown in Fig. 5–8.

Another test coordinator adds an additional seat to the Austin testing site. Now it is possible to test five candidates in Austin at the same time. If the query is issued again. Mary retrieves a different result set which includes seat five as an available seat. Although the application had locked the previously retrieved rows, the application was able to add a new row to the result set, as shown in Fig. 5–9.

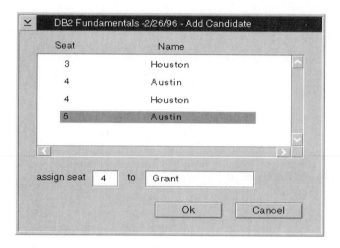

Fig. 5–9 Mary's Query (second time)

Phantom Read Solution

To avoid this behavior, the application has to lock all of the possible qualifying rows. This ensures that no other application can update, delete or insert a row that would affect the result table. This is an important concept to understand. For example, if the query was **SELECT * FROM test WHERE number = '500'**, then all of the rows in the test table would need to be locked to avoid them from being updated by another transaction.

   If DB2 needs to acquire locks for every row in the table to provide the required level of isolation, a table level lock will be obtained instead of multiple row level locks.

Isolation Level

In the previous examples we have seen some of the possible concurrency problems. DB2 provides different levels of protection to isolate the data from each of the database applications while it is being accessed.

These levels of protection are known as **isolation levels** or locking strategies. The DB2 supported isolation levels include

- Uncommitted read
- Cursor stability
- Read stability
- Repeatable read

The **isolation level** is defined, for embedded SQL statements, during the binding of a package to a database. If no isolation level is specified, the **default** level of cursor stability is used.

✍️ Dynamic SQL statements (CLI) have their isolation level defined in the db2cli.ini file.

Uncommitted Read

Uncommitted read (UR), also known as dirty read, is the lowest level of isolation. It can be used to access most uncommitted data changes except tables, views and indexes that are being created or dropped by other transactions.

For example, an application using the uncommitted read isolation level will return all of the matching rows for a query, even if that data is in the process of being modified, and can **never** be committed to the database.

If you decide to use this isolation level, your application might access incorrect data. There will be very few locks held by uncommitted read transactions. Nonrepeatable read and phantom read phenomena are possible when this isolation level is being used.

Cursor Stability

Cursor stability (CS) locks any row the cursor is positioned on during a unit of work. The lock on the row is held until the next row is fetched or the unit of work is terminated. However, if a row has been updated, the lock must be held until the unit of work is terminated. A unit of work is terminated when either a **COMMIT** or **ROLLBACK** is executed.

An application using cursor stability cannot read uncommitted data. It locks the row it has currently fetched. Thus no other application can modify the contents of the current row.

If you decide to use this isolation level, your application will always read consistent data, but non-repeatable read or phantom read situations are still possible.

Read Stability

Read stability (RS) locks those rows which are part of the result table. If you have a table containing 10,000 rows and the query involves 10 rows, then only 10 rows are locked.

An application using read stability cannot read uncommitted data. Instead of locking a single row, it locks all rows that are part of the result table. No other application can change or modify these rows.

If you decide to use this isolation level, your application will always get the 230same result if the query is executed more than once in a unit of work, except for the phantom rows.

Repeatable Read

Repeatable read (RR) is the highest isolation level available in DB2. It locks all rows an application references within a unit of work. If you have a table containing 10,000 rows, locks on all rows are held until the unit of work is complete, even if only 10 rows qualify.

An application using repeatable read cannot read uncommitted data of a concurrent application. Instead of locking the rows that are part of the result table, all rows of the table in the database are locked. No other application can change or lock any row of this table.

If you decide to use this isolation level, none of the mentioned concurrency problems are possible in your application.

Choosing an Isolation Level

Choosing the proper isolation level is very important, because the isolation level influences not only the concurrency, but also the performance of the application. The more protection you have, the less concurrency is available.

Decide which concurrency problems are unacceptable for your application and then choose the isolation level which prevents these problems.

- Use the **uncommitted read** isolation level only if you use queries on read-only tables, or if you are only using only **SELECT** statements and you do not care whether you get uncommitted data from concurrent applications.
- Use the **cursor stability** isolation level when you want the maximum concurrency while seeing only committed data from concurrent applications
- Use the **read stability** isolation level when your application operates in a concurrent environment. This means that qualified rows have to remain stable for the duration of the unit of work.
- Use the **repeatable read** isolation level if the above listed isolation levels are not acceptable for your application.

Locking

DB2 provides isolation levels to control concurrency. In most cases, you do not need to take direct action to establish locks. In general, locks are acquired implicitly by DB2 according to the semantics defined by the isolation level.

Lock Attributes

The resource being locked is called an **object**. The only object you can explicitly lock are tables. Locks on other types of objects, such as rows, table spaces, indexes and sometimes tables are acquired by DB2 according to the isolation level.

 The database itself can be locked if the **CONNECT** statement contains the clause **IN EXCLUSIVE MODE**. This will acquire an exclusive lock on the database and prevent any other applications from connecting.

The length of time a lock is held is called **duration**. It is affected by the isolation level. The type of access or rules is known as the lock **mode**. Some lock modes are only used for locking table objects, while other lock modes are used for row objects. DB2 uses the following hierarchy of lockable database objects:

- Table Spaces
- Tables
- Rows

The different modes of **table** locks are listed in order of increasing control:

- **IN** (Intent None) — The owner of the lock can read any data, committed or non-committed data, in the table.
- **IS** (Intent Share) — The owner of the lock can read any data in the table if an S lock can be obtained on the target row(s).
- **S** (Share) — The owner of the lock can read any data in the table and will not obtain row locks.
- **IX** (Intent Exclusive) — The owner of the lock can read or change any data in the table if an X lock can be obtained on rows to be changed and a U or S lock can be obtained on rows to be read.
- **SIX** (Share with Intent Exclusive) — The owner of the lock can read any data in the table and change rows if it can obtain an X lock on the target row(s).
- **U** (Update) — The owner of the lock can read any data in the table and can change data if an X lock on the table can be obtained.
- **X** (Exclusive) — The owner of the lock can read or update any data in the table. No row locks are obtained.
- **Z** (Superexclusive) - No other application can access the table.

The different modes of **row** locking are listed in order of increasing control over resources:

- **S** (Share) — The row is being read by one application and is available for *read-only* by concurrent applications.
- **U** (Update) — The row is being read by one application which intends to update the data in this row. It is available for *read-only* by concurrent applications. Only one application can possess a U lock on a row.
- **X** (Exclusive) — The row is being changed by one application and is not available for concurrent applications, except for those with uncommitted read isolation level.

Lock Conversion

If an application holds a lock on a data object and the mode of access requires a more restrictive lock, the lock is converted. This process is known as **lock conversion**. During the lock conversion process the more restrictive lock can or can not be granted.

Let's look at an example of lock conversion. Assume that the application fetches a row from the *test_taken* table with the intent to update this row. The intent to update tells DB2 to acquire an update lock on the currently positioned row during the query processing.

```
SELECT * FROM db2.test_taken
WHERE seat_no = '1' AND date_taken = CURRENT DATE
FOR UPDATE OF seat_no
```

The database manager holds an IX lock on the table and a U lock on the specified row. The following SQL statement assigns all test candidates currently scheduled to take the test at *seat_no* 1, to take the test at *seat_no* to 2:

```
UPDATE db2.test_taken
SET seat_no = '2'
WHERE seat_no = '1' AND date_taken = CURRENT DATE
```

Now, the database manager holds an IX lock on the *test_taken* table and an X lock on the changed row.

✍ When rows are being modified an X lock is **always** required.

All the locks are released when your application terminates the unit of work with either **COMMIT** or **ROLLBACK**. The cursor stability isolation level was used in this example.

Lock Escalation

If your application changes many rows in one table, it is better to have one restrictive lock on the entire table rather than many restrictive locks on each of the rows. DB2 requires memory for each lock; therefore if a number of row locks can be replaced with a single table lock, then the locking storage area can be used by other applications.

To avoid lock resource problems DB2 will perform automatic **lock escalation**. Locks will be escalated to a more restrictive object.

✎   Each DB2 lock will consume the same amount of memory.

Two database configuration parameters have a direct impact on the process of lock escalation. They are:

- **locklist** — The locklist parameter defines the amount of memory allocated for the locks.
- **maxlocks** — The maxlocks parameter defines the percentage of the total locklist permitted by a single application.

There are two different situations for lock escalation:

1. One application exceeds the percentage of the locklist as defined by maxlocks. The database manager will attempt to free memory by obtaining a table lock and releasing row locks for this application.
2. Many applications connected to the database fill the locklist by acquiring a large number of locks. DB2 will attempt to free memory by obtaining a table lock and releasing row locks.

You should also note that the isolation level used by the application has an impact on lock escalation as well.

- Cursor stability will acquire row level locks initially. If required, table level locks can be obtained. Usually, a very small number of locks are acquired by each cursor stability application as they only have to guarantee the integrity of the data in the current row.
- Read stability locks all rows in the original result set.
- Repeatable read obtains table locks.

Lock Wait Behavior

What happens if one application requests to update a row that is already locked with an exclusive (X) lock? Assuming the isolation level is not unrepeatable read, the lock will not be granted, as it would compromise the integrity of the data. The application requesting the update will simply wait until the exclusive lock is released by the other application.

To ensure that the waiting application can continue, the **locktimeout** parameter can be set to define the length of the timeout period. The value is specified in seconds. By default, the lock timeout is disabled (set to a value of -1). This means the waiting application will not receive a timeout.

Deadlock Behavior

If two applications are waiting until the lock on an object of the concurrent application is released, this is called **deadlock**. DB2 uses a background process called *deadlock detector* to check if a deadlock has occurred. The process is activated periodically as determined by the **dlchktime** in the database configuration. It is specified in milliseconds (ms).

The deadlock detector will be a thread of execution and not a process for those operating environments that support multi-threaded applications (Windows NT and OS/2).

When the deadlock detector finds a deadlock situation, one of the deadlocked applications will receive an error code and the current unit of work for this application will be rolled back.

Lock Table Statement

You can use the **LOCK TABLE** statement to override the rules for acquiring initial lock modes. It locks the specified table until the unit of work is committed or rolled back. A table can be locked either in **SHARE MODE** or in **EXCLUSIVE MODE.**

Using the **LOCK TABLE** statement in **SHARE MODE,** no other application can update, delete or insert data in the locked table. If you need a snapshot of a table that is frequently changed by concurrent applications, you can use this statement to lock the table for changes without using the repeatable read isolation level for your application.

EXCLUSIVE MODE is more restrictive than **SHARE MODE**. It prevents concurrent applications from accessing the table for read, update, delete and insert. If you want to update a large part of the table you can use the **LOCK TABLE** statement in **EXCLUSIVE MODE** rather than locking each row.

Summary

In this chapter, we have discussed some of the possible concurrency problems that can occur in a multi-user database environment. To protect the data as it is being modified, rules are established and the changes are grouped together in transactions.

The transactions are either made permanent using the **COMMIT** statement, or they are removed using the **ROLLBACK** statement. Each transaction defines an atomic set of SQL statements. The rules of concurrent data access are determined by the isolation level. Isolation levels are set for static and dynamic SQL application modules.

DB2 will implement the isolation level semantics of data access by implicitly acquiring locks on behalf of the applications. Applications can decide to lock a resource for **EXCLUSIVE** or **SHARE** mode. But the only resource which can be directly locked using an SQL statement is a **table**. All row level locks are acquired, according to the isolation level, by DB2.

If a requested lock is more restrictive and another application already has the resource locked, a wait on the release of the lock will occur. The amount of time an application will wait is determined by a database configuration parameter, known as locktimeout. The default amount of lock wait time is indefinite.

If multiple applications require access to data which is held by other applications then a deadlock scenario can occur. DB2 will detect the occurrence of any deadlocks and force one of the transactions to **ROLLBACK**. Every lock requested requires memory on the DB2 server. The amount of lock storage is configurable using the **LOCKLIST** and **MAXLOCKS** parameters.

Questions

1. The application is bound using read stability. You notice that there are a large number of locks being held at any given time, what should you do to decrease the number of locks?

    O   A. Increase the size of the log files.

    O   B. Increase the size of the locklist parameter.

    O   C. Use the BIND option to change the isolation level to cursor stability (CS)

    O   D. Use the BIND option to change the isolation level to repeatable read (RR)

2. Which isolation level would lock the most data?

    O   A. uncommitted read

    O   B. read stability

    O   C. cursor stability

    O   D. repeatable read

Answers

1. (D)
    The repeatable read isolation level must guarantee that none of the rows in a table will change within a single transaction. Row locks will not be obtained, therefore a small number of table locks would be obtained instead. The cursor stability isolation level will acquire more locks, at the row level.
2. (D)
    The repeatable read isolation level would lock the most amount of data records to maintain data consistency.

Exercises

> Note:
> To refresh the **DB2CERT** database issue the following commands
> (from the directory \exercise\chapter5\parta:
>   db2 -tvf create.ddl
>   db2 -tvf data.imp
>   db2 -tvf insert.dml

Part A — Database Concurrency

1. Open two separate CLP window sessions, in this exercise we will refer to these
   sessions as window A and window B. Ensure that there are no active database
   users, to do this issue **db2 FORCE APPLICATIONS ALL**

2. In each of these windows, set the **DB2OPTIONS** environment variable to the fol-
   lowing value: **DB2OPTIONS**=+c
   OS/2 :**SET DB2OPTIONS**=+c
   Windows:**SET DB2OPTIONS**=+c
   AIX:**export DB2OPTIONS**=+c

3. The CLP options set in step 2 are used to **turn off the autocommit** feature.
   By default, every SQL statement issued from the CLP is committed. To examine
   DB2 locking behavior we want to control the commit scope.

4. In window A enter: **db2 CONNECT TO db2cert IN EXCLUSIVE MODE**
   In window B enter: **db2 CONNECT TO db2cert IN EXCLUSIVE MODE**

   What did you notice?
   Window A was successful (SQLCODE was 0) and window B was
   unsuccessful (SQLCODE was SQL1035N). The database is the largest object
   which can be controlled or locked. This type of locking behavior is
   usually only used for administration purposes (e.g., **BACKUP database** (off-
   line)).

5. Issue: **db2 TERMINATE** in each of the CLP windows.

6. In window A enter: **db2 CONNECT TO db2cert IN SHARE MODE**
   In window B enter: **db2 CONNECT TO db2cert IN EXCLUSIVE MODE**

Note that window B received the same error as in step 4. It is impossible for an application to obtain exclusive access to the database if others are using the database (even in share mode).

7. Issue: **db2 TERMINATE** in each of the CLP windows.

Part B — Table Concurrency and Deadlocks

1. Open two CLP window sessions with the same **DB2OPTIONS** setting as in part A.

2. In window A enter: **db2 LOCK TABLE db2.test IN EXCLUSIVE MODE**
    In window B enter: **db2 LOCK TABLE db2.test IN EXCLUSIVE MODE**

    What happened? Window B should be waiting for the table X lock acquired by window A to be released. Now go to window A and type:
    db2 COMMIT
    The transaction in window A has completed and released its lock therefore allowing the transaction in window B to acquire the lock. This is know as lock wait behavior and the lock will wait indefinitely unless the **LOCKTIMEOUT** parameter in the database configuration is set. Issue the
    ROLLBACK command in window B to release the X lock on the *db2.test* table.

3. There are no exclusive table locks at this point.
    In window A enter: **db2 LOCK TABLE db2.test IN SHARE MODE**
    In window B enter: **db2 LOCK TABLE db2.test IN SHARE MODE**

    In this case the table share locks (S) are compatible and both locks were successfully acquired.

4. In window A enter :
    db2 INSERT INTO db2.test
    **   VALUES ('503','DB2 PE','P',NULL,65,0,0)**
    In window B enter :
    db2 INSERT INTO db2.test
    **   VALUES ('504','DB2ADM2','P',NULL,68,0,0)**

    What happened? The first **INSERT** would not complete because an IX lock could not be obtained for the *db2.test* table because it is not compatible with the S lock on the *db2.test* table held by window B.
    The second **INSERT** was blocked on the first **INSERT** as they both had table level S locks and they needed table IX locks (X lock on the new row) to add the data.

    Since the two transactions were dependent on each other a **deadlock** scenario occurred. The DB2 deadlock detector noticed the lock conflict and attempted to resolve the deadlock by performing a rollback on the second transaction. Note the return code for the rolled back transaction it should be: SQLCODE -911 with a reason code of 2.

The **ROLLBACK** of the window B released the S lock on the *db2.test* table. This allowed the first **INSERT** to complete successfully.

Part C — Lock Timeout

1. Issue **db2 TERMINATE** in both windows. In both windows enter : **db2 CONNECT TO db2cert**.

2. In window A enter :
   ```
   db2 UPDATE db2.test SET cut_score = 80
              WHERE CHAR(number) = '500'
   ```
   In window B enter :
   ```
   db2 SELECT * FROM db2.test
   ```

   What happened? The **SELECT** statement waits until the **UPDATE** has been completed as the **UPDATE** is holding X locks on some data rows that need to be read from window B. Now, type **COMMIT** in window A. The **SELECT** statement in window B should contain the new cut_score for exam 500. This provides data READ integrity as the uncommitted data (cut_score of 80) was not available to the transaction in window B until window A completed the transaction. Issue **COMMIT** in window B.

3. Issue: **db2 GET DATABASE CONFIGURATION FOR db2cert**
   Note the value of the **DLCHKTIME** parameter, it is likely set to 10,000 ms. This is the amount of time before a deadlock condition is checked by DB2. You can modify this parameter to perform deadlock checking more or less often.
   Also note the value of the **LOCKTIMEOUT** parameter, it is likely set to -1. This parameter is used to determine how long a straight lock scenario will remain until one of the transactions will be forced to release the resource. A value of -1 represents an infinite amount of time. Let's update the lock timeout parameter.
   Enter: **db2 UPDATE DB CONFIG FOR db2cert USING LOCKTIMEOUT 20**
   This parameter is in units of seconds and not milliseconds as the deadlock detector was.

4. In both CLP windows, perform a terminate and a connect.
   In window A enter: **db2 UPDATE db2.test SET cut_score = 70**
   In window B enter: **db2 UPDATE db2.test SET cut_score = 80**

   What happened? Window B is waiting for window A to release its locks. The

condition is a straight locking scenario and **not** a deadlock condition. Window B will wait for 20 seconds and then DB2 will initiate a **ROLLBACK** of the transaction in Window B. Note the return code,
SQLCODE was -911 and the reason code was 68.

Part D — Row Level Locking

1. Establish a new connection in both CLP windows.

2. In window A enter:
    ```
    db2 UPDATE db2.test SET cut_score = 90
            WHERE CHAR(number) ='500'
    ```
    In window B enter:
    ```
    db2 UPDATE MONITOR SWITCHES USING LOCK ON
    db2 "GET SNAPSHOT FOR LOCKS ON db2cert" > t.out
    ```

    View the file *t.out*. Note that there is a table lock of type intent exclusive (IX) on the *db2.test* table and there is a row lock of type exclusive (X) on a single row of the table. This demonstrates row level locking used by DB2 to maintain a high degree of concurrency.

Part E - Isolation Levels and Cursors

1. From the \exercise\chapter5\parte subdirectory, issue the command:
    ```
    db2 -tvf cursor.ddl
    ```

    Note the definition of the cursor. The cursor is called *cur1* and it is defined for as a **SELECT** statement based on all of the tests taken by candidate with the id '333333333'.

2. Issue: **db2 OPEN cur1**
    Issue: **db2 -a FETCH cur1**

    Note the first qualifying row was returned. Issue the **FETCH** command 3 more times. These are all of the rows defined for the result set. The -a options shows the contents of the SQLCA during each **FETCH**. Note that the SQLCODE is +100 on the last fetch.

3. From this CLP window type: **db2 CLOSE CURSOR cur1**
    Issue the command: **db2 TERMINATE**
    Issue the command: **db2 CHANGE ISOLATION TO RR**

4. Connect to the database and issue the commands:
   db2 -tvf cursor.ddl
   db2 OPEN cur1
   db2 -a FETCH cur1 (repeat until end of result table)

5. In different CLP window issue the command:
   db2 CONNECT TO db2cert
   db2 UPDATE MONITOR SWITCHES USING LOCK ON
   db2 GET SNAPSHOT FOR LOCKS ON db2cert

   Note the locks obtained on the *db2.test_taken* table. For the Repeatable Read (RR) isolation level a Share (S) lock was obtained for the table.

6. Repeat steps 3-5 using the DB2 isolation levels.
   Cursor Stability (**CS**) will obtain an IS lock for the table.
   Read Stability (**RS**) will obtain an IS lock for the table and 3 S locks for the rows which qualified. (phantom rows)
   Uncommitted Read (**UR**) will obtain an IN (intent none) lock on the table. This type of lock is compatible with almost all other locks.

Data Placement

Being able to store and retrieve large amounts of data is the main purpose of any relational database system. The physical placement of the data can directly affect the query performance. It is the responsibility of the database administrator to understand the concepts of data placement and to create an appropriate physical database design.

DB2 Version 2 has very flexible data placement options based on table spaces. A DB2 database consists of three or more table spaces and each table space can be created, modified and recovered independently of each other. The table space concept provides more flexible use of physical devices on the server workstation.

Tables are created within the table spaces according to the physical database design. The table data can be entirely contained in a single table space or multiple table spaces. Tables can be created in pre-allocated storage (within a table space) or the storage can be allocated only when it is required when the data is populated. We will discuss the following concepts:

- Container
- Table Space
- Extent

We will discuss the relationship between these concepts and other database objects, including tables and indexes. The creation and administration of tables and table spaces will be shown, using the Command Line Processor (CLP) and the Database Director.

Containers

A **container** is a generic term used to describe the allocation of physical space.

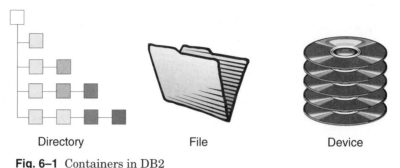

Directory   File   Device

Fig. 6–1 Containers in DB2

Fig. 6–1 shows that a container can be any of the following:

- File
- Directory
- Device

The type of container depends on the type of table space and the platform. For example, in AIX, a device container is a logical volume.

Table Spaces

One of the first tasks in setting up a relational database is mapping the logical database design to physical storage on your system. The database object used to specify the physical location of data is known as the **table space**. The table space is the layer between the database and the actual data stored in tables. Fig. 6–2 shows the relationship between tables, table spaces and databases found in one DB2 instance on a server. The instance is created, and a database called *Database1* is created within the instance. Table spaces are created, and tables are created in the database, as shown. A table space can contain more than one table. For example, table space 3 in Database 1, has three tables created in it. There are two SQL statements that will create table spaces:

```
CREATE DATABASE
CREATE TABLESPACE
```

Table spaces exist in DB2 to provide you with a logical layer between your data and the storage devices. All DB2 tables reside in a table space. This means you will be able to control where table data is physically stored. You can use different kinds of table spaces to store different kinds of data. This gives you the ability to create a more detailed physical database design to fit your particular environment. For example, you can choose slower disks to store less frequently accessed data. You can also specify a table space for the **system catalog tables**, **user tables** and **temporary tables**.

Backup and recovery can be performed at the table space level. This will give you more granularity and control since you can back up or restore each table space individually.

Table Spaces and Containers

There is a one-to-many relationship between a table space and containers. Multiple containers can be defined for a table space. However, a container can only be assigned to one table space.

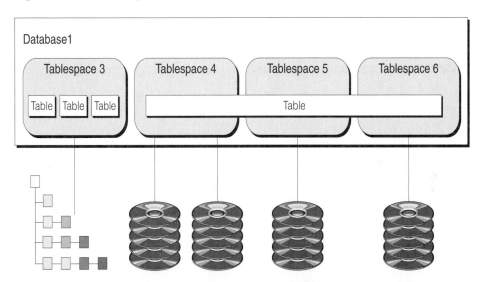

Fig. 6–2 Table Space and Container, One-to-Many Relationship

In Fig. 6–2 tablespace 3 has only one container assigned to it, a directory. tablespace 4 has two containers assigned to it. The containers for tablespace 4, tablespace 5 and tablespace 6 are shown as raw devices. A mixture of containers is possible within a database. You can also mix container types within a table space, though it is not recommended for performance reasons. In Fig. 6–2, a single table spans tablespace 4, tablespace 5 and tablespace 6.

✍ Spanning table data across multiple table spaces can only be performed when DMS table spaces are used.

Extents

An **extent** is an allocation of space within a container of a table space. Database objects are stored in pages within DB2 (except for LOBs). These pages are grouped into allocation units called extents. The extent size is defined at the table space level. Once the extent size is established for the table space, it **cannot** be altered.

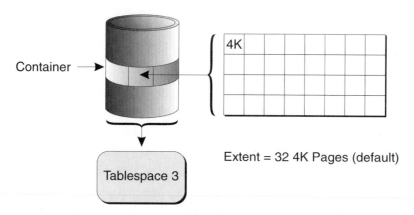

Extent = 32 4K Pages (default)

Fig. 6–3 Extent, Container and Table Space in DB2

Fig. 6–3 shows the relationship between an extent, a container and a table space. The table space is initialized when it is created. As part of this initialization the **extent size** or allocation size is set for the table space. The DB2 physical page size is 4,096 bytes (4K) and the default extent size for table spaces is 32 pages (128 KB).

  Be aware that extents are allocated for DB2 to use for space management purposes and not just for the user table data.

Table Space Types

DB2 supports two kinds of table spaces:

- System Managed Storage (SMS) Table Space
- Database Managed Storage (DMS) Table Space

Both types of table spaces can exist in a single database. SMS table spaces are called **system managed** because DB2 uses the file system mechanism provided by the operating system to manage the location of the database objects.

   For OS/2, the file system type is the High Performance File System (HPFS) or File Allocation Table (FAT).

For Windows NT, the file system type is High Performance File System (HPFS), NT File System (NTFS), or File Allocation Table (FAT).

 For AIX, the file system is the Journaled File System (JFS).

AIX Considerations - Device Usage

In AIX, you can want to create a volume group consisting of specialized disk(s) for your database. The containers will be logical volumes. Additional tasks to be performed when using logical volumes as containers in AIX can be summarized as follows:

1. If you plan to assign a set of hard drives for the exclusive use of DB2, create a volume group within these disks. By doing so, you will not share these drives with other AIX logical volumes.
2. Create as many logical volumes as containers. It is best to place containers on separate physical drives to realize true I/O parallelism. Be careful, as space assigned to the logical volume that is not assigned to the container will be wasted.
3. Assign the devices you have created to the instance owner and group. This will grant DB2 read/write access to the devices.
4. Make sure that all pages in the device are assigned to the container, because they will be unavailable for use by any other application.

System Managed Storage (SMS) Table Spaces

System Managed Storage is based on the storage model where physical storage is acquired as needed from the operating system. Containers in SMS table spaces have some of the following characteristics:

- The container in an SMS table space does not pre-allocate its storage. A small amount of space is allocated during table space creation.
- Containers cannot be dynamically added to an SMS table space after the table space is created.
- The total number of containers in an SMS table space should be specified when creating the table space.
- SMS containers are represented by **directories** in the operating system.

 A table space container layout can be redefined during a **RESTORE** of the table space. This is known as **redirected restore**.

Default Table Spaces

When creating a database, three table spaces will **always** be created. You can choose the characteristics, such as size or type of these three table spaces. If you do not explicitly specify table space characteristics at database creation, default values will be used.

Table spaces contain three types of objects, include:

- System catalogs
- Temporary space
- User data

When a database is initially created, a set of three table spaces will be defined. If you do not specify any table space parameters with the **CREATE DATABASE** command, DB2 will create these table spaces as SMS table spaces. The extent size for these table spaces will be set to the default. Here is an example of the **CREATE DATABASE** command:

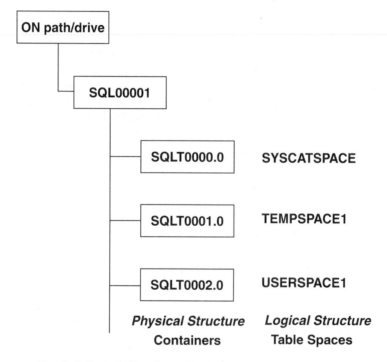

Fig. 6–4 Default Database Configuration

Fig. 6–4 shows the three default SMS table spaces that are created if default values are selected when creating a database. Regardless of platform, the first database will be placed in the SQL00001 directory. The SQL00001 directory consists of three containers assigned to the three default SMS table spaces.

```
CREATE DATABASE yourdb
```

The containers for these table spaces are the following directories.

1. **SQLT0000.0** is the container that holds the system catalogs. The system catalog table space contains all the system catalog tables for the database and cannot be dropped or changed after it is created. This table space is called *SYSCATSPACE*.
2. **SQLT0001.0** is the container that holds temporary tables that are created and removed during normal query processing. This table space is called *TEMPSPACE1*.
3. **SQLT0002.0** is the container that will hold user created tables. This table space is called *USERSPACE1*.

Characteristics of the Default Table Spaces

The table space that holds the system catalogs (*SYSCATSPACE*) cannot be dropped or changed after the database is created. There is only one table space for the system catalogs. The table spaces that hold temporary data or user data can be changed after creating the database or other table spaces. There can be multiple table spaces for temporary data or user data depending on your physical database implementation.

✍   There must be at least one temporary table space for use by the database at all times.

USERSPACE1 can be dropped after creating the database, *SYSCATSPACE* cannot be changed or altered after creating the database. However, you can change the characteristics of *SYSCATSPACE* **during** the creation of the database.

You can add other table spaces for user data or temporary data after the database is created. However, only one temporary table space will be used at any one time. In most situations, you will only create one temporary table space.

✍   It is very likely that you will create multiple user table spaces, especially if you have multiple physical drives.

When to Use SMS Table Spaces

There are two possible advantages of using SMS table spaces for user data:

1. The total amount of disk on your system is limited, and the size of your database is unknown. Storage is not pre-allocated for SMS table spaces; it is obtained from the operating system when it is needed (during **INSERT** or **UPDATE** of data records). When a table space is dropped the physical space used by the table space is immediately available for other resources.
2. SMS table spaces are easier to administer than DMS table spaces. You do not have to pre-allocate space, so there is no need to create containers before using each table space.

Database Managed Storage (DMS) Table Spaces

Database Managed Storage (DMS) table spaces are assigned **pre-allocated** storage. This storage can be a device or a file. DB2 is responsible for the management of this space.

   Do not store any data on physical devices that you have defined as DB2 (DMS) containers.

The storage is allocated to the container when it is created. When working with containers and DMS table spaces, the following apply:

- If the container is a file, it is created when the DMS table space is created and dropped when the DMS table space is dropped.
- Storage is pre-allocated to a container when the container is created for a DMS table space.
- Containers can be dynamically added to a DMS table space using the **ALTER TABLESPACE** statement.

   AIX Note — If the container is a logical volume in AIX, the container must exist before creating the table space. After dropping the DMS table space, the logical volume still exists and must be removed.

One of the main differences and advantages of using DMS table spaces over SMS table spaces is the ability to span data for a single table across multiple table spaces. When creating a table, you can decide to place certain objects of the table in different table spaces. DMS table spaces allow you to store large objects (LF and LOBs) and indexes in different table spaces. A table would then be split across three different table spaces.

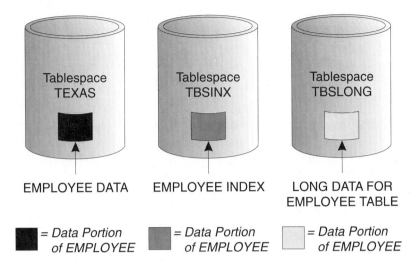

Fig. 6–5 Table Placement in DMS Table Spaces

Fig. 6–5 shows an example of a table called *employee*. It is distributed across three DMS table spaces. The *employee* table contains information such as resumes and photographs. These are stored as **CLOB** and **BLOB** data types. This information is not often updated or accessed, therefore this portion of the table will be placed in a separate table space, *tbslong*, that contains only long field or LOB types of data. The *employee* table also has an index defined in it called *empno*. Most of the table access is done using this index. The index portion of the table has been placed in a DMS table space, *tbsinx*. The *tbsinx* table space was defined using containers on our fastest disk device. The remaining portion of the *employee* table is placed in the *texas* table space. While you can separate long field and LOB data and indexes from regular table data, regular data from a single table cannot be split across different table spaces.

When to Use DMS Table Spaces

The DMS storage model has important benefits when compared to the SMS storage model. The following is a list of possible advantages:

1. You have more control over the placement of database objects according to their type. Tables can be split across multiple DMS table spaces, allowing the separation of table data and its indexes.
2. You have more flexibility over administrative tasks such as backup and restore operations. You can control placement of less-frequently accessed items like BLOBs that can store images on separate table spaces. These BLOBs, can contain data that is neither accessed nor frequently updated.

3. There can be performance benefits in using DMS table spaces because DB2 has more knowledge of the placement of the data. If using devices for DMS table spaces, you can avoid the overhead of using the operating system's file system.

4. DMS table spaces provide easy scalability because you can dynamically add containers to the table space. Rebalancing of the data is done automatically by DB2 when a new container is added.

5. If you know the maximum size of your table space, consider using DMS table spaces. DMS pre-allocates space as database objects are inserted. The database does not have to compete with other applications for disk storage.

Consider the criteria in Table 6–1 to help you determine whether your user table spaces should be SMS or DMS.

Table 6–1   Characteristics of SMS and DMS User Table Spaces

Characteristics	SMS	DMS
Can Dynamically Increase Number of Containers in Table Spaces	No	Yes
Can Store Index Data in Separate Table Spaces	No	Yes
Can Store Long Data in Separate Table Space	No	Yes
One Table Can Span Several Table Spaces	No	Yes
Space Allocated Only When Needed	Yes	No
Table Space Can Be Directed to Different Types of Disk	Yes	Yes
Extent Size Can Be Changed after Creation	No	No

Planning a Table Space Environment

When the logical design of your database is completed, you have to implement the design. This design will depend on the resources, mainly disk space or disk drives you have available for use by the database. The objective of planning your user table space environment is to determine the type of table space and the placement of the user tables in the table spaces.

To efficiently plan your environment, you will need to gather information regarding the size of your tables and indexes. The list of tasks that you will need to accomplish are the following:

1. Determine the logical design of database.
2. Map the database design to the layout of table spaces.
3. Create the database.
4. Size the tables, any indexes and table spaces.
5. Determine the characteristics of the containers in the table spaces.

6. Prepare the physical environment. This may require creating devices.

7. Create the table spaces.

8. Create the tables and indexes within the table space.

Logical Design of Table Spaces

There are several approaches when mapping your database design to your table space layout. This involves deciding how to group tables into table spaces.

- Group tables relative to their access.
  Tables can be grouped together based on their access. For example, tables that are frequently joined could be placed in the same table space using multiple containers to take advantage of parallel I/O.
- Group related tables into table spaces.
  Tables that share relational dependencies through referential constraints or triggers can be grouped together. A backup and restore can be performed at the table space level, reducing the time needed to restore the entire database. Keep referentially related tables together in the same table space.
- Create one table space for each table.
  This policy allows you to make individual backups of each table, as backups can only be performed at either the table space or the database level. You can recover the space allocated to the container after dropping the table space. Since many database may involve a large number of tables, the management of a large number of table spaces can be difficult and is not recommended.

Once you have grouped tables into table spaces, you can wish to further categorize each table space by data type: one table space for index data, one for LOB and **LONG VARCHAR** data, and separate table spaces for regular table data. Thus, if you are going to define indexes or use LOBs and **LONG VARCHAR** data, you will have to create more table spaces than you might otherwise expect.

We will use the *db2cert* database as an example of grouping tables into table spaces. The table spaces were grouped as shown in Fig. 6–6. *SYSCATSPACE* and *TEMPSPACE1* will be SMS table spaces. Regular data is stored in the table space called *ts01*. The BLOBS for the *db2.candidate* table will be placed in a separate table space, *lobs01*, because they are not frequently updated or accessed. The table that has the most activity, *test_taken*, will be placed in a separate table space, *ts03*. The other remaining tables, *test* and *test_center*, have relatively little activity and will be placed in the same table space, *ts02*.

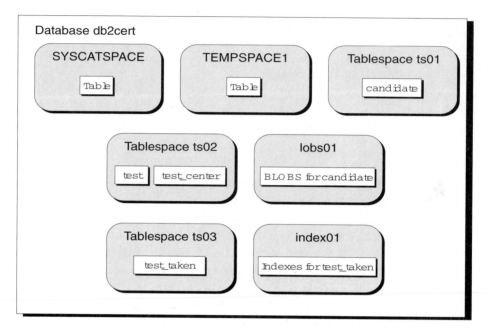

Fig. 6–6 Example Database and Table Space Environment

There are four tables in the database:

- db2.candidate
  This table holds information about test candidates such as name, identification number, address and photograph. The regular data from this table will be placed in table space *ts01* and BLOBs in *lobs01*.
- db2.test
  This table contains information about the individual tests, such as name of test, the cut score and the length of time for the test. This table will be created in the *ts02* table space.
- db2.test_center
  This table describes the various test centers where a candidate can take the DB2 certification tests. This will also be placed in table space *ts02*.
- db2.test_taken
  This table has the most activity. It keeps track of which candidate has taken one of the certification exams at any center. It will be placed in table space *ts03* with indexes in a separate table space, *index01*.

Creating the Database

The **CREATE DATABASE** command lets you create table spaces at the same time as creating the database. The syntax of the **CREATE DATABASE** command is shown in Fig. 6–7.

```
    CREATE DATABASE database-name [ON path/drive]
    [ALIAS database-alias]
    [USING CODESET codeset TERRITORY territory]
    [COLLATE USING {SYSTEM | IDENTITY}]
    [NUMSEGS numsegs] [DFT_EXTENT_SZ dft_extentsize]
    [CATALOG TABLESPACE tblespace-defn]
    [USER TABLESPACE tblspace-defn]
    [TEMPORARY TABLESPACE tblspace-defn]
    [WITH "Comment-string"]

    tblspace-defn:
    MANAGED BY {SYSTEM USING {'string'
        [{,'string'}...]) |
    DATABASE USING {{FILE | DEVICE} 'string'
        number-of-pages
    [{,{FILE|DEVICE} 'string'
        number-of-pages}...])}
    [EXTENTSIZE number-of-pages]
    [PREFETCHSIZE number-of-pages]
    [OVERHEAD number-of-milliseconds]
    [TRANSFERRATE number-of-milliseconds]
```

Fig. 6–7 Create Database Syntax

The **CREATE DATABASE** command initializes a new database with an optional user-defined collating sequence (through the API only), creates three initial table spaces, system tables and allocates the primary recovery log files. A description of the parameters follows:

- database-name
  This is a unique name that will be assigned to the new database. It is 1–8 characters long. It must begin with an alphabetic character, @, # or $. It can contain a–z, A–Z, 0–9, @, # or $.

- **ON** path/drive
  By default, the **DFTDBPATH** environment variable is used to determine the location of the initial database files if a path or drive is **not** specified.

- **ALIAS** database-alias
  An alias for the database. It defaults to the database name.

- **USING CODESET**
  This specifies the code set that will be used for data entered into this database.

- **TERRITORY**
  Specifies the territory to be used for data entered into the database.

- **COLLATE USING**

  Identifies the type of collating sequence to be used for the database. **SYSTEM** indicates that the collating sequence is based on the current territory. **IDENTITY** indicates that the collating sequence is the identity sequence, where strings are compared byte by byte.

- **NUMSEGS**

  Specifies the number of segment directories that will be created for default SMS table spaces. (This parameter is usually **not** used.)

- **DFT_EXTENT_SZ**

  Specifies the default extent size of table spaces in the database.

- **CATALOG TABLESPACE**

  Specifies the table space used for the system catalog tables.

- **USER TABLESPACE**

  Specifies the table space used for all user created tables.

- **TEMPORARY TABLESPACE**

  Specifies the table space used for temporary data, this is used by DB2.

- `tblspace-`**defn**

  Specifies the definition of the table space which will be used to hold the catalog tables (*SYSCATSPACE*), initial user temporary table space (*TEMPSPACE1*) and initial user table space (*USERSPACE1*).

- "comment-string"

  This is a 30 character comment describing the database.

DB2 uses the **CODSET** and **TERRITORY** that are defined in the operating system at the time the database is created as the default codeset and territory. This can be overridden with the **TERRITORY** and **COLLATE USING** parameters.

The **COLLATE USING** parameter can define that either the operating system collating sequence (usually ASCII) or the identity collating sequence (a byte-for-byte string compare). If you want a special collating sequence, the database must be created using an API. The application program can indicate weights for each character in order to supply a user-defined collating sequence. Include files are provided for easy definition of commonly desired collating sequences. The collating sequence will not only affect sorts but also values returned from inequality (greater than or less than, for example) predicate evaluation.

Alternatively, you can use the **CREATE TABLESPACE** statement to create table spaces after the database has been created. For our database, we will use the defaults for creating a database, with one exception. We will specify a different default extent size for the database. The system catalogs and temporary tables will be placed in separate SMS table spaces as subdirectories under the database directory.

If the system catalogs are created in SMS table spaces, they will initially use approximately 1.6 MB of space. If they are created within a DMS table space with the default extent size of 32, over 20 MB of space will initially be allocated. Therefore, it is recommended to use SMS table spaces for the system catalogs.

Let's use the following syntax to create the *db2cert* database:

```
CREATE DATABASE db2cert DFT_EXTENT_SZ 8
```

One of the **CREATE DATABASE** parameters is **DFT_EXTENT_SZ**. It determines how many pages are written to a container before writing to another container. This is the extent size used for table spaces, both Database Managed (DMS) and System Managed (SMS).

The default size for **DFT_EXTENT_SZ** is 32 4K pages. If you do not alter this value, all of your table spaces within the database will have 128 KB extents allocated in the table space containers. The range of values for **DFT_EXTENT_SZ** is between 2 and 256 4KB pages.

You may over ride the extentsize for each table spaces with the **CREATE TABLESPACE** statement is used with a different value for the **EXTENTSIZE**. Care should be taken for determining the correct value for the size of the extents. The extent size can have an impact on space utilization and performance. The data is written, also known as striped, across all containers defined for the table space. This striping is performed automatically by DB2.

Creating Table Spaces

The **CREATE TABLESPACE** statement will create a new table space within the database to which you are connected. It assigns containers to the table space and makes entries into the system catalogs. To execute the **CREATE TABLESPACE** statement you must have SYSADM or SYSCTRL authority and connected to the database. The **CREATE TABLESPACE** statement is shown in Fig. 6–8.

The descriptions of the **CREATE TABLESPACE** options are as follows:

- **REGULAR**
  This is the default value. Regular table spaces store all data except for temporary data.

- **LONG**
  Stores long or LOB table objects. Long table spaces must be DMS table spaces.

- **TEMPORARY**
  Stores temporary tables. One temporary table space is created when the

```
CREATE {REGULAR|LONG|TEMPORARY}
TABLESPACE tablespace-name
MANAGED BY {SYSTEM USING {'string'
       [{,'string'}...]) |
DATABASE USING {{FILE | DEVICE} 'string'
       number-of-pages
[{,{FILE | DEVICE} 'string'
       number-of-pages}...]}]
[EXTENTSIZE number-of-pages]
[PREFETCHSIZE number-of-pages]
[OVERHEAD number-of-milliseconds]
[TRANSFERRATE number-of-milliseconds]
```

Fig. 6–8 Create Table Space Syntax

database is created. The temporary tables are work areas used by DB2 to perform operations such as sorts or joins. A database must always have at least one temporary table space, as temporary tables can only be stored in such a table space. A database can have more than one temporary table space. Temporary objects are allocated between the temporary table spaces in a round-robin fashion.

- **MANAGED BY SYSTEM**
  Defines this table space as a SMS table space.

- **USING** ('container string')
  Identifies the directory used as the container.

- **MANAGED BY DATABASE**
  Defines this table space as a DMS table space.

- **USING (FILE |DEVICE** 'container string' number-of-pages,...)
  Identifies the containers that will belong to this table space and the size of the containers. The container size is specified in 4 KB pages.

- **EXTENTSIZE** <number-of-pages>
  Defines the size of the extent in 4 KB pages. If not specified, the extent size defined for the database will be used. The database parameter for the extent size is **DFT_EXTENT_SZ**. In our example we defined the default extent size to be 8.

- **PREFETCHSIZE** <number-of-pages>
  Specifies the number of pages that will be loaded into the buffer pool prior to their access is required in an SQL statement.

- **OVERHEAD** <number-of-milliseconds>
  This value is only used to determine the cost of I/O during query optimization. Its default value, 24.1, represents the I/O controller overhead and disk and latency time.

- **TRANSFERRATE** <number-of-milliseconds>
  This value is only used to determine the cost of I/O during query optimization. Its default value, 0.9, represents the time to read one 4 KB page from this table space into memory.

Creating Table Spaces Examples

This section gives two examples for creating table spaces, one for an SMS table space, the other for a DMS table space. We'll show the statement syntax for the AIX and the OS/2 and Windows NT environments.

```
AIX:
CREATE TABLESPACE sms01 MANAGED BY SYSTEM USING
('/database/firstcontain',
'/database/secondcontain', '/thirdcontain')

OS/2
-or-
Windows NT:
CREATE TABLESPACE sms01 MANAGED BY SYSTEM USING
('E:\db\firstcnt', 'E:\db\sndcnt', 'F:\thirdcnt')
```

Fig. 6–9 Creating an SMS Table Space

Fig. 6–9 is an example of creating an SMS table space in AIX, OS/2 and Windows NT. The phrase that indicates that this will be an SMS table space is **MANAGED BY SYSTEM**. An SMS table space can only use directories for containers. When specifying the containers in an SMS table space, you must explicitly state the directory paths in the **CREATE TABLESPACE** statement.

It is recommended to create a database, drop the USERSPACE1 table space and create the required user table spaces according to your physical database design.

Fig. 6–10 is an example of creating DMS table spaces. In AIX or Windows NT, the type of container for a DMS table space can be a file, a device or a mixture of the two types. If a device is specified, the path must be a device name.

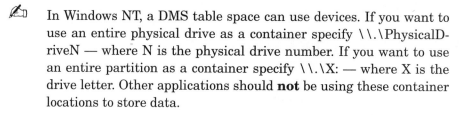   In Windows NT, a DMS table space can use devices. If you want to
use an entire physical drive as a container specify \\.\PhysicalD-
riveN — where N is the physical drive number. If you want to use
an entire partition as a container specify \\.\X: — where X is the
drive letter. Other applications should **not** be using these container
locations to store data.

    AIX note — the creator of the table space must have write access to
the character portion of the device being used.

   In Fig. 6–10, the table space *ts01* did not have a specific extent size specified. The extent size in this case will default to the value of the **DFT_EXTENT_SZ**
as specified when the database was created.

```
AIX:
CREATE TABLESPACE ts01 MANAGED BY DATABASE USING
(DEVICE '/dev/rdata1' 1024,
 DEVICE '/dev/rdata2' 1024)

CREATE LONG TABLESPACE lobs01
MANAGED BY DATABASE USING
(FILE '/db/dmslong.tbs' 500) EXTENTSIZE 16


OS/2
-or-
Windows NT:
CREATE TABLESPACE ts01 MANAGED BY DATABASE USING
(FILE 'E:\db\data1.tbs' 1024,
 FILE 'E:\db\data2.tbs'1024)

CREATE LONG TABLESPACE lobs01
MANAGED BY DATEBASE USING
(FILE 'D:\db\dmslong.tbs' 500) EXTENTSIZE 16
```

Fig. 6–10 Creating DMS Table Spaces

    In OS/2, a DMS table space can only use files as containers.

   Tablespace *lobs01* will contain the LOB and CLOB portion of the db2.*candidate* table. When a DMS table space will only contain large object data you must
specify the **LONG** parameter when the table space is created. Notice that we have
created table space *lobs01* with a different extent size.

One of the advantages gained by splitting your data across different DMS table spaces is that table data and index data can be accessed in parallel, thus improving performance. The next section discusses some other factors that can affect performance.

Performance Considerations

This section examines some parameters defined at the table space level that can affect performance.

Buffer Pool Size

The buffer pool size determines the number of 4 KB pages allocated on the database server to serve as a database cache. This memory is allocated when the first application connects to the database and is released when the last application disconnects. This pool is used as a data cache for database access.

If the buffer pool is large enough, disk I/O activity will be reduced. As a rule of thumb, you can start with 50% of total amount of physical memory available. If the machine is a dedicated database server, you may want to assign a large amount of machine memory to the buffer pool.

✍ The **buffer pool** is the most important parameter that will affect database performance and is defined at the database level. Avoid over allocating the buffer pool, as the operating system can start paging or swapping memory.

Extent Size

The extent size can be specified when a database is created or it can be specified when each of the table spaces are created. By default, the extent size is 128 KB (32*4 KB). You can change the default value at the database level using the **UPDATE DATABASE CONFIGURATION** command. Once the extent size has been set for the table space, it cannot be changed.

If you want to specify a different value for a table space you are about to create, you need to use the **EXTENTSIZE** option of the **CREATE TABLESPACE** statement. The range of **EXTENTSIZE** is from 2 to 256 4 KB pages.

A smaller extent size can be used if you would like the data striped in small extents across a number of containers. The extent size has a direct impact on the amount of prefetching that will take place. All prefetching of data is performed in extents. Therefore if you would like prefetching (asynchronous reads) to occur in larger amounts of data, specify a larger extent size.

A smaller extent size in an SMS table space may use less disk space. Because a disk space used for a table will always increase the size of an extent regardless of the amount of data being inserted into the database.

An extent size of 8 or 16 4 KB pages is usually sufficient for table spaces used for regular data. A larger extent size is recommended for long table spaces. This will help to avoid the overhead derived from allocating a large number of extents each time a new entry is made.

NUM_IOSERVERS

This database configuration parameter specifies the number of processes that will be used to perform asynchronous reads of data from disk into the buffer pool. This is known as I/O prefetching. If prefetching is being used, the value of this parameter should be set to be at least the number of physical disk drives in your physical database design. There is very little overhead if extra I/O servers are allocated.

I/O Prefetch

Query processing is divided into two activities: CPU processing and I/O. The CPU processing is always the 'cheaper' of the two. Therefore, the goal is to eliminate all I/O wait time so that the CPU can be kept as busy as possible. A prefetch request can help eliminate the I/O wait time by anticipating the required data before the CPU asks for it.

Effective prefetching keeps the CPU busy and avoids delays in query processing. The amount of prefetching is expressed by the table space parameter, **PREFETCHSIZE.** This parameter determines the amount of data that is "read-ahead".

✍ In AIX, prefetching will create separate I/O processes. In OS/2 and Windows NT, prefetching is accomplished using threads.

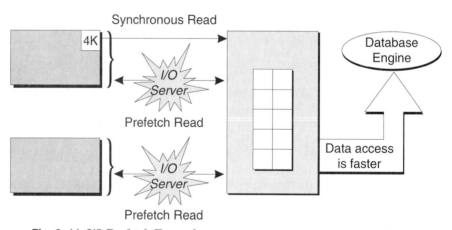

Fig. 6–11 I/O Prefetch Example

Fig. 6–11 shows two types of reads: **synchronous** and **prefetch** reads. A prefetch read is one in which the entire extent is read in a single read operation. A synchronous read only reads a single page (4 KB) at a time from disk.

The **PREFETCHSIZE** table space parameter should be set to a multiple of the **EXTENTSIZE**. The size is determined when the table space is created. If no value is specified when the table space is created, **PREFETCHSIZE** will be set to the default value found in the database parameter **DFTPREFETCH_SZ**. The default size is 128 KB (32* 4 KB).

A table space should be created using multiple container definitions and the containers should reside on different physical disks. The **PREFETCHSIZE** should then be set to the product of the **EXTENTSIZE** and the **number of containers**.

There are two types of prefetch:

- Sequential prefetch is the mechanism which reads consecutive **data** pages into buffer pool before the pages are needed by the application.
- List prefetch (or list sequential prefetch) is a way to access data pages efficiently. This type of prefetching occurs by obtaining a list of data pages required from the index and sorting the index pages so the data pages are in the buffer pool when they are required.

There are situations when it is not obvious whether sequential prefetch will improve performance. DB2 will monitor database access and if sequential page access is occurring, DB2 will activate prefetch activity. Prefetching here is activated and deactivated by DB2 as necessary. This is known as sequential detection. To activate it, set the **SEQDETECT** database parameter to **YES**.

✐ The database configuration parameter **NUM_IOSERVERS** defines the number of asynchronous threads (Windows NT, OS/2) or processes (UNIX) that are available to handle prefetch requests.

During program execution, an SQL statement that requires a large amount of data is executed. DB2 identifies that it would be beneficial to use I/O prefetch. At **DB2START**, the database engine starts separate threads of control. These are called **I/O servers**. The number of threads/processes to be created is specified in the database configuration parameter, **NUM_IOSERVERS**. The database engine informs the I/O server of the application's anticipated data needs.

✐ For any prefetching to occur, the buffer pool also **must** be set to 1100 4KB pages or higher.

Page (I/O) Cleaners

The purpose of buffer pool page cleaners it to help ensure that there are enough available (clean) pages in the buffer pool when a transaction requires space. In this way, the transaction will not have to wait until previously accessed pages are written (flushed) out to disk.

DB2 manipulates data in the buffer pool for performance reasons. The modified data is guaranteed because a log file has been written to the transaction log files. If a page has been modified in the buffer pool eventually it needs to be reflected in the database files on disk. This permanent change of the data will occur when the modified (dirty) pages are written (flushed) to disk, or when a log file is processed during recovery. DB2 may use asynchronous page cleaners to write the dirty pages out to disk. This allows the application agent to process other database requests while the data is written.

Page cleaner activation can be modified using the **MAXCHNGPGS** parameter. They are activated when the number of written pages in the buffer pool is greater than **MAXCHNGPGS** (database configuration parameter). This value acts like a trigger to activate the page cleaners.

The number of asynchronous page cleaners for a database is specified by the database configuration parameter **NUM_IOCLEANERS**. In a query-only database, this parameter should be set to 0, as pages are not modified and therefore are not written to disk. In a transaction environment, the parameter should be set between 1 and the number of physical disk drives used by the database.

The **CHNGPS_THRESH** database configuration parameter determines when page cleaners are activated. It specifies the percentage of changed pages required before the asynchronous page cleaners are started. Page cleaners will write all modified pages to disk and will become inactive until the threshold is again exceeded. This parameter is defined at the database level, and its default value is 60%.

System Catalogs in DB2

Information regarding tables and table spaces is kept in the system catalogs. The database administrator will use DB2 commands to list, alter or create table spaces and tables. Information can also be obtained by querying the system catalogs using SQL statements. These tables also contain information about various database objects and security information about the type of access users have to these objects.

The system catalogs are know by a schema name. A schema name is a fully qualified table name in the form of "schemaname.tablename". There are three system defined schema names that are reserved within DB2:

- SYSIBM
- SYSCAT
- SYSSTAT

The SYSIBM schema refers to the base tables that comprise the system catalogs. You should not use a schema of SYSIBM for any of your user tables. In general, avoid using any schema with the SYS prefix. Over time, these SYSIBM tables have evolved from release to release of the product. They include the base catalogs, built-in types and built-in functions.

Views (SYSCAT schema) of these base tables allow an end-user to query the contents of the catalog tables using more meaningful names. DB2 creates and maintains two sets of catalog views: SYSCAT and SYSSTAT. All of the system catalog views are created when a database is created with the **CREATE DATA-BASE** command. The catalog views cannot be explicitly created or dropped. The views are within the SYSCAT schema, and **SELECT** privilege on all views is granted to PUBLIC by default. A second set of views, formed from a subset of those within the SYSCAT schema, contain statistical information used by the optimizer. Table 6–2 shows the system catalog views.

Table 6–2 Catalog Views

Catalog View	Description
SYSCAT.CHECKS	check constraints
SYSCAT.COLCHECKS	columns referenced by check constraints
SYSCAT.COLDIST	detailed column statistics
SYSCAT.COLUMNS	columns
SYSCAT.CONSTDEP	constraint dependencies
SYSCAT.DBAUTH	authorities on database
SYSCAT.EVENTS	events currently monitored
SYSCAT.EVENTMONITORS	event monitor definitions
SYSCAT.FUNCPARMS	function parameters
SYSCAT.FUNCTIONS	user-defined functions
SYSCAT.INDEXAUTH	index privileges
SYSCAT.INDEXES	indexes
SYSCAT.KEYCOLUSE	columns used in keys
SYSCAT.PACKAGEAUTH	package privileges
SYSCAT.PACKAGEDEP	package dependencies
SYSCAT.PACKAGES	packages
SYSCAT.REFERENCES	referential constraints
SYSCAT.STATEMENTS	statements in packages
SYSCAT.TABAUTH	table privileges
SYSCAT.TABCONST	table constraints
SYSCAT.TABLES	tables
SYSCAT.TABLESPACES	table spaces
SYSCAT.TRIGDEP	trigger dependencies
SYSCAT.TRIGGERS	triggers
SYSCAT.VIEWDEP	view dependencies
SYSCAT.VIEWS	views

The views within the SYSSTAT schema contain columns that can be updated. Table 6–3 shows the views in the system catalogs that are updatable.

Table 6–3 Updatable Catalog Views

Catalog View	Description
SYSSTAT.COLDIST	detailed column statistics
SYSSTAT.COLUMNS	columns
SYSSTAT.FUNCTIONS	user-defined functions
SYSSTAT.INDEXES	indexes
SYSSTAT.TABLES	tables

There are three catalog views directly related to table spaces, tables and indexes:

- SYSCAT.TABLESPACES
- SYSCAT.TABLES
- SYSCAT.INDEXES

The *SYSCAT.TABLESPACES* view contains a row for each table space. Each row maintains information about the name of the table space, the table space id, table space type, type of data this table space stores, extent size and prefetch size.

```
SELECT           TBSPACE, TBSPACETYPE, TBSPACEID,
                 DATATYPE, EXTENTSIZE
FROM             SYSCAT.TABLESPACES


TBSPACE              TBSPACE    TBSPACE    DATA      EXTENT
                     TYPE       ID         TYPE      SIZE
-------------------- ---------- ---------- --------- -------------
SYSCATSPACE          S          0          A         8
TEMPSPACE1           S          1          T         8
USERSPACE1           S          2          A         8
ts01                 D          3          A         8
lobs01               D          4          A         16
ts02                 D          5          A         8
ts03                 D          6          A         16
index01              D          7          A         8
```

Fig. 6–12 Output from SYSCAT.TABLESPACES

The output shown in Fig. 6–12 shows a total of eight table spaces. The first three are SMS table spaces, and the last four are DMS table spaces. The *TBSPACETYPE* column either contains an S for SMS or a D for DMS. The table space id is a unique number that identifies the table space in the database. Values for the *DATATYPE* column show the type of data that can be stored in this table space. "A" is for all types of permanent data and "T" is for temporary tables. Notice that there are different extent sizes for the table spaces.

The *SYSCAT.TABLES* view contains a row for each table, view or alias that is created. Related to table spaces, each row maintains information about the name of the table, the table space where the table is placed, and names of the table spaces where indexes and Long Object Data or LOBs for this table are placed.

```
SELECT              TABNAME, TBSPACEID,
                    INDEX_TBSPACE,LONG_TBSPACE
FROM                SYSCAT.TABLES
WHERE               TABSCHEMA = 'DB2'


TABNAME             TBSPACE    TBSPACE    INDEX_      LONG_
                    ID                    TBSPACE     TBSPACE
-------------       ---------  --------   ----------  -----------


CANDIDATE           3          ts01          -        LOBS01
TEST                5          ts02          -           -
TEST_CENTER         5          ts02          -           -
TEST_TAKEN          6          ts03       index01        -
```

Fig. 6–13 Output from SYSCAT.TABLES

Four tables using the DB2 schema exist in the *db2cert* database as shown in Fig. 6–13. The *candidate* table is placed in table space *ts01*. The tables *test* and *test_center* are placed in table space *ts02*. The table space *ts03* contains the *test_taken* table. The indexes for *test_taken* are placed in a separate table space, *index01*. The BLOBs for *candidate* are placed in table space *lobs01*.

Managing Table Spaces

Table space management includes the tasks of creating, deleting, modifying and monitoring table spaces and containers. DB2 provides commands and utilities to perform these tasks. The commands available to the database administrator are the following:

- **LIST TABLESPACES** — The **LIST TABLESPACES** command lists all the table spaces contained in the database. For each table space, it shows information about type, data type contained, state, extent and prefetch size.
- **LIST TABLESPACE CONTAINERS** — The **LIST TABLESPACE CONTAINERS** command lists all the containers for a specific table space. It shows information about the name, type and size (only DMS table spaces) of the containers of this table space.
- **ALTER TABLESPACE** — The **ALTER TABLESPACE** command enables the database administrator to add containers to a DMS table space. (This is not supported with SMS table spaces.) It also allows modification of the **PREFETCHSIZE, OVERHEAD** and **TRANSFERRATE** of a table space.
- **DROP TABLESPACE** — The **DROP TABLESPACE** command can be used to remove a table space and all of its tables. Database objects that are directly or indirectly dependent on that object are also deleted or marked as inoperative.

   All these tasks can be accomplished using the graphical administration utility known as the Database Director. You can even change the container definitions of table spaces during a restore operation using the Database Director. This is known as a redirected restore operation.

List Table Spaces

The syntax for the **LIST TABLESPACES** command is as follows:

```
                    LIST TABLESPACES [SHOW DETAIL]
```

The **LIST TABLESPACES** command will list all the table spaces for a database including the table space name, type, contents and extent size. If the **SHOW DETAIL** option is specified it will also list information about the size, extent size and prefetch size. The output for the **LIST TABLESPACES SHOW DETAIL** command is similar to that of Fig. 6–14.

Note that when a database is created the creation of the system catalogs will require some storage. The amount of storage depends on the extent size. Here, we have shown another way of setting the extent size for the table space in the database, especially the system catalogs.

```
Tablespace ID                    = 0
Name                             = SYSCATSPACE
Contents                         = System managed space
State                            = Any data
  Detailed explanation:          = 0x0000
    Normal

Total pages                      = 522
Useable pages                    = 522
Free pages                       = Not applicable
High water mark (pages)          = Not applicable
Page size (bytes)                = 4096
Extent size (pages)              = 2
Prefetch size (pages)            = 16
Number of containers             = 2

Tablespace ID                    = 1
Name                             = TEMPSPACE1
Contents                         = System managed space
State                            = Any data
  Detail explanation:            = 0x0000
    Normal

Total pages                      = 1
Useable pages                    = 1
Used pages                       = 1
Free pages                       = Not applicable
High water mark (pages)          = Not applicable
Page size (bytes)                = 4096
Extent size (pages)              = 32
Prefetch size (pages)            = 32
Number of containers             = 1


Tablespace ID                    = 2
Name                             = USERSPACE1
Contents                         = System managed space
State                            = Any data
...                              = 0x0000
```

Fig. 6–14 Output from the **LIST TABLESPACES SHOW DETAIL** Command

We have created the database in Fig. 6–14 with the following SQL statement:

```
CREATE DATABASE DSS
CATALOG TABLESPACE MANAGED BY SYSTEM USING
('/u/bd2/sys', /u/db2/sys2')
EXTENTSIZE 2 PREFETCHSIZE 16
```

This will create a database with three default SMS table spaces. However, the extent size for the system catalogs will be 8KB (2*4KB) with a prefetch size of 128 KB (32*4KB). In our example, the database will be small in size. Therefore setting the extent size small might be a good idea. Also, this is more of a decision support-type database. There will not be much insert, update or delete activity once the database is loaded. The prefetch size of 16 4K pages will allow us to take advantage of prefetching large extents of data. Depending on how the system catalogs are distributed on the disks, this should improve performance. The extent size for *TEMPSPACE1* will be left to the default of 32 4K pages unless otherwise specified. We would want to have a separate physical device for each container for the system catalog table space.

The state of the table space is expressed in a hexadecimal number. The number 0x0000 indicates a normal state. This hexadecimal number can be a combination of more than one state.

✍️ In Fig. 6–14 all of the table space states are set to 0x0000 or normal. This means all of the table spaces are accessible using SQL statements.

Let's examine another example. The *db2cert* database was created with the following command:

```
CREATE DATABASE db2cert DFT_EXTENT_SZ 8
```

The database was created with default table spaces, but with an extent size of 8. Table Space *ts01* is a DMS table space created with the following command:

```
CREATE TABLESPACE ts01 MANAGED BY DATABASE USING
(DEVICE '/dev/rdata1' 1024, DEVICE '/dev/rdata2' 1024)
PREFETCHSIZE 16
```

The **CREATE TABLESPACE** statement is specifying two **DEVICE** containers. The database definition is shown in Fig. 6–15.

Tablespace ID	= 0
Name	= SYSCATSPACE
Contents	= System managed space
State	= Any data
Detailed explanation:	= 0x0000
Normal	
Total pages	= 745
Useable pages	= 745
Free pages	= 745
High water mark (pages)	= Not applicable
Page size (bytes)	= Not applicable
Extent size (pages)	= 4096
Prefetch size (pages)	= 8
Number of containers	= 32
	= 1
Tablespace ID	= 1
Name	= TEMPSPACE1
Contents	= System managed space
State	= Any data
	= 0x0000
....	
Tablespace ID	= 3
Name	= TS01
Contents	= Database managed space
State	= Any data
Detailed explanation:	= 0x0000
Normal	
Total pages	= 2048
Useable pages	= 2032
Used pages	= 24
Free pages	= 2008
High water mark (pages)	= 24
Page size (bytes)	= 4096
Extent size (pages)	= 8
Prefetch size (pages)	= 32
Number of containers	= 2

Fig. 6–15 Output from the **LIST TABLESPACES SHOW DETAIL** Command

Notice in Fig. 6–15 that there is information regarding the total and useable pages for table space *ts01*. When the **CREATE TABLESPACE** command is issued for a DMS table space, the pages needed to create the container are allocated. There are two containers defined for table space *ts01*. After subtracting the page for the container tag, each container has 1,023 pages left. These pages are then divided into extents. There are 1,016 pages for each container or a total of 2,032 for the two containers. The next 24 pages are used for table space creation overhead. This leaves 2,008 pages free. Once a table is created in the table space, other pages are used.

Containers

The complete syntax for the **LIST TABLESPACE CONTAINERS** command is as follows:

```
LIST TABLESPACE CONTAINERS FOR tblspace-id [SHOW DETAIL]
```

The tablespace-id uniquely identifies a table space in the database. The tablespace-id can be obtained using the **LIST TABLESPACE** command or by querying the *SYSCAT.TABLES* table.

If the **SHOW DETAIL** option is not specified, the command will show the container id, name and type (file, disk or path) of every container used by the table space. If specified, the output includes the total number of pages and the number of usable pages if the container(s) belong to a DMS table space.

The output of the **LIST TABLESPACES CONTAINERS** command issued against a DMS table space that is using two containers is shown in Fig. 6–16.

The difference between total pages and usable pages for the containers. The container */dev/rdata1* has 8 pages unusable. Total pages reflects the number of pages that were defined for the containers. Usable pages shows the number of pages that remain for use for user data. Each of these containers are given an id number. In Fig. 6–16 there are 2 containers shown and their corresponding container ids are displayed. Remember, that containers are used by DB2 only, a database administrator cannot place table data directly into a container.

LIST TABLESPACE CONTAINERS FOR 3 SHOW DETAIL

Container ID	= 0
Name	= /dev/rdata1
Type	= Disk
Total pages	= 1024
Useable pages	= 1016
Accessible	= Yes
Container ID	= 1
Name	= /dev/rdata2
Type	= Disk
Total pages	= 1024
Useable pages	= 1016
Accessible	= Yes

Fig. 6–16 Output from **LIST TABLESPACE CONTAINERS**

Alter Table Space

You can increase the size of a table space by adding one or more containers. Once the new container is added, the data will automatically be redistributed. As soon as the commit operation is done for the transaction involving the adding of the container, the data will be rebalanced among the containers.

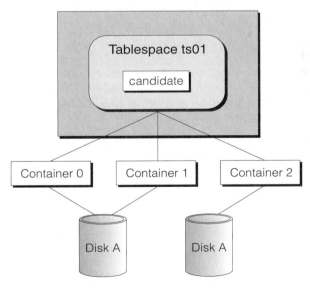

Fig. 6–17 Adding Container to Table Space ts01

Fig. 6–17 shows the table space *ts01* after a third container has been added, usually the new container would be located on a separate disk (unlike the figure indicates). Adding a container is useful when the space is exhausted within the currently defined containers.

✍️   A container can only be added to a DMS table space. Containers cannot be added to an SMS table space.

The syntax for the **ALTER TABLESPACE** statement is shown in Fig. 6–18.

```
         ALTER TABLESPACE tablespace name
          ADD {FILE | DEVICE}
          'container string' number of pages
         PREFETCHSIZE number of pages
         OVERHEAD number-of-milliseconds
         TRANSFERRATE number-of-milliseconds
```

Fig. 6–18 The **ALTER TABLESPACE** Statement

The **ADD** option specifies that a new container is to be added to a DMS table space. Notice that the extent size of a table space cannot be changed. Note also that the size of existing containers cannot be modified. When you add a container to a table space, the data placed in a table space will automatically be distributed among **all** containers. The syntax for adding a container to the ts01 tablespace shown in Fig. 6–18.

```
   ALTER TABLESPACE ts01 ADD
   (DEVICE '/dev/rdata3' 1024) PREFETCHSIZE 48
```

Notice that one of the parameters that can be changed is **PREFETCHSIZE.** Usually, this parameter would be the same as all other containers in the table space.

Drop Table Space

The syntax for the **DROP** statement for table spaces and other database objects is shown in Fig. 6–19.

```
DROP TABLESPACE tablespace-name
```

Fig. 6–19 The **DROP** Statement

For example, suppose you want to create only DMS table spaces and have no need for the default table space, *USERSPACE1*. The statement would be the following:

```
DROP TABLESPACE USERSPACE1
```

When you drop a table space all tables, indexes, primary keys, foreign keys and check constraints referencing the table are also dropped. Views and triggers referencing the table are marked inoperative, and dependent packages will be invalidated. All catalog entries are removed as well as all objects in the table space.

You will not be able to drop a table space if any table stored in the table space has one of its parts (indexes or LOBs) stored in another table space. You will have to drop the table first and then proceed to drop the table space.

It is more efficient to drop an entire table space than to drop all of its objects independently. If a table is dropped and re-created often, store only that table in the table space and drop the entire table space.

User-created containers such as logical volumes in AIX will not be deleted when the table space is dropped. If the container is a file then the disk space should be recovered automatically by DB2. To recover the space used by a DMS container that is not a file, you must reclaim the space manually.

States of Table Spaces

DB2 maintains information about the states of table spaces and will not allow access using SQL (DML) statements, if the table space is not in a "normal state". Table space states are expressed in hexadecimal numbers. Sometimes, a table space can have more than one state associated with it. This will result in a combined hexadecimal number. There should be a description of the state provided with the **LIST TABLESPACES SHOW DETAIL** command.

To view the table space state, issue the **LIST   TABLESPACE** command. Alternatively, you can use a utility that is shipped with the product called **DB2TBST**. Typing db2tbst with the hexadecimal number from the command line will evaluate the table space state. The **DB2TBST** utility can be found in the sqllib directory under the miscellaneous sub-directory of the instance owner.

A table space is placed in a non-normal state during load, backup and recovery operations, or if placed in a quiesced condition via the **QUIESCE TABLESPACE** command. This command is not used very often by itself, but it is used by various DB2 utilities.

The LOAD command will place the table space in a LOAD PENDING state and leave the table space in this pending state until it has completed successfully. The RESTORE command will place the table space in ROLLFORWARD PENDING following a successful restore of the database. The table space will remain in this state until a successful ROLLFORWARD command has been issued. The table space states are important to understand because if the a table space is in any non-normal state (0x0000) no SQL DML (Data Manipulation Language) statements can be issued for any of the related table objects.

A list of some of the possible table space states are as follows:

- (0x0000) — Access to the table space is allowed (normal).
- (0x0001) — Quiesced share.
- (0x0002) — Quiesced update.
- (0x0004) — Quiesced exclusive.

Load related states

- (0x0008) - Load Pending - A table space is in a Load Pending state when a table is being loaded or when the **LOAD** utility fails. After correcting the problem that caused the failure, invoking the **LOAD** utility with the **RESTART** option will continue the load process.
- (0x0010) - Delete Pending - A table space is in a Delete Pending state when a table stored in the table space has been successfully loaded and the **LOAD** utility is processing the delete phase to delete rows with duplicate keys.

- (0x0020) - Backup Pending - A table space will be in this state when a table contained in this table space has been successfully loaded using the **LOAD** utility. Access to the table space will not be allowed until a backup of the database or the table space is taken.
- (0x01000) - Restore Pending - A table space will be in this state when you perform a **LOAD** with **TERMINATE** option. The table space will have to be recovered from a backup. If the backup being restored is a database backup, the database will have to be rolled forward to the end of the log files.

Summary

This chapter discussed the physical placement of objects in a database. There were some concepts that were defined. A table space is created in a database. Table spaces map the logical design of your data to your physical storage. Containers are assigned to table spaces. A container in DB2 can be a file, directory or device. A container has a one-to-many relationship with table spaces. You cannot share containers across table spaces. An extent is an allocation of space within a container of a table space. Database objects are stored in pages within DB2 (except for LOBs). These pages are grouped into allocation units called extents. The extent size is defined at the table space level. Once the extent size is established for the table space, it cannot be altered or changed.

There are two kinds of table spaces in DB2: System Managed Space (SMS) and Database Managed Space (DMS). Each type has different characteristics. System Managed Storage is based on the storage model where storage is acquired as needed. Containers in SMS table spaces are not pre-allocated. Once the number of containers for an SMS table space is set, they cannot be altered. SMS table spaces can only be represented by directories in the operating system.

Database Managed Storage (DMS) table spaces are characterized by table spaces that are assigned pre-allocated storage. This storage can be a device or a file. The Database Manager is responsible for the management of this space. The storage is allocated to the container when it is created.

We discussed how the **CREATE DATABASE** command will create three default table spaces:

- *SYSCATSPACE* holds the system catalogs.
- *TEMPSPACE1* holds temporary tables that are created and removed during normal processing.
- *USERSPACE1*, by default, will hold user tables.

We also talked about commands and statements that are used with table spaces. These include **LIST TABLESPACES**, **LIST TABLESPACE CONTAINERS**, **ALTER TABLESPACE** and **DROP TABLESPACE**.

Questions

1. Which table space characteristic can be altered for a Database Managed
   (DMS) table space?

   O   A. Modify the extent size

   O   B. Modify the prefetch size

   O   C. Change the location of an existing container

   O   D. Change the size of an existing container

2. You have four disk drives (devices) with these characteristics:
   Disk   Speed (Time to read a fixed amount of data into memory)
   -----   -------
   dd1   slowest
   dd2   slow
   dd3   fast
   dd4   fastest

   Which table space characteristic would you set if you wanted DB2 to be
   aware of the relative speed of the different drives?

   O   A. Prefetch size (PREFETCHSIZE)

   O   B. Transfer rate (TRANSFERRATE)

   O   C. Extent size (EXTENTSIZE)

   O   D. Overhead (OVERHEAD)

3. Which of the following can be used as a container in an SMS table space?

   O   A. Raw Device

   O   B. File

   O   C. Logical Volume

   O   D. Directory

4. Which of the following is **not** a characteristic of DMS table spaces?

    ○   A. Can dynamically increase the number of containers

    ○   B. Can store long data and indexes in separate table spaces

    ○   C. Space allocated only when needed

    ○   D. Table space can be directed to different types of disk

5. Which command will show you how many free pages are in a DMS table space?

    ○   A. SHOW TABLESPACES WITH DETAIL

    ○   B. LIST TABLESPACES

    ○   C. LIST TABLESPACE CONTAINERS

    ○   D. LIST TABLESPACES SHOW DETAIL

Answers

1. (B)

   The prefetch size can be modified for DMS table spaces and SMS table spaces.

2. (B)

   The transfer rate (**TRANSFERRATE**) is used to indicate the relative speed of an I/O device.

3. (D)

   A directory is the only valid container type for SMS table spaces.

4. (C)

   SMS table spaces only allocated space when it is required.

5. (D)

   The command **LIST TABLESPACES SHOW DETAIL** will show the used and unused portions of DMS table spaces.

Exercises

Part A — Describing the Environment

This section describes the database design considerations for the DB2CERT
database.

1. Suppose you want to create a database. You have choices as to what kind of
    table spaces will be in the database. Remember, unless you explicitly create
    table spaces when creating your database, three default SMS table spaces
    will be created.
    What kind of table space would you make for your system catalogs?
    There is no wrong or right answer. One option is to use an SMS table space.
    Since the system catalog tables do not generally have high amount of trans-
    actional processing (update, insert or delete statements). There should not be
    a great need for the growth of these tables and therefore many of the prealло-
    cation features of DMS are not beneficial.

2. Approximately how much space is initially needed for the system catalog
    tables when the database is created using an SMS table space?
    The system catalogs take approximately 1.6 MB. The system catalog tables
    will grow as objects are defined including tables, views, indexes, triggers,
    event monitors and application packages are added to the database.

3. In the next several exercises we will create a set of tables in the DB2CERT
    database. These tables will be for a series of books associated with the DB2
    products. The authors of the books also travel to various locations giving
    seminars. We will use these tables as an example of using SMS and DMS
    table spaces in a database. You can type each command from CLP, or use the
    input files provided.

4. There will be five tables. The first one keeps track of the books themselves.
    Information such as title of the book, author id and book number will be kept
    in the **BOOKS** table. There is a **SPEAKER** table which tracks the speaking
    engagements of the various book authors. There is a table that tracks how
    many books are on hand, **STOCK** table, their price and book number. The
    REORDER table tells when to reorder a certain book. There is also an
    AUTHOR table that keeps information regarding each author. We will
    assume that a book only has one author for our examples.

5. The following shows the layout of the various tables. Note, that PK stands
    for primary key. FK is an abbreviation for foreign key.

Table 6–4 BOOKS Table

Colname	Typename	Length
TITLE	varchar	50
AUTHNO (FK)	smallint	2
BOOKNO (PK and INDEX)	smallint	2

6. The next table keeps track of the speaking engagements and seminars given by the book authors.

Table 6–5 SPEAKER Table

Colname	Type	Length
AUTHNO (FK)	smallint	2
DATE	date	4
CITY	varchar	25

7. The stock table keeps track of the amount of books on hand.

Table 6–6 STOCK Table

Colname	Type	
BOOKNO (FK and INDEX)	smallint	2
PRICE	decimal	6
QTY	integer	4

8. The next table is for reorders of the book.

Table 6–7 REORDER Table

Colname	Type	Length
BOOKNO	smallint	2
TIMESTAMP	timestamp	10

9. The author table keeps the personal data about each author.

Table 6–8 AUTHOR Table

Colname	Type	Length
AUTHNO (PK)	smallint	2
NAME (INDEX)	varchar	50

Table 6-8 AUTHOR Table

Colname	Type	Length
SPEAKER	character	1
BIO	CLOB	102400
PICTURE	BLOB	51200

Part B - Determining the Size of the Tables

This section works with the tables from part A and estimates the size of each table.

1. The estimated number of rows for each table can be seen in the following:

Table 6-9 Estimated Number of Rows per Table

Table Name	Number of Rows
BOOKS	300
SPEAKER	200
STOCK	800
REORDER	25
AUTHOR	100

2. To determine how to create the physical tables, you need to consider the following:
    How many table spaces to create?
    What type of table spaces to create?
    The size of each table space.
    In which table space each table will reside.
    What type of containers to use for the table space?

3. The space needed for each user table in a database can be calculated using the following formula: **(average row size + 8) * number of rows * 1.5**. The average row size is the sum of the average column sizes. The factor of 1.5 is for overhead. If a column contains **LONG VARCHAR** or **LONG VARGRAPHIC** data, the column in the base table contains a 20-byte descriptor. If a column contains LOB data, the column in the base table contains a descriptor between 72 and 316 bytes. Use the following information to determine the base table's column length.

Maximum LOB Length	LOB Descriptor Size
1,024	72
8,192	96
65,536	120
65,536	144
524,000	168
4,190,000	200
134,000,000	224
536,000,000	256
1,070,000,000	280
1,470,000,000	316
2,147,483,647	

4. We will make the assumption that all the tables that contain columns with a type of **VARCHAR** are 50% full. Also, we will ignore the space required for null indicators on columns that are not defined as **NOT NULL** (1 byte per field that allows null values). We will also ignore the space required for the length of varying character data and varying graphic data (4 bytes per varying length data). When doing the calculation for your own databases, you can want to include these bytes when calculating row size.

5. Using the formula in Step 12, calculate the space needed for the BOOKS table, the SPEAKER table, the STOCK table, the REORDER table and the AUTHOR table.

    BOOKS Table:
    (TITLE(25) + AUTHNO(2) + BOOKNO(2) + 8) * 300*1.5 = 16,650

    SPEAKER Table:
    (AUTHNO(2) + DATE(4) + CITY(12) + 8) * 200*1.5 = 7,800

    STOCK Table:
    (BOOKNO(2) + PRICE(6) + QTY(4) + 8) * 800*1.5 = 24,000

    REORDER Table:
    (BOOKNO(2) +TIMESTAMP(10) + 8) * 25*1.5 = 750

    AUTHOR Table:
    (AUTHNO(2) + NAME(25) + SPEAKER(1) + BIO(144) +
     PICTURE(144)+8)*100*1.5 = 48,600

6. The space needed for each index can be estimated using the following formula:

    (average index key size + 8) * number of rows * 2

7. Using the formula for calculating index size, let's calculate the index size for the BOOKS table, the STOCK table and the AUTHOR table.

> BOOKS Table:
> (AUTHONO(2) + 8)*300*2 = 6,000
>
> STOCK Table:
> (BOOKNO(2) + 8) * 800 * 2 = 16,000
>
> AUTHNO Table:
> (AUTHNO(2) + 8)*100*2) = 2,000
> (NAME(25) + 8)*100*2) = 6,600
>   Total Index Space   8,600

8. All LOB data for a given table is stored in the same LOB Data Object. In addition to the LOB Data Object, an Allocation Object also will be created. The Allocation Object contains one 4KB page for each 64GB of the LOB data Object and a 4KB page for each 8MB in the LOB Data Object.

Assume that there will only be three biographies and pictures for the BOOKS table.

> LOB Data Object =
> (LOB column sizes * number of rows containing data * 1.5)
>
> LOB Allocation Object =
> ((LOB Data Object / 65,536,000,000) +
> (LOB Data Object / 8,192,000) * 4096)

> Round up to the next whole number for each division

9. Using the above formula, we will calculate the amount of space needed for the LOB data in the AUTHOR table. We will assume that only three rows will contain LOB data.

((BIO(102400) + PICTURE(512000)) * 3 * 1.5)   = 2,764,800

((2764800 / 65536000000) + (2764800 / 8192000) * 4096)   =   8,192

   Total LOB size   = 2,772,992

10. The following table shows the table size information.

Table 6–10 Table Size Information

Table Name	Table Size	Index Size	LOB Size
BOOKS	16,650	6,000	
SPEAKER	7,800		
STOCK	24,000	16,000	
REORDER	750		
AUTHOR	48,600	8,600	2,772,992

Part C - Determining Table Spaces

1. Now, we'll discuss table spaces for our tables. First, we need to determine the type of table spaces that will be used. In this discussion, there is no "correct" answer. For the BOOKS table, you could use a DMS table space. The BOOKS table will probably grow at a predictable rate. Since containers can be added to a DMS table space, the size of the table space can be managed easier than with a SMS table space. The index could also be assigned to its own table space using DMS, also allowing the index to be placed on a faster device. The SPEAKER table could be DMS for the same reason as the BOOKS table. Since both the BOOKS and SPEAKER tables have predictable growth rates, both tables could share the same DMS table spaces.

    The STOCK table will be the largest of all the tables and the most critical since other business applications will want to gain access to the inventory information. To allow for growth, a DMS table space appears to be the best choice.

    Since the STOCK table is a critical table, we might want to back up the STOCK table more often than other tables. Assigning the STOCK table to its own table space makes backup and recovery more efficient. It could also allow separation on different disks.

    You could use an SMS table space for the REORDER table. The REORDER table will be used as a tickler file to notify someone that the stock on a particular time has fallen below a certain level. The REORDER table should never be very large and would be more efficiently managed by the operating system.

    The REORDER table needs its own table space for management purposes. You could use a DMS table space for the AUTHOR table. The AUTHOR table contains LOB data and multiple indexes. If DMS table space is used, the LOB data and index could be placed in their own table spaces.

    Each table space could be supported by different disks.

    The following shows the table spaces for our exercise:

Table 6–11 Table Locations

Table Name	Base TS SMS	Base TS DMS	Separate Index TS	Separate LOB TS
AUTHOR		X	X	X
BOOKS		X	X	
SPEAKER		X		
STOCK		X		
REORDER	X			

2. Based on the above, how many table spaces will you need to create? According to our calculations, there will be seven table spaces. The matrix shown below has assigned names to the table spaces. For Database Managed Storage, we will use the names DMS01-DMSnn. For System Managed Space, we will use the names SMS01-SMSnn. Remember that because we are creating these table spaces in DB2CERT, SYSCATSPACE, USERSPACE1 and TEMPSPACE1 already exist.

Table 6–12 Table Locations

Table Name	Base TS SMS	Base TS DMS	Index TS	LOB TS
AUTHOR		DMS01	DMS02	DMS03
BOOKS		DMS04	DMS05	
SPEAKER		DMS04		
STOCK		DMS06		
REORDER	SMS01			

3. Containers for an SMS table space are directory names. The directory names can be located in a single file system or in multiple file systems. If all the directories are located in the same file system, then the largest table space that can be created is the maximum size the operating system supports for a file system size.
   If all the directories are located in different file systems, then the largest table space that can be created would be:
   (number of directories * maximum file system size supported by the operating system)

4. The space for containers used for a DMS table space is specified in numbers of pages. However, space is allocated for tables in terms of extents. An extent represents a certain number of pages. The extent size ranges from 2 to 256, with the default being 32. Since space is allocated by extents in a DMS table space, the size of the extent must be used in determining the size of the table space. The following rules apply:

   One page in every container is reserved for overhead and the remaining pages will be used one extent at a time. Only full extents are used in a container. The size of a container can be calculated with the following formula:
   (extent size * n) + 1
   where n is the number of extents to be stored in a container.
   The minimum number of extents required to create a DMS table space are:

   - Three extents in the table space are reserved for overhead
   - At least two extents are required to store any user table data. Each object requires an extent map of at least one extent.

- A container must have enough space to hold at least five extents, or the table space will not be created.
- If the table space will contain indexes, Long Field Data or LOBs, two additional extents are required for each type.

5. The next thing to consider is the types of containers to assign to table spaces. SMS table spaces can only be allocated using directories as containers. SMS containers can increases in size up to the operating system file system limit, but new containers cannot be added.

    DMS table spaces can be allocated using a file or a device container, depending on the operating system. If a file is used, the actual disk space allocated will be on a page basis. If a device can be used in AIX and Windows NT. DMS containers can be added to a table space, but the size of an existing container cannot be increased.

    For this exercise, we will only use files and directories. Remember that your operating system can support devices as containers.

6. The following matrix shows the container type and number that we have selected for this exercise.

    Table 6–13 Containers Used

Table Space	Container Type	Number of Containers
DMS01	file	1
DMS02	file	1
DMS03	file	1
DMS04	file	1
DMS05	file	1
DMS06	file	1
SMS01	directory	2

Part D — Creating and Managing the Table Spaces

1. Go to the \exercise\chapter6\partd directory.
    Note: there is a separate sub-directory for Windows, OS/2 and AIX.

2. Connect to the DB2CERT database. You can issue the commands individually or execute the CLP file called **create.tst**. If you use the command file, you must edit the file first to specify the path/drive for the containers. Use the **CREATE TABLESPACE** command to create the DMS01 table space. Create the file container in a subdirectory under the instance. Call the subdirectory

dms. (In Windows and OS/2 use the syntax X:\DMS\.... in these examples.) The command is the following:

CREATE REGULAR TABLESPACE dms01 MANAGED BY DATABASE USING (FILE '/home/db2/dms/dms01' 29) EXTENTSIZE 4

where db2 is the instance owner (AIX only).

3. Use the same subdirectory, dms, and place the dms02 table space there.

CREATE REGULAR TABLESPACE dms02 MANAGED BY DATABASE USING (FILE '/home/db2/dms/dms02' 13) EXTENTSIZE 2

4. Create DMS03 the same way.

CREATE LONG TABLESPACE dms03 MANAGED BY DATABASE USING (FILE '/home/db2/dms/dms03' 721) EXTENTSIZE 8

5. Create DMS04 with 19 pages and an extent size of 2.

CREATE REGULAR TABLESPACE dms04 MANAGED BY DATABASE USING (FILE '/home/db2/dms/dms04' 19) EXTENTSIZE 2

6. Create DMS05 with an extent size of 2 and 11 pages.

CREATE REGULAR TABLESPACE dms05 MANAGED BY DATABASE USING (FILE '/home/db2/dms/dms05' 11) EXTENTSIZE 2

7. Write the CREATE TABLESPACE command you would use to create the DMS06 table space. Use a file container.

CREATE REGULAR TABLESPACE dms06 MANAGED BY DATABASE USING (FILE /home/db2/dms/dms06' 33) EXTENTSIZE 4

8. For the SMS table space, use two containers. Use the directory names of sms/sms01 and sms/sms02. Place the SMS table space in a subdirectory of the instance. The command is the following:

CREATE REGULAR TABLESPACE sms01 MANAGED BY SYSTEM USING ('/home/db2/sms/sms01', '/home/db2/sms/sms02') EXTENTSIZE 4

9. Make sure you are connected to the DB2CERT database. Issue the command to show the table spaces.

LIST TABLESPACES SHOW DETAIL

10. Notice how many pages are used for DMS05.

11. Issue the command to show the detail on the SMS table space you have created in this exercise.

LIST TABLESPACE CONTAINERS FOR X SHOW DETAIL

where X is the table space ID.

12. Query the system catalogs to find information about the name of the table space, the table space ID, table space type, type of data the table space stores, extent size and prefetch size.
    SELECT TBSPACE, TBSPACETYPE, TBSPACEID, DATATYPE, EXTENTSIZE FROM SYSCAT.TABLESPACES

13. Use the **ALTER TABLESPACE** statement to add a container to dms03. Use 723 pages as the size of the file. Use a file name of "more".
    ALTER TABLESPACE dms03 ADD (file '/home/dms/more' 7213)

14. Change the prefetch size for table space dms05. First, you need to know the current prefetch size for the table space. Use the following command:
    LIST TABLESPACES SHOW DETAIL

15. Use the **ALTER TABLESPACE** command to change the prefetch size for table space dms03 from 32 to 64.
    ALTER TABLESPACE dms05 ADD PREFETCHSIZE 64

16. Next, create the tables in the table spaces. There is a command file called book.tab that you can use.

17. After creating the tables, check the number of pages used in DMS05. Can you account for this? Remember that if the table space contains indexes, two extents are required for this type of data. One extent is required for the Extent Map.

18. From the appropriate <platform> sub directory in \exercise\chapter6\partd\<platform> issue the commands:
    db2 -tvf cr8db.ddl
    db2 -tvf create.tst
    db2 -tvf book.tab

    Examine that the tables were created properly in the proper table spaces. Issue the commands:
    db2 LIST TABLESPACES
    db2 LIST TABLESPACES SHOW DETAIL
    db2 LIST TABLESPACE SHOW CONTAINERS FOR 1

    If you would like to drop all of the database objects isse the command:
    db2 -tvf drop.tbs

Data Management

Data management involves consistency, reliability and security of your data. Your hardware in time will be obsolete. You might even change operating systems. Applications may change as user requirements dictate. However, the data in your database has the greatest longevity. As such, the protection of the data in your database requires the database administrator to perform management tasks such as backing up the database or table space, so that if a system error occurs, a previous version of the data can be recovered. In this chapter, we discuss how to protect your data should you need to return to a previous version of your data. In database terminology, this involves backing up and being able to restore your database or table space. Should a disaster occur, you'll need to perform some type of recovery on your data. There are different methods for recovery. We will talk about the files that can assist in the recovery process. These files are called log files. We will discuss them and their usage in backup and recovery both at the table space and at the database level.

We will also talk about how to populate tables with data in DB2 databases and in particular using the **LOAD**, **IMPORT** and **EXPORT** commands.We'll look at the differences between these utilities and when you would want to use one utility versus another.

We will cover maintenance topics involving the control of the database management system. Some of the utilities we'll look at are **REORGCHK, REORG, RUNSTATS, REBIND** and **BIND**. These utilities are useful in controlling the system on-line. We'll also cover commands to control the access of users to the database, specifically the **LIST APPLICATIONS** and **FORCE** commands.

Populating Tables

There are two utilities that populate tables in DB2 databases:

- The **LOAD** utility
- The **IMPORT** utility

The **LOAD** utility is used for the initial load or append to a table where large amounts of data will be inserted. The **LOAD** utility can move data into tables, create an index and generate statistics. The **LOAD** utility is significantly faster then the **IMPORT** utility because load writes formatted pages directly into the database while import performs SQL inserts. Also, the **LOAD** utility does a minimal amount of logging. Data that is moved from one table using the **EXPORT** utility can be loaded into another table with the **LOAD** utility.

Using the **IMPORT/EXPORT** utility, you can move data between a table or view and another database and between DB2 common server databases as well as between DB2 common server databases and host databases.

The LOAD Utility

There are three phases of the load process shown in Fig. 7–1.

1. **Load**, when the data is written into the table.
2. **Build**, when the indexes are created.
3. **Delete**, when the rows that caused a unique key violation are removed from the table.

All phases of the load process are part of one operation which is completed only after all three phases complete successfully. The **LOAD** utility will generate messages during the progress of each phase. One of the ways these messages can assist you is if the load process fails. Should a failure occur during one of the phases, then these messages can assist you in deciding the recovery actions you'll want to consider. We'll talk about the **LOAD** utility in detail, starting with each of the three phases, showing examples as we proceed.

Load Phase

During the load phase, data is stored in a table and index keys are collected. Save points or consistency points are established at intervals specified by you in the **SAVECOUNT** parameter of the **LOAD** command. Messages let you know how many input rows have been successfully loaded during the operation. If a failure occurs, you can use the **RESTARTCOUNT** option set to the value indicated by the last load consistency/save point indicated in the message file. If the failure occurs near the beginning of the load, you can also restart the load from the beginning of the input file.

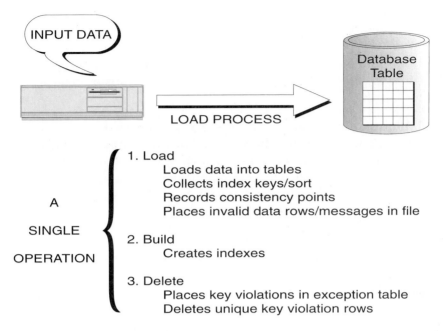

Fig. 7–1 Three Phases of LOAD

Build Phase

During the build phase, indexes are created based on the index keys collected in the load phase. The index keys are sorted during the load phase. If a failure occurs, the build is restarted from the beginning of the build phase.

Delete Phase

During the delete phase, all rows that have violated a unique key are deleted. If a failure occurs during this phase, you should restart the **LOAD** utility from the beginning of the delete phase. Once the database indexes are rebuilt, information about the rows containing the invalid keys is stored in an exception table, if the exception table was created before the load began. The exception table must also be identified in the syntax of the **LOAD** command. Rows that violate any unique key defined on the table are placed in the exception table. Messages on these rejected rows are placed in the message file. Finally, any duplicate keys that are found are deleted.

The input data for the load process must be in one of three file formats:

- **Integrated Exchange Format (IXF)**
  This is the preferred method for exchange between relational database managers. You can export a data file from a host database to the DB2 server. In general, a PC/IXF file consists of an unbroken sequence of variable-length records.

  ✍ If the host file contains packed fields, you will have to convert these fields before transferring the file to a DB2 common server database. To perform this conversion, create a view in a host database, DB2 for MVS, for example, for all the columns that you require. A view automatically forms character fields out of the packed fields. From the view, you can export the required data as an IXF file.

- **Delimited ASCII (DEL)**
  This type is used for exchanging files with a wide variety of industry applications, especially other database products. This is a commonly used way of storing data that separates column values with a special delimiting character. An example of a delimited ASCII file is shown in Fig. 7–2.

"Smith, Bob",4973,15.46
"Jones, Suzanne",12345,16.34
"Williams, Sam",452,192.78

Fig. 7–2 Example of a DEL File Type

- **Non-delimited ASCII (ASC)** Non-delimited ASCII files are used for loading data from other applications that create flat text files with aligned column data, such as those produced by word processing programs. Each ASCII file is a stream of ASCII characters consisting of data values organized by row and column. Rows in the data stream are separated by a line feed. An example of a non-delimited ASCII file is shown in Fig. 7–3.

Smith, Bob	4973	15.46
Jones, Suzanne	12345	16.34
Williams, Sam	452	193.78

Fig. 7–3 Example of an ASC File Type

Creating the Target Table and the Exception Table

The **LOAD** utility moves data into a target table whose definition must exist within the database prior to the start of the load process. The target table may be a new table which you have just created or an existing table to which you will be appending or replacing data. Indexes on the table may or may not already exist. However, the load process only builds indexes that are already defined on a table.

In addition to the target table, it is recommended that an exception table be created to write any rows that violate unique index key or constraint violations.

Using an exception table is an optional parameter of the **LOAD** command. However, if the exception table is neither created nor specified with the **LOAD** utility, any rows that violate unique index rules will be discarded without any chance of recovering or altering them.

Using The LOAD Utility

There are a large number of parameters which can be used during a load operation. The **LOAD** command can be issued from the Command Line Processor (CLP) or from an Application Programming Interface (API). It is recommended that the **LOAD** command be placed in a file that can be edited and executed from the CLP using the following syntax:

```
db2 -tvf filename
```

✍️   The input data file for the **LOAD** command must exist on the same workstation as the database.

The **LOAD** command has four possible actions associated with it. While performing a **LOAD** operation, the table space in which the table resides will be placed in a load pending state. A sample **LOAD** command is shown in Fig. 7–4.

* **INSERT**
  When loading into an empty table, you should specify an insert operation. Also when appending data to an existing table with data, specify **INSERT** to add data to the table without changing the existing table data.

* **REPLACE**
  If you specify **REPLACE** in the **LOAD** command all the existing data in a table will be deleted and new data from the input file will be loaded into the target table. The table definition and the index definitions are not changed.

* **RESTART**
  After a load has been interrupted, this action is used to restart the load process. In such a situation it is important to note the last consistency point. This information is stored in the message file and the remote file.

- **TERMINATE**

  This action terminates a previously interrupted load and moves the table space in which the target table resides, from a load pending state to a restore pending state. The table space cannot be used until a backup has been restored and the log files have been applied.

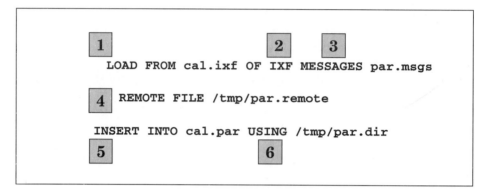

Fig. 7–4 Example LOAD Command

1   The input file for the **LOAD** command is *cal.ixf*.

2   The file type is **IXF**.

3   Messages will be directed to a file called *par.msgs*. This file can be viewed after the load has completed.

4   The temporary remote file built during the load process will be prefixed with *par.remote*. The remote file will be generated in the /tmp filesystem.

5   The action of the load is **INSERT**. In this example, the table was empty before the load. The *cal.par* table is the target table.

6   The **USING** option will place any temporary sort files in the */tmp/par.dir* directory/filesystem.

The load process turns off constraint checking. If you have created and specified an exception table and rows have been placed in that exception table, your target table will be placed in a check pending state. Before using the table, this check pending state must be removed with the **SET CONSTRAINTS** statement. If the target table has referential constraints that involve other dependent tables, then those dependent tables are also placed in a check pending state.

The **LOAD** command also allows you to load large objects or LOBs into a table. If the LOBs are contained within the load input file or device, then the **LOAD** command requires no additional parameters to include the LOBs.

Syntax of the LOAD Command

The full syntax of the **LOAD** command is shown in Fig. 7–5. We'll examine some of the parameters of the command. The most important **LOAD** options are discussed below. For a complete description of the options and parameters, check the *DB2 Command Reference*.

```
LOAD FROM file/pipe/dev[{,file/pipe/dev}...]OF{ASC|DEL|IXF}
[LOBS FROM lob-path [{,lob-path} ...] ]
[MODIFIED BY filetype-mod...]
[METHOD {L (col-start col-end [{,col-start col-end}...])
[NULL INDICATORS (col-position [{,col-position}...])] |
 N (col-name [{,col-name}...]) |
 P (col-position [{,col-position}...])}] [SAVECOUNT n]
[RESTARTCOUNT {n | B | D}] [ROWCOUNT n] [WARNINGCOUNT n]
[MESSAGES msg-file] [REMOTE FILE remote-file]
{INSERT | REPLACE | RESTART | TERMINATE}
 INTO table-name [( insert-column [{,insert-column}..])]
[FOR EXCEPTION table-name] [STATISTICS {YES
[WITH DISTRIBUTION [AND [DETAILED] INDEXES ALL] |
{AND | FOR} [DETAILED] INDEXES ALL] | NO}]
[COPY {NO | YES [USE ADSM [OPEN num-sess SESSIONS] |
 TO dir/dev [ {,dir/dev}...] | LOAD lib-name
[OPEN num-sess SESSIONS]]}] [USING directory
[{,directory}...]] [HOLD QUIESCE]
[WITHOUT PROMPTING] [DATA BUFFER buffer-size]
[SORT BUFFER buffer-size]
```

Fig. 7–5 Syntax of the LOAD Command

- filename, pipename, device
  This parameter identifies the source of the data being loaded. The source file, pipe or device must be on the same node as the database being loaded. If several data sources are identified, they will be loaded sequentially.

- **METHOD L, N** or **P**
  There are three possible load method options. If the source data is an ASCII file, use L to identify the first and last byte of each column of data to be loaded. If the source data is an IXF file, use N to identify the name of the column to be loaded. If the data is a delimited ASCII file, use P to identify the numbers of the columns to be loaded.

- **SAVECOUNT n**

  This parameter is used to establish consistency points during a load after every n rows. The benefit of specifying this parameter is only realized in a recovery situation where you can restart the load from the last consistency point. You should only consider using consistency points when loading large amount of data (>1 hour for the duration of the load). The default is for no consistency points, **SAVECOUNT** equaling 0.

- **RESTARTCOUNT n**

  This parameter can have the following values, used with the **RESTART** action of the load utility:

  B — The load will be restarted at the beginning of the build phase.

  D — The load will be restarted at the beginning of the delete phase.

  n — The load is restarted at n+1. The n is determined from the last consistency point found in the **SAVECOUNT** option.

- **message-file**

  Specifies the location for warning and error messages that occur during the load.

- **remote-file**

  Identifies a base file name from which the system will create three internal temporary files (basename.rid, basename.log, basename.msg) during the **LOAD** process. These files are destroyed upon completion of the **LOAD** process, but some of their contents are copied to the message file.

- **INTO table-name**

  Specifies the target table within the database and, optionally, the table columns into which the data is to be loaded.

- **EXCEPTION table-name**

  Specifies the exception table into which rows in error will be placed. An exception table is a user-created table which mimics the definition of the target table being loaded. This table is used to store copies of rows that violate unique index rules, have check-constraint violations of foreign keys or have invalid rows from a previous load operation.

- **COPY YES/NO**

  If you specify the **COPY NO** option and have archival logging enabled for the database, the table space in which the table resides will be placed in backup pending state after loading. The data will not be accessible until a table space backup is made. If you choose the **COPY YES** option and have archival logging enabled for the database, a copy of the changes caused by the load process will be saved either to a tape, directory or ADSTAR Distributed Storage Manager (ADSM). This option does not apply to a database that uses circular logging.

- **USING** directory

  When loading into a table that contains indexes, temporary files will be created in the sort directory. With this parameter, you can select which directory to use.

What Happens If a LOAD Fails?

Diagnosing a load failure situation is a non-trivial exercise. Should the **LOAD** utility fail, the table space will be either in a load pending or delete pending state, which must be corrected to access the table space and the tables. The following points may be helpful in determining the problem:

1. An SQLCODE and a short explanation will be returned when an error occurs. This return code can be misleading since it can only yield information for a symptom, rather then a cause of the problem.

2. By viewing the message file, you may get information about the progress of the load operation. This is where warning and error messages that occur during the load will be written. However, the messages file may not be available for viewing, depending on the failure and the phase in which the failure occurred. The remote file can be viewed using the **LOAD QUERY** command that returns diagnostic and recovery information to speed up the restart/recovery process. The remote files are temporary internal files. Information from the remote file is written to the messages file.

3. Finally, you could check the **db2diag.log** file to understand the sequence of events taking place within the database. The path of the **db2diag.log** is set in the **DIAGPATH** environment variable.

Recovery from a LOAD Failure

If a load fails, you have several options. You can restart the **LOAD** utility at either the beginning of the load or at a point during the load process. Alternatively, you can recover the table to a previous state, should a table space or database level backup be available to you.

You will have to select an option to recover from the load failure. The table space in which the target table resides will be left in an inconsistent state. The actual state can be determined using the **LIST TABLESPACES** command. The table space will more than likely be either in a load pending or delete pending state. Before any access to the table space is allowed, the table space must be returned to a "normal" state. This state is indicated by the hexadecimal number 0x0000.

If a failure occurs while loading data, you may be able to restart the load from the last save point. In order to do this, you must have specified the **SAVECOUNT** option during the initial invocation of the **LOAD** utility. Then you can use the **RESTARTCOUNT** option to re start the **LOAD** operation from the last save point. The **RESTARTCOUNT** option uses the value as specified in the **SAVECOUNT** parameter. You'll be able to see the status activity of the load operation by viewing the messages generated during the   load. What is specified in **RESTARTCOUNT,** is a counter that is incremented by one, specifying that the load is to be restarted at the n+1 record. n is the last **SAVECOUNT** point that specifies that the load will set consistency points at intervals of n rows.

If the load fails in the build phase, the **RESTARTCOUNT** parameter should supply a B for its value. This says to restart the load at the build phase. Similarly, if **RESTARTCOUNT** has a value of D, the delete phase will be restarted.

Optimally, to ensure that you can recover from any load failure, a backup copy of the table space or database should be available. When a load fails and you want the database returned to the state immediately before the load transaction, you must restore the backup image. Either a full database image or a table space backup image of all table spaces affected by the failed load can be used. The backup image must have a timestamp prior to the start of the load.

TERMINATE terminates a previously interrupted load and moves the table spaces in which the table resides from load pending state to recovery pending state. The table spaces cannot be used until a backup has been restored and the log files of the database applied. As a first step in deciding which course of action to take to recover from a failed load, a restart of the load should be considered.

LOAD Statistics

The **LOAD** utility allows for building indexes and gathering statistics for a table as part of the **LOAD** process. This is more efficient than executing each of these steps separately. Keys are sorted and statistics are collected during the load phase, which removes some of the overhead involved in issuing separate **CREATE INDEX** and **RUNSTATS** statements. But for larger tables, total load time is largely a product of the number of indexes and whether statistics are collected. You can specify the option to gather statistics during the load phase only if you are in **REPLACE** mode.

LOAD Performance Considerations

There are some performance considerations for the **LOAD** utility:

- Executing the **LOAD** utility in **REPLACE** mode improves performance, but if you are loading into an empty table, **INSERT** will perform better.
- If you have to load a table containing data and later create the index, using **IMPORT** may be faster than using **LOAD.** Creating entirely new indexes can take much more time than simply updating existing indexes.

- The **COPY** option can affect performance. This option only pertains to a database that has archival logging or log retain enabled. When attempting a load into such a database, the default is **COPY NO**. This will place the table space in a backup pending state. You must perform either a table space or database level backup to remove the backup pending state to allow access to the table space.   The **COPY YES** option can reduce performance because there is a backup copy created at the same time the load operation is being performed. However, this choice may be faster than using **COPY NO** that requires a separate invocation of the backup utility before accessing the table space and thus the table.

LOAD Example One — Index Key Violations

This load example involves an input file of type IXF as shown in Fig. 7–6. A user has prepared an input file named *category.ixf,* a target table named *category* and an exception table named *cat.parexp*. The target table has a unique key defined on the first column. In this situation, we want to replace records in the target table and we want to save any records that violate the unique key in the exception table. We will use the file *cat.msg* for the messages and *cat.remote* as the base name for the three internal temporary files that will be placed in the *tmp* directory. The syntax of the **LOAD** command is as follows:

```
LOAD FROM category.ixf OF IXF MESSAGES cat.msg
REMOTE FILE /tmp/cat.remote
REPLACE INTO category FOR EXCEPTION cat.parexp
USING /tmp/cat.dir
```

Notice that we are using the **REPLACE** mode of the **LOAD** command. This means that if the load fails, the original data will be lost. Should we want to return to the same state as before the load, we need to restore a backup image of either the table space containing the table *category*, or the entire database.

During the load operation, messages similar to those in Fig. 7–7 will be displayed on the screen. When a table with a unique index is loaded, rows causing a violation of the index will be deleted from the table during the delete phase. This message provides information on how many rows have been deleted.

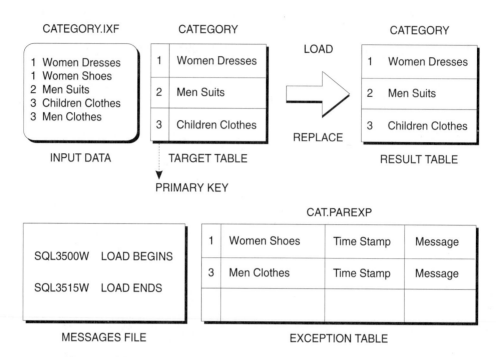

Fig. 7–6 LOAD with an Index Key Violation

The load has ended successfully, but **two** input rows have been written into the exception table because they violated the index key. You need to decide if these rows, do indeed contain the correct data, or if they need to be modified.

The end of the message file shown in Fig. 7–7 shows the delete phase of the load operation. Following a successful load operation, the table may still be unavailable to the user because the DB2 constraint mechanisms were bypassed during the load. Therefore, to ensure complete data integrity all of the constraints defined for the table need to be applied. This task is performed using the **SET CONSTRAINTS** SQL statement.

The SET CONSTRAINTS Statement

Check pending is a table state, not a table space state. It means that some of the rows, in this case from the load operation, have violated a constraint condition. If you try to access a table that is in check pending, you will receive an error code of SQL0668N.

This message indicates that some of the rows attempted by the load violated a constraint. In Fig. 7–6 a unique key was defined on the first column. The load operation identified two rows that violated the unique key constraint defined on the table and placed them in the exception table called *cat.parexp*.

SQL3500W The utility is beginning the "LOAD" phase at time "03-29-1996 10:40:32.654674".

SQL3519W Begin Load Consistency Point. Input record count = "0".

SQL3520W Load Consistency Point was successful.

SQL3109N The utility is beginning to load data from file "/home/db2/category.ixf".

SQL3153N The H record in the PC/IXF file has product "DB2 01.100", date "19960327", and time "111045".

SQL3153N The T record in the PC/IXF file has name "category.ixf", qualifier", and source "

SQL3110N The utility has completed processing. "5" rows were read from input file.

SQL3519W Begin Load Consistency Point. Input record count = "5".

SQL3520W Load Consistency Point was successful.

SQL3515W The utility has finished the "LOAD" phase at time "03-29-1996 10:40:33.599667".

SQL3500W The utility is beginning the "BUILD" phase at time "03-29-1996 10:40:36.600457".

SQL3515W The utility has finished the "BUILD" phase at time "03-29-1996 10:40:40.279589".

SQL3500W The utility is beginning the "DELETE" phase at time "03-29-1996 10:40:43.788941".

SQL3509W The utility has deleted "2" rows form the table.

SQL3515W The utility has finished the "DELETE" phase at time "03-29-1996 10:40:48.276650".

Fig. 7–7 Messages from the LOAD Operation

To verify the status of tables, you can query the *SYSCAT.TABLES* system catalog using the following SQL statement:

```
SELECT TABNAME, STATUS, CONST_CHECK
FROM SYSCAT.TABLES
WHERE TABNAME IN ('category')
```

The following is a sample of the output of a table, *category*. The value 'C' in the *status* column indicates that the table is in a check pending state

```
TABNAME          STATUS          CONST_CHECKED
--------         ------          -------------
CATEGORY         C               NYYYYYYYYY
```

Fig. 7–8 Check Pending State on a Table

To remove the check pending on the table, use the **SET CONSTRAINTS** statement:

```
SET CONSTRAINTS FOR category IMMEDIATE CHECKED
FOR EXCEPTION IN cat.parexp
```

The **SET CONSTRAINTS** statement will generate the following message:

```
SQL3602W Check data processing found constraint violations
moved them into the exception table. SQLSTATE-01603
```

Fig. 7–9 Result of **SET CONSTRAINTS** Statement

Even though the load process has completed, you cannot access the table until the **SET CONSTRAINTS** statement is issued. You can also verify that the status of the table in the *SYSCAT.TABLES* system catalog is normal. As a final step, you can make a decision about the rejected rows that were placed in the exception table, *cat.parexp*. You could correct the data and either load or import them back into the target table.

LOAD Scenario Two — Referential Constraints

This load example involves a table with constraints defined, as can be seen in Fig. 7–10. A user has prepared an input file named *product.ixf* and a target table called *product*. In this case, the target table has a parent table named *category*, containing a unique key on the first column. The target table was created with a foreign key referencing the parent table. This represents a scenario that can occur while you are loading data into a table with referential constraints.

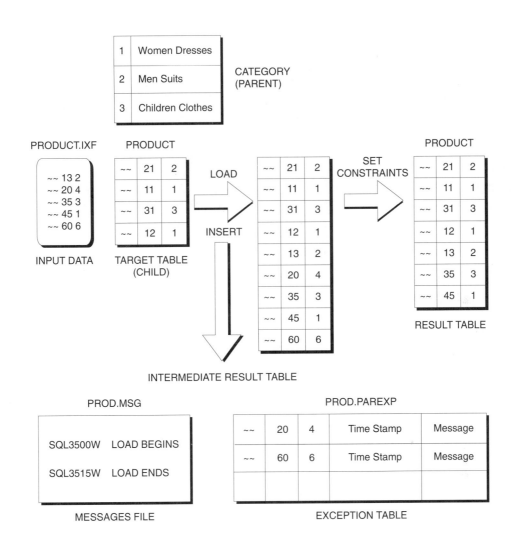

Fig. 7–10 LOAD with a Constraint Violation

The **LOAD** command for the example in Fig. 7–10 is as follows:

```
LOAD FROM product.ixf OF IXF MESSAGES prod.msg
    REMOTE FILE /tmp/prod.remote USING /tmp/prod.dir
    INSERT INTO product FOR EXCEPTION prod.parexp
```

If you look at the message file listing, it would seem to indicate that the **LOAD** command has completed successfully.

The message file will contain status information regarding the load operation. An sample of the message file is shown here:

```
Number of rows read           = 5
Number of rows skipped        = 0
Number of rows loaded         = 5
Number of rows rejected       = 0
Number of rows deleted        = 0
Number of rows committed      = 5
```

These messages still do not indicate that the load has encountered any difficulty. Next, you should check the table space state by using the DB2 command **LIST TABLESPACES**.

The output of this command shows a table space state 0x0020, the table space in which the table resides. The database has log retain enabled. The default **COPY** option of the **LOAD** utility for a database with log retain enabled is **COPY NO**. This will place the table space in a backup pending state. You must perform either a table space level or full database level backup to remove the backup pending. This will change the state of the table space to 0x0000, which indicates a normal state.

However, if you try to retrieve rows from the table with a check pending, the following error message may be received:

```
SQL0668N Operation not allowed when the underlying table
is in Check Pending. SQLSTATE=57016
```

Again to remove the check pending on the table, you must issue the **SET CONSTRAINTS** statement. This will place the rows in the exception table, *prod.parexp*. You can then decide how to proceed with data contained in the exception table.

The IMPORT/EXPORT Utility

This section provides detail on the utilities that allow you to import and export data. Some of the functions provided are to move data from an input file into a table or view. The input file may contain data from another database. You can copy data from a table or view to an output file to be used by another database. You can import or export data between other DB2 common server databases or with a DB2 host database.

The **IMPORT** and **EXPORT** commands support another data type for files that can be imported or exported that are not supported in the **LOAD** utility. This format is **WSF** or Worksheet which is used with spreadsheet products.

The EXPORT Utility

The **EXPORT** utility is used to export data from a database into a file. Data can be exported in several different file formats that can be used with other programs to manage databases, file systems or other DB2 tables. You must already be connected to the database from which data is being exported.

✍ You must have SYSADM or DBADM authority, or CONTROL or SELECT privilege.

The full syntax of the **EXPORT** command is as follows:

```
EXPORT TO filename OF {IXF | DEL | WSF}
   [LOBS TO lob-path [{,lob-path} ... ] ]
   [LOBFILE lob-file [{,lob-file} ... ]
   [MODIFIED BY {filetype-mod ... }]
   [METHOD N ( column-name [{,column-name} ... ] )]
   [MESSAGES message-file]
```

Fig. 7–11 Syntax of the EXPORT Command

Some of the parameters of the **EXPORT** command are as follows:

- `filename` — Specifies the name of the file to which data is exported. If the path is omitted, the current working directory is used.
- `filetype` — Specifies the format of the data in the output file:

  IXF (Integrated Exchange Format, PC version) makes it possible to import into the same or another type of database manager table. What is different from the **LOAD** utility is that the definition of the table as well as any existing indexes are saved in the IXF file.

  DEL (Delimited ASCII Format) is the same format that you can use with the **LOAD** utility. DEL makes it possible to exchange a wide variety of files between different database managers and file manager programs.

  WSF format allows you to use data from spreadsheet applications.

- **filetype-mod** — Specifies additional information unique to DEL or WSF file formats that was specified in the **filetype** parameter. This parameter is ignored with IXF file types.

For the **DELIMITED ASCII** (DEL) file format, **filetype-mod** selects characters to override the following options:

Column delimiters, which are commas (,) by default. Specifying **COLDEL** followed by one character causes the specified characters to be used to signal the end of a column in place of a comma. For example, you can specify that the **EXPORT** utility interpret any semicolon (;) it encounters as a column delimiter by using the following:

```
EXPORT TO myfile.del of DEL MODIFIED BY COLDEL;
SELECT NAME, CREATOR FROM SYSIBM.SYSTABLES
```

The output would be similar to the following:

```
SQL3104N The Export utility is beginning to export data
to file "myfile.del".

SQL3105N The Export utility has finished exporting "14"
rows.
```

Character string delimiters are double quotes (") by default. Specifying **CHARDEL** followed by one character causes the specified character to be used to enclose a character string. For example, you can specify that the **EXPORT** utility interpret any single quote (') it encounters as a character string delimiter by using the following:

```
EXPORT TO myfile.del of DEL MODIFIED BY CHARDEL''
SELECT * FROM db2.test
```

Decimal point characters are periods (.) by default. Specifying **DECPT** followed by one character causes the specified characters to be used to enclose a character string.

For example, you can specify that **EXPORT** interpret any single quote (') it encounters as a character string delimiter and any semicolon (;) it encounters as a decimal point by using the following:

```
EXPORT TO myfile.del of DEL MODIFIED BY CHARDEL'DECPT;
MESSAGES msg.txt SELECT * FROM db2.test_taken
```

Plus sign characters are used as a prefix to positive numbers. The default is the plus sign (+). Specifying **DECPLUSBLANK** causes **EXPORT** to prefix positive decimal numbers with a blank space (in place of the + sign) as shown in the following:

```
EXPORT TO myfile.del of DEL MODIFIED BY DECPLUSBLANK
SELECT * FROM DB2.TEST
```

Date format specifies what format to use for date values. Specifying **DATESISO** in the string causes dates to be exported in ISO date format (yyyy-mm-dd):

```
EXPORT TO myfile.del of DEL MODIFIED BY DATESISO
MESSAGES msgs.txt SELECT * FROM db2.test_taken
```

The values for the column delimiter (COLDEL), character string delimiter (CHARDEL), and decimal point (DECPT) must be different characters so that each delimiter can be uniquely identified. Table 7–1 contains a list of all possible delimiter overrides for **EXPORT**.

- **METHOD N** — This parameter indicates that the specified column names are to be used for the output file. If this parameter is not specified, the default names (column names of the existing table) are used for the columns. This parameter is only valid for IXF and WSF files.
- **msgfile** — Specifies the destination for warning and error messages that occur during the export. If msgfile is omitted, the messages are written to the screen. If you do not specify the complete path to the file, **EXPORT** uses the current directory and the default drive as the destination. If you specify the name of a file that already exists, export overwrites the file.
- **SELECT statement** — This specifies that the select statement will be used to extract the information that will be exported.

Table 7-1 Character Delimiters

HEX	CHAR	CHAR DESCRIPTION
X'22'	"	Double Quotes
X'25'	%	Percent Sign
X'26'	&	Ampersand
X'27'	'	Apostrophe
X'28'	(	Left Parenthesis
X'29'	)	Right Parenthesis
X'2A'	*	Asterisk
X'2C'	,	Comma
X'2E'	.	Period (not valid for character string delimiters)
X'2F'	/	Slash
X'3A'	:	Colon
X'3B'	;	Semicolon
X'3C'	<	Less Than Sign
X'3D'	>	Greater Than Sign
X'3F'	?	Question Mark
X'5F'	_	Underscore (for SBCS environment only)
X'7C'			Vertical Bar

Note: The characters are the same for all code pages.

Examples Using the EXPORT Utility

Let's look at some examples using the **EXPORT** utility. We will place each example in a CLP input file called export.cmd. Then we will execute the commands from the file as follows:

```
db2 -tvf export.cmd
```

- The first example shows how to export information from the *candidate* table in the *db2cert* database. You must be connected to the database before you issue the command. We will export to the file *myfile.ixf*, with the output in IXF format:

```
EXPORT TO myfile.ixf OF IXF MESSAGES msgs.txt
   SELECT *
   FROM db2.candidate
```

- The next example shows how to export the information about candidates who live in Canada from the *db2.candidate* table.

```
EXPORT TO myfile.ixf OF IXF MESSAGES msgs.txt
   SELECT *
   FROM db2.candidate
   WHERE COUNTRY='Canada'
```

- The following is an example of using a semicolon as a column delimiter:

```
EXPORT TO myfile.del OF DEL MODIFIED BY COLDEL';'
   SELECT LNAME, FNAME
   FROM db2.candidate
```

This produces the following in the *myfile.del* file:

```
"Hutchison";"Grant"
"Janacek";"Calene"
"Mantesso";"Greta"
```

- The next example uses a single quote as a character field delimiter (instead of using the default double quotes).

```
EXPORT TO myfile.del OF DEL MODIFIED BY CHARDEL''
   SELECT lname, fname
   FROM db2.candidate
```

The output changes in two ways: the separator between columns is a comma (,) and single quotes surround each column.

```
'Hutchison','Grant'
'Janacek','Calene'
'Mantesso','Greta'
```

- The last **EXPORT** example we'll show uses **DATESISO** to export date fields in ISO format. ISO format is yyyy-mm-dd, instead of the default yyyymmdd.

```
EXPORT TO myfile.del OF DEL MODIFIED BY DATESISO
MESSAGES msg.txt
   SELECT cid, date_taken
   FROM db2.test_taken
```

The output from executing this command is the following:

```
"111234589","1996-01-01"
"112345678","1996-01-01"
"220123456","1996-02-04"
```

EXPORT Considerations

The following information is required when exporting data:

- A **SELECT** statement specifying the data to be exported.
- The path and name of the operating system file that stores the exported data.
- The format of the data in the input file (**IXF**, **DEL** or **WSF**).
- A message file name.

You can also specify the following:

- A method that allows you to specify new column names when exporting to **IXF** or **WSF** files.
- A file type modifier to specify additional format when creating **DEL** and **WSF** files.

The IMPORT Utility

The **IMPORT** utility inserts data from an input file into a table or view. You can either replace or append data if the table or view already contains data.

✍ If the existing table contains a primary key data cannot be replaced, only appended.

With the **IMPORT** command or utility, you can specify how to add or replace the data into the target table. You must be connected to the database to use the utility. If you want to import data into a new table using the **CREATE** option, you must have SYSADM or DBADM authorities or **CREATETAB** authority for the database. In order to replace data to a table or view you must have SYSADM or DBADM authorities or **CONTROL** privilege for the table or view. If you want instead only to add data to an existing table or view, you must have **SELECT** and **INSERT** privileges for the table or view. The complete syntax of the **IMPORT** command is shown in Fig. 7–12.

Many of the parameters of the **IMPORT** command have the same definition as those of the **EXPORT** command. The parameter **filetype** is the same. The **IMPORT** command supports the same file types as does **EXPORT**. However, some of the parameters are different:

- **filetype-mod** — This specifies additional information unique to the file format (DEL, WSF or IXF) that was specified in the **filetype** parameter. For all file formats, if you specify lobsinfile within the filetype-mod string, ASC, DEL or IXF input files contain the names of the files that have LOB data in the LOB column.

  For the ASC file format, **filetype-mod** is used to indicate that the trailing blanks after the last non-blank character are to be dropped when importing into a variable-length database field. If you specify a T within the **file-**

```
IMPORT FROM filename of {IXF | ASC | DEL | WSF}
  [LOBS FROM lob-path [{,lob-path} ... ] ]
  [MODIFIED BY filetype-mod ...]
  [METHOD {L(col-start col-end [{,col-start col-end}...])
  [NULL INDICATORS (col-position [{,col-position}...])] |
  N ( col-name [{,col-name} ... ]) |
  P ( col-position [{,col-position} ... ] )}]
[COMMITCOUNT n] [RESTARTCOUNT n] [MESSAGES message-file]
{INSERT|INSERT_UPDATE|REPLACE|CREATE|REPLACE_CREATE}
  INTO table-name [( insert-column , ... )]
```

Fig. 7–12 Syntax of the IMPORT Command

type-mode string, this indicates that trailing blank spaces are to be truncated. If the **filetype-mod** parameter is not specified within the command string, blank spaces are kept.

For the **DEL** (delimited ASCII) file format, **filetype-mod** selects characters to override column delimiters, character string delimiters and decimal point characters.

For **WSF**, **filetype-mod** is ignored.

For **IXF**, you can suspend the comparison of the code page values in the input file with the application and the database. There are two options to consider. The **FORCEIN** option will tell the **IMPORT** utility to accept all code pages even if they do not match and perform no translation on them. The **INDEXIXF** option tells **IMPORT** to drop all the indexes that are currently defined on the existing table. New ones will be created using the index definition found in the PC/IXF file. You can only use this option when replacing existing data. You cannot use this option with a view or when **insert-column** is specified.

- **METHOD L** — The **METHOD** parameter with the L option specifies the start and end column number from which to import the data. This option must be used for ASC files.
- **METHOD N** — This parameter specifies the names of the columns to be imported.
- **METHOD P** — The **METHOD** parameter with the P option specifies the order of column numbers to be imported. If no method is selected, then the default columns are used during the import.
- **COMMITCOUNT n** — A commit will be done every n records.
- **RESTARTCOUNT n** — This specifies that an import will be started at record n+1. The first n records are skipped.
- **INSERT** — Adds the imported data to the table without changing the existing table data.

- **INSERT_UPDATE** — Adds rows of imported data to the target table or updates existing rows of the target table with matching primary keys.
- **REPLACE** — This option deletes all existing data in the table and inserts the imported data. The table definition and index definition are not changed. You can use **REPLACE** only on an existing table.
- **CREATE** — This option creates the table definition and row contents. If the data is exported from another DB2 database, indexes are also created. This can only be used with IXF files.
- **REPLACE_CREATE** — If the table exists, all the data in that table is deleted and the imported data is inserted without changing the table and index definitions. If the table does not exist, the table definitions are created and data is inserted. Also, if data is exported from a DB2 database, indexes are also created.

IMPORT Considerations

The following information is required when importing data to a table or view:

- The path and the input file name where the data to import is stored.
- The name or alias of the table or view where the data is imported
- The format of the data in the input file. This format can be IXF, DEL, ASCII or WSF.
- Whether the data in the input file is to be inserted, updated, replaced or appended to the existing data in the table or view.
- A message file name.

You can also provide the following:

- The method to use for importing the data
- The number of rows to insert before committing changes to the table
- The number of records in the file to skip before beginning the import
- The names of the columns within the table or view into which the data is to be inserted.

The **IMPORT** utility will issue a **COMMIT** or a **ROLLBACK** statement. Therefore before you use **IMPORT**, be sure that all database activity in the current transaction has completed and all locks are released by doing a **COMMIT** or **ROLLBACK.**

The **IMPORT** and **LOAD** utilities have many different capabilities. These are compared in Table 7–2.

Table 7–2 Import vs. LOAD

The IMPORT utility	The LOAD utility
Significantly slower than the **LOAD** utility on large amounts of data.	Significantly faster than the **IMPORT** utility on large amounts of data because the **LOAD** utility writes formatted pages directly into the database.
Creation of table and indexes supported with IXF format.	Table and indexes must exist.
WSF format is supported.	WSF format is not supported.
Can import into views, tables and aliases.	Can load into tables or aliases.
The table spaces that the table and its indexes reside in are on-line for the duration of the import.	The table spaces that the table and its indexes reside in are off line for the duration of the load.
All rows are logged.	Minimal logging is performed.
Triggers will be fired.	Triggers are not supported.
If an import is interrupted and a commitcount was specified, the table is usable and will contain the rows that were loaded up to the last commit. The user has the choice to restart the import or use the table as is.	If a load is interrupted and a savecount was specified, the table remains in load pending state and cannot be used until the load is restarted or the table space is restored from a backup image created some time before the load.
Space required is approximately the size of the largest index plus about 10%. This space requirement is used from temporary table spaces within the database.	Space required is approximately the sum of the size of all indexes of the database. The space required is temporary space outside of the database.
All constraints are validated during an import.	Uniqueness is verified during a load, but all other constraints must be checked using the **SET CONSTRAINTS** statement.
The keys of each row are inserted into the index one at a time during import.	During load, all the keys are sorted, and the index is built after the data has been loaded.
RUNSTATS must be run afterwards.	Statistics can be gathered during the load.
You can import into a host database.	You cannot load into a host database.
Files that are imported must reside on the node where import is invoked.	Files/pipes that are loaded must reside on the node where the database resides.
No backup image is required.	The backup image can be created during load procedure.

Data Maintenance

The physical distribution of the data stored in a table can improve or decrease the performance of the applications. The way the data is stored in a table is affected by the update, insert and delete operations. For example, a delete operation will leave empty pages of data that may not be reused later. Also, updates done to variable-length columns may result in the new column value not fitting in the same data page. This can cause the row to be moved to a different location. This also will produce internal gaps or unused space in the tables. As a consequence, DB2 will read more physical pages to retrieve the same information stored in the tables.

These scenarios are almost unavoidable. However, as the database administrator, you can use the data maintenance commands provided in DB2 to optimize the physical distribution of the data stored in your tables.

There are three related utilities or commands that help you organize the data in your tables. These commands are

- **REORGCHK**
- **REORG**
- **RUNSTATS**

Analyzing Data's Physical Organization: REORGCHK

We have said that update, insert and delete operations can produce internal gaps in your tables. So the question you may ask is how can you know the physical organization of your tables or indexes? How can you know how much space is currently being used and how much is free?

Questions like these are answered by the **REORGCHK** utility. This utility is used to analyze the system catalog tables and gather information about the physical organization of your tables or indexes.

The **REORGCHK** utility uses the **RUNSTATS** utility to collect the statistics about the space allocation of your tables and indexes.

With the information collected from the system catalog tables, the **REORGCHK** utility displays the space allocation characteristics of your tables and indexes. The utility uses six formulas to help you decide if your tables and indexes require a physical reorganization.

These formulas are general recommendations that show the relationship between the allocated space and the space that is being used for the data in your tables. Three formulas are used for tables, and three are used for indexes.

It is recommended that you establish a data maintenance policy to ensure that your tables are correctly using disk space. If you don't, you may discover that your applications will start to suffer performance degradation. This can be caused by the poor physical organization of your data, so before this happens, it is better to do preventive maintenance on your tables.

The following is an example of the **REORGCHK** utility. We'll use it to check the physical organization of the table *db2.candidate*.

REORGCHK ON TABLE db2.candidate

By default, **REORGCHK** will call the **RUNSTATS** utility before it executes. The output of the **REORGCHK** utility is shown in Fig. 7–13.

The output of **REORGCHK** is divided in two sections. The first section will show you the table statistics and formulas. The second section displays information about the table's indexes.

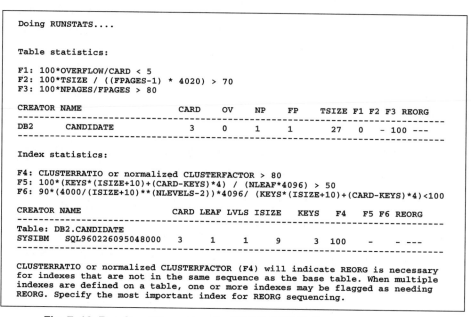

```
Doing RUNSTATS....


Table statistics:

F1: 100*OVERFLOW/CARD < 5
F2: 100*TSIZE / ((FPAGES-1) * 4020) > 70
F3: 100*NPAGES/FPAGES > 80

CREATOR NAME                        CARD   OV    NP    FP    TSIZE F1 F2 F3 REORG
-----------------------------------------------------------------------------
DB2       CANDIDATE                  3     0     1     1      27    0  - 100 ---
-----------------------------------------------------------------------------

Index statistics:

F4: CLUSTERRATIO or normalized CLUSTERFACTOR > 80
F5: 100*(KEYS*(ISIZE+10)+(CARD-KEYS)*4) / (NLEAF*4096) > 50
F6: 90*(4000/(ISIZE+10)**(NLEVELS-2))*4096/ (KEYS*(ISIZE+10)+(CARD-KEYS)*4)<100

CREATOR NAME                      CARD LEAF LVLS ISIZE   KEYS    F4   F5 F6 REORG
-----------------------------------------------------------------------------
Table: DB2.CANDIDATE
SYSIBM    SQL960226095048000   3     1     1     9       3    100    -   - ---
-----------------------------------------------------------------------------

CLUSTERRATIO or normalized CLUSTERFACTOR (F4) will indicate REORG is necessary
for indexes that are not in the same sequence as the base table. When multiple
indexes are defined on a table, one or more indexes may be flagged as needing
REORG. Specify the most important index for REORG sequencing.
```

Fig. 7–13 Results of Executing the REORCHK Utility.

Interpreting the Output from REORGCHK

The **REORGCHK** utility uses six formulas that can help you decide if a table requires reorganization or not. In this section, we'll look at the table related formulas in more detail.

Let's first explain the elements that are used to calculate those formulas. These elements are shown in Fig. 7–14.

```
Table statistics:

F1: 100*OVERFLOW/CARD < 5
F2: 100*TSIZE / ((FPAGES-1) * 4020) > 70
F3: 100*NPAGES/FPAGES > 80

CREATOR NAME                 CARD    OV    NP    FP    TSIZE F1 F2 F3 REORG
-------------------------------------------------------------------------
DB2        CANDIDATE           3     0     1     1       27  0  - 100 ---
```

Fig. 7–14 REORCHK Table Information.

- **CREATOR** — This column indicates the schema to which the table belongs. Remember that the creator of an object is used as the default schema.
- **NAME** — This column indicates the name of the table for which the **REORGCHK** utility has been run. **REORGCHK** can check a set of tables at one time.
- **CARD** — Indicates the number of data rows in the table.
- **OV** — This is the overflow indicator. It indicates the number of overflow rows. An overflow can occur when a new column is added to a table or when a variable-length value increases its size.
- **NP** — Indicates the total number of pages that contain data.
- **FP** — Indicates the total number of pages that have been allocated to the table.
- **TSIZE** — Indicates the table size in bytes. This value is calculated from the result of multiplying the number of rows in the table times the average column length allowing for an overhead of eight bytes for each row.
- **REORG** — This column has a separate indicator for each one of the first three formulas. A hyphen (-) indicates that reorganization is not recommended. An asterisk (*) indicates that reorganization is recommended.

The formulas F1, F2 and F3 provide guidelines for the table reorganization. The formulas are shown in the **REORGCHK** output.

F1 works with the overflow rows. It recommends a table reorganization if more than 5 percent (5%) of the total number of rows are overflow rows.

F2 works with the free or unused space. It recommends a table reorganization if the table size (**TSIZE**) is less than 70% the size of the total space allocated to the table. In other words, it recommends reorganizing a table when more than 30% of the space allocated is unused.

F3 works with free pages. It recommends a table reorganization when more than 20% of the pages in a table are free. A page is considered free when it has no rows in it.

Whenever the formulas find that table reorganization is needed, it will be shown with an asterisk in the **REORG** column of the output.

For example, if the overflow rows of a table exceed the recommended value, the **REORG** column will look Fig. 7–15.

REORG

- - - - -

*- -

Fig. 7–15 F1 Threshold Has Been Exceeded

Remember, these values are only general guidelines. You can use your own thresholds. However, most of time, you will find these values adequate for your environment.

Interpreting the Index Output from REORGCHK

Another part of **REORGCHK** involves interpreting the output gathered from indexes. To do this, we need some information about the structure of indexes in DB2.

Indexes in DB2 are created using a B+ tree structure. These data structures provide an efficient search method to locate the entry values of an index.

The logical structure of a DB2 index is shown Fig. 7–16.

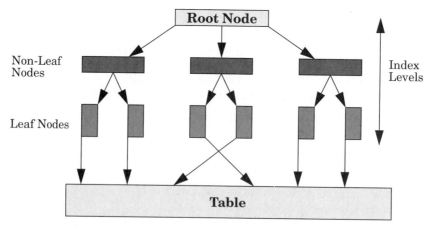

Fig. 7–16 DB2 Index Structure

An index can have several levels. The fewer levels an index has, the more quickly DB2 can access the table or data pages. The index shown in Fig. 7–16 has two levels. Now let's review the **REORGCHK** index information.

```
Index statistics:

F4: CLUSTERRATIO or normalized CLUSTERFACTOR > 80
F5: 100*(KEYS*(ISIZE+10)+(CARD-KEYS)*4) / (NLEAF*4096) > 50
F6: 90*(4000/(ISIZE+10)**(NLEVELS-2))*4096/ (KEYS*(ISIZE+10)+(CARD-KEYS)*4)<100


CREATOR NAME                    CARD LEAF LVLS ISIZE   KEYS   F4    F5 F6 REORG
--------------------------------------------------------------------------------
Table: DB2.CANDIDATE
SYSIBM   SQL960229150128970       3    1    1     9      3   100    -   - ---
```

Fig. 7–17 REORGCHK Index Information

- **CREATOR** — This column indicates the schema to which the index belongs. Remember that the creator of an object is used as the default schema.
- **NAME** — This column indicates the name of the index. **REORGCHK** is only specified at table level. It will show statistics about all the indexes of a table. The information is also collected for system defined indexes, such as primary key indexes.
- **CARD** — Indicates the number of rows in the associated table.
- **LEAF** — Indicates the number of LEAF nodes of the index.
- **LVLS** — Indicates the total number of levels of the index.
- **ISIZE** — Indicates the average column length of the key columns. This column **does not** provide space allocation information.
- **KEYS** — Indicates the number of different key values in the index. With a **UNIQUE** index the **KEY** and **CARD** columns should have the same value.
- **REORG** — This column has a separate indicator for each one of the index formulas. A hyphen indicates that the reorganization is not recommended, and an asterisk indicates that reorganization is recommended.

The formulas F4, F5 and F6 provide guidelines for the data reorganization. The formulas are shown in the **REORGCHK** output.

F4 indicates the **CLUSTERRATIO** or normalized **CLUSTERFACTOR**. This ratio shows the percent of data rows that are stored in same physical sequence as the index.

F5 calculates used space. It says that less than 50% of the space allocated for the index should be empty.

F6 measures the usage of the indexes pages. It indicates the number of index pagees it should be more than 90% of the total entries that **NLEVELS** can handle.

Whenever the formulas find that table reorganization is needed, it will be shown with an asterisk in the **REORG** column of the output.

For example, if the **CLUSTERRATIO** of an index is below the recommended level, the **REORG** column will appear as in Fig. 7–14.

```
                              REORG
                              - - - - -
                               * _ _
```

Fig. 7–18 CLUSTERRATIO Threshold Has Been Exceeded

  The **REORGCHK** utility is an analysis tool provided with DB2. To reorganize your tables you must use the **REORG** utility.

REORGCHK Options

You can use the **CURRENT STATISTICS** option of the **REORGCHK** utility. For example, to analyze the current statistics of table *db2.test_taken*:

```
REORGCHK CURRENT STATISTICS ON TABLE db2.test_taken
```

To review the current statistics of all the tables in a database, including the system catalog and user tables:

```
REORGCHK CURRENT STATISTICS ON TABLE ALL
```

You can also verify the organization of the system catalog tables using the **SYSTEM** option. You can select all the tables under the current user schema name by specifying the **USER** keyword.

```
REORGCHK CURRENT STATISTICS ON TABLE SYSTEM
```

If you don't specify the **CURRENT STATISTICS** parameter, **REORGCHK** will call the **RUNSTATS** utility.

Table Reorganization: REORG

After using the **REORGCHK** utility, you may find the physical reorganization of a table necessary.

✎   In order to use the **REORG** utility, you must have one of the following authorities: SYSADM, SYSCTRL, SYSMAINT, DBADM or CONTROL privilege over the table.

The **REORG** utility will delete all the unused space and write the table data in contiguous pages. With the help of an index, it can also be used to place the data rows in the same physical sequence as the index. These actions can be used to increase the **CLUSTERRATIO** of the selected index.

Let's say that after running the **REORGCHK** utility, you find that it is necessary to reorganize the *db2.test_taken* table.

```
REORG TABLE db2.test_taken
```

This command will reorganize the *db2.test_taken* table and all of its indexes.

✎   When using **REORG**, it is mandatory to use the qualified name of the table.

Using an Index to Reorganize a Table

With the help of an index, **REORG** will put the data in the same physical order as the selected index. This operation can help improve the response time in the execution of your applications. This is because the data pages of the table, will be placed in sequential order according to an index key. This will help DB2 find the data in contiguous space and in the desired order, reducing the seek time needed to read the data.

If DB2 finds an index with a very high cluster ratio, it can use it to avoid a sort, thus improving the performance of applications that require sort operations.

When your tables have only one index, it is recommended to reorganize the table using that index. If your table has more than one index defined on it, you should select the most frequently used index for that table.

As an example, we will assume that the table *db2.test_center* has an index called *by_country*. We will also assume that most of the queries that use the table are grouped by country. Therefore, you might want to reorganize the *db2.test_center* table using the *by_country* index.

The **REORG** command is as follows:

```
REORG TABLE db2.test_center INDEX BY_COUNTRY
```

The **INDEX** option tells the **REORG** utility to use an index to reorganize a table. After the **REORG** command has completed, the physical organization of the table should match the order of the selected index. This way, the key columns will be found sequentially in the table.

In Fig. 7–19, the *HIGH CLUSTER RATIO INDEX* was used to **REORG** the table shown. A high cluster ratio index is onw which the index pages closely match the corresponding data pages. The links into the data pages are known as record ids or RIDs. These RIDs are used to locate the corresponding data page for an index key. The *LOW CLUSTER RATIO INDEX* is shown to emphasize the difference between using or not using an index to perform the reorganization.

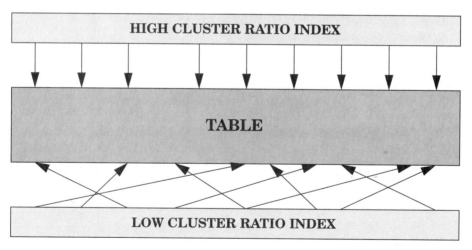

Fig. 7–19 Cluster Ratio Index

The arrows in Fig. 7–19 illustrate the position of the index keys in the table. In a HIGH CLUSTER RATIO INDEX, the keys will be in sequential order. In a LOW CLUSTER RATIO INDEX, the index page order does not correspond with the physical data page order.

After reorganizing a table using the index option, DB2 will not force the subsequent inserts or updates to match the physical organization of the table. You may wish to run the **REORG** utility on a regular basis.

 It is recommended you use the **REORGCHK** utility before attempting a reorganization of a table.

Using a Temporary Table Space for Reorganization

While **REORG** is executing, it creates temporary files in the table space where the table resides. However, you can specify a different table space to create these files. If you want to have control over the location of the files, you need to specify the **USE** option.

 If the table is very large then it is recommended that a temporary table space is used during **REORG**.

In our example, we will place the temporary tables created during the processing of the **REORG** utility in the temporary table space, tempspace1.

```
REORG TABLE db2.test_center INDEX BY_COUNTRY
   USE tempspace1
```

 In the event of a failure, **DO NOT DELETE** the temporary files created by **REORG**. DB2 will use them for recovery purposes.

Recommended Actions after Reorganizing a Table

Table reorganization can help to improve the performance of your applications. There are some additional steps that you should follow. These actions will allow your existing applications to benefit from the table reorganization. Here is a list of recommended actions:

1. Use the **RUNSTATS** utility on your table and its indexes. This will provide the optimizer with the information about the new physical organization of the table and its indexes. We will examine the **RUNSTATS** command in the next section of this chapter.

2. Use the **REBIND** utility on the packages that access the reorganized table. This will allow your applications to take advantage of any changes selected by the optimizer to improve the access strategy of your SQL statements.

RUNSTATS

The system catalog tables contain different information about columns, tables and indexes. They contain information such as the number of rows in a table, the use of the space for a table or index and the number of different values in a column.

However, this information is not actualized automatically. It has to be collected by a special utility called **RUNSTATS**.

The statistics collected by the **RUNSTATS** utility can be used in two ways: to show the physical organization of the data and to provide information that the DB2 optimizer needs in selecting the best access path for executing SQL statements.

We have seen that the **REORGCHK** utility calls the **RUNSTATS** utility to review the information about the physical organization of tables and indexes. We'll talk about some of the options of the **RUNSTATS** utility and how **RUNSTATS** is involved in query optimization.

Updated statistics that reflect the actual state of your tables, indexes and columns is the key to having efficient access paths to data. Whenever you issue an SQL statement, DB2's SQL optimizer reads the system catalog tables to review the available indexes, the size of each table, the characteristics of a column and other information used to select the best access path available for executing a query.

If you have statistics that do not reflect the current state of your tables, the DB2 optimizer will not have the correct information to make the best choice in selecting an access path to execute your query. This becomes more crucial as the complexity of your SQL statements increases. When you access only one table without indexes, there are fewer choices available to the optimizer. However, when your SQL statement involves several tables, each one with one or more indexes, the number of choices available to the optimizer increases dramatically.

Choosing the correct access path can reduce the response time considerably. Depending on the size of the tables, the indexes available and other considerations, the selected access path can affect the response time, varying from minutes to hours. You may also want to consider the physical and logical design in your database. The next step in improving performance involves the use of the **RUNSTATS** utility.

It is recommended to perform **RUNSTATS** on tables that have a large number of updates, inserts or deletes. For tables with a great deal of insert or delete activity, you may decide to run statistics after a fixed period of time or after the insert or delete activity.

✍🏻   It is recommended to issue the **RUNSTATS** command following a
table reorganization.

An important feature of DB2 is that it allows you to reorganize and use the
RUNSTATS utility on the system catalog tables. This feature of DB2 will improve
the access plans generated when querying the system catalog tables. DB2 may
access these tables when you issue an SQL statement, even though you are
referencing only user tables. Therefore, it is very important to have statistics on
the system catalog tables.

Using the RUNSTATS Utility

In order to use the **RUNSTATS** utility, you must have one of the following
authorities: SYSADM, SYSCTRL, SYSMAINT, DBADM or CONTROL privilege
on the table.

Suppose you are the database administrator and have noticed that every
time your application attempts to resolve a user request, it takes a considerable
amount of time before data is retrieved. You decide to investigate by using the
RUNSTATS utility on some of the system catalog tables. We will use the
SYSIBM.SYSCOLUMNS table for the following example:

```
RUNSTATS ON TABLE SYSIBM.SYSCOLUMNS
```

The **RUNSTATS** utility does not produce any output. You can only see its results
by querying the system catalog tables. More importantly, the performance of
your applications can be improved.

As we said before, after executing the **RUNSTATS** utility, the system catalog
tables are updated with the information gathered by the utility.

Fig. 7–20 shows some of the data updated by **RUNSTATS**. This output was
obtained by selecting all the columns of the *SYSSTAT.TABLES* catalog view.

TABSCHEMA	TABNAME	CARD	NPAGES	FPAGES	OVERFLOW
SYSIBM	SYSCOLUMNS	927	32	32	1
SYSIBM	SYSTABLES	-1	-1	-1	-1

Fig. 7–20 Reviewing the SYSSTAT.TABLESTable after RUNSTATS

In Fig. 7–20, the -1 (minus one) value indicates that there are no statistics available for that object. The columns of the *SYSSTAT.TABLES* table have the same meaning as those of the **REORGCHK** utility.

- **CARD** — Indicates the number of data rows in the table.
- **NPAGES** — Indicates the total number of pages that contain data.
- **FPAGES** — Indicates the total number of pages that have been allocated to the table.
- **OVERFLOW** — Indicates the number of overflow rows. An overflow can occur when a new column is added to a table or when a variable length value increases its size.

Identifying Updated Statistics

It is not difficult to identify the absence of available statistics for a specific object. The -1 (minus one) value in the statistical information columns indicates this state. However, it is also important to identify the time of the last update of the object's statistics.

When you perform **RUNSTATS** on an object, the utility records the timestamp of its execution in the system catalog tables. Depending on the type of object, you can find the timestamp information in *SYSCAT.TABLES* or *SYSCAT.INDEXES*. In both views, the information is stored in the *STATS_TIME* column.

Old statistics can also affect the access path selection. They can mislead the optimizer to choose a bad access plan for an SQL statement.

In summary, only actualized statistics can help the optimizer choose the best access path for a particular SQL statement.

Collecting Statistics for Tables and Indexes
It is possible to perform **RUNSTATS** on a table and all of its indexes at the same time. This is shown in the following command:

```
RUNSTATS ON TABLE db2.test_taken AND ALL INDEXES
```

The **REORGCHK** utility executes the command shown when it calls the **RUNSTATS** utility. The **ALL INDEXES** option indicates that statistics for all the indexes of a table are required. The **AND** option specifies that you want statistics for the table and for the indexes as well.

Collecting Statistics for Indexes Only

After creating a new index on a table, you may find it useful to gather statistics only for the indexes of a table. **RUNSTATS** allows you to collect the statistics for indexes only. This way, the table information will not be updated.

```
RUNSTATS ON TABLE db2.test_taken FOR INDEXES ALL
```

Collecting Distribution Statistics on Table Columns

There can be some columns in which the values are not distributed in a uniform way. For example, salary data would likely not be evenly distributed from zero to $100,000 within a company.

This kind of non-uniform distribution of data can confuse the optimizer in choosing the most appropriate access method. However, the **RUNSTATS** utility provides the ability to show this non-uniform distribution to the optimizer. This will improve the access plans for such kinds of tables.

Let's suppose that 75% of the DB2 Certification Program Exams are taken in one testing center. The other 25% are distributed in other test centers. This is a non-uniform distribution of values. This information is stored in the *db2.test_taken* for which you want to collect distribution information.

```
RUNSTATS ON TABLE db2.test_taken WITH DISTRIBUTION
```

The **WITH DISTRIBUTION** option is used to instruct DB2 to collect data about the distribution of values for the columns in a table. This option is related to three database configuration parameters: **NUM_FREQVALUES**, **NUM_QUANTILES** and **STAT_HEAP_SZ**. These parameters will limit the action of the **WITH DISTRIBUTION** option.

NUM_FREQVALUES — Indicates the number of most frequent values that DB2 will look for. For example, if it is set to 10, only information for the 10 most frequent values will be obtained.

NUM_QUANTILES — Indicates the number of quantiles that DB2 will look for.

STAT_HEAP_SZ — Indicates how much memory DB2 uses for collecting these statistics. It is recommended to increase the size of this parameter if use the **DETAILED** option during **RUNSTATS**.

This procedure is demanding, and it is not recommended for all your tables. Only tables presenting a high volume of non-uniform values are candidates for this option.

Collecting Detailed Information about Indexes

It is also possible to collect data that will give more information about an index. This information is used to model the number of I/O operations required to read data pages into the buffer pools.

Now, let's say that you want to collect detailed information about the indexes of the table, *db2.test_taken*:

```
RUNSTATS ON TABLE db2.test_taken FOR DETAILED
INDEXES ALL
```

The **DETAILED** option is used to gather this information. The statistics collected are stored in the **CLUSTERFACTOR** and **PAGE_FETCH_PAIRS** columns of the *SYSIBM.SYSINDEXES* system catalog table.

The **CLUSTERFACTOR** and **PAGE_FETCH_PAIRS** data is a more detailed measurement of the relationship between the index and the data pages. These two values can give the optimizer a more better method of modeling the I/O operations and chose a better access path for a SQL statement. The **DETAILED** option is also affected by the **STAT_HEAP_SZ** database parameter.

Recommended Actions after RUNSTATS

Now that the system catalog tables have been updated, you should perform the following procedures. This will give your applications the benefit of the recently collected statistics about your tables.

Do a **REBIND** on the packages that access the reorganized table. This will provide your applications with any changes selected by the DB2's SQL optimizer to improve the access strategy for your SQL statements.

Dynamic SQL statements will experience immediate benefits from the execution of the **RUNSTATS** utility. Packages in this situation do not need to be rebound.

The REBIND Utility

The **REBIND** utility provides you with the ability to re-create a package with the information available in the system catalog tables. This will allow your embedded SQL applications to use a different access path as selected by the optimizer.

The **REBIND** utility is recommended after doing **REORG** or **RUNSTATS**. The DB2 SQL optimizer will use the new organization and recently collected statistics to generate an access path. This access path will be better suited for the new physical organization of your data.

For example, suppose you have an application called *db2cert* that uses the table *db2.test_taken*. You have just created a new index for the table, and you need to use **REBIND** so that the *db2cert* application uses the new index for data access.

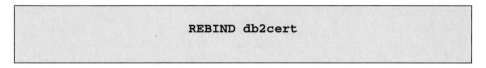

REBIND db2cert

✍️ The **REBIND** utility does not have any options.

Data Maintenance Process

As shown in Fig. 7–21, the data maintenance process starts with the **REORGCHK**

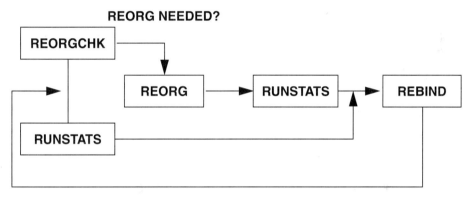

Fig. 7–21 The Data Maintenance Process

utility. The **REORGCHK** utility can execute the **RUNSTATS** utility at the same time. However, it is recommended issuing **RUNSTATS** separately, so that you can control the utility's options to customize for your environment. After performing the **RUNSTATS** utility, the **REORGCHK** utility reviews the statistics collected, applies six formulas and then gives you the recommendations about **REORG**.

If reorganization is recommended, you will use the **REORG** utility on the selected objects and then do **RUNSTATS** and **REBIND**. You also must perform a **REBIND** on any packages affected by the above operations, so that they can take advantage of the benefits of the new physical organization and updated statistics of your data. After new update, insert and delete operations, as part of the data maintenance process, repeat by first executing the **REORGCHK** utility.

You may want to establish a routine for doing the **RUNSTATS** and the **REBIND** processes. Updated statistics will give you the precise information about your database state.

Modeling a Production Environment

You can use the *SYSSTAT* schema to update system catalog statistical information. You can enter values for statistics such as table cardinality, column distribution or index cluster ratio. By doing this, you will be able to model different volumes of data on smaller databases.

This is useful when you want to be sure that the access plan your applications are using in your production environment are the same as those in your development environment. The access paths selected by the optimizer in each environment may differ because of the different data volumes.

By updating the *SYSSTAT* views, you will be able to provide the optimizer with the same environment that you will find in a different database. The update procedure is made by using the SQL **UPDATE** statement.

There are five updatable views under the *SYSSTAT* schema. These views are:

- *SYSSTAT.TABLES*
- *SYSSTAT.COLUMNS*
- *SYSSTAT.INDEXES*
- *SYSSTAT.COLDIST*
- *SYSSTAT.FUNCTIONS*

These catalog views can also be used to provide a "what-if" analysis for your database applications. For example, you can increase the cardinality of a table or the cluster ratio of an index.

You can use the **REBIND** utility to model the behavior of your static SQL applications in the "what-if" analysis process. You can create or drop an index and then use the **REBIND** utility to see how the access plan is affected by it.

As a general recommendation, only update the *SYSSTAT* schema view in a development environment.

User Maintenance

This section looks at some of the ways that an instance or database administrator can control users accessing the database. We'll also look at how the administrator of the instance can control how and where certain applications are executed.

Fenced and Not-Fenced Procedures and Functions

The administrator of the instance can also control where an application is executed. This control pertains to stored procedures and user-defined functions or UDFs.

A stored procedure or function that is fenced runs isolated from the storage and control blocks of DB2. Fig. 7–22 shows the basic differences between a fenced or not-fenced function.

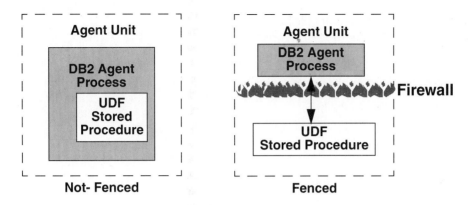

Fig. 7–22 Fenced and Not-Fenced Functions and Procedures

User-defined functions and stored procedures are created as fenced by default and do not need any special privilege for creation. The execution of a fenced procedure or function needs more resources than those of not-fenced ones due to the extra cost associated with building, maintaining and communicating between the two isolated address spaces.

A not-fenced procedure or function, as shown in Fig. 7–22, executes in the same address space as the database manager. Fenced functions or procedures require more memory on the database server. Not-fenced functions do have the benefit of increased performance when compared with a fenced procedure or function. However, there is the danger that user code could accidentally or even maliciously damage the database control structures. Because of these risks, the ability to create not-fenced procedures is a special privilege.

The authority **CREATE_NOT_FENCED** is required for a user other than the instance administrator to create. Only the instance administrator can grant this privilege to a user.

If a stored procedure or user-defined function is defined as not-fenced or not-fenced, it should only be done to maximize the performance benefits. It should be thoroughly tested prior to running as a not-fenced procedure. The procedure or function should first be defined as a fenced one that has undergone exhaustive testing. Then, the procedure must be dropped and re-created as not-fenced.

The LIST APPLICATIONS Command

The **LIST APPLICATIONS** command will display information about the applications executing within the instance. The type of information you'll receive is the name of the application, the auth-id, the agent-id, the application-id and the database that the application is accessing.

The complete syntax of the command is shown in Fig. 7–23.

```
LIST APPLICATIONS [FOR DATABASE database-alias]
                  {SHOW DETAIL}
```

Fig. 7–23 The LIST APPLICATIONS Command

The database administrator can use the output of this command as a tool for controlling users or problem determination. A common usage of the command is in conjunction with the **FORCE** command.

The FORCE Command

The **FORCE** command will force local or remote users or applications off the DB2 system. A database administrator can use the **LIST APPLICATIONS** command to find a particular agent-id and then force that user off the system. Fig. 7–24 shows these two commands.

```
 $ db2 list applications

Auth Id Application Name  Agent Id Application Id          DB Name
------- ----------------- -------- -------------------- -------

  DB2        db2bp_32      9878     *LOCAL.db2.960426161832 DB2CERT

  DB2        db2bp_32      27134    *LOCAL.db2.960426161005 DB2CERT


 $ db2 "force application ( 9878 )"
 DB20000I The FORCE APPLICATION command completed successfully.
 DB21024I This command is asynchronous and may not be effective
 immediately.

Auth Id Application Name  Agent Id Application Id          DB Name
------- ----------------- -------- -------------------- -------

  DB2        db2bp_32      27134    *LOCAL.db2.960426161832 DB2CERT
```

Fig. 7–24 Controlling Users within DB2

From Fig. 7–24, you can see that there are two applications executing. Both are from the same user, *db2*. They both access the same database, *db2cert*. To remove the second application, the **FORCE APPLICATION** command specifying the agent-id of the application to terminate is supplied with the command parameters.

Database Recovery

Recovering your environment can be very important in preventing loss of critical data. A number of tools are available to help you manage your environment and to ensure that you can perform adequate recovery of your data.

We'll discuss the concept of logging in a relational database system as it pertains to the recovery of a database. Log files are files which are used by DB2 to ensure the integrity of your database even when the system crashes due to some unforeseen problem, such as a power failure. To fully understand the purpose of logging, the concepts of *unit of work* and *transaction* must first be explained.

Unit of Work

In order to ensure consistency of the data in a database, it is often necessary for applications to apply a number of changes all at once. Likewise, it may be necessary to inhibit all changes. This is called the unit of work. A unit of work is a recoverable sequence of operations within an application process. The unit of work is the basic mechanism that an application uses to ensure that it doesn't introduce inconsistent data in a database. At any time, an application process has a single unit of work, but the life of an application process may involve many units of work.

Transaction

In relational databases such as DB2, the unit of work is called the transaction. A transaction is a recoverable sequence of SQL operations within an application process. Any reading or writing to a database is done within a transaction.

Any application that successfully connects to a database automatically starts a transaction. The application must end the transaction by issuing an SQL **COMMIT** or an SQL **ROLLBACK** statement. The SQL **COMMIT** statement tells the database manager to apply all database changes (inserts, updates, deletes) in the transaction to the database at once. The SQL **ROLLBACK** statement tells the database manager not to apply the changes but to return the affected rows to their original state just before the beginning of the transaction.

Use of Log Files

DB2 has implemented a write ahead logging scheme to ensure the integrity of your data. The basis for write ahead logging is that when an SQL call is made which deletes, inserts or updates any data in the database, the changes are first written to the log files. When an SQL commit is issued, DB2 ensures that all log files required for replay are written to disk. In case of a mishap such as power failure, for example, the log files would be used to bring the database back to a consistent state. All committed transactions would be redone, and all uncommitted transactions would be rolled back.

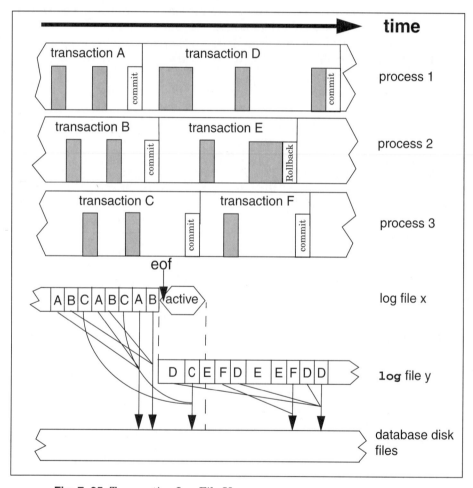

Fig. 7–25 Transaction Log File Use

All databases have log files associated with them. Log files have a predefined length. Therefore, when one log file gets filled, logging continues in another log file.

Fig. 7–25 shows how multiple log files are being used to manage concurrent transactions. The top part of the diagram represents the evolution in time of three user processes (1–3) accessing the same database. The boxes represent database changes such as inserts or updates. You can see the life of every transaction (A–F). The lower-middle of the diagram shows how the database changes are synchronously recorded in the log files (x,y). The letter in each box indicates the transaction to which the database change belongs.

When an SQL **COMMIT** is issued, the log buffer containing the transaction is written to disk. This is represented by the arrows and the small wavy lines. Transaction E is never written to disk because it ends with an SQL **ROLLBACK** command. When log file x runs out of room to store the first database change of transaction D, the logging process switches to log file y. Log file x remains active until the writing of all changes of transaction C to the database disk files is complete. The period of time during which log file x remains active after the moment logging switched to log file y is represented by the hexagon.

Log Management Configuration Parameters

There are a series of parameters that are used by the logging process with DB2. Every time you change the value of these parameters, you have to terminate the database connection and then re-establish it so that the database configuration file is read with the updated changes. Fig. 7–26 shows the parameters that affect logging.

- **LOGBUFSZ**

  The log buffer size parameter determines how much database shared memory will be allocated to buffer the log records before they are written out to disk. The value for this parameter will indicate the number of 4K pages up to a maximum of 128 4K pages.

- **LOGFILSIZ**

  This value determines the number of pages to be allocated when a log file is requested. Combined with LOGPRIMARY and LOGSECOND, this value determines the disk space required to support logging. It is measured in units of 4K pages.

- **LOGPRIMARY**

  This value represents the number of primary log files that will be allocated to support database logging. Each one will be of **LOGFILSIZ** in size.

- **LOGSECOND**

  This parameter specifies the maximum number of secondary log files that can be created when needed by the system. When the primary log files become full, the secondary log files of size **LOGFILSIZ** are allocated one-at-a-time as needed. The default number of secondary log files is two.

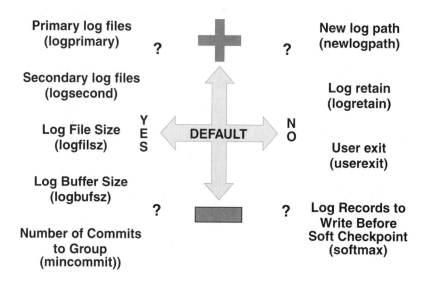

Fig. 7–26 Logging Configuration Parameters

- **NEWLOGPATH**

  The default subdirectory for the log files is defined in *SQLOGDIR* which is a subdirectory of the database directory. For recovery purposes it is better to place log files on a different physical disk than the database files. This parameter identifies a new path for placement of log files. Remember that the new path does not become active until all connections to the database end and the database is in a consistent state.

- **SOFTMAX**

  When a database is restarted, the log control file is used to determine which records from the log file need to be applied to the database. This value is a percentage of the **LOGFILSIZ** that determines if a log control file should be written more frequently than the default to the disk. The default is that the control log file is always written to disk when it is full, known as a hard checkpoint.

- **LOGRETAIN**

  Indicates if the log retention or archival logging is to be used.

- **USEREXIT**

  Setting this value **enables** archival logging and roll forward recovery.

- **MINCOMMIT**

  This value indicates that a grouping of commits issued by multiple applications is to be attempted if the value is set greater than 1.

- **OVERFLOWLOGPATH**
  Specify an alternative log path to search for archived logs. The default is null.

- **NUM_IOCLEANERS**
  Specify the number of asynchronous page cleaners for a database.

 The page cleaners examine the buffer pool, looking for pages which need to be written to disk. In this way, the regular database agents can more likely find empty space in the buffer pool.

Types of Logging

Now we will see the two types of logging that can occur in DB2:

- **Circular logging**
- **Archival logging**

Circular Logging

With this type of logging, log files are used in sequence. They can be reused when all units of work contained within them are committed or rolled back. The committed changes are reflected on the disks supporting the database. The circular logging method is shown in Fig. 7–27.

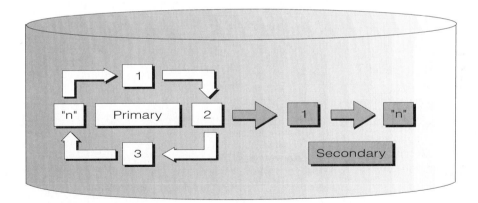

Fig. 7–27 Circular Logging

Circular logging uses two type of log files:

- **Primary log files**
- **Secondary log files**

Primary log files are pre-allocated, while secondary log files are only allocated when necessary. If the database manager requests the next log in the sequence and it is not available for reuse, a secondary log file will be allocated. Secondary log files will be allocated until the primary log file becomes available for reuse or the number of secondary logs permitted for allocation is exceeded. Secondary log files are de-allocated once the database manager determines that they are no longer needed. Primary log files are allocated when the database becomes active.

The number of primary log files and secondary log files is determined by the database parameters **LOGPRIMARY** and **LOGSECOND**.

When a database is first created, circular logging is enabled as the default logging method.

Databases configured with circular logging are only recoverable to the point at which the backup was taken. All work done on the database since the backup was taken is lost when the database is restored. For this reason, circular logging works best for query-only databases.

Archival Logging

Archival logging is the log file management technique where log files are archived when they became inactive. There are three types of log files associated with this method. They are shown in Fig. 7–28.

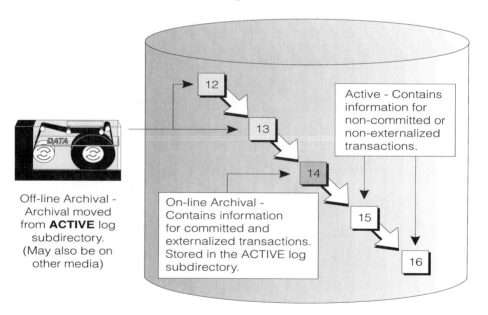

Fig. 7–28 Archival Logging

1. **Active** (Indicated by numbers 15 and 16)

   These files contain information related to transactions that have not yet committed (or rolled back) work. They also contain information about transactions that have been committed but whose changes have not yet been written to the database files.

2. **On-line Archival** (Indicated by number 14)

   These files contain information related to completed transactions no longer required for crash recovery protection. They are called "on-line" because they reside in the same subdirectory as the active log files.

3. **Off-line Archival** (Indicated by numbers 12 and 13)

   These files have been moved from the active log file subdirectory. The method of moving these files could be a manual process such as that invoked through a **user exit**. Archived log files can be placed off-line simply by moving them to another directory, storing them on tape or elsewhere.

Two configuration parameters allow you to configure a database for archival logging:

- **LOGRETAIN**
- **USEREXIT**

When the **LOGRETAIN** database configuration parameter is enabled, log files are not deleted when they become inactive. When the **user exit** database configuration parameter is enabled, the database manager will call a program named *db2uexit* each time a log file is no longer needed for log writes. The database name and path of the log file are passed to the program.

Archival logging is not the default logging method, but it is the only method that will allow you to perform roll forward recovery.

Log File Usage

The log files are used for the following situations:

1. **Rollback**
2. **Crash Recovery**
3. **Roll Forward Recovery**

The **ROLLBACK** command uses log files to terminate a unit of work and back out of the database changes that were made by that unit of work.

Crash Recovery

If your system experiences a disk crash, power outage or other kind of failure, crash recovery is needed to bring the database back to a consistent usable state. Crash recovery consists of two phases. The first phase reapplies all transactions to the database regardless of whether they were committed or not. This phase completes when the end of the active log files is reached.

The second phase is to roll back all uncommitted transactions. The database configuration parameter that sets the crash recovery is **AUTORESTART**. By default, this parameter is ON.

Roll Forward Recovery

The **ROLLFORWARD DATABASE** command is invoked every time a table space backup or a database backup is restored. Roll forward applies transactions recorded in the database log files. Every time an I/O error occurs while reading or writing to a disk, the table space where the page resides is disabled and placed in a "roll forward pending" state. If the pending state cannot be cleared with just a roll forward of the table space, a restore followed by a roll forward is required.

Here's the syntax for the **ROLLFORWARD DATABASE** command:

```
ROLLFORWARD DATABASE database-alias
[USER username [USING password]] [TO {isotime |
END OF LOGS} [AND STOP] | STOP | QUERY STATUS]
[TABLESPACE on-line] [OVERFLOW LOG PATH log-directory]
```

Fig. 7–29 Syntax of **ROLLFORWARD DATABASE** Command

The description of the parameters, as shown in Fig. 7–29, are the following:

- **database**-alias
  Database name which will be rolled forward.

- **username**
  The authorized user id under which the database will be rolled forward.

- **password**
  The password for the supplied user name.

- **TO isotime**
  The point in time to which all committed transactions are rolled forward. This parameter is only valid for full database restore.

- **TO END OF LOGS**
  This will cause the roll forward to process as many log files as it can locate in the current log path directory.

- **STOP | AND STOP**

  This will indicate that you have processed all of the log files and you want to make the database consistent.

- **QUERY STATUS**

  List the log files which have been rolled forward, the next archival log file required and the timestamp of the last committed transaction since roll forward processing began.

- **TABLESPACE on-line**

  Indicates that the roll forward will be done at the table space level.

- **OVERFLOW LOG PATH**

  Specifies an alternative log path to search for archived log files.

Backup and Restore

This section describes the backup and restore utilities which are used to safeguard and recover databases in the event of failure. We will talk about both database and table space backup and restore considerations.

Performing a Database Level Backup

You can back up your database while it is either on-line or off-line. The default is off-line. If the backup is performed off-line, only the backup task can be connected to the database. The stored data must be consistent. This level of backup is a requirement for disaster recovery and should be an essential part of any backup/restore strategy.

If the backup is performed on-line, other applications or processes can continue to connect to it while the backup task is running. on-line backups are supported only if roll forward recovery is enabled.

You must have SYSADM, SYSCTRL or SYSMAINT authority to use the **BACKUP DATABASE** command. The database manager must be started (**DB2START**) before issuing the **BACKUP DATABASE** command. If you are using the Database Director, you do not need to explicitly start the database manager. The **BACKUP DATABASE** command uses the database alias name, not the database name itself, as a parameter to the command.

The database can be local or remote. You can back up a database or table space to disk, tape or a location managed by a utility like ADSTAR Distributed Storage Manager (ADSM). If you change a database configuration parameter to enable roll forward recovery, you must take an off-line backup of the database before it is usable.

Multiple files can be created to contain the backed image up. During the backup procedure, an internal buffer is filled with data to be backed up. When this buffer becomes full, the data is copied to the backup medium.

You can specify the number of pages to use for the backup buffer(s) when you invoke the **BACKUP DATABASE** command. The minimum number of pages is 16. If a system crash occurs during a critical stage of backing up the database, you cannot successfully connect to the database until you re-issue the **BACKUP DATABASE** command.

The syntax of the **BACKUP DATABASE** command is as follows:

```
BACKUP DATABASE database-alias
    [USER username [USING password]]
    [TABLESPACE tblspace-name [{,tblspace-name}.. ]]
    [ONLINE]
    [USE ADSM [OPEN num-sess SESSIONS]] |
    TO dir/dev [ {,dir/dev} .. ]   |
    LOAD lib-name [OPEN num-sess SESSIONS]]
    [WITH num-buff BUFFERS]
    [BUFFER buffer-size] [WITHOUT PROMPTING]
```

Fig. 7–30 Syntax of the BACKUP DATABASE Command

The parameters, as shown in Fig. 7–30, are explained further:

- **DATABASE database-alias**
  Specifies the alias name of the database to back up.

- **USER username**
  Identifies the user name under which the backup is processed.

- **USING** password
  The password used to authenticate the user name.

- **TABLESPACE tablespace-name**
  Lists one or more table spaces within the database to be backed up.

- **ONLINE**
  Specifies on-line processing; the default is off-line. on-line processing requires that the database be enabled for roll forward processing.

- **USE ADSM OPEN num-sess SESSIONS**
  Specifies that ADSM will be the backup target for this backup and "num-sessions" ADSM sessions will be used throughout the backup.

- **TO target-area**
  Specifies where the target placement for the backup will be. This can be a directory or tape device name. If backing up to a directory, the full path name must be specified. If no parameter is issued, the backup will be placed under the current directory.

- **LOAD library-name OPEN num-sess SESSIONS**
  Specifies that a third-party vendor product will be used as the target for this backup and that "num-sessions" will be used.

- **WITH num-buffers BUFFERS**
  The number of buffers to be used.

- **BUFFER buffer-size**
  The size in pages of the buffer used for the appropriate process. The minimum value for this is 16 pages. The default is 1,024 pages.

- **WITHOUT PROMPTING**
  Perform the backup without prompting for new media.

The Backup File

Depending on your platform, the naming conventions used for files can be different. The naming of backup files in DB2 is not identical across platforms. However, the format for the file is easy to understand. Fig. 7–31 shows the format of the backup file for the AIX and OS/2 platforms.

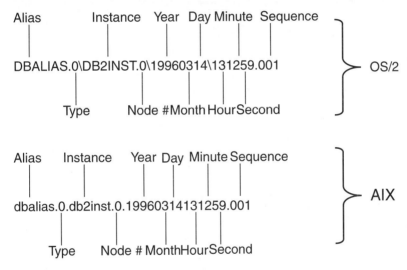

Fig. 7–31 Backup File Format

There are three possible ways that data has been saved in the backup file:

1. Type 0 is for full database
2. Type 3 is for a table space backup
3. Type 4 is for a copy from a table load

The number after the instance name is reserved for the node number. Tape images for backups are not named but contain the same information on the header for verification purposes.

Performing a Database Level Restore

The database to which you perform the restore operation may be different or it may be the same one from where the data was originally backed up from. You may restore the data to a new or an existing database. In order restore to an existing database from a full database or table space backup, you must have SYSADM, SYSCTRL or SYSMAINT authority. To restore to a new database, you must have SYSADM or SYSCTRL authority. The database manager must be started before restoring a database. You can only use the **RESTORE DATABASE** command if the database or table space has been backed up with the **BACKUP DATABASE** command.

You can select, at the time of the restore, which type of restore is to be performed. You can select from the following types:

1. A full restore of everything from the backup image.
2. A table space restore (using a backup image that only includes table spaces).
3. A restore of only the recovery history file from the backup image.

The database may be local or remote. The restore requires an exclusive connection so no applications can be running against the database when the task is started. The size and number of buffers used to support the restore can be specified as a command option. During the restore procedure, you may have the ability to optionally elect to use **multiple buffers** to improve the performance of the restore operation. You may specify the number of pages to use for each restore buffer when you invoke the **RESTORE DATABASE** command. The minimum number of pages is 16.

The backup copy of the database or table space to be used by the restore database command may be located on disk, tape or in a location managed by products like ADSTAR Distributed Storage Manager (ADSM).

✍️   In OS/2, the restore copy also may be located on diskette.

We said that when you restore the database, you can specify whether to restore to an existing database or to a new database as shown in Fig. 7–32.

Once the database level restore starts, the database is not usable until the command completes successfully. It is also possible that a roll forward will be required before access is permitted. If a failure occurs during the restore operation, you cannot connect to the database until you re-issue the restore command and successfully complete the restore.

There are certain considerations for each case:

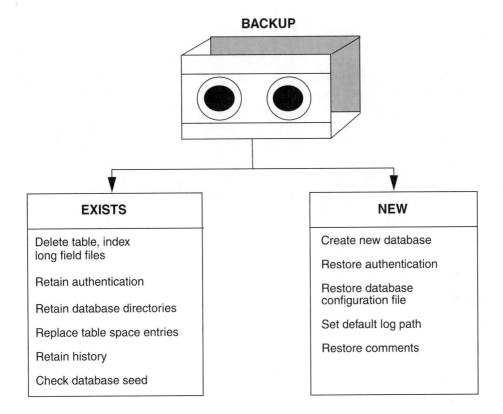

Fig. 7–32 Restoring a Backup Image to a Database

- Restoring to an existing database
  You may restore an image of a full database backup or table space backup to an existing database of one or more table spaces. The restore task deletes table, index and long field contents from the existing database and replaces them with the contents from the backup image. Then, it retains the authentication and the database directories that define where the database resides and how it is cataloged for the existing database. Finally the restore replaces the table space table entries for each table space being restored and retains the recovery history file unless the one on disk is damaged.

- Restoring to a new database

  You may create a new database and then restore the backup image of the data. In this case, the restore task creates a new database using the database name and database alias name that was specified by the target database alias parameter. Then, it restores the authentication type and the database configuration file from the backup image. It also modifies the database configuration file to indicate that the default log file path should be used for logging and, finally, restores the database comments from the backup image for the database directories.

If the target alias that you are restoring to and the alias in the backup image are the same, the database seed is checked. If the database seeds are different, the backup image was not made from the database being restored. The restore process continues deleting logs associated with the existing database, copying the database configuration file from the backup image and changing the database configuration file to indicate that the default log file path should be used for logging. If the database seeds are the same, the backup image was created from the database being restored. Restore will continue retaining the current database configuration file unless the file is corrupted, and deleting the logs if the image is of a non-recoverable database. Otherwise the log files will be kept.

Here's the **RESTORE DATABASE** command syntax:

```
RESTORE DATABASE source-database-alias [USER username
   [USING password]] [TABLESPACE on-line | HISTORY FILE]
   USE ADSM [OPEN num-sessions ]] | FROM dir/dev
   [{.dir/dev} ..] LOAD shared-lib [OPEN num-sess SESSIONS]}
   [TAKEN AT date-time] [TO target-directory]
   [INTO target-database-alias] [WITH num-buff BUFFERS]
   [BUFFER buffer-size] [WITHOUT ROLLING FORWARD]
   [WITHOUT PROMPTING]
```

Fig. 7–33 Syntax of **RESTORE DATABASE** Command

The parameters are described as follows:

- **DATABASE source-database-alias**

  Specifies the alias name of the database to restore.

- **USER username**

  Identifies the user name under which the database is to be restored.

- **USING password**

  The password used to authenticate the user name.

- **TABLESPACE ONLINE**

  Specifies that this is an on-line process; the default is off-line. Other users can connect while the backup is being restored. Once the restore process begins for a table space, that table space is not usable until the restore completes and a successful roll forward to the end of log files has occurred. On-line table space processing requires that the database be enabled for roll forward processing.

- **HISTORY FILE**

  Specifies that only the history file from the backup image will be restored.

- **USE ADSM OPEN num-sess SESSIONS**

  Specifies that the database is to be restored form ADSM managed output using "num-sessions".

- **FROM dir/device**

  Specifies the device or directory on which the backup image resides.

- **LOAD library-name OPEN num-sess SESSIONS**

  Specifies that a third-party vendor product will be used as the target for this backup and that a specific number of I/O sessions will be used.

- **TAKEN AT date-time**

  This is a parameter allows you to choose between several backup images. You must issue the full timestamp to indicate which database image is being restored.

- **TO target-directory**

  Specifies the path to be used to create the target database. This path must exist on the server.

- **INTO target-database-alias**

  Specifies the name of the database to restore into so you can change the name or the database at restore time.

- **WITH num-buff BUFFERS**

  The number of buffers to be used.

- **BUFFER buffer-size**

  The size in pages of the buffer used for the appropriate process. The minimum value is 16 pages; the default value is 1,024 pages.

- **WITHOUT ROLLING FORWARD**

  This option is valid with an off-line backup image of a recoverable database. This will indicate that you do not want to roll forward and the database should be made consistent to the end of the backup.

- **WITHOUT PROMPTING**

  Perform restore without prompting for new media.

Performing a Table Space Level Backup or Restore

A table space level backup and restore cannot be run at the same time even if they cover different table spaces. If you have to back up tables that span more than one table space, you should back up or restore the set of table spaces together. A table space backup can contain a single or multiple table spaces. However, the restore is not selective.

The table space level restore must be to the same database in which the table space backup was made. The name and seed for a table space restore must be identical A table space level restore can be performed using a backup image that contains one or more table space level backups.

To ensure that restored table spaces are synchronized with the rest of the database, the table spaces must be rolled forward to the end of the log files. For this reason, table space level backup and restore can only be performed if roll forward recovery is enabled.

Another important consideration is that you must manually retrieve any archived log files. This is not done automatically for a table space level roll forward.

In cases where it cannot be determined that the backup is valid (if, for example, the database has been restored and rolled forward, thus creating a new log sequence), the restore may be successful; the broken restore set will be detected during the roll forward recovery. This technique does not require the backup restored in phase one of the recovery process to reflect a point of consistency.

Fig. 7–34 shows the backup of the table space reflecting a point of consistency. Here, the backup image of the table space(s) was taken. Logging continued with transactions being recorded in the log files at the point in time after the backup completed. At a later point in time, a crash occurred that required the table space backup to be restored. The roll forward must take place and go to the end of the log files to ensure a point of consistency within the table space and database.

Each component of a table may be backed up and restored with the table space in which it resides, independently of the other components of the table. An exception to this general rule concerns recovery strategies for tables involving LOB and long field data. If the roll forward phase of such a restore process includes a **REORG** of such tables, the backup image previously restored must contain all related LOB and long field data. This could mean that the backup image must contain more than one table space if the LOB and long field data were placed in separate table spaces.

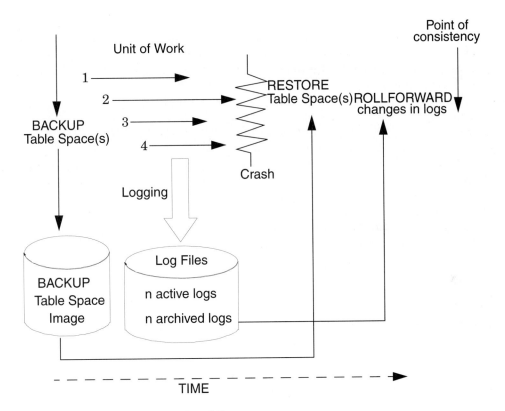

Fig. 7–34 Table Space Level Restore

Summary of Backup/Restore Consideration

There are some items for consideration in your backup/restore strategy:

1. Consider the type of logging to be used - circular versus archival.
2. Decide what type of access you can live with for both the backup and restore operations.
3. Realize that your recovery action may include a roll forward operation.
4. Understand the point in time to which a roll forward must take place.

Fig. 7–35 summarizes the considerations for backup and restore, at both the table space and full database level.

Limitations and Restrictions of Backup					
	Full Database Backup Off-line		Full Database Backup On-line	Table Space Backup Off-line	Table Space Backup On-line
Logging Type Allowed	Archival	Circular	Archival	Archival	Archival
Access Allowed During Backup Process	N/A		Full Access to Database	No Access to Database	Full Access to Database
Database State Following Restore	Database in Rollforward Pending	Database Consistent	Database in Rollforward Pending	Database in Rollforward Pending	Database in Rollforward Pending
Rollforward Required	Any Point in Time	N/A	Any Point in TIme Past End of Backup	End of Log Files	End of Log Files

Fig. 7–35 Limitations and Restrictions of Backup

The Recovery History File

A **recovery history file** contains historical information for a database. The file is maintained at the database level and resides in the same directory as the database configuration file. If the database is dropped, the history file is removed.

The recovery history file is updated every time a full database or table space(s) backup or restore is performed or when a load of a table occurs.

The recovery history file provides a summary of backup information useful in the event that a database or table space must be restored. The backup information includes:

- The part of the database that has been copied by a backup, load or copy operation
- When the database was copied
- The location of the copy
- Time of the last restore

To list all the backups, restoreS and loads that have been done for *db2cert* database, the command would be:

```
            LIST HISTORY ALL FOR db2cert
```

There is a **RESTORE** option that permits only the history file in a backup image to be restored.

The history file is automatically written to whenever a backup, restore or load is performed. You cannot insert records into the history FILE directly.

You will get a warning if the history file cannot be inserted into or updated, due to either a full file system, a damaged history file or an I/O error. If the file system is full, the current entry will be lost.

You can manage the recovery history file using the **PRUNE HISTORY** command. It can be used to delete entries from the recovery history file. The syntax of the command is shown in Fig. 7–36.

```
    PRUNE HISTORY timestamp [WITH FORCE OPTION]
```

Fig. 7–36 Syntax of the PRUNE HISTORY Command

All entries with timestamps equal to or less than the timestamp provided are deleted from the recovery history file. The **WITH FORCE OPTION** specifies that the file will be pruned according to the timestamp specified, even if some entries from the most recent restore set are deleted from the file.

You must have SYSADM, SYSCTRL, SYSMAINT or DBADM authority to use the **PRUNE HISTORY** command. There will be a recovery history file for every database. The size of this file depends on the **REC_HIS_RETENTN** database configuration parameter and the frequency of backups, restores and table loads. **REC_HIS_RETENTN** is used to set the retention period of the history file (the default is 366 days). If you want to keep the recovery history file indefinitely, set this parameter to -1. By default, it is automatically pruned after recording a full database backup. The contents of the recovery history file is shown in Table 7–3.

Table 7–3 Format of the Recovery History File

Column Name	Type	Description
OPERATION	Char(1)	type of operation performed: B = Backup, R = Restore, L = Load
OBJECT	Char(1)	Granularity of operation: D = Full Database, P = Table Space, T = Table.
OBJECT_PART	Char(17)	First 14 characters = timestamp = yyymmddhhnnss. Next 3 characters = Sequence Number. Backup can save to multiple files/tapes. Restore/Load always '001'.
OPTYPE	Char(1)	Additional operation qualification: F = off-line backup, N = on-line backup, R = Load Replace, A = Load Append, C = Load Copy, Blank for other operations.
DEVICE_TYPE	Char(1)	D = Disk, K = Diskette, T = Tape, A = ADSM, U = UserExit, O = Other vendor device support.
FIRST_LOG	Char(12)	Earliest Log File ID (S0000000 to S9999999) required for roll forward recovery after full database/table space backup.
LAST_LOG	Char(12)	Latest log file id.
BACKUP_ID	Char(14)	Timestamp 'yyyymmddhhnnss' that references one or more file lines representing backup operation. For full database restore, references full database backup that was restored. For table space, references table spaces backup or full database backup used to restore specified table spaces.
SCHEMA	Char(8)	Table name qualifier for load.
TABLE_NAME	Char(18)	Name of loaded table.
NUM_TABLESPACES	Char(3)	Number of table spaces involved in backup/restore. If non-zero, next lines in fill contain one line for each table space.

Table 7–3 Format of the Recovery History File

Column Name	Type	Description
LOCATION	Char(255)	Where data is saved for backups/ load copy. For restore/loads, where first part of data was saved. Refers to DEVICE_TYPE. if D or K, then fully qualified file name. If T, then tape volume label. If A, then ADSM server name. If U or O, then free-form text.
COMMENT	Char(30)	Free-form text.

If the current database is unusable or not available and the associated recovery history file is damaged or deleted, an option on the **RESTORE DATABASE** command allows only the recovery history file to be restored. Then, it can be reviewed to provide information on which backup image to use to restore the database.

Graphical Management Tools

This section discusses two of the graphical interfaces that help you to display database objects and their relationship to one another, simplifying tasks such as configuration or backup and recovery of a database. These two graphical interfaces are

- The Recovery Jobs Tool
- The Database Director

The Recovery Jobs Tool

This graphical tool is available on AIX and OS/2 platforms. The command used to invoke the recovery jobs window is **db2jobs**. An example of the Recovery Jobs tool is shown inFig. 7–37.

From this window, you can monitor backup, recovery, roll forward and restart jobs that are running, waiting, completed, stopping or stopped. You can choose which type of jobs you want to see by clicking on the appropriate button on the *Include Jobs* panel.

Each toggle button in the Include jobs panel can be selected to provide different types of information:

- All — shows all types of jobs
- Running — shows all jobs that are running
- Succeed — shows all jobs that completed successfully
- Failed — shows all jobs that completed with errors

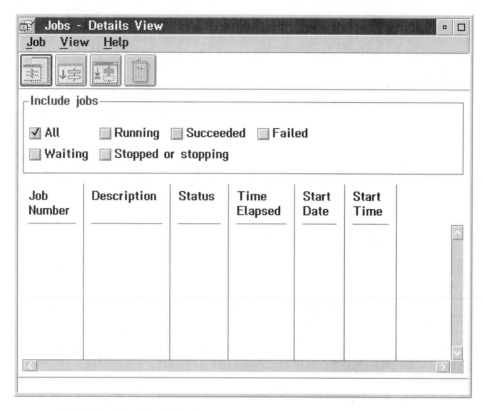

Fig. 7–37   The Jobs Window

- Waiting — shows all jobs that are waiting for operator intervention
- Stopped or stopping — shows jobs that are stopped or stopping

From the menu bar, you can select *Job* or *View*. Job lets you view output information from a selected job, continue a job in waiting state, stop a running or waiting job or delete a successful, failed or stopped job from the job list. View lets you sort the entry according to a particular column. You can also refresh a window with the latest information.

The Database Director

The Database Director provides a graphical interface that helps you to perform common database administration tasks. Using it, you can create, modify or delete DB2 objects like tables or table spaces.

From the Database Director, you can also invoke the Visual Explain and Performance Monitor tools. The Database Director can also be started from the command line by typing **db2dd.**

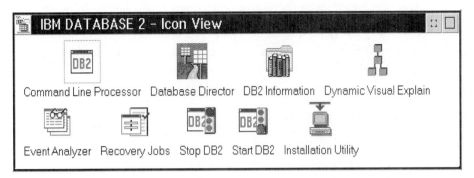

Fig. 7–38 Invoking the Database Director from the DB2 Folder

In OS/2 or Windows environments, you may double-click on the Database Director icon in the DB2 folder. The first window you'll see is similar to Fig. 7–38. A sample of the database directory tool is shown in Fig. 7–39.

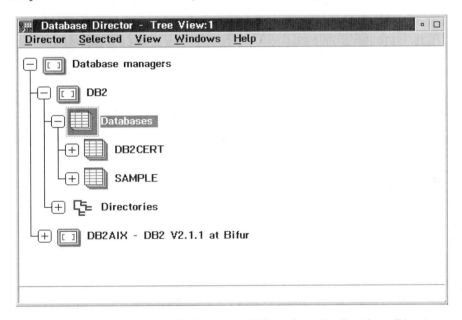

Fig. 7–39 Tree View of the Database Objects from the Database Director

Both the tree format and the view format display objects of the same type. There are three areas that can be accessed using the Database Director: instances, databases and directories. Fig. 7–39 shows two instances: **DB2** and **DB2AIX**. The instances may be either local or remote. In the DB2 instance, two databases are displayed: **DB2CERT** and **SAMPLE**.

Configuring DB2 Instances

The Database Director allows you to modify any of the DBM configuration parameters by using a pop-up menu for the instance you wish to configure (Fig. 7–40). The parameters are grouped by type; this is useful in understanding how they relate to each other. You can also see the database manager configuration release level (0x0600). You can configure any local or remote instance which has been cataloged where the database manager is active.

Configuring DB2 Databases

The Database Director also allows you to modify the database configuration parameters by using the pop-up menu for the database you wish to configure (see Fig. 7–41). The parameters for each database, as at the instance level, are grouped by type; it is useful to understand how they are related to each other.

Some of the configuration tasks that can be changed in the database configuration file are the following:

- Setting resources for the database, including:
  Buffer pool size
  Setting the size, number and location of the log files for the database
  Changing the number of applications that can connect to the database
- Determining the code page defined for the database
- Examining some of the values used when creating the database such as the number of containers and the extent size for table spaces.

Catalog/Uncatalog Databases

There are four directories which can be accessed using the Database Director:

- System database directory
- Node directory
- Database connection services directory
- Local database directory

The advantage of using the Database Director to catalog your databases is in its integration of the various DB2 directories, as shown in Fig. 7–40. The Database Director makes the task easier as it will display the available nodes to catalog a remote database.

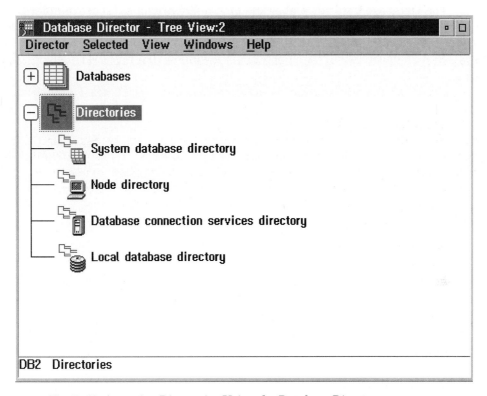

Fig. 7–40 Accessing Directories Using the Database Director

Creating/Modifying DB2 Objects

This section discusses how to create or modify DB2 objects using the Database Director. Specifically, the following operations may be performed:

- Create a Database
- Drop a Database
- Create a Table Space
- Back up a Database
- Back up a Table Space
- Restore a Database and Change Container Definitions
- Examine Database Packages
- Use the Performance Monitor

Creating a Database

The Database Director makes the task of creating a database simpler than remembering the complete syntax of the **CREATE DATABASE** command. You select the database icon, and then select *Create* from the pull-down menu in the *selected* item on the menu bar. You will get a window like Fig. 7–41.

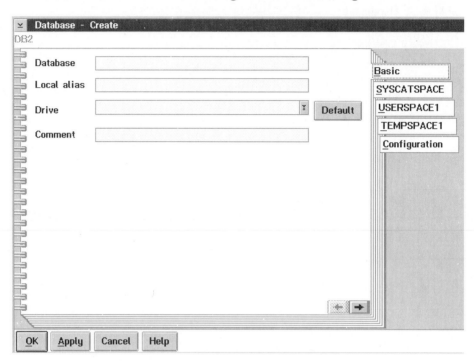

Fig. 7–41 Pop-up Menu for Creating Database

Characteristics of the new database can be easily defined, including

- The location of the three default table spaces
- The number and location of the containers for the table spaces
- The collating sequence

Dropping a Database

You can select the *drop* option from the pull-down menu after selecting the database object that you want to delete. The Database Director will warn you before the database is actually dropped as shown in Fig. 7–42.

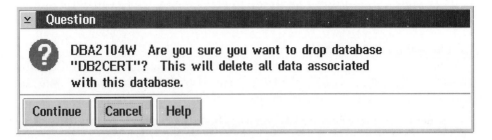

Fig. 7–42 Question Window — Drop Database

Creating a Table Space

With the Database Director, you can also create a new table space within a database.

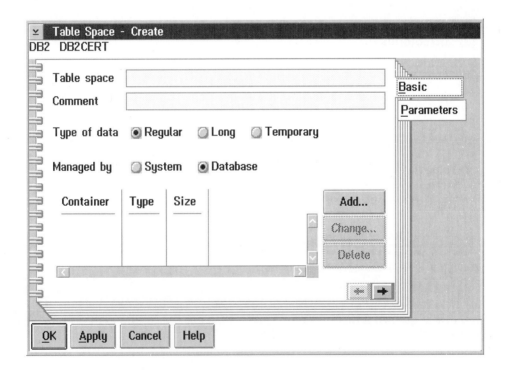

Fig. 7–43 Creating a Table Space

You can specify the type of table space, the type of data it will store and the size and number of containers as shown in Fig. 7–43. You also can add containers to an existing DMS table space.

Backing Up a Database

This is also an easy-to-use interface for performing backups of a database or table space as shown in Fig. 7–44. You can start the backup process and then monitor its progress using the **db2jobs** interface.

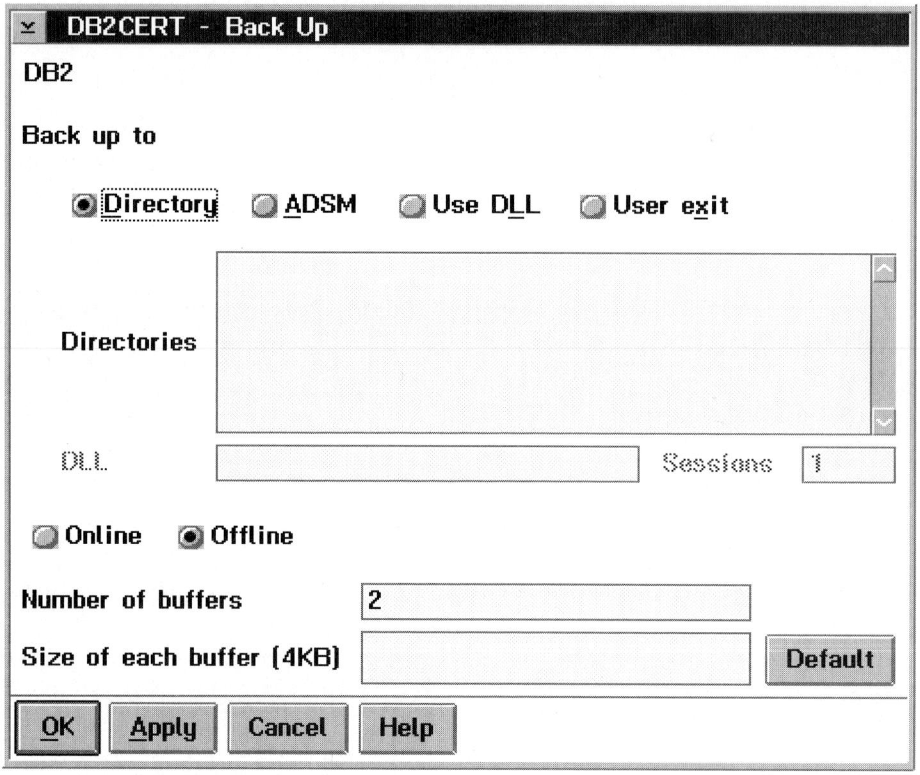

Fig. 7–44 Backing Up a Database

You can specify parameters such as where to place the backup image, whether the backup is off-line or on-line and the size and number of buffers used in the operation.

Restoring a Database

The task of restoring a previously backed up database image can become complicated, especially if archival logging is being used. The Database Director allows you to perform the restore and as part of the process, perform a roll forward recovery (see Fig. 7–45).

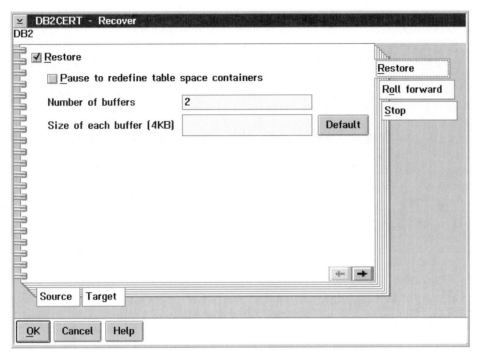

Fig. 7–45 Restoring a Database

You also have the ability to select the **Pause to redefine table space containers** option. This option allows you to add a new container or change the container locations for both SMS and DMS table spaces. This is called a **redirected restore**, and it is unique to the Database Director. This option is not possible when using the Command Line Processor (CLP) or an API. The redirected restore option will prompt the database administrator to redefine the container definitions before the restore task is started. Containers can be added or dropped during the restore.

After the list of containers has been redefined, a confirmation or revalidation of the list takes place. If there is a problem, you will return to the previous window until the list is correct, or until you decide to cancel the operation.

You can change the container definition for a table space, but not the table space type. For example, if you want to change your SMS table space to a DMS table space, you must drop the SMS table space and create a new DMS table space.

Following a successful database restore, the Database Director can then be used to perform the recovery phase of database restore.

Summary

In this chapter, we have talked about the data management tasks that the database administrator has to perform in order to ensure the recoverability of data in the database. We discussed the utilities used to populate tables in databases, namely, the **IMPORT/EXPORT** utility and the **LOAD** utility. We discussed in detail the three phases of the **LOAD** utility: load, build and delete. We also looked at examples of these utilities and differences between them.

We also discussed some utilities for data maintenance. **REORGCHK** lets you know if a table needs to be reorganized in order to improve query performance. **REORG** will actually reorganize the data in the table. **RUNSTATS** collects statistics about the physical characteristics of a table and the associated indexes. These statistics are then used by the optimizer when determining the access path to the data into the table. The **REBIND** utility updates packages after a **RUNSTATS** or a **REORG** has been performed. The **LIST APPLICATIONS** and **FORCE** commands can be used to control users to the database. A function or procedure may be executed within the same address space as the database manager requiring less memory, but greater risk.

We talked about the differences between circular and archival logging, the recovery procedures, in particular what roll forward recovery means and how to enable it. The use of the **BACKUP** and **RESTORE** commands at either database and table space level were also discussed. There are different types of backup, on-line and off-line, that can be performed under certain conditions. The recovery history file contains information about the backup, restore and load operations that can be useful in recovery situations.

Finally, we saw two graphical interfaces, the Recovery Jobs and Database Director. The Recovery Jobs tool helps in monitoring tasks and displays database objects and their relationships to one another, simplifying tasks such as configuring databases and table spaces and backup and recovery operations.

Questions

1. Which DB2 utility are you using if a table space is in delete pending state?

  ○ A. **REORG**

  ○ B. **RUNSTATS**

  ○ C. **IMPORT**

  ○ D. **EXPORT**

  ○ E. **LOAD**

2. Which DB2 utility requires exclusive access to the table space in which the table resides?

  ○ A. **IMPORT**

  ○ B. **EXPORT**

  ○ C. **RUNSTATS**

  ○ D. **LOAD**

  ○ E. **REORG**

3. What action may be specified from the **LOAD** command?

  ○ A. **REORG** of the table

  ○ B. **ROLLFORWARD** of the database

  ○ C. **COPY** the table space **BACKUP**

  ○ D. **CREATE** table if it does not exist

4. Why might data exist in the exception table following a **LOAD** operation?

○   A. Primary key constraint violations

○   B. Triggers may have fired and populated the exception table

○   C. Referential integrity constraint violations occurred

○   D. The data types from the **LOAD** file do not match the data types defined in the table

5.   Which database objects can be reorganized using the **REORG** command?

○   A. Table Spaces

○   B. Views

○   C. Tables

○   D. Columns

6.   Following a successful RUNSTATS execution, what should be performed?

○   A. A database backup

○   B. REORG for all the database objects

○   C. REBIND applications

○   D. RESTART the database

7.   Where will DB2 create temporary storage required when using the **REORG** command?

○   A. In the tmp directory of the active DB2 instance

○   B. In the path specified by the **REORGTMP** environment variable

○   C. In the buffer pool allocated for the database

○   D. In the table space specified in the **REORG** command

8. Which action establishes a point of consistency for database recovery?

    ○   A. Performing a table space level **RESTORE** only

    ○   B. Performing a database level **RESTORE**

    ○   C. Performing a **QUIESCE TABLESPACE** command

    ○   D. Performing a **FORCE APPLICATIONS** command

9. What commands would update the database recovery history file?

    ○   A. **ROLLFORWARD**

    ○   B. **IMPORT**

    ○   C. **BACKUP**

    ○   D. **RUNSTATS**

    ○   E. **REORG**

10. A database is enabled for roll forward recovery. What is true about the database recovery time if the time between full database backup images increases?

    ○   A. **RESTORE** database time will increase

    ○   B. **RESTORE** database time will decrease

    ○   C. **ROLLFORWARD** database time will increase

    ○   D. **ROLLFORWARD** database time will decrease

11. When is table space level recovery available?

    ○   A. Always

    ○   B. When log retain is disabled

    ○   C. When log retain is enabled

12. What dictates where errors encountered during an **IMPORT** are reported?

○   A. the **DB2MESSAGES** environment variable

○   B. the **MESSAGES** parameter specified during **IMPORT**

○   C. the database configuration file

○   D. the errors are placed in the specified exception table

Answers

1. (E)
   The **LOAD** utility.
2. (D)
   The **LOAD** utility.
3. (C)
   You can copy the table space backup
4. (A)
   Rows which have violated primary key constraints can be placed in the exception table.
5. (C)
   The **REORG** command is used on tables.
6. (C)
   Do a rebind on the packages that access the reorganized table.
7. (D)
   REORG creates temporary files in the table space where the table resides.
8. (B)
   Performing a database level **RESTORE**.
9. (C)
   Backup. Only backup, restore and copies from a load are placed in the recovery history file.
10. (C)
    The time required to **ROLLFORWARD** the database will increase.
11. (C)
    Table Space level recovery is available only if the database is enabled for log retain and/or user exits.
12. (B)
    The **MESSAGES** parameter of the **IMPORT** command specifies the destination for warning and error messages that occur during export.

Exercises

Part A— Moving Data Into a DB2 Database

1. Go to the directory \exercise\chapter7\parta

2. This section uses the database the SAMPLE database. If you don't have the SAMPLE database created then you can use the DB2CERT database. You may need to edit the command files to change the database alias name and/ or the path or drive.

3. When a database is created certain defaults are assigned. Check the contents of the database configuration file to see what type of logging is the default. Connect to the SAMPLE database and use the following command:
    db2 GET DB CFG FOR sample

4. Change from the default of circular logging to archival logging. You can do this by setting either the **LOGRETAIN** or the **USEREXIT** parameter or by setting both. Let's issue the following command:
    db2 UPDATE DB CFG FOR sample USING LOGRETAIN YES

    This command will now enable roll forward recovery. The log files will be used to handle transactions and the log files will not be re-used. Since a userexit was not enabled, the log files will remain in the default log path. It is important **not** to delete any of these log files until a verified **FULL** (Off-Line) database backup has been performed.

5. There are two things you must do to make this change take effect. First, you must disconnect all users from the database. Secondly, you must take a full database backup. You might also consider changing the path where logging will take place. This is recommended and should be done before any users start performing transactions against the database. The commands you'll need are:
    db2 FORCE APPLICATIONS ALL
    db2 BACKUP DATABASE sample TO <PATH/DRIVE>

    Don't worry about the various **BACKUP** command options at this point.

6. Connect to the sample database and run the file create.tab. This file will create three tables: **customer**, **customer.exp** and **nation**.
    db2 -tvf create.tab

7. This CLP input file also places referential constraints on the **nation** and the
    customer table. Either examine the command file or issue the following
    statement.
    db2 "SELECT * FROM SYSCAT.TABCONST"

8. You should see that there are two constraints defined. The **nation** table has
    a primary key, **nk**. The **customer** table has a foreign key, **fknk**, that refer-
    ences the primary key in the **nation** table. Next, we will load data into the
    nation table. There should be two files in the directory, *nation.load* and
    nation.tbl. The file *nation.lod* contains the **LOAD** commands. The *nation.tbl*
    file contains the data to be loaded, it is in delimited ASCII format. Issue the
    following command:
    db2 -tvf nation.lod

    You should have encountered an error stating that the table did not exist.
    The error is referring to the exception table called nation_exp. We have not
    created this exception table yet and it is an important component of using
    the **LOAD** command.

9. Next we will create an exception table for the nation table using the **IMPORT/
    EXPORT** commands. We will use **EXPORT** create an empty file containing the
    table definitions. We will then use the output file from the **EXPORT** to perform
    an **IMPORT** command using the **CREATE** option. Then we can **ALTER** the table
    to add the required **TIMESTAMP** and message columns. (Make sure that you
    are connected to the database.)
    **db2 "EXPORT TO nation.ixf OF IXF MESSAGES nation.txt
    SELECT * FROM nation WHERE 0=1"**

10. This creates a file called *nation.ixf*. Use the import utility to import the DDL
    in the export file, *nation.ixf* and create an exception table called nation_exp.
    **db2 "IMPORT FROM nation.ixf OF IXF MESSAGES nation.txt
    CREATE INTO nation_exp"**

11. Use the **ALTER TABLE** statement to add the TIMESTAMP and CLOB column
    to the *nation_exp* table. Issue the following commands:
    db2 ALTER TABLE nation_exp ADD COLUMN ts TIMESTAMP
    db2 ALTER TABLE nation_exp ADD COLUMN msg CLOB(1M)

    Now, you can use the LOAD command to load the nation table, issue :
    db2 -tvf nation.lod

12. Now, let's use the **LOAD** command to load data into the **customer** table. There
    is a file called *customer.lod* that uses the input file *customer.tbl*. The com-
    mand is as follows:
    db2 -tvf customer.lod

13. The LOAD failed as we didn't create the exception table for the customer table. Create the proper exception table as in the previous steps and complete the LOAD.
    This loads data into the customer table. Try to select rows from the customer table. You first need to be connect to the database. Does this work?
    db2 "SELECT * FROM CUSTOMER"

14. If you look at the two files that load data to the tables, nation and customer, you should see a difference. The file nation.load uses the **COPY YES** option, while customer.lod takes the default of **COPY NO**. Can you explain what happened? Use the **LIST TABLESPACES** command to help you.
    db2 LIST TABLESPACES

15. When a database is enabled for archival logging and the default option of the **LOAD** utility is used, the table space is placed in a backup pending. Remove the backup pending by performing a table space backup of the table space in question or a full database backup.
    db2 BACKUP DB sample TABLESPACE userspace1 TO PATH/DRIVE

16. You should be able to connect to the database. Try selecting rows from the customer table. Were you successful?
    db2 "SELECT * FROM CUSTOMER"

    You should receive a message SQL0668N that the operation is not allowed when the underlying table is in Check Pending. Query the system catalogs to show the status of the nation and the customer table using the following command:
    **db2 "SELECT TABNAME, STATUS, CONST_CHECKED
         FROM SYSCAT.TABLES
         WHERE TABNAME IN ('NATION', 'CUSTOMER')"**

17. You should see a 'C' in the status column for the customer table. You must remove the underlying check pending on the table customer with the **SET CONSTRAINTS** command:
    **db2 SET CONSTRAINTS FOR customer
         IMMEDIATE CHECKED
         FOR EXCEPTION IN customer
         USE customer.exp"**

18. The **SET CONSTRAINTS** command should move the rows in question to the exception table. You should see the following warning message:
    SQL3602W Check data processing found constraint violations and moved them to exception tables. SQLSTATE=01603

19. Run the file *drop.tab* to clean up :**db2 -tvf drop.tab**

Part B — Backup and Recovery

1. Next, back up just the system catalogs for the *DB2CERT* database. Place the backup copy in a different directory from the database and other backup copies. List the contents of the history file when the backup is complete.
    Change the drive/path for the backup image to one on your system (/dir).

    db2 BACKUP DATABASE db2cert
        TABLESPACE SYSCATSPACE to /dir
        LIST HISTORY FOR db2cert

    If you get an error message, make sure that the database is enabled for table space level backup. Change the database configuration and do a full backup. Then backup just the system catalogs.

2. Now, using the Database Director, look at the activity for the db2cert database in the History File (db2jobs). You should see that the same information is found, but the display is slightly different. To get to the history file using the Database Directory, follow these steps:
    From the Database Director Tree View, select the Database Manager db2. Then select the database under the instance. The database should be *DB2CERT*.
    Doubel click on the database, db2cert and you will find the Recovery history file listed.

3. We are going to make some changes in the candidate table. You will find an import file of type del that will do an insert update into the candidate table. Use the **IMPORT** commond with the **INSERT_UPDATE** option to update the candidate table. Alternatively, there is a file, candidat.imp that will connect to the database and make the changes in the candidate table. The command to enter the commands:

    db2 -tvf create.ddl
    db2 -tvf candidat.imp

4. Now connect to the database and perform a select. Look for all candidates whose last name begin with a 'C'. Display last name, first name and country.

    db2 "SELECT lname, fname, country
        FROM db2.candidate WHERE NAME LIKE 'C%'"
    You should get one row where the last name is Coldicott

5. Create a table in the db2cert table. Use the following table definition:
    CREATE TABLE A(C1 (CHAR(1))

6.   Now, let's restore the backup of the system catalogs that you made in Step 17. You can either use the Database Director or the command line.
     RESTORE DATABASE db2cert FROM /PATH/DRIVE

     where path/drive is where the backup was placed.

7.   Try to connect to the db2cert database. You should receive an error message similar to the following:
     SQL0290N Table space access is not allowed.   SQLSTATE=55039
     Remember that when you restore a table space, you must perform a roll forward of the database to the end of the log files.

     ```
     db2 ROLLFORWARD DATABASE db2cert QUERY STATUS
     db2 ROLLFORWARD DATABASE db2cert TO END OF LOGS AND STOP
     ```

8.   Now connect to the db2cert database and issue the following statements:
     ```
     db2 CONNECT TO db2cert
     db2 "SELECT lname, fname, country
         FROM db2.candidate
         WHERE lname LIKE 'C%'"
     db2 "SELECT * FROM A"
     ```

9.   Did the statements work? You should be able to issue all of the statements. The user with the last name Coldicott should still be in the candidate table. The table A should still exist, but have no data since none was ever inserted into the table.

10. Drop the A table.
     ```
     db2 DROP TABLE A
     ```

Database Monitoring and Tuning

*U*nderstanding a database and the applications in a dynamic environment requires interactive monitoring. This means that a database administrator should gather information regarding the usage of the database. An application programmer may also require SQL statement execution information. We will discuss gathering database information via database monitoring and information regarding the SQL statement processing.

DB2 provides different facilities for monitoring the database manager. The Explain Facility, Snapshot Monitor and Event Monitor are the main tools used to monitor and tune DB2 databases and SQL statements. These tools may be used to perform the following tasks:

- improve database and application performance
- tune configuration parameters
- determine the source and cause of problem
- better understand how an SQL statement is processed
- understand user and application activity within the database manager.

Monitoring and tuning a database should be performed using the following process:

- define your objectives
- determine the information you will analyze
- determine which type of monitoring to use
- obtain the monitor data
- analyze the monitor information
- determine what changes are required
- implement the changes

This chapter will give you the information to decide which of the existing facilities is the best for your needs. It shows how to capture data using the Explain Facility, the Snapshot Monitor and Event Monitor and how to interpret the collected information.

Obtaining Database Access Information

The first step in the database monitoring process is defining your objectives. Defining the objectives is very important in selecting the best facility to meet your requirements. An objective can be:

- Understanding how a specific query will be executed in a specific environment. For example, there is a query used in an application that does not perform well.
- Understanding how applications use database manager resources at a specific point of time. For example, the database concurrency is reduced if a special application is started.
- Understanding which database manager events have occurred when running applications. For example, you notice a degradation in overalll performance when certain executing applications are used.

There are various methods to obtain the required information. The following is a description of the information provided by the explain facility and the database monitors:

- Choose the Explain facility if you want to analyze the access plan for an SQL statement or a group of SQL statements.
- Choose the Snapshot Monitor if you want to gather disk activity, buffer pool usage, amount of prefetch, lock usage and record blocking.
- Choose the Event Monitor if you want to analyze the resource usage over a period of time by tracing the database activity.

Explain Facility

If you want to analyze the access plan of a specific query, the **Explain** facility will provide the required information. Before describing the capabilities and the features of the explain facility, you should understand how SQL statements are processed by the DB2 database engine at a high level. An executable form of the query is created by DB2 either during a static bind or dynamically. The component within DB2 which determines the access path to be used is known as the **optimizer** or the **compiler** (as the output of this component is an 'executable' form of the SQL statement).

During the static preparation of the SQL statements the SQL compiler is called to generate an executable **access plan**. The access plan contains the data access strategy including index usage, sort methods, locking semantics and join methods. The executable form of the SQL statements is stored in the system catalog tables when the **BIND** command is executed (assuming deferred binding method).

Sometimes, the complete statement is not known at application development time. In this case, the compiler is invoked during program execution to generate an access plan for the query that can be used by the database manager to access the data. The access plan is **not** stored in the system catalogs. It is stored in memory (known as the package cache).

Query Compilation

The SQL compiler performs a number of tasks during the creation of the compiled form of the SQL statements. These phases are described below and also shown in Fig. 8–1. You may notice in the referenced figure; the representation of the query is stored in a structure known as a graph, this is known as the **Query Graph Model** (QGM) form of the SQL statement. This representation corresponds to the explain snapshot information which is analyzed using the Visual Explain utility.

1. **Parse Query**
   Parse the SQL statement to validate its syntax. If no error is detected, an initial QGM graph is created. Otherwise processing will be stopped and an appropriate SQL error is returned to the calling application.

2. **Check Semantics**
   Verify the SQL statement and identify any constraints. These constraints could include referential integrity (RI) contraints, table check constraints, triggers, and views. The QGM is modified to include these constraints.

3. **Rewrite Query**
   The query can be modified (as QGM) to a new form which can be more easily optimized in the next phase of query processing.

4. **Optimize Access Plan**
   Use the QGM graph as input to generate alternative execution plans. The optimizer estimates the execution cost of each alternative plan, using the statistics of tables, indexes, columns and functions to choose the plan with the smallest estimated cost. The output of this task is known as the access plan.

5. **Generate Executable Code**
   Create an *executable access plan* for the SQL statement. This access plan will either be stored in the system catalog tables or in memory. Static SQL statements will be stored in the system catalog tables and dynamic SQL statements will be stored in memory. Therefore, the dynamic SQL statements are only available while they remain in memory. The executable access plan is part of a **package**. The amount of memory used to store packages is configurable using the database configuration parameter known as **pckcachesz**.

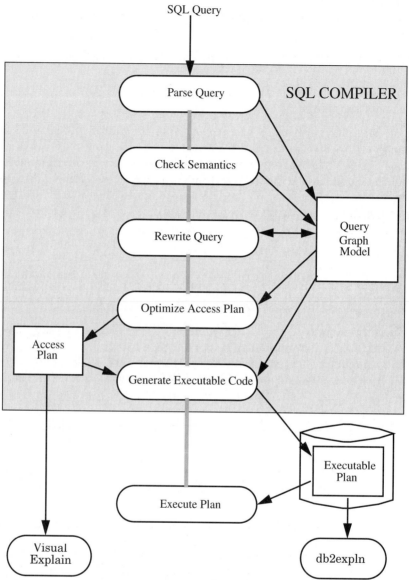

Fig. 8–1 Diagram of Steps Performed by SQL Compiler

While the query is being processed, you can decide to capture detailed information regarding the access plan. This is known as capturing the explain information for the query. The information can be captured into a file using a tool called **db2expln** or special tables known as **explain tables**. In Fig. 8–1 there are two explain interfaces shown: **Visual Explain** and **db2expln**. It is recommended that you use Visual Explain.

Explain Tables

There are a number of explain tables which are used to store the access plan information:

- **EXPLAIN_ARGUMENT** — represents the unique characteristics for each individual operator.
- **EXPLAIN_INSTANCE** — main control table for all Explain information. It contains basic information about the source of the SQL statements being explained as well as information about the environment in which the explain took place.
- **EXPLAIN_OBJECT** — contains data objects required by the access plan generated to satisfy the SQL statement (objects can include tables, indexes, etc.).
- **EXPLAIN_OPERATOR** — contains all the operators needed to satisfy the SQL statement (the operators may include table scans, index scans, etc.)
- **EXPLAIN_PREDICATE** — identifies which predicates are applied by a specific operator.
- **EXPLAIN_STATEMENT** — contains the text of the SQL statement in two forms. The original version entered by the user is stored as well as the re-written version.
- **EXPLAIN_STREAM** — contains the input and output streams between individual operators and data objects.

The explain tables have to be created before any explain information can be gathered. The CLP input file called **explain.ddl**, located in the **misc** subdirectory of the current instance, contains the definition of the explain tables. Connect to the database and use the following command to create the explain tables:

```
db2 -tf EXPLAIN.DDL
```

✏️   The location of subdirectory **misc** depends on the operating system.

DB2 provides two levels of gathering SQL statement information. The explain information is always stored in these relational tables, but there may be Visual Explain information also stored in the tables. The amount of data stored in the tables is determined using the following keywords:

EXPLAIN — captures detailed information of the access plan and stores the information in the explain tables. There is no visual representation of the QGM for the SQL statement stored in the tables. Therefore, the Visual Explain facility cannot be used if this option is used.

EXPLAIN SNAPSHOT — capture of the current internal representation of an SQL query and related information. This information is required by the visual explain facility. There is a column called *snapshot* within the *explain_statement* table which stores the visual representation of the access plan (in a binary large object data type).

Gathering Explain Data

There are three general methods of populating the explain tables:

EXPLAIN SQL Statement — gather explain data for an SQL statement

Special Register — gather explain data for dynamic SQL statements

BIND options — gather explain data for static and/or dynamic SQL statements in a database package using appropriate **BIND** options.

These methods will provide explain data for any **SELECT**, **UPDATE**, **INSERT** and **DELETE** statements, as well as data definition (DDL) statements. The following statements will **not** be explained:

BEGIN/END DECLARE SECTION

BEGIN/END COMPOUND

INCLUDE

WHENEVER

COMMIT and ROLLBACK

CONNECT

OPEN cursor

FETCH

CLOSE cursor

PREPARE

EXECUTE

EXECUTE IMMEDIATE

DESCRIBE

dynamic DECLARE CURSOR

SET (all types)

EXPLAIN Statement

Use the **EXPLAIN** statement if you want to gather information for a single query. The **EXPLAIN** statement can be invoked either from the command line processor or within an application. You can specify the amount of explain data captured using the following keywords:

WITH SNAPSHOT — in addition to the regular explain information, an explain snapshot is to be taken.

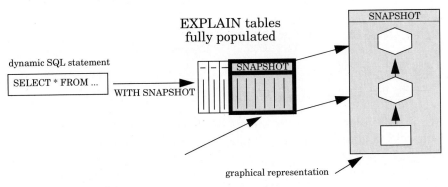

FOR SNAPSHOT — only an explain snapshot is to be taken and placed into the explain tables. No other information is captured.

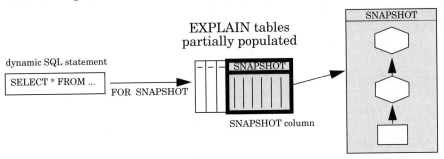

Otherwise, the **EXPLAIN** statement will gather the explain data and place the output in the explain tables. Therefore, the visual explain facility may not be used to interpret the access plan.

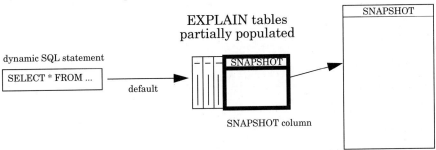

To issue the **EXPLAIN** statement the current authorization id must have **INSERT** privilege on the explain tables.

✍🏻 The SQL statement being explained using the **EXPLAIN** statement will not be executed; only the explain data is captured.

Let's examine some examples of gathering access plan information using the **EXPLAIN** statement.

```
EXPLAIN ALL WITH SNAPSHOT FOR
        "SELECT * FROM candidate"
```

Fig. 8–2 Using the EXPLAIN Statement

In Fig. 8–2 the explain statement is shown. This example would populate the snapshot column within the explain tables. The snapshot represents the QGM (access plan) as shown in Fig. 8–1. This statement will actually populate a number of explain tables; including the *snapshot* column because the **WITH SNAPSHOT** phrase was used. If the phrase **WITH SNAPSHOT** were not specified, then the access plan details would be stored in the explain tables and no snapshot information (Visual Explain) would be obtained. There is a column called *SNAPSHOT_TAKEN* in the *EXPLAIN_INSTANCE* table which will correspond to the existence of a visual explain snapshot for each explained statement.

The **EXPLAIN** statement is useful for gathering access plan information for a single dynamic SQL statement. The statement could also be used in an application to populate the explain tables. Once the explain tables are populated they can be queried. Special operators can be examined to determine if the ideal access plan was used for the query (e.g., IXSCAN — Index Scan operator).

Explain Special Register

There are two special registers used by DB2 for gathering explain information for SQL statements. These registers can be set interactively or they can be used in a dynamic SQL program. The values of special registers are modified using the **SET** statement.

To change the value of these special registers use the following statements:

```
SET CURRENT EXPLAIN MODE [NO | YES | EXPLAIN]
SET CURRENT EXPLAIN SNAPSHOT [NO | YES | EXPLAIN]
```

NO — No explain information is captured for dynamic SQL statements.

YES — Explain tables will be populated for dynamic SQL statements while executing the SQL statement and the result is returned.

EXPLAIN — Explain tables will be populated for dynamic SQL statements without executing the SQL statement. Use this state to obtain explain information without actually executing the SQL statement.

Once you have set a register to **YES** or **EXPLAIN**, any subsequent dynamic SQL statements will be explained until the register is reset to **NO**.

✍ If the **EXPLAIN MODE** register is used only the explain tables are populated. If the **EXPLAIN SNAPSHOT** register is used then the explain tables are populated including the snapshot column (used by visual explain).

Explain BIND Options

There are two explain **BIND** options which can be specified: **EXPLAIN** and **EXPLSNAP**. As previously discussed, explain snapshots are used by the Visual Explain facility. If you are planning to view the access plan using Visual Explain only then use the **EXPLSNAP** option; if you are planning or querying the explain tables directly then use the **EXPLAIN** option. Fig. 8–3 shows, according to the **BIND** parameter used, when the Explain tables are populated.

✍ Explain snapshots cannot be performed for DRDA database servers.

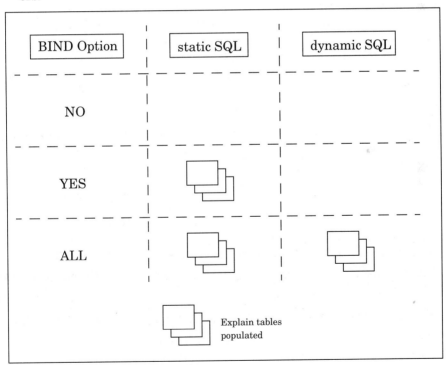

Fig. 8–3 Using the EXPLAIN or EXPLSNAP BIND Option

Let's capture explain data using a bind option:

```
BIND checkid.bnd EXPLSNAP ALL
```

During the bind phase the explain tables will be populated for all of the static SQL statements defined in the *checkid.bnd* package. An explain snapshot will also be obtained and stored in the explain tables. Because the **ALL** option was specified the dynamic SQL statements issued during package execution will also be explained in the Explain tables.

The bind method of obtaining explain information is useful for an administrator to determine the access plans of static SQL packages. To examine the access plan for dynamic SQL statements the special register technique is an easier method.

Using the Explain Report Tools

There is an alternative method of gathering explain data which stores the explain data in a report and not in relational tables. The utilities are called: **dynexpln** and **db2expln**. These utilities are located in the *misc* subdirectory of the *sqllib* directory. The utilities are useful as a quick and easy method of gathering access plan information. The explain output is stored in a readable report file which can be examined.

 It is not recommended using the **dynexpln** or the **db2expln** utilities for detailed access plan analysis as more information is provided in the explain tables.

Examining EXPLAIN Data

Visual Explain

Visual Explain is a utility that gives the database administrator or application developer the ability to examine the access plan determined by the optimizer. Visual Explain can only be invoked for access plans which have been explained using the snapshot option.

To use visual explain you must have created the explain tables and gathered explain snapshots. You can invoke visual explain either from the **Database Director** or by using command **db2vexpl**.

 The utility **db2vexpl** is useful to explain a single dynamic SQL statement.

From the Database Director interface click on the database involved in the explain data capture. You will notice that there is an option called **Explained Statements History** as shown in Fig. 8–4.

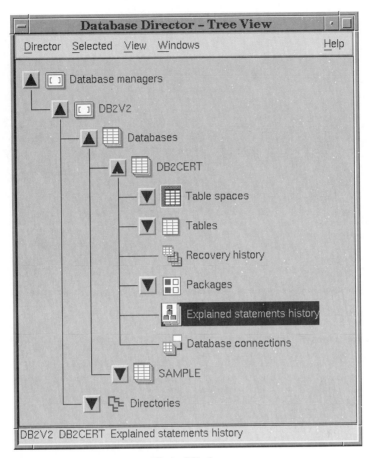

Fig. 8–4 Database Director Main Window

Once the **Explained Statements History** window has been opened, all of the explained statements will be shown, as shown in Fig. 8–5. The displayed information can differ as it may be customized to your environment. In Fig. 8–5 the total costs and the SQL statement are shown.

To examine the access plan detail simply double-click on the explained statement or use the menu and select **Statement - Show access plan**.

All of the explain statements will be displayed in the list, but only the explained statements with **SNAPSHOT** information can be examined using Visual Explain.

To add a comment describing the query shown in Fig. 8–5 select **Statement - Change**. This option can be used to provide a query tag, which can be used to help track the explain snapshot information. You may also wish to remove explain snapshots. The snapshots can be removed from the explain tables by selecting **Statement - Delete**.

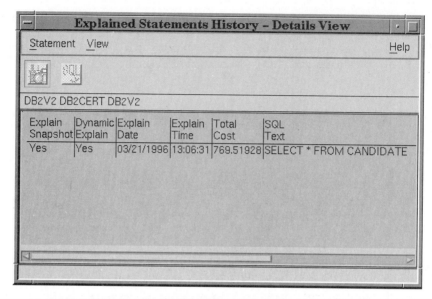

Fig. 8–5 Customized Display of Explained Statements History

The Visual Explain output displays a hierarchical graph representing the components of the SQL statement. Each part of the query is represented as graphical objects. These objects are known as **nodes**. There are two basic types of nodes: **operator** nodes and **operand** nodes.

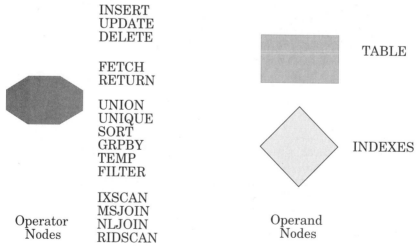

Fig. 8–6 Operators and Operands Displayed in Visual Explain

An operator is an action which is performed on a group of data. An operand is an object which the operators act upon. These objects are usually tables and indexes. There are many operators which can be used by the DB2 optimizer to determine the best access plan. You may notice in Fig. 8–6 the operators are grouped according to their usage. The first group corresponds to the SQL statements **INSERT**, **UPDATE**, **DELETE**. The **other** operators are used when indexes are being used (e.g., **IXSCAN** and **RIDSCAN**). Operators such as **GRPBY** and **SORT** can be used when the **GROUP BY** clause or the **ORDER BY** clause is specified in the SQL statement.

Arrows on the arc/line between the nodes show the flow of data from operation to operation. The final operation is always a **RETURN**. You can examine the details at each node by double-clicking on the node or choosing **show details** from the pop-up menu.

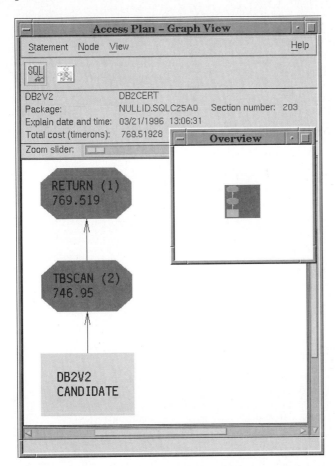

Fig. 8–7 Graphical Access Plan for SQL Statement Including Overview

The access plan shown in Fig. 8–7 is a simple SQL statement: "**SELECT * FROM db2v2.candidate**". In this example there are two operators and a single operand. The operand is the *db2v2.candidate* table and the operators include a relational table scan (**TBSCAN**) and a **RETURN** operator.

The analysis of the statement in Fig. 8–7 would conclude that indexes were not used, as there are no index operands (diamond shape). This does not mean that all statements of this form would result in a relational table scan. If there were a single column in the *db2v2.candidate* table and an index existed then an index scan would likely be performed. It is impossible to determine the exact access plan strategy by simply examining the SQL statement as the DB2 optimizer is very advanced and therefore the explain output is required to understand the access plan.

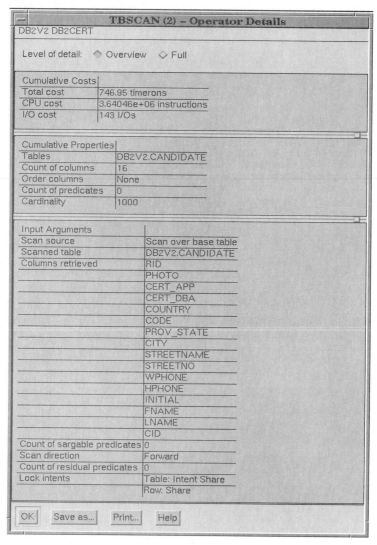

Fig. 8–8 Operator Details

To display the details of the table scan operation select the **TBSCAN** operator node and select **show detail** from the pop-up menu. Information about the **TBSCAN** operation is displayed in Fig. 8–8. This window contains sections of detailed information:

cumulative costs — contains information about the estimated costs calculated using statistics stored in the system catalog tables.

cumulative properties — contains information about the table and columns used to satisfy the query.

input arguments — contains information about the input arguments used for this operation.

In Fig. 8–8 information regarding the operator details (**TBSCAN**) is shown. You may also want to examine operand details. Fig. 8–9 shows operand details for the *db2v2.candidate* table.

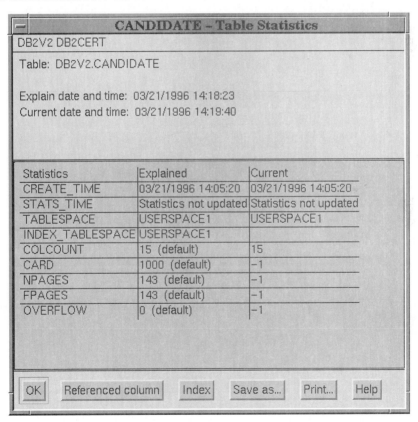

Fig. 8–9 Statistics for an Operand Node

Table statistic information includes table space information, number of columns selected and the number of rows in the table. Fig. 8–9 shows the current statistics existing in the system catalog tables. These statistics are used by the DB2 optimizer to determine the access plan. Therefore, if we were to create an index on a table, the optimizer would not fully utilize the index until statistics are gathered for the table. There were no statistics gathered for the *db2v2.candidate* table. Therefore, default values are used by the optimizer.

To ensure the latest statistics are available for the optimizer a DB2 utility must be used. To gather the statistics for this table use the **RUNSTATS** command. An example of gathering statistics is shown here:

```
RUNSTATS ON TABLE db2v2.candidate
        AND DETAILED INDEXES ALL
```

The gathered statistics for the *db2v2.candidate* table are stored in the system catalog tables. If you gather statistics and re-explain the SQL statement you will note that the values for current statistics have changed and more than likely the total cost of the access plan generated would change. Fig. 8–10 shows that the statistics have changed.

CANDIDATE – Table Statistics

DB2V2 DB2CERT

Table: DB2V2.CANDIDATE

Explain date and time: 03/21/1996 14:18:23
Current date and time: 03/22/1996 16:17:27

Statistics	Explained	Current
CREATE_TIME	03/21/1996 14:05:20	03/21/1996 14:05:20
STATS_TIME	Statistics not updated	03/22/1996 16:12:50
TABLESPACE	USERSPACE1	USERSPACE1
INDEX_TABLESPACE	USERSPACE1	
COLCOUNT	15 (default)	15
CARD	1000 (default)	3
NPAGES	143 (default)	1
FPAGES	143 (default)	1
OVERFLOW	0 (default)	0

OK   Referenced column   Index   Save as...   Print...   Help

Fig. 8–10 Table Statistics after RUNSTATS

To ensure that the updated current statistics will be used for static SQL statements, you must recreate the packages (use the **BIND** command to update the packages in the database). For dynamic SQL statements, the SQL compiler will always use the current statistics to calculate the access plan.

Note that the total cost in Fig. 8–11 shows the revised cost of the statement is much less than the cost prior to performing the **RUNSTATS** command. The previous explain was based on default table statistic values. The default table statistics indicated that 143 pages would be accessed (see Fig. 8–10 under the **Explained** column). The second explain was based on a single data page access.

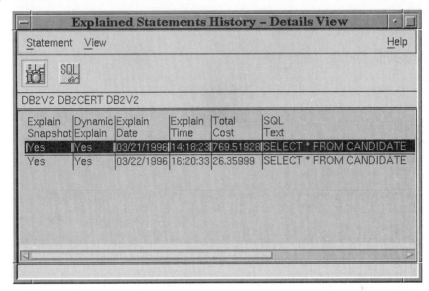

Fig. 8–11 List of Explained Statements

Database Monitoring

The explain facility will provide access plan information, but it does not provide detailed resource usage information. Explain does not provide information regarding locking, connections, buffer pool usage, table space usage and memory usage. To gather detailed resource usage information, the DB2 database monitors must be used. Monitoring may be performed from a DB2 client or a DB2 server. The monitor interface is invoked using CLP commands, graphical Performance Monitors, or the provided monitoring APIs.

Snapshot Monitoring provides information regarding database activity for a specific point in time. It is a picture of the current state of the DB2 activity. The amount of data returned to the end user when a snapshot is taken is determined using the monitor switches. These switches can be set in the DBM configuration file or at an application level.

Event monitoring records the occurrence of specific milestones of DB2 events. This can allow you to collect information about transient events, including: deadlocks, connections, SQL statements.

The performance impact of monitoring is based on the frequency of monitored events and the amount of data captured for each event. Each snapshot monitor is invoked immediately and event monitors are invoked by DB2 according to the event monitor definition.

    If excessive amounts of monitoring are performed, the performance of the DB2 database and its applications will be negatively impacted.

Snapshot Monitoring

The Snapshot Monitor provides cumulative information in the form of counters. These counters can be reset using an API. The snapshot information is provided in special data structures which can be examined by the application issuing the snapshot. The amount of data returned in the monitoring data structures is set according to the switches defined in Table 8–4. The switches can be turned on and off at the instance (DBM configuration) level or at the application level (**UPDATE MOINTOR SWITCHES**). Table 8–4 includes a summary of the information provided when a snapshot is performed. There is also base information provided by the Snapshot Monitor.

Table 8–4 Available Groups of Information for Taking Snapshots

Group	Information Provided	Monitor Switch	DBM Parameter
Sorts	number of heaps used, overflows, sorts performance	SORT	DFT_MON_SORT
Locks	number of locks held, number of deadlocks	LOCK	DFT_MON_LOCK
Tables	measure activity (rows read, rows written)	TABLE	DFT_MON_TABLE
Buffer pools	number of reads and writes, time taken	BUFFERPOOL	DFT_MON_BUFPOOL
Unit of work	start times, end times, completion status	UOW	DFT_MON_UOW
SQL statements	start time, stop time, statement identification	STATEMENT	DFT_MON_STMT

Setting the DBM (instance) configuration parameters for monitor switches will affect all databases within the instance. Every application connecting to a database will inherit the default switches set within the DBM configuration.

 SYSADM, **SYSCTRL**, **or SYSMAINT** authority is required to use the DB2 Snapshot Monitors. Event Monitors require **SYSADM** or **DBADM** authority for the monitored database.

Let's examine the necessary command to turn on the monitor switch to capture all of the SQL statements for each application at the DB2 instance level.

```
UPDATE DBM CONFIGURATION USING DFT_MON_STMT ON
```

OR

```
UPDATE MONITOR SWITCHES USING STATEMENT ON
```

The first command will modify the DBM configuration and therefore statement information will be captured for all applications accessing all database within the instance. The second command will only capture SQL statements for the application which activated the switch (in this case the application is the command line processor). This means if the **UPDATE MONITOR SWITCHES** command is used, only the subsequent SQL statements are considered within the CLP interface.

 Even if none of the switches are turned on, there will be some basic information captured for each database snapshot.

Most of the data values returned during a database monitor snapshot are based on counters. These counters can be used to determine the amount of database activity. The counters are initialized or reset when one of the following activities occur:

- When the application connects to the database, gathering of information is dependent on the level defined for taking snapshots:
  At the application level, this is when the application connected
  At the database level, this is when the first application connected
  At the table level, this is when the table was accessed
  At the table space level, this is when the table space was accessed
- Last counter reset
- Responsible monitor group turned on

If you turn on the switch, then the data is collected. The data is externalized when a snapshot is requested. There is a minor performance impact when the data is recorded. Issuing a snapshot affects performance more.

A snapshot can be requested using the command **GET SNAPSHOT**. The monitor data is displayed to the screen or it can be captured into a file using the output file option within CLP. You may decide to code your own monitoring application using the APIs provided (refer to the *Database System Monitor Guide and Reference*).

There is a graphical Performance Monitor provided with DB2. The graphical Performance Monitor is integrated with the database director interface. Before we examine the output of the Snapshot Monitor, let's discuss how the snapshot information is captured. We will first use the CLP interface to capture database monitor snapshots.

While taking a snapshot, it is possible to define the area of interest. When database monitoring is required there is usually a specific need. We introduced some reasons for monitoring database activity at the start of this chapter. Therefore, if there is a problem with concurrency (locking) behavior for a specific database, then the lock level may be specified. If you are interested in the activity of all applications accessing a database, then the application level should be specified. Information regarding the table activity (**INSERT/UPDATE/SELECT**) can be captured if the **STATEMENTS** switch is turned on and the snapshot is taken at a database level. The database activity for each of the tables within a database can also be captured. The following snapshot levels are available:

Database Manager — captures information for an active instance

Database — capture information for all databases or a single database

Application — captures information for all applications or a single application.

Table Space — captures information for table spaces within a database

Table — captures information for tables within a database

Lock — captures information for locks held for applications using a database.

Let's gather a database monitor snapshot using the following CLP command:

```
GET SNAPSHOT FOR LOCKS ON db2cert2
```

The output of the snapshot will be displayed to the screen; therefore it is recommended capturing the output to a file for analysis. The output of the snapshot for locks is shown in Fig. 8–12. Analysis of the snapshot would conclude that first application (application id *LOCAL.DB2.960828124715) is holding an exclusive (X) row level lock (lock object — 67108864) and the second application (application id *LOCAL.DB2.960828124725) is in Lock-Wait status attempting to acquire a row lock on the same row. The resolution involves completing the transaction for the first application (**COMMIT** or **ROLLBACK**).

```
                          Lock Snapshot
Database name                            = DB2CERT2
Database path                            = G:\SQL00001\
Input database alias                     = DB2CERT2
Locks held                               = 16
Applications currently connected         = 2
Applications currently waiting on locks  = 1
Snapshot timestamp          = 08-28-1996 08:52:08.934836
Agent ID                                 = 14
Application ID                 = *LOCAL.DB2.960828124715
Sequence number                          = 0001
Application name                         = DB2BP.EXE
Authorization ID                         = DB2
Application status                       = UOW Waiting
Status change time          = 08-28-1996 08:50:39.575823
ID of code page used by application      = 437
Locks held                               = 12

Object Name Object Type Table Schema Table Name  Mode Status
----------- ----------- ------------ ----------- ---- ------
654311427   Row         DB2          T500        X    Granted
167772163   Row         DB2          T500        X    Granted
889192450   Row         DB2          T500        X    Granted
1006632961  Row         DB2          T500        X    Granted
503316481   Row         DB2          T500        X    Granted
251658241   Row         DB2          T500        X    Granted
637534208   Row         DB2          T500        X    Granted
67108864    Row         DB2          T500        X    Granted
4           Table       DB2          T500        IX   Granted
5           Row         SYSIBM       SYSTABLES   S    Granted
2           Table       SYSIBM       SYSTABLES   IS   Granted
0           Internal                             S    Granted

Agent ID                                 = 15
Application ID                 = *LOCAL.DB2.960828124725
Sequence number                          = 0001
Application name                         = DB2BP.EXE
Authorization ID                         = DB2
Application status                       = Lock-wait
Status change time          = 08-28-1996 08:52:06.001614
ID of code page used by application      = 437
Locks held                               = 4
Agent ID holding lock                    = 14
Application ID holding lock    = *LOCAL.DB2.960828124715
Sequence number holding lock             = 0001
Table Schema of lock                     = DB2
Table Name of lock                       = T500
    Lock object type waited on            = Row Lock
    Lock object name                      = 67108864

Object Name Object Type Table Schema Table Name  Mode Status
----------- ----------- ------------ ----------- ---- -------
4           Table       DB2          T500        IX   Granted
218103813   Row         SYSIBM       SYSTABLES   S    Granted
2           Table       SYSIBM       SYSTABLES   IS   Granted
0           Internal                             S    Granted
```

Fig. 8–12 Monitor Snapshot (lock information)

The information provided by the Snapshot Monitor is a valuable resource to resolve many problems. In Fig. 8–12 the problem was a concurrency problem and therefore the **LOCKS** level was used to capture the snapshot.

```
                    Application Snapshot

Agent ID                                  = 16
Application status                        = UOW Waiting
Status change time          = 08-28-1996 08:43:14.967444
ID of code page used by application       = 437
Country code of database                  = 1
DUOW correlation token         = *LOCAL.DB2.960828124245
Application name                          = DB2BP.EXE
Application ID                  = *LOCAL.DB2.960828124259
Sequence number                           = 0001
Authorization ID                          = DB2
Execution ID                              = DB2
Configuration NNAME of client             = OS2
Client database manager product ID        = SQL02011
Process ID of client application          = 864
Platform of client application            = OS2
Communication protocol of client          = Local Client
Database name                             = DB2CERT2
Database path                             = G:\SQL00001\
Client database alias                     = db2cert2
Input database alias                      = DB2CERT2

Locks held by application                 = 0
Lock waits since connect                  = 1
Time application waited on locks (ms)     = 9977
Deadlocks detected                        = 0
Lock escalations                          = 0
Exclusive lock escalations                = 0
Number of Lock Timeouts since connected   = 1
Total time UOW waited on locks (ms)       = 9977
Commit statements                         = 1
Rollback statements                       = 0
Dynamic SQL statements attempted          = 1
Static SQL statements attempted           = 1
Failed statement operations               = 1
Select SQL statements executed            = 0
Update/Insert/Delete statements executed  = 1

DDL statements executed                   = 0
Internal commits                          = 1
Internal rollbacks                        = 1
Internal rollbacks due to deadlock        = 0

Rows read                                 = 7
Rows written                              = 0

Previous UOW completion timestamp 08-28-1996 08:42:58.877556
UOW start timestamp            = 08-28-1996 08:43:02.658573
UOW stop timestamp             = 08-28-1996 08:43:14.967496
UOW completion status          = Rolled back - Lock Timeout
```

Fig. 8–13 Monitor Snapshot (application information)

Let's examine another snapshot output file. The information shown in Fig. 8–13 was taken based on the **APPLICATION** level. The snapshot indicates that an excess (relative) amount of time 9,977 ms (almost 10 seconds) was spent waiting for locks. In this example, the **locktimeout** database configuration parameter was set to a value of 10 ms. Examining the output in Fig. 8–13, the value for **Unit of Work - Completion Status** is *Rolled Back - Lock Timeout*. To determine more information regarding the table or row involved in the lock timeout, a snapshot based on locks should be performed (as in Fig. 8–12).

Let's examine one more snapshot output file. The information shown in Fig. 8–14 was taken based on tables. Using a table snapshot we can determine the most active table in our database and how the table is being used; either the table is being read frequently or it is being updated frequently.

```
                        Table Snapshot

First database connect timestamp   = 08-28-1996 08:47:02.855887

Last reset timestamp               =
Snapshot timestamp                 = 08-28-1996 08:49:55.875226
Database name                      = DB2CERT2
Database path                      = G:\SQL00001\
Input database alias               = DB2CERT2
Number of accessed tables          = 6

Table   Table             Table     Rows     Rows   Overflows
Schema  Name              Type      Written  Read
------  ------------      -------   -------  -----  ---------
DB2     T500              User      8        257    0
SYSIBM  SYSTABLES         Catalog   0        1      0
SYSIBM  SYSTABLESPACES    Catalog   0        6      0
SYSIBM  SYSPLAN           Catalog   0        2      0
SYSIBM  SYSEVENTMONITORS  Catalog   0        2      0
SYSIBM  SYSDBAUTH         Catalog   0        6      0
```

Fig. 8–14 Monitor Snapshot (tables)

The SQL statement which caused the output report in Fig. 8–14 is:

```
UPDATE test_taken SET INTEGER(score) = 90
           WHERE lname = 'HUTCHISON'
```

Examining the snapshot output and the SQL statement, it is likely that there were 8 tests taken by people with the last name of HUTCHISON. Note, that other system tables were read during the processing of the **UPDATE** statement.

The final snapshot output that we will examine is based on table space activity (**TABLESPACES**).

```
                          Tablespace Snapshot

First database connect timestamp  = 08-28-1996 08:47:02.855887
Last reset timestamp                =
Snapshot timestamp                = 08-28-1996 09:01:17.849480
Database name                     = DB2CERT2
Database path                     = G:\SQL00001\
Input database alias              = DB2CERT2
Number of accessed tablespaces    = 2

Tablespace name                   = SYSCATSPACE
  Buffer pool data logical reads        = 37
  Buffer pool data physical reads       = 13
  Asynchronous pool data page reads     = 0
  Buffer pool data writes               = 0
  Asynchronous pool data page writes    = 0
  Buffer pool index logical reads       = 58
  Buffer pool index physical reads      = 20
  Buffer pool index writes              = 0
  Asynchronous pool index page writes   = 0
  Total buffer pool read time (ms)      = 232
  Total buffer pool write time (ms)     = 0
  Total elapsed asynchronous read time  = 0
  Total elapsed asynchronous write time = 0
  Asynchronous read requests            = 0
  Direct reads                          = 62
  Direct writes                         = 0
  Direct read requests                  = 5
  Direct write requests                 = 0
  Direct reads elapsed time (ms)        = 63
  Direct write elapsed time (ms)        = 0
  Number of files closed                = 0

Tablespace name                   = USERSPACE1

  Buffer pool data logical reads        = 43
  Buffer pool data physical reads       = 4
  Asynchronous pool data page reads     = 0
  Buffer pool data writes               = 0
  Asynchronous pool data page writes    = 0
  Buffer pool index logical reads       = 0
  Buffer pool index physical reads      = 0
  Buffer pool index writes              = 0
  Asynchronous pool index page writes   = 0
  Total buffer pool read time (ms)      = 28
  Total buffer pool write time (ms)     = 0
  Total elapsed asynchronous read time  = 0
  Total elapsed asynchronous write time = 0
  Asynchronous read requests            = 0
  Direct reads                          = 0
  Direct writes                         = 0
  Direct read requests                  = 0
  Direct write requests                 = 0
  Direct reads elapsed time (ms)        = 0
  Direct write elapsed time (ms)        = 0
  Number of files closed                = 0
```

Fig. 8–15 Monitor Snapshot (Tablespace Information)

The snapshot in Fig. 8–15 is based on the same SQL statement, but the information provided is quite different. A table space snapshot is organized according to the I/O activity for each tablespace and the buffer pool (shared for all tablespaces within a database). The analysis of the data captured shows the amount of time (in milliseconds, ms) spent accessing the **SYSCATSPACE** (system catalog tablespace) and the **USERSPACE1** (user tablespace). It is interesting to note that more time was spent reading from the system tables than the user tables. The size of the user table was very small and did not represent a large number of tests taken. As the number of records in the *test_taken* table increases, the proportion of time spent accessing the **USERSPACE1** tablespace increases.

In Fig. 8–15, the buffer pool usage can be determined (if the **BUFFERPOOL** switch is on) for each tablespace. Any I/O prefetching is shown as **asynchronous reads** and any buffer pool asynchronous page cleaning is shown as **asynchronous writes**. The term **direct read/write** corresponds to large object manipulation.

At any time you can determine the current settings of database monitor switches by issuing the following command:

```
GET MONITOR SWITCHES
```

The switch states are shown in Fig. 8–16. The timestamps correspond to the last time the switches were reset or turned on.

```
                 Monitor Recording Switches

Buffer Pool          (BUFFERPOOL)= ON   08-28-1996 08:46:59.039126
Lock Information          (LOCK)= ON    08-28-1996 08:46:59.039126
Sorting Information       (SORT)= ON    08-28-1996 08:46:59.039126
SQL Statement        (STATEMENT)= ON    08-28-1996 08:46:59.039126
Table Activity           (TABLE)= ON    08-28-1996 08:46:59.039126
Unit of Work              (UOW)= ON     08-28-1996 08:46:59.039126
```

Fig. 8–16 Monitor Switch Settings

The switches can be reset at anytime by issuing the command:

```
RESET MONITOR FOR DATABASE db2cert
```

Resetting the monitor switches effectively starts all of the counters at zero and further snapshots are based on the new counter values.

Event monitoring

While Snapshot Monitoring records the state of database activity when the snapshot is taken, an Event Monitor records the database activity when an **event** or **transition** occurs. Some database activities, which need to be monitored, cannot be easily captured using the Snapshot Monitor. An example of these activities include deadlock scenarios. When a deadlock occurs, DB2 will resolve the deadlock by issuing a **ROLLBACK** for one of the transactions. Information regarding the deadlock event cannot be easily captured using the Snapshot Monitor, as the deadlock has likely been resolved before a snapshot can be taken.

Event Monitors are similar to other database objects, as they are created using SQL DDL (Data Definition Language). The main difference is that an Event Monitor can be turned on or off, much like the Snapshot Monitor switches.

✍🏻   **SYSADM** or **DBADM** authority is required to create an Event Monitor.

When the Event Monitor is created, the type of event to be monitored must be stated. The event records are recorded when the following events occur:

DATABASE — records an event record when the **last** application disconnects from the database

TABLES — records an event record for each active table when the last application disconnects from the database

DEADLOCKS — records an event record for each deadlock event

TABLESPACES — records an event record for each active table space when the last application disconnects from the database

CONNECTIONS — records an event record for each database connection event when an application disconnects from a database

STATEMENTS — records an event record for every SQL statement issued by an application (dynamic and static)

TRANSACTIONS — records an event record for every transaction when it **completes** (**COMMIT** or **ROLLBACK**)

The output of an Event Monitor is stored in a directory or in a named pipe. The existence of the pipe or the file will be verified when the Event Monitor is activated. If the target location for an Event Monitor is a named pipe, then it is the responsibility of the application to read the data promptly from the pipe. If the target for an Event Monitor is a directory, the stream of data will be written to a series of files. The files are sequentially numbered and have a file extension of evt (e.g. 00000000.evt, 00000001.evt, etc.). The maximum size and number of Event Monitor files is specified when the monitor is defined.

✍🏻   An Event Monitor will turn itself off if the defined file space has been exceeded.

Let's create an Event Monitor which will store its event records in a directory. In Fig. 8–17 an Event Monitor called *evmon1* has been created. The Event Monitor is not active at this time because it has not been turned on. It has been defined to store the event information in the directory '/evmon1'.

✍   The Event Monitor output directory will **not** be created by DB2, it must be created by the database administrator.

The monitor in Fig. 8–17 is defined to allocate up to 3 files each 4 MB (4*1000*4096) in size, for a total monitor storage area of 12 MB. Other Event Monitor options include: specifying the size of the write buffer, synchronous (**BLOCKED**) writes, asynchronous (**UNBLOCKED**) writes, **APPEND** the Event Monitor data to existing records, or **REPLACE** the Event Monitor data in the directory when the monitor is activated. The Event Monitor may be defined to be automatically started when the database is active, but the default is manual start.

```
CREATE EVENT MONITOR evmon1 FOR DEADLOCKS
WRITE TO FILE '/evmon1' MAXFILES 3 MAXFILESIZE 1000
```

Fig. 8–17 Event Monitor Definition

Two system catalog tables are used to store Event Monitor definitions:

SYSCAT.EVENTMONITOR
Contains a record for each Event Monitor including the current state of the Event Monitor.

SYSCAT.EVENTS
Contains a record for each event being monitored. A single Event Monitor can be defined to monitor multiple events (e.g. **DEADLOCKS** and **STATE-MENTS**).

Event Monitors can be defined to monitor many different types of database activities. A condition can also be specified for an Event Monitor. The condition can be based on the **APPL_ID**, **AUTH_ID** or **APPL_NAME** (e.g. **AUTH_ID** = 'DB2', **APPL_NAME** = 'PROGRAM1'). There is no limitation in the number of defined Event Monitors, but there is a limitation of 32 **active** Event Monitors.

Once the Event Monitor has been defined, using the **CREATE EVENT MONITOR** statement, it must be activated. An Event Monitor can be started automatically each time the database is started using the **AUTOSTART** option, or can be started using the statement shown in Fig. 8–18.

```
SET EVENT MONITOR evmon1 STATE = 1
```

Fig. 8–18 Event Monitor Activation

When the Event Monitor has been activated, Event Monitor records are written to the files contained in the defined directory (e.g., *levmon1* in our example). The Event Monitor files cannot be analyzed directly, an application must be used. There are a few application alternatives provided by DB2 which we will discuss, but let's first examine some of the Event Monitor records.

 To ensure that all of the event records have been written to disk (some may be buffered), simply turn the Event Monitor off.

The Event Monitor is similar to tracing as each event is recorded as it occurs and it is appended to the event record log files (to be analyzed later). An Event Monitor file will contain a number of event records. Table 8–5 shows all of the event record types and when they are used.

Table 8–5 Event Monitor Records

Record Type	Collected for Event Type
Event Monitor Log Header	All
Event Monitor Start	All
Database Header	All
Database Event	Database
Table Space Event	Table Space
Table Event	Table
Connection Header	Connection
Connection Event	Connection
Connection Header	Transaction
Transaction (Unit of Work) Event	Transaction
Connection Header	Statement
Statement Event	Statement
Dynamic Statement Event	Statement
Connection Header	Deadlock
Deadlock Event	Deadlock
Deadlock Connection Event	Deadlock
Event Monitor Overflow	All (if any)

 Some event records are created when any application disconnects from the database and others are only created when the **last** application disconnects from the database.

If the Event Monitor is monitoring database, table space, or table events, it will only write event records when the last application using the database disconnects. If database, table space, or table monitoring data is required before the last application disconnects, use the Snapshot Monitor.

To flush all of the event records, turn the monitor off using the command:

```
SET EVENT MONITOR evmon1 STATE = 0
```

The Event Monitor is still defined in the system catalog tables, but it is not actively recording event information. To determine if an Event Monitor is active or inactive, use the SQL function **EVENT_MON_STATE**. In Fig. 8–19 an example SQL statement is shown. It can be used to determine which Event Monitors are active. A value of 1 indicates that the Event Monitor is active and a value of 0 indicates that the monitor is inactive.

```
SELECT evmonname, EVENT_MON_STATE(evmonname)
FROM SYSCAT.EVENTMONITORS WHERE evmonname = 'EVMON1'
```

Fig. 8–19 Using the EVENT_MON_STATE Function

To remove the definition of an Event Monitor the **DROP** statement must be used. Removing the definition would remove the associated rows in the *SYSCAT.EVENTMONITORS* and *SYSCAT.EVENTS* system catalog tables. An example of removing the *evmon1* Event Monitor is shown:

```
DROP EVENT MONITOR evmon1
```

Analyzing Event Monitor Output

There are two utilities available to analyze Event Monitor data. The **db2evmon** utility is located in the misc sub-directory of the sqllib directory. It is a text-based tool which will read the event records and generate a report. To generate an Event Monitor report issue the following command:

```
db2evmon -path /evmon1
                or
db2evmon -db db2cert -evm evmon1
```

The output of the **db2evmon** utility will be displayed on the screen by default. It is recommended redirecting the output to a file for analysis. Let's examine a portion of the Event Monitor output for a **DEADLOCK** Event Monitor.

```
----------------------------------------------------------
                       EVENT LOG HEADER
     Event Monitor name: EV1
     Server Product ID: SQL02011
     Version of event monitor data: 2
     Byte order: LITTLE ENDIAN
     Size of record: 76
     Codepage of database: 437
     Country code of database: 1
     Server instance name: DB2
----------------------------------------------------------

17) Deadlock Event ...
   Number of applications deadlocked: 2
   Deadlock detection time: 08-28-1996 12:52:21.371051

18) Deadlocked Connection Event ...
   Application Id: *LOCAL.DB2.960828165204
   Sequence number: 0001
   Appl_id of connection holding lock: *LOCAL.DB2.960828165159
   Seq. no. of connection holding the lock: 0001
  Waited on Lock:
   Table Name of lock waited on: T500
   Table Schema of lock waited on: DB2
   Tablespace Name of lock waited on:
   Type of lock: Table
   Mode of lock: S
   Lock object name: 4
  Timestamps:
   Lock wait start time: 08-28-1996 12:52:20.939347
   Deadlock detection time: 08-28-1996 12:52:21.371051

19) Deadlocked Connection Event ...
   Application Id: *LOCAL.DB2.960828165159
   Sequence number: 0001
   Appl_id of connection holding lock: *LOCAL.DB2.960828165204
   Seq. no. of connection holding the lock: 0001
  Waited on Lock:
   Table Name of lock waited on: T500
   Table Schema of lock waited on: DB2
   Tablespace Name of lock waited on:
   Type of lock: Table
   Mode of lock: S
   Lock object name: 4
  Timestamps:
   Lock wait start time: 08-28-1996 12:52:17.469732
   Deadlock detection time: 08-28-1996 12:52:21.371051
```

Fig. 8–20 Deadlock Event Monitor Records

In Fig. 8–20 a deadlock event record and a deadlock connection event records are shown. The information identifies the two applications involved in the deadlock and the reason for the deadlock.

In this example the deadlock involves two shared locks on the *db2.t500* table. Using an Event Monitor to capture deadlock information is just one use of Event Monitors. For example, you can monitor every SQL statement which is issued against a database.

Visual Performance Monitors

We have discussed the steps involved in obtaining snapshot and Event Monitor data. There are graphical interfaces for both of these monitoring facilities. DB2 provides an **Event Analyzer** and **Performance Monitor**.

✍️   These tools are represented as icons in Windows NT and OS/2.

Event Analyzer

If you have gathered Event Monitor data, as described in the previous section, you can use the **Event Analyzer** to analyze the data. The event analyzer is an alternative to the db2evmon tool.

The event analyzer displays the Event Monitor records which have been previously collected. To invoke the Event Analyzer, double-click the icon or issue the following command:

```
db2eva -evm evmon1 -db db2cert
```

If you do not include the database name and monitor name, you will be prompted for the path or location of the event records. When the Event Analyzer is initialized, a screen similar to Fig. 8–21 will be displayed.

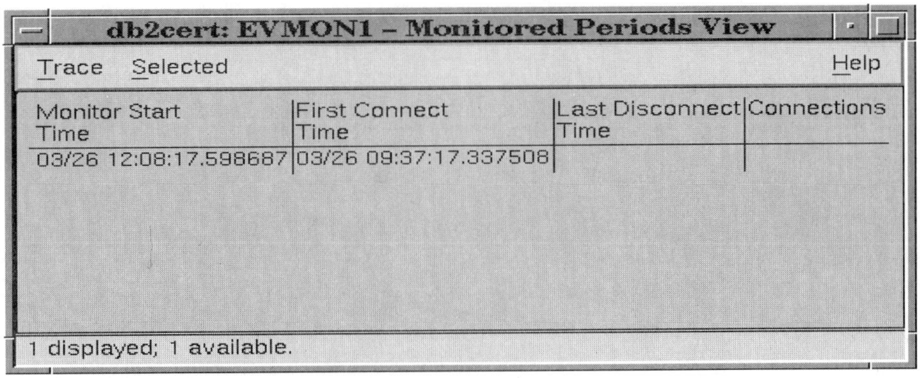

Fig. 8–21 List of Monitored Sessions

Fig. 8–21 shows the event record data. This data could have been captured at any time prior to the analysis. In this example there is only one period for monitoring the database as the monitor was turned on and off once.

Type	Operation	Package Name	Creator	Section Number	Start Time	Elapsed Time	Total CPU Time	Total Sort Time	S
Static	EXECUTE	CHECKID	DB2V2	1	03/26 12:08:40.617028	0.005094	0.01	0.0	0
Static	EXECUTE	DRIVER2	DB2V2	2	03/26 12:08:40.624426	0.027367	0.01	0.0	0
Static	EXECUTE	DRIVER2	DB2V2	3	03/26 12:08:46.188693	0.005552	0.01	0.0	0
Static	COMMIT	DRIVER2	DB2V2	0	03/26 12:08:46.196009	0.085646	0.0	0.0	0

db2cert: 12:08:17 – SQL Statements View

Period   Selected   View   Help

4 displayed; 21 available. Static SQL text not available from "db2cert".

Fig. 8–22 Statement Event Records

To analyze event records for each SQL statement, select the monitoring period and click **Open as Statements** from menu option **Selected**. Fig. 8–22 shows the statements captured in the event record files.

DB2V2: DRIVER2: 2 – Data Elements View

Data Element	Value
Application ID	*LOCAL.db2v2.960326180832
Package Name	DRIVER2
Application Creator	DB2V2
Section Number	2
Statement Type	Static
Statement Operation	EXECUTE
Cursor Name	
Sequence Number	0001

Data Element	Value
Event Start Time	03/26 12:08:40.624426
Event Stop Time	03/26 12:08:40.651793
User CPU Time	0.01
System CPU Time	0.0
Number of Successful Fetches	0
Total Sorts	0
Total Sort Time	0.0
Sort Overflows	0
Rows Read from Table Since Connect	3
Rows Written in Table Since Connect	0
Internal Rows Deleted	0
Internal Rows Updated	0
Internal Rows Inserted	0
SQL Return Code (SQLCODE)	0

Fig. 8–23 Database Event Records

If you want additional information regarding the execution of a single SQL statement, highlight the statement and click **Open as Data elements** from menu option **Selected**. Fig. 8–23 shows the data which is available regarding the processing of the SQL statement.

✍ The Event Analyzer will only display previously captured data. Therefore, there is no overhead in using the event analyzer as there is with the snapshot Performance Monitor. The event analyzer may not contain the desired information as it can only display the event records that have been previously captured. For example, if you select **Open as Statements** and no statement information was defined for the Event Monitor, then the display will not contain SQL statement information.

Performance Monitor

The Performance Monitor can be used to display snapshot information at predefined intervals (default interval is 20 seconds). It can be used to analyze the activity of a specific instance, database, tablespace, or table. The Performance Monitor is initiated from the Database Director.

You can start monitoring by selecting the database object you want to monitor, from the pop-up menu click **Start monitoring**. A window similar to Fig. 8–24 will display the monitoring results for the selected object.

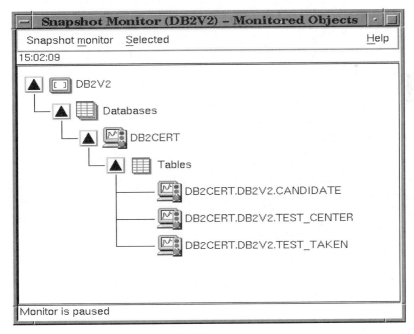

Fig. 8–24 List of monitored objects

The Performance Monitor will turn on the appropriate monitor switches, according to the performance variables. **Performance variables** are used to define important calculations to monitor database activity. These performance variables are defined in a file called **db2sm.pv**. In Fig. 8–24, the *db2cert* database and the tables *candidate*, *test_center* and *test_taken* are being monitored.

Additional monitor information can be displayed by selecting an object and selecting 'Open as Performance graphs' from menu option **Selected**. A monitoring session graph, like the one shown in Fig. 8–25, will be displayed. You may decide to monitor different values and display only the values which you are interested in. Some useful performance variables include the following:

Buffer Pool Hit Ratio — This value indicates how often DB2 could read buffer pool data directly from memory instead of reading the page from disk. The greater the value of buffer pool hit ratio, the less amount of disk access time required to satisfy the query.

Catalog Cache Hit Ratio — This value indicates if the system catalog information describing the reference objects was found in memory (**CATALOGCACHE_SZ** database parameter). The higher the ratio, the less amount of disk activity required.

Lock Escalation — This value indicates how many lock escalations have occurred. The amount of lock escalation activity depends on the **maxlocks** and **LOCKLIST** parameters. If lock escalation occurs, the amount of database concurrency is reduced. Usually, escalations occur as locks are escalated from row level locks to table level locks.

Deadlocks — This value indicates the total number of deadlocks that have occurred since the monitor switches have been set.

Average Lock Wait Time — This value indicates how long (average) an application requesting a lock had to wait because the resource was being used by another application. If the average wait time is high, end-user query response time will be adversely affected.

SQL Statements per Second — This value indicates how many SQL statements are processed per second. A low value may indicate complex query processing or concurrency problems.

Sort Overflowed — This value indicates the total number of sorts that ran out of the sort heap and may have required disk space for temporary storage.

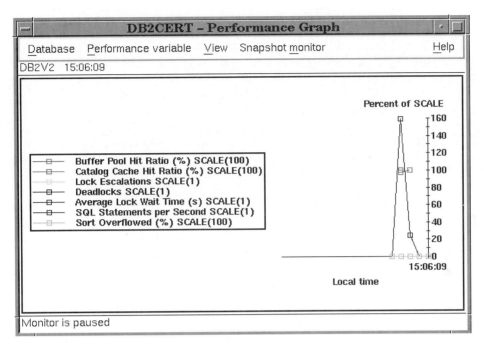

Fig. 8–25 Performance Graph for a Database

In the monitor graph shown in Fig. 8–25 there were no lock escalations, no deadlocks, no sort overflows and the buffer pool and catalog cache hit ratio was nearly 100 percent.

Detailed information about the current, average and maximum value for the monitored performance variables is shown in Fig. 8–26. From the data in Fig. 8–26, we notice that prefetching was not being used and the maximum amount of **LOCKLIST** memory used was 1,692 bytes. This information is invaluable for tuning database configuration parameters.

Performance Issues

Monitoring database activity is performed with a purpose. The purpose of monitoring may involve greater concurrency or reduce the amount of disk access wait time. Another key purpose of monitoring database activity includes configuring various DB2 (instance) and database parameters to optimize memory utilization and increase performance.

Let's examine some of the key DBM and DB configuration parameters and how they relate to each other. Some of these parameters are used to determine the memory allocated for each DB2 instance, database, or application.

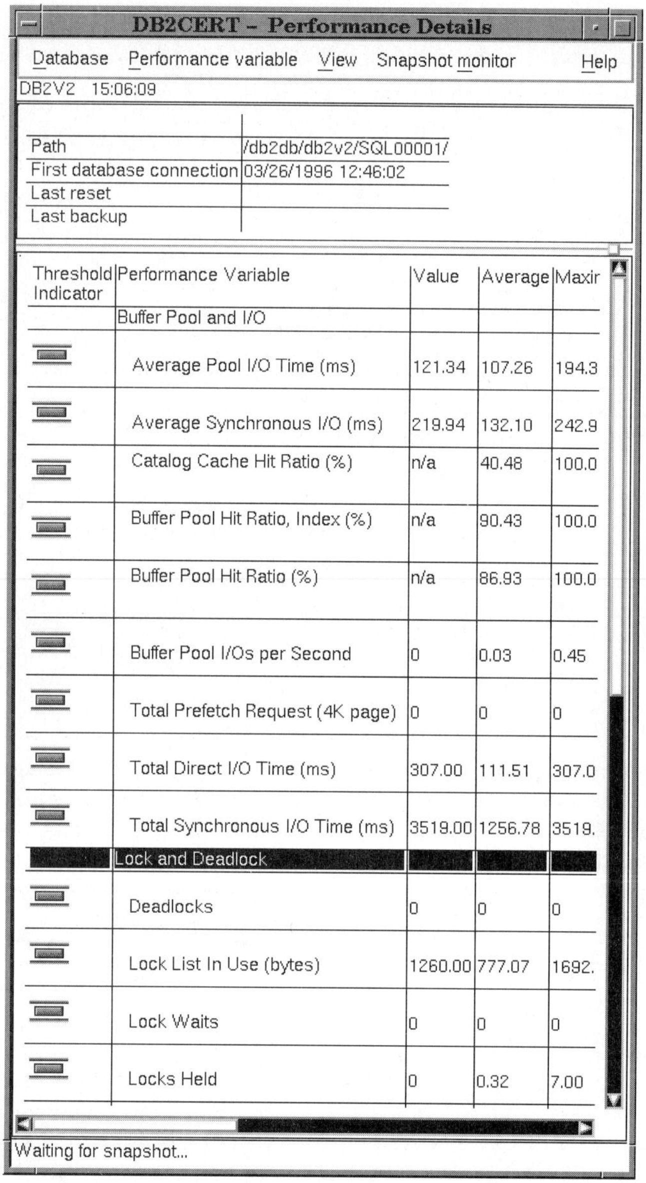

Fig. 8–26 Example of Performance Details Display

Database activity involves disk access (I/O) and memory access (CPU). Each of the DB2 configuration parameters affect either the memory or disk resources. Since disk access is much slower than memory access, the key database performance tuning criterion is to decrease the amount of disk activity. If you are able to eliminate I/O wait time, the database requests are CPU bound and increasing performance would then require faster CPUs or multiple CPUs.

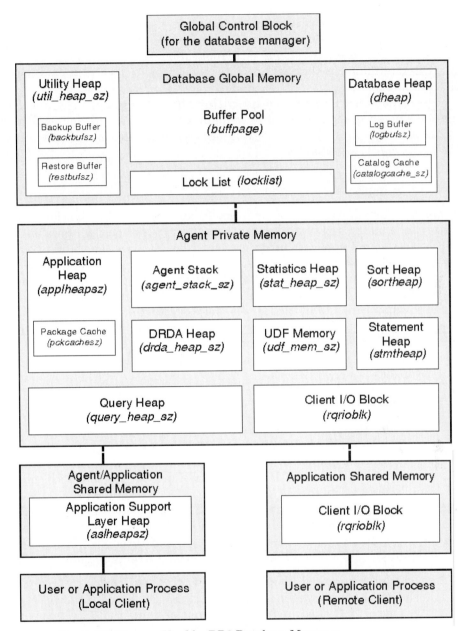

Fig. 8–27 Memory Used by DB2 Database Manager

Fig. 8–27 shows the relationship of the various configurable memory parameters. Memory will be allocated on the server or the client. The number of memory segments allocated for the **database global memory** depends on the number of currently active databases.

Each DB2 application has an associate DB2 server agent. The database agent accesses the database resources on behalf of the application. Therefore, there are tuning parameters to adjust resource usage of the database agent. The **agent private memory** exists for each application connect to the database and the size is determined by the agent private memory heap. The DBM parameter is called **APPLHEAPSZ**.

The memory area known as **application shared memory** is used to determine the amount of memory used to communicate between the application and its DB2 agent process. Record blocking occurs within this memory area. The DBM parameter is **ASLHEAPSZ**.

Configuring Database Resources

The **most** important configuration parameter affecting database performance is the size of the buffer pool (**BUFFPAGE**). There is one buffer pool per database and it will be used by **all** applications connected to the database. The buffer pool is a large data **cache** between the applications and the physical database files.

If there were no buffer pool, then all database activity would result in disk access. If the size of the buffer pool is too small, the buffer pool hit ratio will be low and the applications will wait for disk access activity to satisfy SQL queries. If the buffer pool is too large, memory on the sever will be wasted. If the buffer pool is larger than the physical memory available on the server, then operating system paging (disk activity) will occur. Accessing a buffer pool which has been paged out to disk is **very** inefficient.

✍️   Each page in the buffer pool is 4 KB in size.

The DB2 optimizer will utilize the buffer pool to achieve the best query performance. There is a parameter which provides the optimizer with information regarding the average number of active applications (**AVG_APPLS**). This parameter is used by the optimizer to determine how much of the buffer pool may be used for each application.

Another memory block shared at the database level is called the **database heap** (**DBHEAP**). Most of the database related resources are allocated out of the **dbheap**. There are many I/O caches which can be configured, including a log file cache (**LOGBUFSZ**) and a system catalog table cache (**CATALOGCACHE_SZ**).

The **log buffer** is used as a buffer for writing log records to disk. Every transaction involves writing multiple log records. To optimize disk write performance, the writes are buffered in memory and periodically flushed to disk.

The **catalog cache** is used to store the system catalog tables in memory. As a SQL statement is compiled or referenced, the database object information needs to be verified. If the information is in memory, then there is no need to perform disk activity to access the data.

Record blocking is a client/server caching technique used to send a group of records across the network to the client instead of a single record at a time. The decrease in network traffic increases application performace and allows for better network throughput.

The records are blocked by DB2 according to the cursor type and bind parameter. If the optimizer decides to return the query output in blocks, then the amount of data in each block is determined by the **ASLHEAPSZ** parameter.

✍️   If the DB2 client is configured with a different value for the **RQRIOBLK** parameter, the **RQRIOBLK** parameter is used as the record blocking size.

The **application heap** (**APPLHEAPSZ**) contains a number of memory blocks which are used by DB2 to handle requests for each application. The package cache (**PCKCACHESZ**) is allocated from this heap and is used to reduce the need to reload access plans (sections) of a package. This caching can improve performance when the same section is used multiple times within a program.

✍️   The access plans are cached for static and dynamic SQL statements in the **package cache**.

The sort heap (**SORTHEAP**) is allocated from the agent private memory and determines the number of private memory pages that can be used for each sort. This parameter is used by the optimizer to determine if the sorting can be performed in memory or on disk. DB2 will always attempt to perform the sort in memory. The **sheapthres** parameter is used to control the number of sort heaps allocated for a DB2 server.

Let's modify one of the key performance parameters which affects the amount of memory used on the DB2 server as a data cache (database level). The buffer pool is updated to a size of 2 MB in Fig. 8–28.

✍️   Allocating half of the physical memory to the buffer pool is usually a good starting point when adjusting its size. This assumes a dedicated DB2 database server workstation and a single database active at any given time. For example, if the database server had 40 MB of RAM, then a buffer pool size of 20 MB would usually be effective.

```
UPDATE DB CONFIG FOR db2cert USING BUFFPAGE 500
```

Fig. 8–28 Modifying the Database Buffer Pool Size

Any modification to the database configuration file will not be effective until all applications using the database are disconnected. The subsequent database connection will use the new database configuration parameters.

If you change the DBM (instance) configuration parameters, the new values will not be effective until the instance has been stopped and restarted.

Let's change the size of the amount of memory used to perform record blocking. The memory area used for record blocking is known as the application support layer heap (**ASLHEAPSZ**). The following command would set the record blocking to be 200 KB in size (the units are 4 KB):

```
UPDATE DATABASE MANAGER CONFIGURATION USING ASLHEAPSZ 50
```

Therefore, when the instance is restarted, records will be sent across the network from the DB2 server to the application in 200 KB blocks (likely more than a single row). If the average row length were 1 KB, then 200 records would be returned in a single block of data (assuming more than 200 records are in the final result table).

✍️   Record blocking occurs for remote and local DB2 client applications.

Any changes to the database manager configuration (instance) will not take effect until all of the applications have disconnected. The instance must then be stopped (**DB2STOP** command) and started using the **DB2START** command.

✍️   In a Windows NT environment each instance is a Windows NT service. Therefore, to ensure any changes to the instance have taken effect, the Windows NT service should be stopped and restarted.

DB2 Sorting Methods

When an SQL query requires the data to be returned in a defined sequenced. The result may or may not require sorting. DB2 will attempt to perform the ordering through index usage. If an index cannot be used, the sort will occur in memory or on disk. A sort is called a **piped** sort if it does not require a temporary table to be created. This is usually the preferred method of sorting as there is much less I/O activity involved. If a temporary table is required, the sort is considered to be **non-piped**.

The DB2 optimizer will determine if a piped sort can be used by comparing the result set with the value of the **SORTHEAP** database configuration parameter.

✎ To obtain an ordered result set, a sort is not always required. If an index scan is the access method used, then the data is already in the order of the index and sorting is not required.

Visual Explain can be used to determine the access method used for sorting. In Fig. 8–29 we notice that an index was used to provide the ordered result from the *db2.candidate* table. From the name of the index, we can determine that the index is a primary key index (SQL960724223103590 — timestamp indicates when the index was created).

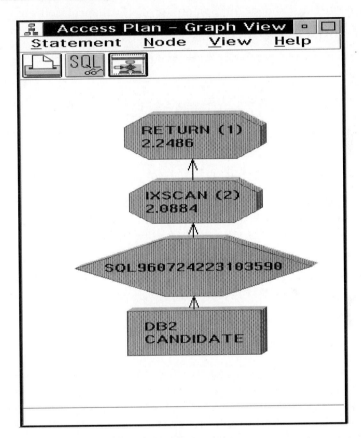

Fig. 8–29 Sort Request Satisfied by an Index

The sort heap is used for each application sort request. The DB2 optimizer may decide to attempt to perform a piped sort, but at runtime if there is not enough available memory to allocate another sort heap, then the sort may be performed on disk instead.

There is a database manager parameter which is used to control the total amount of memory allocated for sorting on the DB2 server. The parameter is called **SHEAPTHRES**. The **SHEAPTHRES** parameter should be set to the maximum number of sort heaps which should be allowed to be allocated at any given time. If the sort heap threshold is reached, the amount of memory allocated for sorting is reduced and therefore the number of accepted piped sort requests will decrease.

The Visual Explain output shown in Fig. 8–30 shows a sort operator. If the detailed information for the sort operator is displayed, the type of sort and the columns involved are shown. Accompanying Performance Monitor information could be used to determine if the sort operation was piped or non-piped. Note that there are two relational table scan operators. The first table scan is reading the base table *db2.candidate* and the second table scan is reading from a temporary sort table.

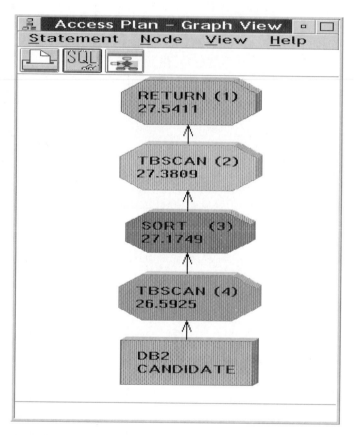

Fig. 8–30 Visual Explain with Sort Operator

There are a number of sorting related performance variables which can be monitored using the graphical Performance Monitor. These parameters include:

Percentage of overflowed sorts — This variable can be monitored to determine if the optimizer is attempting to use a sort heap and fails. If the percentage is low, consider increasing the **sortheap** and/or **sheapthres** values.

Percentage of piped sorts accepted — This variable can be monitored to determine if piped sorts are being chosen by the optimizer, but not accepted. If the percentage is low, consider increasing the sortheap and/or **sheapthres**.

Post threshold sorts — This variable can be monitored to determine if the threshold is being reached for piped sort requests. If the value is increasing, then consider increasing the **sheapthres** parameter or decreasing the **sortheap** parameter.

✍ As with the buffer pool allocation, it is important to allocate as much memory as possible to the sort heap (and set the threshold accordingly) without over allocating memory and causing memory paging to occur.

DB2 Server Resources

The process model or server architecture for DB2 is known as an "n-n process model". The main feature of this architecture is its ability to ensure database integrity. It isolates all database applications from critical database resources. These resources include database control blocks and critical database files.

During the database connection process, a database server agent is assigned to each database application. Each database server agent works on behalf of the database application and handles all of the SQL requests. The application and database agents communicate using InterProcess Communication (IPC) techniques (e.g., message queues, shared memory, and semaphores).

✍ The database server agents are threads in Windows NT and OS/2, but they are processes in UNIX operating systems.

This architecture provides a **firewall** to protect the database resources from an errant application.

✍ These database agent processes are scheduled by the operating system and **not** by DB2. Therefore, you can tune the DB2 process scheduling using regular operating system tuning techniques.

Fenced / Not Fenced Resources

A database **stored procedure** is a dynamically loadable library which can be invoked from a database application using the **CALL** statement. The library is stored on the DB2 database server and it can execute as a **fenced** resource or a **not fenced** resource. A fenced resource is one which executes in a separate process from the database agent. A not fenced resource will execute in the same process as the database agent.

✍️   A DB2 stored procedure is also called a **DARI** or Dynamic Application Remote Interface process.

A not fenced resource will have better performance than a fenced resource as there is less interprocess communication overhead. However, a not fenced resource can damage critical database files and control blocks, if it is not well tested (debugged).

✍️   User-defined Functions (UDFs) can also be defined to execute as a fenced or unfenced resource.

Problem Diagnosis

As a DB2 database administrator, you will undoubtedly have to perform problem diagnosis at some point. Fortunately, DB2 provides diagnosis information at the point of failure in most cases.

The first error log which should be examined is the DB2 error log. This error log is named **db2diag.log**. When errors are encountered, one or more entries are written into this file. The default location for the error log is within the instance directory (sub-directory called db2dump on UNIX platforms).

The location of the db2diag.log can be changed by updating the value of the **DIAGPATH** parameter in the DBM configuration file, for example:

```
UPDATE DBM CONFIG USING DIAGPATH '/diagpath'
```

You can also determine how much error/informational data is written into the db2diag.log file. The DBM configuration parameter called **DIAGLEVEL** is set to 3 (ALERTS / SEVERE ERRORS / ERRORS) by default. If you would like to capture more detailed (INFORMATIONAL) data, then you can set the value to level 4. The following command would provide the most amount of problem diagnostic data:

```
UPDATE DBM CONFIG USING DIAGLEVEL 4
```

Let's examine the output of the db2diag.log and discover the diagnostic information provided. In Fig. 8–31 an example DB2 error log is shown. The error log provides very detailed information regarding the initialization of the NET-BIOS protocol on a DB2 server. The detail includes the DB2 server workstation name (nname) and the allocated names on the network adapter. The db2diag.log shown in Fig. 8–31 is only a portion of the file. Much more detail was provided but is not shown here.

```
Fri Aug 30 15:39:07 1996
DB2 pid(94) tid(3) process (DB2SYSC.EXE)
common_communication  sqlccnbconnmgr_child Probe:35
DIA3411I "NETBIOS" protocol support: Workstation name (nname)
for this server is "OS2".

Fri Aug 30 15:39:08 1996
DB2 pid(94) tid(3) process (DB2SYSC.EXE)
common_communication  sqlccnbgetadapters Probe:2
DIA3402I "NETBIOS" protocol support: adapter "0" initialization
will be attempted.

DB2 pid(94) tid(3) process (DB2SYSC.EXE)
common_communication  sqlccnbaddnames Probe:11
DIA3401I "NETBIOS" protocol support "ADDNAME" was successful for
name:"S$SQLOS2#DB    " for adapter "0".

Fri Aug 30 15:39:18 1996
DB2 pid(94) tid(3) process (DB2SYSC.EXE)
common_communication  sqlccnbaddnames Probe:31
DIA3401I "NETBIOS" protocol support "ADDNAME" was successful for
name:"S$SQLOS2#IB    " for adapter "0".

Fri Aug 30 15:39:22 1996
DB2 pid(94) tid(3) process (DB2SYSC.EXE)
common_communication  sqlccnbaddnames Probe:41
DIA3401I "NETBIOS" protocol support "ADDNAME" was successful for
name:"$SQLOS200    " for adapter "0".

Fri Aug 30 15:39:23 1996
DB2 pid(94) tid(1) process (DB2SYSC.EXE)
common_communication  sqlccnb_start_listen Probe:62
DIA3000I "NETBIOS" protocol support was successfully started.
```

Fig. 8–31 DB2 Error Log (db2diag.log)

The information in the error log includes a timestamp and process/thread information. This information indicates when and where the error was detected. The messages provide more details regarding the error condition and they should be used to supplement any SQL error information obtained (SQLCA).

✍ The main source for DB2 error information is the **db2diag.log** file.

Performance Tuning Scenario

Let's examine a straightforward DB2 performance tuning scenario. A database application user telephones you because he has observed that around 2:00 pm everyday the application is much slower than at other times. The response is slow and sometimes he has to wait to obtain his database requests.

You assume that this problem occurs because there are many applications accessing the database around 2:00 pm. So you decide to use the Performance Monitor to gather information around 2:00 pm. The first resources you decide to monitor are the **buffer pool activity** and the number of **lock escalations**. You will obtain this information if you capture snapshots before, during and after 2:00 pm and compare the output. Snapshots are taken every 30 seconds for a period of time.

You begin to notice that the buffer pool hit ratio decreases below 50%, the number of lock escalations increases and the average lock wait time is increasing around 2:00 pm.

You decide to capture a snapshot of the currently active applications for the *db2cert* database. The CLP command **LIST APPLICATIONS**, as shown below, is actually a database monitor snapshot for applications.

```
           LIST APPLICATIONS FOR DATABASE db2cert
```

Auth Id	Application Name	Agent Id	Application Id	DB Name
DB2V2	db2bp_32	12172	*LOCAL.db2v2.960328211650	DB2CERT
USER1	db2bp_32	13254	*TCPIP.09030158.960329211654	DB2CERT
USER5	db2bp_32	2655	*TCPIP.09031183.960329154357	DB2CERT
BATCH1	data_imp	8366	*TCPIP.09030827.960329211650	DB2CERT
USER9	db2cert	32084	*LOCAL.db2v2.960328211650	DB2CERT

The **LIST APPLICATIONS** command will list all of the currently active applications connected to the database. You note that *user9*, the user who was complaining about performance, was using the *db2cert* application, shown as the last line in the output.

Taking snapshots based on locks for each of the other applications, you note that the *db2v2* user has a large number of row locks allocated and is using most of the locking memory, as defined by the **locklist** parameter.

Snapshots are then taken based on statements for the **APPL_ID** *LOCAL.db2v2.960328211650. It is discovered that the application is performing a large number of inserts on the *test* table.

You decide to increase the amount memory allocated for locks, because lock escalation occurs when an application starts exhausting the available lock list.

The lock memory is defined in the database configuration file. The value can be modified using the CLP or the Database Director. The CLP command to obtain the current database configuration settings is:

```
GET DATABASE CONFIGURATION FOR db2cert
```

Some of the most important database configuration parameters are shown in Fig. 8–32. The first step for resolving the locking problem is to increase the size of the **LOCKLIST** and the value for **MAXLOCKS**. You can issue the following CLP commands to perform the update:

```
UPDATE DB CONFIG FOR DB2CERT USING LOCKLIST 250
UPDATE DB CONFIG FOR DB2CERT USING MAXLOCKS 30
```

```
Database heap (4KB)                        (DBHEAP) = 1200
Catalog cache size (4KB)         (CATALOGCACHE_SZ) = 64
Log buffer size (4KB)                    (LOGBUFSZ) = 8
Utilities heap size (4KB)           (UTIL_HEAP_SZ) = 5000
Buffer pool size (4KB)                   (BUFFPAGE) = 500
Max storage for lock lists (4KB)        (LOCKLIST) = 100

Sort list heap (4KB)                     (SORTHEAP) = 256
SQL statement heap (4KB)                 (STMTHEAP) = 2048
Default application heap (4KB)         (APPLHEAPSZ) = 128
Package cache size (4KB)               (PCKCACHESZ) = 36
Statistics heap size (4KB)          (STAT_HEAP_SZ) = 4384

Interval for checking deadlock ms     (DLCHKTIME) = 10000
Percent. of lock lists per application  (MAXLOCKS) = 10
Lock timeout (sec)                    (LOCKTIMEOUT) = -1

Changed pages threshold            (CHNGPGS_THRESH) = 60
Number of async. page cleaners      (NUM_IOCLEANERS) = 1
Number of I/O servers               (NUM_IOSERVERS) = 3
Index sort flag                          (INDEXSORT) = YES
Sequential detect flag                   (SEQDETECT) = YES
Default prefetch size (4KB)        (DFT_PREFETCH_SZ) = 32

Default number of containers                       = 1
Default tablespace extentsize (4KB)(DFT_EXTENT_SZ) = 32

Max number of active applications         (MAXAPPLS) = 40
Average number of active applications    (AVG_APPLS) = 1
Max DB files open per application         (MAXFILOP) = 64
```

Fig. 8–32 Important Database Configuration Parameters

You may also decide to change the average number of active applications to match the database activity. The **AVG_APPLS** parameter will affect the usage of the buffer pool as determined by the optimizer. Since, there were only 5 applications using the database according to the **LIST APPLICATIONS** command, we will set the value to 8 (allow a few extra connections). The following CLP command will modify the **AVG_APPLS** parameter:

```
UPDATE DB CONFIGURATION FOR DB2CERT USING AVG_APPLS = 8
```

After all these modifications, you should create new application packages (creates new access plans for any static SQL). Use the **REBIND** command to update the package information. Now you should verify that the changes were beneficial. In this example, you should determine if the lock escalations occur the next day and verify that the user (*user9*) is obtaining acceptable response time. Remember, that some performance problems must be addressed within the application or the database design itself.

Summary

Understanding the DB2 database environment is an important part of any database administrator's job. To gain this understanding there are various facilities which can be used.

The DB2 optimizer is one of the most advanced in the relational database industry. The optimizer will generate an access plan during query compilation. Access plans are stored in the system catalog tables for static SQL applications. Access plans for dynamic SQL statements are generated at query execution time and stored in memory.

To gain an understanding of the access plan (strategy) chosen by the DB2 optimizer, the **Explain Facility** may be used. The **Explain Facility** will populate relational tables with detailed information for the SQL statements. These tables can then be queried to determine the plan information regarding index usage and other database resources. There is a snapshot column in the explain tables which is used to store a graphical representation of the access plan. This graphical version of the plan can be examined using **Visual Explain**.

There are two types of monitors available to analyze the database activity, they are called the **Snapshot Monitor** and the **Event Monitor**. A Snapshot Monitor provides point-in-time information regarding resource usage. Many of the elements returned from a snapshot are counters and high-water marks. An Event Monitor is defined using a DDL statement. Once activated, the monitored events will be written to disk or to a named pipe.

Graphical monitoring tools are provided with DB2. The **graphical Performance Monitor** uses the Snapshot Monitor API to gather database activity and display the activity as a graph. The **Event Analyzer** is a graphical interface to help analyze the collected Event Monitor records.

In this chapter the topics of record blocking, sorting and database parameter tuning were discussed.

Questions

1. What is the advantage of creating a not-fenced stored procedure instead of a fenced stored procedure?

    ○   A. It decreases connect time.

    ○   B. It increases database security.

    ○   C. It increases application performance.

    ○   D. It decreases disk space required on the DB2 server.

2. Which command should you use to update a package after the developer has modified the application executable?

    ○   A. **REBIND**

    ○   B. **BIND**

    ○   C. **OPTIMIZE PACKAGE**

    ○   D. **EXPLAIN**

3. Where would you specify the size of the buffer pool?

    ○   A. in the database configuration file

    ○   B. in the database manager configuration file

    ○   C. in the DB2 node directory

    ○   D. in the DB2 system directory

    ○   E. in the DB2 system catalogs

4. When is the buffer pool allocated for a database?

    ○   A. during the start of the DB2 instance for the database

    ○   B. during each SQL statement for the database

    ○   C. during each **COMMIT** statement for the database

    ○   D. during the first connection to the database

5. Which statement about the buffer pool is correct?

     ○   A. The buffer pool is shared memory for all databases within a DB2 instance.

     ○   B. The buffer pool is shared memory for all applications using a database.

     ○   C. The buffer pool is private memory allocated for each application.

     ○   D. The buffer pool is an operating system file used for caching of query request for each database.

6. What must be done prior to capturing an EXPLAIN snapshot?

     ○   A. Update the EXPLAIN directory.

     ○   B. Create the EXPLAIN database.

     ○   C. Rebind the EXPLAIN tool.

     ○   D. Create the EXPLAIN tables.

7. Which SQL statement can be analyzed using the EXPLAIN facility?

     ○   A. **COMMIT**

     ○   B. **DESCRIBE**

     ○   C. **ROLLBACK**

     ○   D. **UPDATE**

     ○   E. **GRANT**

8. Why would a database administrator use the EXPLAIN facility?

     ○   A. Determine how an SQL statement is being processed.

     ○   B. Determine the amount of buffer pool resources being used by each application.

     ○   C. Determine when the last database backup was performed.

     ○   D. Determine the number of applications using the database.

9. What step is required to gather EXPLAIN information for an application
    which contains static SQL?

    ❍   A. Update the DB2CLI.INI file.

    ❍   B. Update the database manager configuration file.

    ❍   C. Issue **SET CURRENT EXPLAIN SNAPSHOT YES**

    ❍   D. Use the **EXPLSNAP YES** bind option.

10. What is the minimum required authority to obtain a DB2 monitor snapshot?

    ❍   A. SYSADM

    ❍   B. DBCTRL

    ❍   C. DBADM

    ❍   D. PUBLIC

11. Given the Snapshot Monitor output:

Total sort time (ms)	= 153
Total buffer pool read time (ms)	= 3015
Total elapsed asynchronous read time (ms)	= 1960
Direct reads elapsed time (ms)	= 81

    How much time was spent prefeteching data?

    ❍   A. 153 ms

    ❍   B. 3,015 ms

    ❍   C. 1,960 ms

    ❍   D. 81 ms

12. Given the Snapshot Monitor output:

Rejected Block Remote Cursor requests   = 2
Accepted Block Remote Cursor requests   = 4

What action would you perform to attempt to increase the number of accepted block remote cursors?

  ○   A. Bind the client application using **BLOCKING NO**.

  ○   B. Bind the client application using **BLOCKING YES**.

  ○   C. Decrease the parameter aslheapsz on the database server.

  ○   D. Decrease the parameter buffpage on the database server.

13. If a query is to provide a sorted result how might DB2 perform the sorting operation?

  ○   A. DB2 will not sort the result

  ○   B. DB2 will sort the data within the buffer pool

  ○   C. DB2 will always sort the data on disk

  ○   D. DB2 will attempt to perform the sort in memory

14. If a DB2 Event Monitor has been defined for a database and it is active, where would its output be found?

  ○   A. in the TEMPSPACE1 table space

  ○   B. in a user-defined database table

  ○   C. in the EXPLAIN tables

  ○   D. in a user-defined directory location

15. If you wanted to record details of each occurrence of a deadlock within a database, what should be performed?

    O   A.   obtain a periodic database monitor snapshot

    O   B.   use the EXPLAIN facility

    O   C.   examine the DB2DIAG.LOG for each occurrence

    O   D.   create an Event Monitor and examine its output

16. Where would the SQL error code (SQLSTATE/SQLCODE) be reported?

    O   A.   in the SQLDA data structure

    O   B.   in the SQLCA data structure

    O   C.   in the DB configuration file

    O   D.   in the Event Monitor log

Answers

1. (C)
   A not-fenced (unfenced) resource will increase the application performance as there is less overhead to communicate between the application
   process and the DB2 agent process.

2. (B)
   If a new bind file has been created for an application then the **BIND** command must be used to store the package in the database.

3. (A)
   The size, amount of memory, allocated for the buffer pool is specified in
   the database configuration file. The buffer pool is shared between all
   applications connected to the database.

4. (D)
   The buffer pool is allocated during the first application **CONNECT** to the
   database. The buffer pool may be preallocated if the **ACTIVATE DATABASE**
   command is issued prior to the first application connect.

5. (B)
   The buffer pool is shared memory for all applications. It contains most of
   the recently read and updated data from the database. Any modified pages
   in the buffer pool will be flushed (written) to the database files over time.

6. (D)
   To obtain an explain snapshot the explain tables must be created. These
   tables can be created using the explain.ddl CLP file, located in the sqllib/
   misc directory of the DB2 instance.

7. (D)
   The **UPDATE** statement will be represented in the explain data which is
   captured. The other statements, (**COMMIT, DESCRIBE, ROLLBACK, GRANT**) do
   not involve query processing and therefore cannot be explained.

8. (A)
   A DB2 database administrator would use the explain facility to determine
   how an SQL statement is being processed (e.g. index usage).

9. (D)

   To capture explain information for an application containing static SQL
   the explain bind options must be used. The **EXPLSNAP YES** bind option
   would gather the snapshot data for all static SQL statements in the package being bound.

10. (A)

   To obtain a DB2 database monitor snapshot the issuer requires **SYSCTRL**,
   SYSMAINT or **SYSADM** authority. In this question the **SYSADM** authority is the
   only option which would be able to perform snapshots.

11. (C)

   Prefetching data corresponds to asynchronous reading. In the data provided in the question the only value representing asynchronous reading is
   the 1,960 ms.

12. (B)

   Cursor blocking is controlled by the bind option called **BLOCKING**. Therefore, the **BLOCKING YES** option would attempt to group the query return
   data into blocks. If the **BLOCKING NO** option is used, record blocking is
   effectively turned off. The **aslheapsz** parameter affects the amount of data
   (number of rows) in each of the returned data block, but it does not affect
   the number of blocked cursors accepted.

13. (D)

   Sorting may be performed in memory of using temporary files on disk.
   The sort will perform in memory if the **sortheap** parameter is large
   enough.

14. (D)

   The output of Event Monitor is specified during the definition of the
   Event Monitor. Therefore, the output is a user-defined location (path/
   directory).

15. (D)

   To determine the applications involved in a deadlock scenario the best
   detection method would be to create an Event Monitor to monitor deadlock activity.

16. (B)

All SQL errors are reported in a special data structure called an SQLCA. Within this structure the error code is recorded in the SQLCODE element and the SQLSTATE element. The SQLCODE is a numeric value and the SQLSTATE is a character string. You may use either element to determine the success or failure of each SQL statement.

Exercises

Part A — Snapshot Monitoring

1. Perform the following steps (similar to part D of chapter 5 Exercises).
   Set the DFT_MON_LOCKS parameter in the DBM configuration to ON.
   Connect to the db2cert database.
   Issue the following commands:

   ```
   db2 +c UPDATE test SET cut_score = 90
            WHERE CHAR (number) = '500'


   db2 "GET SNAPSHOT FOR LOCKS ON db2cert" > out
   ```

   Examine the file to determine the type and number of locks acquired. You
   should notice that row locks were obtained. This exercise demonstrates
   the usage of the Snapshot Monitor to monitor lock behavior.

2. Now instead of using the CLP interface to obtain lock information, use
   the graphical Performance Monitor. Remember, the graphical Performance Monitor is integrated with the database director. Choose the
   db2cert database and open a monitor for the object. Open the database
   monitor for lock information as a performance graph.

   The graphical Performance Monitor can be configured to take snapshots
   at time intervals. You may also set threshold values for performance variables within the monitor. When a threshold has been reached, you may
   decide to record it in a file or database table.

Part B — Event Monitoring

1. Create an Event Monitor for deadlocks. Call the monitor *dead1* and store
   the event records in a directory of your choice.

2. Turn the Event Monitor on, using the command:
   ```
   SET EVENT MONITOR dead1 STATE = 1
   ```
   Note: If you encounter an error, the directory may not exist.

3. Perform the steps in part B of chapter 5 Exercises.

4. Use the event analyzer to examine the captured data.
   `db2eva -db db2cert -evmon dead1`

5. Can you determine the reason for the deadlock? Can you determine the SQL statement involved in the deadlock?
   The reason for the deadlock involves share locks on the db2.test table (as explained in the chapter 5 Exercises). If you attempt to open the monitor to examine SQL statements there is no SQL statement, information displayed as the dead1 Event Monitor was not defined to record this information.

Part C — Sorting and Visual Explain

1. Create the explain tables. Issue: `db2 -tvf explain.ddl`.
   Note: You must be in the misc subdirectory in the sqllib directory.

2. Turn on the special register for explain snapshots.
   `SET CURRENT EXPLAIN SNAPSHOT YES`

3. Issue the statement:
   `SELECT cid FROM db2.candidate ORDER BY 1`

4. Open the visual explain of the statement (from the database director interface). Examine the access plan. Was a sort performed? Was an index scan or a table scan operator used?
   You should have noticed that a sort operator was not involved and an index scan was used instead.

5. Issue the statement:
   `SELECT cid FORM db2.candidate ORDER BY 1 DESC`

6. Open the visual explain of the statement (from the database director interface). Examine the access plan. Was a sort performed? Was an index scan or a table scan operator used?

   You should have noticed that a sort operator was involved and two table scans. The index could not be used because of the requested sort order. If an index was created involving the cid column and it was a descending index then it would likely have been used.

7. Issue the following statement:
    ```
    INSERT INTO db2.test_taken VALUES
        ('111111111', 'TR01','502',
          '04/04/1996', '12:00',NULL,99,NULL, '1')
    ```

8. Examine the visual explain for this statement.
    Why is the access plan so large?
    The access plan includes all of the triggered activity. We defined a number
    of INSERT triggers on the db2.test_taken table when the database was
    created.

DB2 Application Programming

Applications represent the interface to the database, and as a DB2 application developer, it is your responsibility to provide users with the functionality they require. As a DB2 application developer, you must decide which application programming language and operating system are the most appropriate for your skills and the end users' expectations. DB2 does not have its own programming language. Instead DB2 allows applications to be developed using many popular programming languages including COBOL, FORTRAN and C/C++. A precompiler for each of these programming languages is provided with the DB2 Software Developer's Kit (SDK). The precompiler is used to convert embedded SQL statements into a series of API (Application Programming Interface) requests.

The DB2 application can perform ad hoc queries or process well-defined transactions. An application which performs transaction processing is sometimes referred to as an OLTP (On-line Transaction Processing) application. An application which performs ad hoc queries is sometimes referred to as a DSS (Decision Support System) application. DB2 can be used as the database server for both types of applications.

Depending on the type of application, one or more programming techniques can be used. The application can contain static or dynamic embedded SQL statements or dynamically prepared statements using the DB2 Command Line Interface (CLI). Another application development option is to create the application using the REXX interface to DB2 (available on OS/2 and AIX platforms).

In a static embedded SQL application, data is exchanged between DB2 and the application using host variables. These variables are defined in the native programming language such as C, COBOL or FORTRAN. You will become familiar with the proper declaration and usage of host variables.

Data is stored in DB2 databases as tables or a set of records. This unordered set is retrieved from the database using the **SELECT** statement. The output of the **SELECT** statement is known as the result set or result table.The result set is examined using cursors. You will examine how to declare cursors and use them to read, update, and delete a single record at a time.

DB2 Application Development Environment

When you are starting a DB2 application development project, there are a few details which should be decided early in the planning stages. Let's start with a checklist of questions which should be considered:

1. Where will the database(s) reside (including the choice of operating system)?
2. Which operating system will the client application be designed for?
3. What is the nature of the application: OLTP or DSS?
4. Will the application be required to perform a single transaction across multiple database servers?
5. How many developers are coding the application, and what are their programming language skills?

Client/Server Platform

DB2 application developers require a DB2 Software Developer's Kit (SDK), as it contains the necessary programming libraries and header files.

The DB2 Software Developer's Kit is unique for each **client** development platform. The platform of the database **server** does not affect the application development process.

For example, let's suppose you have been asked to develop an application which would allow an OS/2 user to access a DB2 for AIX database. The user needs an OS/2 application. You would require the DB2 SDK for OS/2 to develop the application as the DB2 programming libraries and the precompiler are provided in the SDK product.

If the database were moved to another DB2 server, such as DB2 Server for OS/2, the application would likely require no changes. However, you would have to bind the application to the new database. We will discuss the bind process in more detail later. Usually, the DB2 SDK product would be installed on each developer's workstation. This can be avoided in multi-user environments like DB2 for UNIX systems.

DB2 for UNIX systems can be configured to allow a group of developers to share a single installation of the SDK product. However, there are licensing considerations to keep in mind if you decide to implement this type of environment.

Connection Types

Every DB2 application can connect to one or more DB2 databases. The method of establishing a connection to a remote database does not change across the DB2 Family (AIX, MVS, etc.).

The physical location of the database server is contained in the DB2 directories on the client workstation. Once the proper information is stored in the DB2 directories using the **CATALOG** command, a connection is established using the following SQL statement:

```
CONNECT TO dbname USER user1 USING pw1
```

If another database server is to be used, then the SQL statement to release the current connection is:

```
CONNECT RESET
```

The **CONNECT RESET** will perform an implicit **COMMIT** if there is an outstanding unit of work. If the application needs to perform a single transaction (unit of work) involving more than one database, then the application must use a **TYPE 2 CONNECT**. The behavior of the **CONNECT** statement is dependent on **PRECOMPILE** parameters.

Transactions Involving Multiple Databases

If a transaction requires access to more than one database, then it is considered a **Distributed Unit of Work (DUOW)** transaction. A DUOW application must use a special type of database connection known as a **TYPE 2** connection. The default **CONNECT** behavior is known as a **TYPE 1** connection. Since the syntax of SQL statements is verified during the precompile phase of application development, the connection options are set using precompile options. The **PREP** options which are used for **TYPE 2** connections include:

- **CONNECT (1 | 2)** - The **CONNECT** 2 option will allow a connection to another database within a unit of work
- **DISCONNECT (EXPLICIT | AUTOMATIC | CONDITIONAL)** — This option will be used to determine when a connection will be released at **COMMIT**. The **EXPLICIT** keyword is used to specify only those connections marked to be released at **COMMIT** using the **RELEASE** command. The **CONDITIONAL** keyword is used to specify that connections marked using the **RELEASE** command and any transactions using non **WITH HOLD** cursors, will be released at commit time. The **AUTOMATIC** keyword is used to specify that all connections will be released at commit time.
- **SQLRULES (DB2 | STD)** — This option is used specify the syntax for a **TYPE 2 CONNECT**. The **DB2** keyword will specify the **CONNECT** statement to establish new and dormant connections. The **STD** keyword will specify the **SET CON-**

NECTION statement to be used to establish a connection.

- SYNCPOINT (NONE | ONEPHASE | TWOPHASE) - This option is used to specify the method of transaction control in a multi-database transaction. The **NONE** keyword is used to specify that the transaction will not be coordinated using a Transaction Manager (TM). The **ONEPHASE** parameter is used to specify that no TM will be used for transaction control, and a commit will be sent to each of the participating databases. The **TWOPHASE** parameter is use to specify a TM, which will be used to perform two-phase commit transactions.

✍️   If the DB2 database resides on a DB2 DRDA Application Server, such as DB2 for MVS, the database must have been cataloged via a DDCS gateway.

Usually, a database is created using the Database Director or the Command Line Processor (CLP). The creation of the database and its objects are often performed by a database administrator. These database objects will be referenced by the DB2 application. If the database will reside on the same workstation as the application program being developed, then a local database connection is required. A local database connection is usually a desirable development environment as it eliminates any network communications.

Once you have successfully created a database and all of its objects, the next step is to establish a database connection. The proper authority is required to establish this connection. Therefore, specific user ids can need to be created for application developers or a separate DB2 instance could be established for database programming environments.

One of the first tasks performed by a DB2 application is the establishment of a database connection. Therefore, you should verify that your environment has been set up properly by establishing a connection to the database using the Command Line Processor (CLP). Also verify that the Software Developer's Kit has been installed on each of the development workstations. The Software Developer's Kit contains sample programs using all of the supported DB2 programming interfaces.

Most DB2 applications are written using the COBOL or the C/C++ language. Therefore, you must ensure that the proper programming language tools are installed on each of the development workstations. Since each compiler has different attributes, ensure that the compiler that you wish to use for application development is a supported DB2 compiler. The supported compilers are documented in the DB2 manual *Building Applications Using SDK*.

Choosing a DB2 Programming Method

There are many programming methods available to a DB2 application developer. These are:

- Static Embedded
- Dynamic Embedded
- REXX / Interpreted
- Command Line Interface (CLI)
- Open Database Connectivity (ODBC)
- Native DB2 Application Programming Interfaces (APIs)

Why are there so many different programming methods? Each programming method has unique advantages. We will examine each of the methods and provide examples of their advantages and disadvantages.

Static Embedded SQL

Static embedded SQL applications will be explained in detail later in this chapter. The development process involves the execution of pre defined SQL statements which have been bound to the database as application packages. There are many performance benefits to having ready-to-execute database logic stored within the database. The package is in a form which is understood by the database server. As you might have guessed already, this method of developing applications is not the most flexible, as you must understand every SQL statement that the end user would require during the development process.

The transactions are grouped into packages and stored in the database. The applications can be coded using COBOL, C/C++, or FORTRAN, and the SQL statements are embedded within programming modules. The program modules, which contain embedded SQL statements, must be precompiled. The modified program modules, created by the precompiler, are then compiled and linked to create the application. During the precompile phase, the SQL statements are analyzed and packages are created. Later in this chapter, we will examine all of the steps to create static embedded DB2 applications.

Advantages

- Optimized packages available at runtime.
- Utilize programming skills in COBOL, C/C++ or FORTRAN.

Disadvantages

- Must define SQL statements during development.
- Requires a precompile.

✍ There is also a precompiler available for the PL/1 programming language.

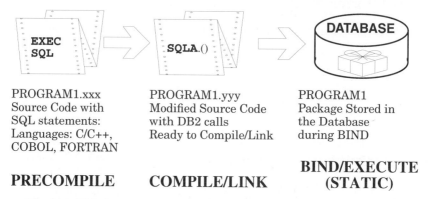

PROGRAM1.xxx   PROGRAM1.yyy   PROGRAM1
Source Code with   Modified Source Code   Package Stored in
SQL statements: with DB2 calls   the Database
Languages: C/C++,   Ready to Compile/Link   during BIND
COBOL, FORTRAN

PRECOMPILE   COMPILE/LINK   **BIND/EXECUTE
                                       (STATIC)**

Fig. 9–1 SQL Statements Prepared during Application Development

Dynamic Embedded SQL

Dynamic Embedded SQL, as shown in Fig. 9–2, still requires the precompile/
compile/link phases of application development. The binding or choosing of the
most effective data access plan is performed at program execution time, as the
SQL statements are **dynamically prepared**. Choosing the access path at
program execution time has some advantages and some drawbacks.

The database objects being accessed needed to exist when a static
embedded application module was bound to the database. Dynamic embedded
SQL modules do not require that these database objects exist when the
application is bound to the database.

An embedded static SQL module will determine the data access method
during the static bind phase, using the database statistics available at bind time.
An embedded dynamic SQL module will determine the data access method
during the statement preparation and therefore can utilize the database
statistics available at query execution time.

Therefore, there is no need to bind dynamic embedded SQL modules to the
database following a collection of database statistics. The database statistics are
collected when the **RUNSTATS** command is issued, and the results are stored in
the system catalog tables. There is, of course, a query execution time overhead to
choose the access path, as each dynamically prepared SQL statement needs
resolved.

In Fig. 9–2, the development steps for embedded dynamic SQL program
modules are shown. Embedding dynamic SQL statements does not remove the
precompile phase of development, but it does provide the execution of dynamic
SQL statements.

Languages: C/C++,
COBOL, FORTRAN

PRECOMPILE   **COMPILE/LINK**   **BIND/EXECUTE (DYNAMIC)**

Fig. 9–2 SQL Statements Prepared during Application Execution

Advantages

- Current database statistics are used for each SQL statement.
- More flexible SQL statements are possible than with static SQL.

Disadvantages

- Access control cannot be performed at the package level.
- Since queries are optimized at run time, the query can take more time to execute.

Call Level Interface (CLI)

The DB2 Call Level Interface (CLI) provides an application development environment where precompiling and static binding are no longer required. CLI is referred to as a callable SQL interface, because database resources are directly accessed from a native programming language using APIs (Application Programming Interfaces).

DB2 CLI is a dynamic SQL application development environment. The SQL statements are issued using the C/C++ Application Programming Interfaces (APIs) provided with DB2. The necessary data structures used to communicate between the database and the application are allocated by DB2. Since the SQL statements are issued through direct API calls, there is no need to precompile the program modules.

The DB2 Call Level Interface is based on the Microsoft Open Database Connectivity Standard (ODBC) specification and the X/Open Call Level Interface specification. A CLI application is more easily ported to other database servers as many of these APIs are supported for other database servers.

There exist many differences between developing an embedded SQL application module and developing a Call Level Interface (CLI) module. Since an application is usually comprised of a number of program modules, the modules can use different DB2 programming techniques. It can be beneficial to use different DB2 programming interfaces in a single application.

The CLI application development environment is shown in Fig. 9–3. A detailed discussion will follow in chapter 10.

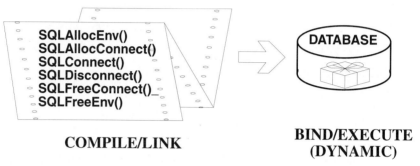

SQLAllocEnv()
SQLAllocConnect()
SQLConnect()
SQLDisconnect()
SQLFreeConnect()
SQLFreeEnv()

DATABASE

COMPILE/LINK   **BIND/EXECUTE (DYNAMIC)**

Fig. 9–3 Application Development Using CLI

Advantages

- Precompiler is **not** required.
- Binding an application package to the database is **not** required.
- Current database statistics are used.
- Can store and retrieve sets of data.
- Easy porting to other database platforms.

Disadvantages

- Must have C/C++ programming skills.
- Dynamic binding results in slower query execution.
- Cannot use embedded SQL features, such as compound SQL statements.

Native DB2 Application Programming Interfaces (APIs)

DB2 supplies Application Programming Interfaces (APIs) which can be used to directly manipulate DB2 instances and databases. Some tasks, such as performing a backup or copy of a database, must be coded using these APIs. There is no method of embedding an SQL statement to perform this operation because the **BACKUP DATABASE** command is not part of SQL.

The DB2 APIs are provided in many programming languages, including C/C++, COBOL and FORTRAN. Information is exchanged between the application and database using special data structures. If the source program module contains only DB2 APIs, there is no need to precompile, and a database package is not created.

You can wish to use the DB2 APIs in an embedded SQL or a CLI application. For example, the function **sqlaintp()** is commonly used to retrieve the complete text for a DB2 error message, so the application can then display the error message to the end user. The DB2 APIs are grouped by functional category. (see Table 9–1). For details on using these APIs, see the *DB2 API Reference*.

Table 9–1 DB2 Application Program Interfaces (Areas)

Backup/Recovery	Database Monitoring
Database Control	Operational Utilities
Database Manager Control	Data Utilities
Database Directory Management	General Application Programming
Node Directory Management	Application Preparation
Network Support	Remote Server Utilities
Database Configuration	Table Space Management

Advantages

- Advanced features of DB2 can be utilized (for example, table space administration).
- No precompiling or binding required.
- Utilize your host language programming skills (C, COBOL, FORTRAN).

Disadvantages

- Requires host language compiler/linker, unlike REXX.
- can be more difficult to implement.
- Cannot issue SQL statements.
- Not easily ported to other database servers.

Accessing Data from an Application

Before we start writing DB2 applications, we must take a step back and ensure that we understand how data is stored and referenced within SQL statements.

Using Schemas

The objects stored within a DB2 database are organized into groups called schemas. The schema name is actually part of the full name of the object being accessed. When database objects are being defined using the SQL **CREATE** <database object> statement, a qualifier or schema-name should be provided in the name of the database object.

Schema names are associated with many database objects, including tables, views, indexes and packages. For application development purposes, the table, view, and package objects are of primary concern as indexes cannot be directly referenced in SQL DML statements (**INSERT, UPDATE, DELETE**). Specifying the schema name for each database object is important, as each database object will be implicitly given a schema. If the creator of a database object does not include the schema name in the database object definition, then the object will be created using the creator's schema name. For example, let's assume that a user called Mark created a table using the statement: **CREATE TABLE** *table1* (**C1 CHAR(3)**). The complete name of the database object would be *MARK.TABLE1* and the application would have to specify the entire name.

✎ **Avoid** using unqualified table or view names in SQL statements.

In Fig. 9–4, the schema for the table called *test* is *db2*. If you refer to this table in an embedded SQL application, you should reference the table using its fully qualified name, *db2.test*. Failure to include the schema name can result in unexpected behavior.

In an embedded SQL application, unqualified database objects are qualified with the user id of the person who performed the **BIND** command to bind the application package. In a dynamic SQL application, unqualified database objects are qualified with the user id of the person who is executing the statement. This difference is a major consideration during application development, as it affects the required data access privileges.

The fully qualified name of a database object must be unique within the database. Thus, from the previous example, another table can exist with the name *test,* if the schema name is something other than *db2*. Another term used for schema name is *collection*.

```
CREATE  TABLE        db2.test  (
                     Number       test_id      NOT  NULL,
                     Name         VARCHAR(30)  NOT  NULL,
                     Type         CHAR(1)      NOT  NULL,
                     AvgScore     score        NOT  NULL,
                     CutScore     score        NOT  NULL,
                     Length       minutes      NOT  NULL,
                     TotalTaken   INTEGER      NOT  NULL,
                     TotalPassed  INTEGER      NOT  NULL,
                     CONSTRAINT
                                  PRIMARY  KEY(Number))
```

Fig. 9–4 Creating a Table Specifying a Schema

Using an Alias

An alias can be used to refer to a table within the database. If an application contained SQL statements which accessed tables based on an alias, then the alias could be defined to represent different tables without modifying the application. An alias can be created for a table, as in the example, or it can be another alias.

For example, let's assume a user named Greta created a table called prices and a user named Volker created a table called prices. Each of these tables reside in the same database and they are named *greta.prices* and *volker.prices*. Suppose you were asked to develop an application which would access both of these tables and produce summary reports. Let's also assume that you will be using an embedded SQL technique. Your application would require two sets of queries, one for each schema name: *greta* and *volker*. This is not a very desirable programming technique and it is prone to error. Later you can find a problem with one of the SQL statements, but you also forget to make the change in the statement which accesses the other table. An alias can be used as the target table name for your SQL statements in your application. If the referenced object in your application is an alias, it can be defined to represent the table *volker.prices* or *greta.prices*.

Let's create the alias objects which could be used in the example scenario.

```
CREATE ALIAS db2.prices FOR volker.prices
CREATE ALIAS db2.prices FOR greta.prices
```

The application could then be developed simply referencing the table object as *db2.prices*. The application would then access whichever table has been defined as the source for the *db2.prices* alias. There can only be one definition for the *db2.prices* alias at any given time within the database. However, the same alias name could be used in different databases.

Another example of using aliases involves creating multiple aliases to the same source table or view. Let's assume that the database object was called *db2.prices* and we wanted to allow the users Calene and Frank to issue the following SQL statement from the Command Line Processor (CLP):

```
SELECT * FROM prices
```

The **SELECT** statement did not explicitly qualify the table name using the table's schema name. Since the CLP interface is an embedded dynamic SQL interface, the table is implicitly qualified with the current user ids. The target table for this query would be *calene.prices* and *frank.prices*. These are two different tables. However, the goal of the **SELECT** statement was to access the data in the *db2.prices* table. Let's create two aliases to provide the desired results:

```
CREATE ALIAS calene.prices FOR db2.prices
CREATE ALIAS frank.prices FOR db2.prices
```

To create the aliases shown above, you would require DBADM or SYSADM authority, as you are creating the aliases outside of your schema. Once created, an alias does not provide access control. The privileges on the referenced table or view are used to determine if access is allowed.

Creating Packages

A package is database object which contains optimized SQL statements. A **package** corresponds to a single source program module and a **section** corresponds to the SQL statements contained in the source program module.

A program module which contains embedded static SQL statements requires precompiling. The precompiler will generate a package. This package contains a number of sections. Each of these sections corresponds to an embedded SQL statement. An optimized **access plan** will be stored in the section. The package canbe stored in a bind file or directly in the database. Creating a bind file and binding the package in a separate step is known as *deferred binding*.

A program module which contains embedded dynamic SQL statements still has an associated package and sections, but the sections are used as placeholders for the SQL statement which will be dynamically prepared. There are no access plans stored in the sections as there are in embedded static SQL modules.

Like views and tables, packages also have an associated schema name. The fully qualified name of a package is *schema-name.package-name.*

In most cases, application developers will use deferred binding. Deferred binding requires a two-step process:

- Creating a bind file (which contains a package).
- Binding the package to the database.

Let's examine these steps. First, we need to create a bind file. The bind file is generated by the precompiler. The precompiler is invoked using the Command Line Processor (CLP). The command is called **PREP** or **PRECOMPILE**.

The precompiler input is always a source program module with embedded SQL statements. Each DB2 supported programming language has its own precompiler provided with the Software Developer's Kit. The file extension of the source program module is used to determine which precompiler (e.g., C, C++, COBOL, FORTRAN) will be invoked.

In Table 9–2 , the input host language source file extensions and the modified source output extensions are provided. The examples in this book will be written in C. Therefore, the embedded SQL program files will be named *program-name.sqc,* and the precompiler output files will be named *program-name.c.* The name of the original source module is important, as the precompiler will use this as the name of the package unless otherwise specified.

Table 9–2 Precompile File Extensions

Host Language	File Extension (input - source)	File Extension (output - modified source)
C	.sqc	.c
C++ (case sensitive - AIX)	.sqC	.C
C++ (case insensitive - OS/2)	.sqx	.cxx
COBOL -use TARGET and/ or OUTPUT options to use other extensions	.sqb	.cbl
FORTRAN (UNIX)	.sqf	.f
FORTRAN (OS/2, Windows)	.sqf	.for

If you were to issue the following DB2 commands,

```
CONNECT TO db2cert USER db2 USING db2
PRECOMPILE prog1.sqc
CONNECT RESET
```

you would be creating an application package called *db2.prog1* in the *db2cert* database. This package would contain all of the necessary information, with the exception of host variable values, required to execute all embedded SQL statements which were contained in the file *prog1.sqc*. There are additional steps required before you have a usable application. All database objects (tables, views, etc.) must exist during the precompile in this example because deferred binding is not being used. The other inconvenient aspect of not creating a separate bind file is that the entire database would need to be provided with the application to the end user, as the package only exists in the database. The package is not contained in a separate bind file in this example.

Let's look at an example of deferred binding with the DB2 commands:

```
CONNECT TO db2cert USER db2 USING db2
PRECOMPILE prog1.sqc BINDFILE
CONNECT RESET
```

This example demonstrates the use of the precompiler option **BINDFILE**. This option is used to generate an output file which contains all of the package information for the source module. By using this option, the package is stored in a file called *prog1.bnd*. You can change the name of the output bind file, but in this example we did not rename the bind file. To avoid confusion relating source program modules, bind files, and package names, try to avoid renaming any of these objects. If you want to create the package using a different name, use the option **PACKAGE USING <package-name>**. If you want to create the package using a different schema name, use the option **COLLECTION <schema-name>**.

The name of the package is determined when the *prog1.bnd* file is bound to the database. If the same user were to bind this package, the name of the package would be *db2.prog1*. If the database objects do not exist during precompile, only warnings will be generated, and the bind file is created. The **BIND** command will verify the existence and access privileges of database objects.

✍🏻   Database objects referenced in embedded static SQL programs must exist during package creation in the database (**PRECOMPILE** without **BINDFILE** option or **BIND**).

For each source program module containing embedded static SQL statements, a corresponding package must exist in the database. Let's assume that we are creating an application which accesses two different DB2 databases. The objects referenced in the application must exist in the database for the package to be bound successfully. Therefore, we will develop the application using two different program modules. Each program module, or source file, represents a database package. If we keep the SQL statements for each database in separate packages, the bind will be successful. We can then compile and link the program modules together into a single executable.

Any **PRECOMPILE** error messages will be reported to the display or to a message file. The error message file can be specified using the **MESSAGES** option when issuing the **PRECOMPILE** command. It is recommended to send the messages to an output file so you can examine the file to determine the cause of the errors. Errors during precompile could include invalid host variable definitions and incorrect SQL statements.

It is important to remember that an embedded dynamic SQL program module does have an associated packages, but it **does not** contain access plans or executable sections. For example, suppose an SQL program contains four static SQL statements and two dynamic SQL statements in a single source module. There would be four SQL sections or access plans created and stored in the database within a single package.

Binding Applications

The most common method of binding used during application development is *deferred* binding. When deferred binding is used, the package must be bound using the **BIND** command to store the package in the database. Once the package exists in the database, there is no longer any need to bind the application.

The package from the bind file is examined during the bind process, and the current database statistics are used to determine the best method of data access. At this point, an access plan is chosen by the DB2 optimizer. This access plan is then stored in the database system catalog tables. An access plan is **only** created for static embedded SQL statements. Embedded dynamic SQL statements have a package and a section number assigned, but there is **no** access plan created until the statement is executed.

The bind process needs to be performed following each successful precompile of the application source modules. When the bind file is created, a timestamp is stored in package. The timestamp is sometimes referred to as a *consistency token*. This same timestamp is also stored in the database when the bind has been completed. The timestamp is used to ensure that the resulting application executes the proper SQL statement.

The modified source module (output from the precompile) will attempt to execute the SQL statements by package name and section number. If the required package and section are not found, the application will return the following error message:

```
SQL0805N Package "pkgschema.pkgname" was not found.
SQLSTATE=51002.
```

If the required package and section exist in the database system catalogs, the timestamp is then checked. If the timestamp in the application executable does not match the timestamp stored in the system catalog tables in the database, the application will return the following error message:

```
SQL0818N A timestamp conflict occurred.
SQLSTATE=51003.
```

Unqualified database objects in embedded static SQL programs are qualified using the authorization user id of the person who bound the package. If the database being accessed is a DRDA host, such as DB2 for MVS, the unqualified objects can be qualified using the **OWNER** and **QUALIFER** keywords. It is not possible to specify a schema or qualifier name for all unqualified database objects if the database being accessed is a DB2 common server database.

The person who binds the packages must have **BINDADD** authority for the database. They also must have the proper privileges for all of the referenced objects in the bind file. Once the package exists in the database, any person with **EXECUTE** privilege on the package can issue any of the SQL statements contained in the package, even if the individual does not have direct privilege on the database object. This is a unique feature of embedded static SQL program modules. It allows end-users access to a portion of data contained in a table without defining a view or define column level privileges.

    DB2 does not provide column level privileges.

Examining Packages and Timestamps

We have briefly discussed packages and timestamps. Let's examine how we can verify that the bind file and the packages in the database match. When the **BIND** command is successful, a single entry in the system catalog **SYSCAT.PACKAGES** is created. There are a number of columns defined for this table. We will not go into a complete explanation here. But let's look at the timestamp column. The timestamp associated with a package is actually stored in the column named *unique_id*. If you were to successfully issue the command,

```
BIND connect.bnd MESSAGES msg1.out
```

the **SYSCAT.PACKAGES** table would have a new entry for this bind file with the package name *connect* and the package schema as your authorization user id. Any error or warning messages would be written to the file called *msg1.out*. To examine the timestamp contained in the *connect.bnd* file, there is a utility provided with DB2 called **db2bfd**. The tool is located in the sqllib directory under the misc sub-directory. Fig. 9–5 contains the output of the **db2bfd** tool and the timestamp associated with the package.

Note that the timestamp is encoded as DA6eLWCM but the decoded timestamp is also shown. This timestamp is the exact time when the **PRECOMPILE** command was used to generate the bind file.

```
connect.bnd:  Header Contents

Element name              Description                Value
------------              -----------                -----
bind_id                   Bind file identifier       :BIND V02:
relno                     Bind file release number   :0x300:
application               Access package name        :CONNECT :
timestamp                 Access package timestamp   :DA6eLWCM:
                                                     1996/02/22 11:30:57:003

creator                   Bind file creator          :USERID  :
```

Fig. 9–5 Contents of a Bind File (db2bfd connect.bnd -b)

If you want to confirm that this bind file (*connect.bnd*) has been previously bound to the database, issue the SQL statement:

```
SELECT pkgschema, pkgname, unique_id
       FROM SYSCAT.PACKAGES
       WHERE pkgname = 'CONNECT'
```

The output of the above statement should contain a single row result which should have a matching timestamp to the bind file as shown in Fig. 9–5.

PKGSCHEMA	PKGNAME	UNIQUE_ID
USERID	CONNECT	DA6eLWCM

The *unique_id* and the timestamp contained in the bind file match. Therefore, you know that this bind file has been successfully bound to the database.

✎ A User Defined Function has been provided to decode the timestamp (in chapter 10).

Binding Utilities

The Command Line Processor is an embedded dynamic SQL application which is provided with DB2. The packages associated with the utilities, like the DB2 CLP, are included in the sqllib directory in the bnd sub-directory. There are five bind files associated with the CLP: db2clpcs.bnd, db2clprr.bnd, db2clpur.bnd, db2clprs.bnd, db2clpnc.bnd.

Each of the CLP bind files is created with different isolation levels. This allows a user the ability to change their isolation level when using the CLP utility, using the **CHANGE ISOLATION** command.

These bind files must have been bound to the database you wish to access using the DB2 Command Line Processor (CLP).

 To bind the DB2 utilities (e.g. **CLP, IMPORT, EXPORT**) issue the command **BIND** @*db2ubind.lst* **BLOCKING ALL**

To bind a number of packages using a single **BIND** command, add the @ character in front of the source file. When this character is encountered, DB2 will assume that the file contains a list of bind files and not a bind file itself.

Important Application Development Bind Considerations

There are a large number of options which can be specified when you are binding your application to the database. These **BIND** options differ slightly between DB2 common server databases and DRDA host databases like DB2 for MVS. The *DB2 Command Reference* contains all of these options, but we will describe the options that affect application development directly.

Blocking

Record blocking is a feature of DB2 database servers which reduces data access time across networks when an application is retrieving a large amount of data. The record blocking is based on cursor type and the amount of storage allocated on the DB2 server to perform record blocking. Cursors are used in applications to manipulate multi-row result sets from a DB2 server.

The DBM configuration parameter known as *aslheapsz* specifies the amount of memory used to buffer the data on the server for applications requesting multiple data records. For applications executing on remote clients, the buffer is specified by the DBM configuration parameter known as *rqrioblk*.

You can think of record blocking as data retrieval caching. The record blocking options are described in Table 9–3. Usually, you would specify **BLOCKING ALL** for applications that perform many queries. An *ambiguous cursor* is a cursor which has been defined without any reference to its intended usage in an SQL statement. As we will see, all cursors are defined using a **SELECT** statement. They are used in a **SELECT, DELETE,** or **UPDATE** statement.

The default blocking option for static embedded applications is **BLOCKING UNAMBIG**. The default blocking option for CLI applications and the Command Line Processor is **BLOCKING ALL.**

Record blocking affects the way you, as an application developer, declare your cursors within your application. The more specific you are with your cursor declaration, the more likely DB2 will use record blocking appropriately.

Table 9–3 Record Blocking Options

BLOCKING <option>	Record Blocking Behavior
UNAMBIG	All cursors except those specified as FOR UPDATE are blocked.
ALL	Ambiguous cursor are blocked.
NO	No cursors are blocked.

If record blocking is enabled, the cache is allocated when the cursor is opened. It is deallocated when the cursor has been closed. Therefore, to avoid wasting memory resources on the server, avoid keeping cursors open if they are no longer required.

 All cursors used for dynamic SQL statements are assumed to be ambiguous.

Parts of a DB2 Embedded Static SQL Application

Host Variables

Host variables are used to pass data between an application and the database. These variables are declared in a special manner in the host language program module. During precompile, the host variables are converted to corresponding host language variables (C variables, COBOL data items). One of the major output files generated during precompile is the modified source module. Within this module, precompile runtime function calls are used to actually manipulate the host variables.

When you use host variables in SQL statements, you must prefix the host variable name with a colon (:).

Remember that the host variable is used in two ways in a program:

- Within SQL statements (always precede the variable by a colon).
- Outside of SQL statements (treat host variables like any other variable).

Host variables can only be used within static SQL statements. Dynamic embedded SQL statements use parameter markers instead of host variables. Each programming language has slightly different rules for declaring host variables, but there are many similarities. Every host variable must be declared in an **EXEC** SQL **DECLARE** section.

 REXX does not support host variables. REXX is not considered a static SQL application development environment.

Two types of host variables:

- **Input Host Variables**

  Input host variables specify values to be passed to the database manager from the application during statement execution. For example, an input host variable would be used in the following SQL statement:

  ```
  SELECT name FROM candidate
  WHERE name = <input host variable>
  ```

- **Output Host Variables**

  Output host variables specify values to be returned from the database manager to the application during statement execution. For example, an output host variable would be used in the following SQL statement:

  ```
  SELECT INTO <output host variable> FROM candidate
  WHERE name = 'HUTCHISON'
  ```

Host variables must be defined within the **BEGIN DECLARE SECTION** and the **END DECLARE SECTION**. You can decide to have multiple declare sections in a single source module. This really depends on your coding preference. Be sure that all of the host variables used in your SQL statements have been defined within a **DECLARE** section. During precompile, the programming language scope of data variables is not taken into account. This means that all host variables must be unique within a single source module being precompiled, even if they are locally scoped, as in the C programming language. You can decide that small program modules are better suited to your programming style. This will help avoid incorrect host variable declaration. A host variable can not be redefined within the same program module. Its definition must be compatible with the DB2 data type to which it corresponds in the SQL statement.

Fig. 9–6 demonstrates an example of declaring host variables in the C programming language. The host variable *name* corresponds to the DB2 data type of **CHARACTER.** The host variable *age* corresponds to the DB2 data type **SMALLINT.** From the figure, we see that the actual declaration of the variable *name* follows C language variable definition rules. Note that the programmer should **not** declare any other C variable as *name*. The **EXEC SQL** clause lets the precompiler know that this data is to be interpreted and replaced with a C API call to the DB2 engine. The ending semi-colon (;) lets the precompiler know that the SQL statement is complete.

```
EXEC SQL BEGIN DECLARE SECTION;
/* place all host variables here */
                char        name[9];
                short       age;
EXEC SQL END DECLARE SECTION;
```

Fig. 9–6 Host Variables using C

✍ When developing C applications, host variables for **CHARACTER** column types should be defined one character more than the column definition. The extra character will store the null-termination character. If you do not provide for the null-termination character, the resulting variable can be truncated.

Fig. 9–7 is an example of declaring host variables in a COBOL application. As in the C example, do not declare a variable outside of the **BEGIN DECLARE** and **END DECLARE** section. This example is defining a host variable *name*. This variable would correspond to the DB2 **CHAR** data type.

```
EXEC SQL BEGIN DECLARE SECTION END-EXEC.
* place all host variables here
                 01 name      PIC X(8).
EXEC SQL END DECLARE SECTION END-EXEC.
```

Fig. 9–7 Host Variables using COBOL

Fig. 9–8 is an example of establishing a connection to a DB2 database using host variables. The example is a C program module which takes two arguments as its input: szUserid and szPassword. Since the user id and password will be supplied by the end user, the programmer must use host variables.

Also note that the input arguments are copied to the local variables user id and password. The variables user id and password are local to this function, but remember that to the DB2 precompiler they are valid DB2 host variables and they must be unique in the entire source module.

The return code of this module is an **SQLCODE**. The SQLCODE is a error number contained in the SQL communications area data structure called the **SQLCA**. If the database connection is unsuccessful, the SQLCODE will be a negative number. If the database connection is successful, the SQLCODE will be a value of zero. A positive value for SQLCODE indicates a warning condition.

✍ When declaring host variables in C that will be used for string data, an extra character in the array should be defined to contain the null termination character.

Connecting to the Database Server from an Application

In Fig. 9–8, a connection to a database called *db2cert* was established. This connection should be explicitly performed by your application. The connection will establish the authorization id for this session. In this example, the authorization id is passed into the module as the variable *szUserid*. Usually, your application will only use the resources of a single database at a time. This is known as a **CONNECT TYPE 1** application. If more than one database needs to be utilized, then other items need to be considered. A special user variable called *current server* is assigned by DB2 following a successful connection.

```
/**************************************************************
** Source File Name = connect.sqc
**
** PURPOSE: This program will establish a database connection
**          as defined by the dbname host variable.
** STATEMENTS Used:
**        - CONNECT TO ....
** Concepts:
**        - Establishing a database connection
**************************************************************/

#include <stdio.h>
#include <stdlib.h>
#include <string.h>
#include "cert.h"
int Establish_Connection ( char *szUserid, char *szPassword )
{
   EXEC SQL BEGIN DECLARE SECTION;
       char userid[9];
       char passwd[19];
       char dbname[19];
   EXEC SQL END DECLARE SECTION;

   strcpy (userid,szUserid);
   strcpy (passwd,szPassword);
   strcpy (dbname,"db2cert");

   EXEC SQL CONNECT TO :dbname user :userid USING :passwd;
   return SQLCODE;
}
```

Fig. 9–8 Establishing a Database Connection Using Host Variables

You can establish a database connection implicitly using the default database. The default database is defined using the environment variable **DB2DBDFT**. When the application is initialized and the first SQL statement is being executed, an **implicit connect** will occur.

Implicitly establishing a database connection is not the recommended approach as it is based on a user environment setting which is difficult to maintain. Therefore, **always** code an explicit database connection in your application. You should also include the user id and password as shown in Fig. 9–8.

Once the database connection has been established, it will remain until:

- **CONNECT RESET** is issued to drop the database connection.
- **CONNECT TO** is issued to another database.
- **DISCONNECT** is issued (available in **CONNECT TYPE 2** applications).

When your application terminates, you should always issue a **CONNECT RESET** upon termination to release your connection to the database and explicitly complete any outstanding transactions.

✍ The DB2 CLP utility will perform a **CONNECT RESET** when **TERMINATE** command is issued.

SQL Communications Area SQLCA (Part 1)

As with most application development environments, proper error handling is essential for creating and maintaining a quality program. Every SQL statement issued from an application can result in a successful condition or an error condition. The primary means of determining the result of an SQL statement is for the application developer to examine the contents of the SQL Communications Area (SQLCA). The SQLCA is a host language data structure which is defined by DB2. It contains many data elements which are populated by DB2 during SQL processing.

✍ The SQLCA is automatically provided in the DB2 REXX environment.

Your application must declare an SQLCA prior to the issuing of any SQL statements. There are two methods of defining the SQLCA in your program:

* Use **EXEC SQL INCLUDE SQLCA.**
* Declare a structure called **sqlca** as defined in the DB2 header files.

The SQLCA data structure shown in Table 9–4 is used as the primary means of error handling between the application and DB2. It is **critical** that your application check the contents of the SQLCA following the processing of each SQL statement. Failure to examine the SQLCA contents can cause unexpected errors to occur. For many errors which can occur, a corresponding action is usually suggested (and can be coded into your application). For example, suppose you attempt to connect to a database server and receive an error that the database manager has not been started. The application could then issue a **DB2START** to start the database manager and attempt to connect to the database server again.

Table 9–4   SQLCA Data Structure

Element Name	Data Type	Description
sqlcaid	CHAR(8)	An eye-catcher to help visually identify the data structure. It should contain the string 'SQLCA '.
sqlcabc	INTEGER	Contains the length of the SQLCA. This should always contain the value 136.
sqlcode	INTEGER	Probably the most important element of the SQLCA structure. This value contains the error code or zero if the SQL statement was processed successfully. If the value is positive, then a warning was returned and the SQL statement was processed. If the value is negative, then an error occurred and the SQL statement was not processed. If the value was zero (0), then no errors or warnings occurred and the SQL statement was processed.
sqlerrml	SMALLINT	Contains the length of the character string in the element sqlerrmc.
sqlerrmc	VARCHAR(70)	Contains one or more message tokens separated by the value X'FF'. These tokens provide more details about the error/warning which has occurred. The separator is used to pass multiple arguments/tokens.

sqlerrp	CHAR(8)	Usually, this element contains the product signature. The product signature is a character string which represents the type of DB2 database server which is currently being used. For example, SQL02010 states that the current server is a Version 2.1.0 of DB2 common server. Other DB2 database servers are:
		`DSN - DB2 for MVS`
		`QSQ - DB2 for OS/400`
		`ARI - DB2 for VM/VSE (SQL/DS)`
		The format is *pppvvrrm* where:
		`ppp - product`
		`vv  - version`
		`rr  - release`
		`m   - modification level (fixes applied)`
		
		If the sqlcode is not zero, then this element usually contains an 8-character representation of the program module that caused the error.

Table 9–4   SQLCA Data Structure

Element Name	Data Type	Description

sqlerrd	Integer Array	This array of 6 integer values can contain extra diagnostic information when error conditions occur.
		SQLERRD(1) - Internal return code
		SQLERRD(2)
		  Internal return code
		  Compound SQL - # of failed
		SQLERRD(3)
		  PREPARE - # of returned rows (estimate)
		  UPDATE/DELETE/INSERT - # of affected rows
		  Compound SQL - sum of all rows
		  CONNECT - 1 if database is updatable, 2 if it is not
		SQLERRD(4)
		  PREPARE - cost estimate
		  Compound SQL - # of successful sub-statements
		  CONNECT
		    0 - one-phase commit from down-level client
		    1 - one-phase commit
		    2 - one-phase commit read-only
		    3 - two-phase commit
		SQLERRD(5)
		  DELETE/INSERT/UPDATE - # of rows (due to constraints)
		  Compound SQL - # of rows (due to constraints)
		SQLERRD(6) - Reserved (not used)

sqlwarn	Character Array	A set of indicators corresponding to various warning conditions. SQLWARN0 - Global indicator, '' if no warnings, 'W' otherwise. SQLWARN1 - 'W' if string was truncated, 'N' if null was truncated SQLWARN2 - 'W' if null values were not used in function SQLWARN3 - 'W' if # of host variables does not match select list SQLWARN4 - 'W' if DELETE/UPDATE doesn't contain WHERE SQLWARN5 - Reserved SQLWARN6 - 'W' if the result of a date was adjusted SQLWARN7 - Reserved SQLWARN8 - Reserved SQLWARN9 - Reserved SQLWARNA - 'W' if conversion error assigning data into SQLCA
sqlstate	CHAR(5)	A cross-platform (SQL92) error code. The value of the sqlstate corresponds to a sqlcode. Some sqlcodes can not have a corresponding sqlstate as there is no equivalent sqlstate for the specific error condition.

Error Handling — Message Retrieval (Part 2)

The SQLCA data structure is useful in determining if errors have been encountered in your application. How do you get this information recorded for problem analysis by an application support person? DB2 provides translated message files which can be referenced using a specific DB2 API called **sqlaintp**. Fig. 9–9 contains the prototype for this error message function.

```
SQL_API_RC SQL_API_FN
sqlaintp(
        short BufferSize,
        short LineWidth,
        struct sqlca * pSqlca,
        char * pBuffer);

Input   - Size of input buffer that was allocated
Input   - Line width to return formatted message
Output - Updated SQLCA
Output - String containing the formatted message
```

Fig. 9–9 Syntax of Message Retreival DB2 API (C syntax)

The **sqlaintp** API provides a formatted text string based on the input SQLCA data structure. You must allocate a buffer prior to calling sqlaintp to store the message string. The length of the error message string returned by sqlaintp is provided in the output of the function. You can display this message to the end user directly or write it in a file for future reference.

✍🏻   The recommendation is to record severe (negative SQLCODE) errors in a file and provide a timestamp with each error. This provides a historical record of any SQL errors that the application has encountered.

In our example application, we recorded all of the DB2 errors in a file called *db2cert.err* (see Appendix E for the **db2cert** application source code). Be sure to examine the error file, using an editor, if you encounter any errors while using the db2cert application.

SQLCODE vs. SQLSTATE

The sqlcode is an integer value and, therefore, is easy to check for a negative or positive value. However, the sqlcode for an error condition is **not** consistent across the entire DB2 family of database servers. To help alleviate this problem, the **sqlstate** field is populated with a character representation of the same error condition. The **sqlstate** conforms to the SQL92 standard (which in turn conforms to all DB2 database servers).

Program Logic for Error Handling

Application modules can contain numerous SQL statements to be processed. After each SQL statement, the application should verify its success by checking the SQLCA contents. This can make for some interesting coding techniques, because the flow of control for the program can suddenly be interrupted due to an SQL error. If you wish to avoid coding a call to an error checking routine after each SQL statement, you can use the statement:

```
SQL EXEC WHENEVER SQLERROR GO TO procname;
```

This embedded SQL statement only needs to be defined once in your source module. Every statement that returns with a negative SQLCODE program control will be transferred to the procedure name specified (in the example, the procedure would be *procname)*. There are other variations on the usage of the **WHENEVER** statement, such as:

```
SQL EXEC WHENEVER NOT FOUND GO TO lastrow;
SQL EXEC WHENEVER SQLWARNING CONTINUE;
```

When processing a multi-row result set, you can wish to implement a common display routine. This can be accomplished with the above example, which checks the **NOT FOUND** condition (**SQLCODE 100**). If positive values are returned as the **SQLCODE**, you can wish to go to a specific routine or in the example, continue program execution.

You should note that we chose not to implement these common error handling routines in the *db2cert* application (Appendix E). In Fig. 9–18 the sample program called **REORGIT** specified the **WHENEVER** statements, but the **CONTINUE** option was used. Therefore, there was not default error handling routine indentified.

We decided to check the SQLCODE following each SQL statement and use an error handling routine if the SQLCODE was negative. The error handling routine writes data to the *db2cert.err* file (Appendix E). The reasoning behind this was to promote structured coding techniques and avoid any 'GO TO' program logic flow.

✍ The **WHENEVER** statements, once precompiled, are expanded to conditional branching (GO TO) structures.

Indicator Variables

An **indicator** variable is a special type of host variable which is used to represent the null or non-null value of a column. When the host variable is used as input into the database, it should be set by the application before the SQL statement is executed. When the host variable is used as output from the database, the indicator is defined by the application, but it is updated by DB2 and returned. The application should then check the value of the indicator variable after the result has been returned.

```
SELECT score INTO :hv1 INDICATOR :hvind
            FROM test_taken;
SELECT score INTO :hv1 :hvind score
            FROM test_taken
```

Fig. 9–10 General Host Variable Declaration

Fig. 9–10 shows two example methods of populating an indicator variable. Both of the queries return the value for the *score* column. We have defined two host variables, one called *hv1* and the other is called *hvind*. Both host variables are identified by the colon (:). The *hv1* host variable would have to represent a compatible host language data type for the *score* column.

✍ There are **NO** commas between the column host variable and its corresponding null indicator host variable.

The second host variable, called *hvind*, is used to indicate the nullability of the value retrieved into the host variable *hv1*. We have defined the *score* column to accept null values. Null values for the score column represent that the candidate is scheduled to take an exam, but has not yet taken the exam Therefore, there is no score.

The indicator host variable is either identified using the keyword **INDICATOR**, or simply by a blank space as shown in the second **SELECT INTO** statement in Fig. 9–10. All indicator host variables are defined using the host language data type which corresponds to the DB2 data type **SMALLINT**.

✍ In C, a variable of type **SHORT** should be used as an indicator variable.

Null indicators must be checked when an application is retrieving data from a nullable column. It is likely that most of the columns in your database schema will contain the **NOT NULL** specification. Therefore, null indicator host variables are not required for **NOT NULL** columns.

In the *db2cert* database design, there are some columns that do not contain the **NOT NULL** specification. The column *cut_score* in the *test* table and the column *score* in the *test_taken* table both accept null values. These columns could represent the non-presence of a value, otherwise known as a null value.

A test that is in a **beta** status does not have a *cut_score* associated with it. Therefore, any reference to a beta test should not have a score. This is represented using the null column value. Similarly, the test_taken table serves a dual purpose. Test scheduling is controlled by this table and the test results are also stored in this table. A candidate who is scheduled to take an exam does not have a score. So a scheduled test candidate would have a null value for their score.

The return of a null value into an application is different than querying the null status of a column within SQL. SQL statements which check for null values have been discussed in Chapter 4. As an application developer, it is important to note any nullable columns and always check the null indicator host variable in the application.

Interpreting an indicator host variable requires that you test its value. If the indicator host variable is negative, then the column contains a null value and the contents of the corresponding host variable is ignored. If the indicator host variable is any non-negative value, then the input or output host variable contains a *real* non-null value.

If the application does not provide a null indicator host variable, an SQL error could be returned by the DB2. When nullable columns are referenced during **UPDATE** or **INSERT** statements, the column will be set to null if the indicator variable is negative.

Data Retrieval Methods

The majority of SQL statements used in database applications are used to retrieve data from the database. The **SELECT** statement is used to perform the data retrieval, but if you remember from Chapter 4, the **SELECT** statement returns a set of rows. There was no method of determining the number of rows that would be returned from any given **SELECT** statement.

When coding a **SELECT** statement in an application, the data must be handled by the application. Therefore the data is returned into native language host variables. In static SQL programs, there are two methods of retrieving the data:

- Use the **SELECT INTO** or **VALUES INTO** clause.
- Use a cursor and the **FETCH INTO** clause.

Single Row Results — SELECT INTO

When the result of an SQL statement is a single row, the application can store the data directly into host variables. The **SELECT** statement requires the phrase **INTO** followed by an equal number of host variables for the number of columns being retrieved.

It is important to remember that a **single** row must be returned. Other conditions for a **SELECT INTO** statement are:

- If the number of host variables does not match the number of columns specified, a warning flag in the SQLCA will be set.
- If the row does not exist, SQLCODE +100 or SQLSTATE 02000 is returned.
- If the result set contains more than one row, an SQLCODE -811 is returned

A **SELECT INTO** statement should be used if an equality predicate is specified on a primary key column. This action will always retrieve a single row result. We have used a number of these statements in the *db2cert* application. When the test candidate id is provided by a *db2cert* application end user, a **SELECT INTO** is used to retrieve the remaining candidate information. This is easier to code than declaring and positioning a cursor.

Single Row Result — VALUES INTO

The structure of a **SELECT** statement is easily understood. It has a logical form which reads much like a language: "I want the book from the fiction section called Moby Dick". This translates into the following **SELECT** statement:

```
SELECT title
            FROM fiction
            WHERE title = 'Moby Dick'
```

The structure of a **VALUES INTO** statement is different than the **SELECT** statement as the information being retrieved is not database objects, but **special registers**, **constants**, and **host variables**. *Special registers* are used to contain current information about the application. The DB2 special registers are shown in Table 9–5 .

Table 9–5 Special Registers

Name	Description
CURRENT DATE	Contains the day when the SQL statement is executing on the DB2 server.
CURRENT EXPLAIN MODE	Contains an 8 character string which corresponds to the amount of EXPLAIN data is being capture in the explain tables. (BIND option - EXPLAIN)
CURRENT EXPLAIN SNAPSHOT	Contains an 8 character string which corresponds to the amount of EXPLAIN snapshots, used by Visual Explain, that are being captured. (BIND option - EXPLSNAP)
CURRENT FUNC-TION PATH	Contains a varying length string of up to 254 characters which represents the schema names used for SQL function resolution. (BIND option - FUNCPATH)

Table 9–5 Special Registers

Name	Description
CURRENT QUERY OPTIMIZATION	Contains an integer value which represents the amount of query optimization which will be performed by DB2. (BIND option - QUERYOPT)
CURRENT SERVER	Contains a varying length string of up to 18 characters which represents the database alias currently active.
CURRENT TIME	Contains the time, on the DB2 server, when the SQL statement is being executed.
CURRENT TIMES-TAMP	Contains a complete timestamp, on the DB2 server, when the SQL statement is being executed.
CURRENT TIME-ZONE	Contains an integer representing the difference between UTC (Coordinated Universal Time) and the local time at the DB2 server.
USER	Contains an 8-character string which represents the currently active user id.

If you want to obtain the value of any of these special registers, use the **VALUES INTO** statement as shown in Fig. 9–11.

```
VALUES (CURRENT DATE) INTO :hvdate
VALUES (CURRENT SERVER) INTO :svrName
```

Fig. 9–11 Using the Values INTO Clause

The **VALUES** clause can also be used with constants in the **INSERT** statement or when constant values need to be included in the result set. For example:

```
SELECT tcid
            FROM test_center
UNION       VALUES ('999999999')
```

This query will always return at least one row with the value of 999999999 for test center id, even if the *test_center* table is completely empty. The **VALUES** clause is a similar to a **SELECT** statement. It also provides an easy-to-use interface to invoke User-Defined Functions (UDFs).

```
VALUES ( Send_Certificate (cid,lname,fname))
```

Fig. 9–12 Using VALUES to Invoke a User-Defined Function

In Fig. 9–12, the statement will invoke a UDF called **Send_Certificate** and pass the column values of candidate id, last name, and first name to the function. The result of the user-defined function would be a single result (scalar value).

Multiple Row Results

When the **SELECT** statement does not resolve to precisely one row, the application must be written to handle an arbitrary number of rows. A **cursor** is used to retrieve the results from the **SELECT** statement. A cursor is associated with an SQL statement using the **DECLARE** cursor statement in the application. The name of the cursor is provided during the **DECLARE** statement.

```
DECLARE c1 CURSOR FOR
          SELECT cid, lname, fname
          FROM CANDIDATE
          WHERE lname IN (:hvLastName)
```

Fig. 9–13 Cursor Declaration with an Input Host Variable

In Fig. 9–13, the cursor *c1* is being declared to retrieve the test candidate ids and first and last names according to an input host variable called *hvLastName*. Since the predicate (**WHERE** clause) is not an equality predicate using the candidate id (cid), it must be assumed that the result of this statement could be 0, 1 or more rows (depending on the value of *hvLastName* during the **OPEN** cursor processing). The steps involved in the usage of cursors are as follows:

1. **DECLARE** the cursor, specifying its name and type. The location of the declare statement in the application must be any place before the usage of the cursor.
2. **OPEN** the cursor to retrieve the matching rows of the result set. The locks, depending upon isolation level, are placed at this time. The **input** host variables have been evaluated to determine the result set. Following a successful open cursor, the cursor is logically positioned before the first result row.

3. **FETCH** the results one row at a time. A check should be made to ensure that the end of the set has not been encountered (e.g., SQLCODE +100, SQLSTATE 02000). The **FETCH** statement will initialize the host variables with the last row retrieved. At this time, indicator host variables should also be analyzed.

4. (Optional) Use the **DELETE** or **UPDATE** statement to remove or modify the contents of the row where the cursor has just retrieved. This is known as cursor positioned deletes/updates.

5. **CLOSE** the cursor (by name) to release any locks.

Using Cursors

Cursors are used to manipulate a multi-row result set. The manipulation can involve simply retrieving data using a **SELECT**. It also can involve a cursor positioned **DELETE** or **UPDATE**. The concept of a cursor is not often externalized in SQL end-user query tools as it is too abstract for an end-user. When the DB2 Command Line Processor (CLP) is used, each SQL statement is dynamically prepared (see Chapter 10) and each resulting row is displayed via multiple fetch operations using a cursor.

Cursors within DB2 are like **one-way** streets. They can only be used in one direction: **Forward**. There is currently no backward fetching capability provided with DB2. Cursors which can be used to fetch in two directions are also known as *scrollable cursors*.

It is important to remember that the **result set** of the **SELECT** statement is usually determined during the processing of the **OPEN** cursor. There are circumstances when the result set is derived during the **FETCH**. But in this case, the data must not have been modified since the **OPEN** cursor processing. Multiple cursors can be open on the same result set and positioned independently. This can be useful to provide backward-like scrolling. If a cursor is re-opened, its current position is at the beginning of the result set.

The name of a cursor is only known by the application which declared it. It cannot be a host variable. The cursor name must be unique within the application module.

Cursor Types

A cursor type is determined by the declaration of the cursor, its usage and the record blocking **BIND** parameters. There are three types of cursors:

1. **Read-Only** — The **SELECT** statement is a read-only **SELECT** statement (e.g., **SELECT** cid **FROM** candidate). There can be performance advantages, especially when the data is retrieved across a network, as record blocking will likely be performed.

2. **Updatable** — The **FOR UPDATE** clause is use during the cursor declaration. Only a single table or view can be referenced in the **SELECT** statement.

3. Ambiguous — The cursor type cannot be determined by its declaration or the **SELECT** statement being used. The amount of record blocking for these types of cursors is determined by the **BIND** parameter.

If the cursor is going to be used in an **UPDATE WHERE CURRENT OF** statement, specify the **FOR UPDATE** clause during the cursor declaration. The optimizer will pick the best possible access path. Also, if you know that the cursor is only used to retrieve data, add the clause **FOR READ ONLY** or **FOR FETCH ONLY.** This will encourage record-blocking to occur and avoid extra locks on the result set.

The phrases **FOR UPDATE ONLY, FOR FETCH ONLY,** and **FOR READ ONLY** are actually part of the SQL statement and **not** part of the **DECLARE** cursor syntax. Let's look at an example cursor declaration and usage in the db2cert application.

In Fig. 9–14, all of the host variables are initialized in the **BEGIN DECLARE** section. The cursor is then defined. Remember, cursors are always defined as **SELECT** statements. Cursors can be used to delete or update during the manipulation of the cursor. The cursor type is defined within the **SELECT** statement. In Fig. 9–14, the cursor is defined as a read-only cursor. The phrase **FOR FETCH ONLY** is specified at the end of the SQL statement.

We could have specified the **WITH HOLD** option to maintain the cursor position across transactions. Since we did not specify this option, the cursor will no longer be accessible following the **CLOSE** cursor statement. Cursors specified as **WITH HOLD** are useful when a large number of rows need to be examined and modified. However, the application cannot afford to lock all of the rows over the entire unit of work.

For example, let's suppose the *db2cert* application provides a facility for a testing administrator to change all the scores for the candidates who took test number '500'. Let's also suppose that a searched **UPDATE** statement could not be used. Therefore updatable cursors are needed to satisfy this requirement. The application could provide the administrator with the ability to retrieve all of the candidates who took the exam and proceed to update their scores. After updating the scores for each testing center, the administrator would like to ensure that the changes have been committed to the database. The updating of the scores could be accomplished a number of ways.

One method could involve a single cursor for all test candidates declared **WITH HOLD.** When the updates were made for a particular testing center, the changes could be committed and the subsequent fetch would retrieve the next test candidate.

Another method could involve a cursor declaration not using the **WITH HOLD** declaration. This option would involve much more effort on the application developer's part. It would not be as efficient.

```
EXEC SQL BEGIN DECLARE SECTION;
  char szTCID[7];
  char szTCName[41];
  char szPhone[11];
  char szStreetNo[9];
  char szStreetName[21];
  char szCity[31];
  char szProvState[31];
  char szCode[7];
  char szCountry[21];
  char cTCType;
  short iNoSeats;
  char szCitySearch2[21];
EXEC SQL END DECLARE SECTION;


  EXEC SQL DECLARE c1 CURSOR FOR
          SELECT TCID, NAME,STREETNO,
                 STREETNAME,CITY,PROV_STATE,
                 COUNTRY, CODE, TYPE, PHONE,NOSEATS
          FROM
                 TEST_CENTER
          WHERE CHAR(city) LIKE :szCitySearch2
          FOR FETCH ONLY;

  EXEC SQL OPEN c1;
    EXEC SQL FETCH c1 INTO :szTCID,
                           :szTCName,
                           :szStreetNo,
                           :szStreetName,
                           :szCity,
                           :szProvState,
                           :szCountry,
                           :szCode,
                           :cTCType,
                           :szPhone,
                           :iNoSeats;
    if (SQLCODE == SQL_RC_OK) {
        printf ("Center Number\t:%s\n",szTCID);
        printf ("Center Name\t:%s\n",szTCName);
        printf ("City\t\t:%s\n",szCity);
        }
  EXEC SQL CLOSE c1;
  EXEC SQL COMMIT;
```

Fig. 9–14 Using Cursors

Let's examine the cursor specific phrases in the **SELECT** statement. In Fig. 9–15, the **FOR UPDATE** clause shows that it is possible to specify the column name to update,. The column tcid is optional, but, if supplied, it can help the optimizer during statement execution.

```
EXEC SQL DECLARE c1 CURSOR FOR
          SELECT tcid,name,streetno,
                 streetname,city,prov_state,
                 country,code,type,phone,noseats
          FROM
                 test_center
          WHERE CHAR(city) LIKE :szCitySearch2
          FOR UPDATE OF noseats;
```

Fig. 9–15 Updatable Cursor

✍ The column name in the **FOR UPDATE** clause should be unqualified and it must be the first table or view referenced in the **FROM** clause.

If the **SELECT** statement is not involved in an update or delete, then add the phrase **FOR FETCH ONLY** or **FOR READ ONLY** to the end of the statement.

Cursor Positioning

A cursor, regardless of type, can have three positions depending on its current state.

1. An open cursor prior to the first fetch is positioned **before** a record and the contents of the output host variables are undefined at this point.
2. Following a fetch, the cursor is considered **on** the record. The output host variables contain the values of the current row. This is the row that will be changed if a positioned **UPDATE** or **DELETE** is performed at this time.
3. The third possible cursor position is following the last row. At this point, the host variables contain the values of the current (last) row, and the **SQLCA** contains the value of (SQLCODE +100, SQLSTATE '02000').

✍ Remember to **COMMIT** or **ROLLBACK** transactions even if they involve read-only cursors as there are locks held on the system catalogs for the **SELECT** statement.

In Fig. 9–16, the result set contains four test candidates. The candidates are in no particular order because there is no **ORDER BY** clause in the SQL statement. Examine the three cursor positions shown in Fig. 9–16. The cursor is either before a record, on a record or after the last record. Since the example is a read only cursor, a positioned update or delete would result in an SQL error. The only valid operation on a **CLOSED** cursor (not defined **WITH HOLD**) is **OPEN**.

Let's examine cursor positioning when a cursor is declared as a **WITH HOLD** cursor. This type of cursor will maintain its position since the last fetch operation even after the transaction has been committed. This allows you to commit changes for other applications to read without losing your current cursor position.

SQL Statement

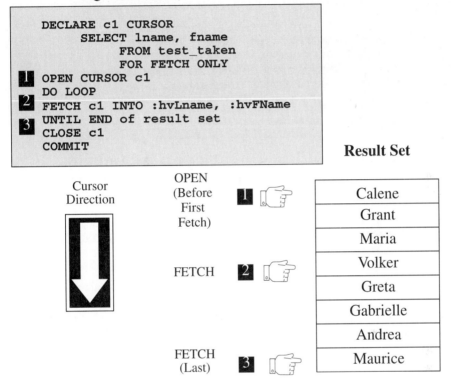

```
DECLARE c1 CURSOR
     SELECT lname, fname
          FROM test_taken
          FOR FETCH ONLY
1 OPEN CURSOR c1
  DO LOOP
2 FETCH c1 INTO :hvLname,  :hvFName
3 UNTIL END of result set
  CLOSE c1
  COMMIT
```

Result Set

Cursor Direction	OPEN (Before First Fetch)		Result Set
			Calene
			Grant
			Maria
	FETCH		Volker
			Greta
			Gabrielle
			Andrea
	FETCH (Last)		Maurice

Fig. 9–16 Cursor Positioning (not WITH HOLD)

If the unit of work was completed using the **ROLLBACK** statement, all of the open cursors including any **WITH HOLD** cursors are closed and the resources are released. If the unit of work ends in a **COMMIT**, then the **WITH HOLD** cursors will remain open as in Fig. 9–16.

The example in Fig. 9–16, shows that a positioned **UPDATE** is being performed on the second row fetched from the result set. The update of the score for test candidate *Grant* is committed and then the loop is terminated. The new score will then be accessible by all other applications, as the **UPDATE** has been committed. Since the cursor was not closed, we can still fetch data using the cursor.

SQL Statement

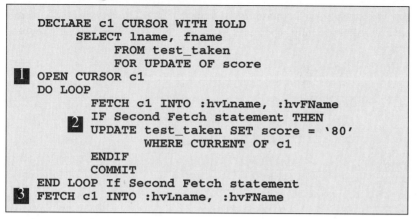

```
    DECLARE c1 CURSOR WITH HOLD
        SELECT lname, fname
            FROM test_taken
            FOR UPDATE OF score
 1  OPEN CURSOR c1
    DO LOOP
        FETCH c1 INTO :hvLname, :hvFName
      2 IF Second Fetch statement THEN
        UPDATE test_taken SET score = '80'
            WHERE CURRENT OF c1
        ENDIF
        COMMIT
    END LOOP If Second Fetch statement
 3  FETCH c1 INTO :hvLname, :hvFName
```

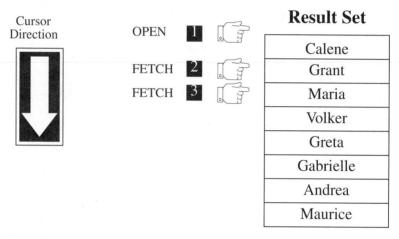

Cursor Direction

OPEN **1**

FETCH **2**

FETCH **3**

Result Set

| Calene |
| Grant |
| Maria |
| Volker |
| Greta |
| Gabrielle |
| Andrea |
| Maurice |

Fig. 9–17 Cursor Positioning (WITH HOLD)

The cursor is opened and the subsequent **FETCH** will give us the data record for test candidate Maria. If the **WITH HOLD** option was not specified, the second **FETCH** statement would be in error. The cursor would have been implicitly closed during the **COMMIT** statement.

The example would be more appropriate if the results were in descending order and the objective was to update the score for the second-highest score of all candidates. This type of update cannot be performed in a single SQL statement. The SQL language has no concept of ordered updates or restricted results by the number of entities. For example, suppose you were asked to generate a report of the top 10 scores for a particular test. Would you use the **SELECT INTO** statement or cursors? Declaring a cursor with an appropriate **ORDER BY** clause and subsequently fetching 10 rows would provide the desired results.

Advanced Cursor Usage

Scrolling in a single direction through data is a simple use of cursors. But how can an application allow more flexible scrolling techniques? Usually, advanced scrolling techniques involve multiple cursors and/or keeping a copy of the retrieved data in application memory.

The program example provided at the end of this chapter demonstrates the technique of maintaining a result set in an array, see "Sample Program to REORG all User Tables" on page 483.

Using multiple cursors can allow the end-user to re-position within the data being retrieved. Let's say that an application provides the end-user with the ability to examine record one and then record two. Then the application allows a modification of record one. With a single cursor, this would be difficult, as the cursor would have to be reopened to position the cursor to record one, and the record at position one can have been already modified by another application.

Suppose two cursors are declared for the same result set. The second cursor is always one record behind the first cursor. By using this two cursor technique, the end-user could update the previous record without closing the first cursor.

✍️   Keep in mind that the order of a result set without an **ORDER BY** clause is arbitrary.

Keeping a copy of the data in application memory does not guarantee that the application is displaying the proper data values. However it does provide the application developer with the most flexibility to scroll through data. Usually this technique involves a buffer (storage area) within the application. The end-user is allowed to examine all of the contents of this buffer. When the end-user wants to change the contents of the buffer, an update is attempted. There is no guaranteed result. To ensure that the contents will not change, either explicitly lock the table using the **LOCK TABLE** statement or use an isolation level. The isolation level should use appropriate locking semantics, such as repeatable read.

Application Level Locking

Locking semantics are usually specified by choosing an appropriate isolation level for the application during the bind process. As an application developer, you should understand a few statements that dramatically affect the amount of locking of database objects.

The **LOCK TABLE** statement can be used to enforce a table level lock in either **exclusive** (X) mode or **share** (S) mode. As with all types of database locking, the larger the object being locked, the less concurrency is available.

✍️   Concurrency is usually a high priority for transaction processing database applications.

Obtaining an explicit table lock can improve the performance for batch applications which involve changes to a large percentage of the table. If a table lock is acquired, equivalent row locks will not be acquired.

All locks use approximately the same amount of storage in the `locklist`. Remember that the `locklist` is shared by all applications accessing the database. An explicit table lock will avoid filling the `locklist` and thus, defer lock escalation for other tables.

Searched Updates/Deletes

We have discussed positioned **UPDATE** and **DELETE** statements using cursors in the previous section. If a row can be uniquely identified, then a searched **UPDATE** or **DELETE** can be used instead of cursors. Adding an appropriate **WHERE** clause to the end of an **UPDATE** or **DELETE** statement with proper input and/or output host variables can provide enough flexibility for the end-user.

The *db2cert* application can uniquely identify key entities. In the certification program, candidates can be identified using the unique *candidate_id* attribute. This allows a searched update if modifications are required for any of the attributes of a candidate. This implementation allows a test center administrator to update any of the columns for a candidate, except the *candidate_id* column and the derived columns (*CertDBA* and *CertAPP*). The derived columns are updated by a triggered **UPDATE** statement based on the *test_taken* table.

An **UPDATE** statement requires the application developer to specify the columns and their corresponding values to be updated. A static embedded SQL statement **cannot** use host variables to represent column names in an update or select list. Therefore, to avoid having to prepare any single column **UPDATE** statement dynamically, we decided to use an **UPDATE** statement where every column is updated. The previously fetched retrieved values are used for the update. The updated column has a new user-input value. This is not the most efficient method of updating records in DB2, but it is a valid method. We will discuss how to modify this part of the application using dynamic embedded SQL and Call Level Interface (CLI) in the next chapter.

Handling Application Termination

When an application that utilized DB2 resources has completed, the remaining DB2 activity is determined by the program termination.

If the application terminated abnormally, then the current unit of work will issue the **ROLLBACK** statement to undo any changes.

If the application terminated normally, then the current unit of work issues the **COMMIT** statement to apply changes to the database. It is good programming practice to close open cursors, free LOB locators and free dynamically allocated memory. Ensure that the last transaction is in a known state (**COMMIT/ ROLLBACK**).

Interrupt Handling

An **interrupt, exception,** or **exit list handler** (depending on the operating environment) is a routine which is registered with the operating environment by the application. This routine will be invoked on the application's behalf when the operating system detects an interruption in normal program execution.

A default DB2 signal handler is provided via the interrupt API (**sqleintr/ sqlgintr**). This routine should be included in the application interrupt handling sequence of events. This is platform specific.

✍️   Avoid coding any SQL statements in the application interrupt handling routine. The results are unpredictable.

Sample Program — REORGIT

The following program (Fig. 9–18) contains many aspects of DB2 programming. The program can be quite useful for a DB2 database administrator to automate some of their table maintenance activities.

Following transaction processing (INSERT/UPDATE/DELETE) activity the database files can become somewhat fragmented. Fragmenation can result in wasted disk space and poor performance. The DB2 REORGANIZE TABLE (REORG) command can be issued to defragment the table. Not only can you defragment the table, you can also sort the table as it is stored on disk. The index pages are always kept in order so if you REORG a table using a sort order similar to the index then the index can be much more clustered.

The REORGIT program (Fig. 9–18) is used to REORG all of the user tables within a database using the primary key index definition during the REORG. The syntax for the program is:

```
REORGIT dbname userid password reportfile
```

Let's examine some of the DB2 interfaces in the embedded SQL program. Note the sqlutil.h and the sqlenv.h header files have been included. These are necessary as the sqlutil.h file defines the function prototype for the REORG API and the sqlenv.h file is required for all DB2 applications.

The SQLCA structure has been defined as a global structure (one sqlca per application). The name of the variable must be sqlca. We could have used the EXEC SQL INCLUDE SQLCA phrase instead.

Section 1 of the program defines some of the host variables for the program. Note that some of the host variables involve C structures. A varying-length character string host variable can be defined using this method.

Section 2 uses **SQL WHENEVER** statements, but we did not define an error handling function here (these statements could be removed without affecting the application).

Section 3 uses the DB2 API **sqleisig**() to install the default signal handler provided by DB2. This will help ensure that any outstanding transactions will be rolled back during abnormal termination.

Section 4 is the database connection step. This step is required before any SQL statements can be processed (for obvious reasons). Note that if the SQLCODE is not zero then the check_error() routine is called to record the error and stop program execution.

Section 5 is the start of the first transaction (unit of work). A cursor called c1 is declared (always an SQL **SELECT** statement). The cursor has been defined as a **READ ONLY** cursor and is therefore, not an ambiguous cursor. There is an initial **FETCH** and then a **WHILE** loop is entered (if there were no errors up to this point).

Section 6 involves locating the primary index corresponding to the table which is to be reorganized. Note a **SELECT INTO** statement can be used as it the **SELECT** statement guarantees that no more than one row will be returned. The next table name is retrieved (using cursor c1) and the loop continues until all of the user tables and their primary indexes have been read and stored into the array called tables.

Section 7 closes the cursor. This will free some of the cursor (application level) resources, but a **COMMIT** at this point would ensure that any share locks (S) have been released.

Section 8 calls the DB2 API to reorganize the tables. The return code of DB2 APIs should be checked. If they are negative then the SQLCA should be examined for details.

✍️ Some DB2 APIs (including **REORG**) cannot be issued within a transaction. This is why we decided to use an array to store the results from the cursor fetching.

Section 9 releases or disconnects from the database using the **CONNECT RESET** command.

Section 10 is the error handling function check_error(). This function calls the DB2 message API sqlaintp() to retrieve the full text of the error. The message is then written to the standard output (screen).

```
/****************************************************************************/
/*                                                                        */
/* Program:    Reorgit.sqc                                                */
/* Purpose:    This tool reorgs all user-created tables. (Aliases, views, */
/*             and system-created tables are ignored).  If there is a     */
/*             primary key associated with the table, the table will be   */
/*             reorganized using the primary key.                         */
/****************************************************************************/
/*                                                                        */
/*            THIS PROGRAM IS IN EXERCISE\CHAPTER9\PARTA on the CD-ROM.   */
/*                                                                        */
/****************************************************************************/

/* Include C and DB2 header files ******************************************/

#include <stdio.h>                              /* For I/O functions       */
#include <time.h>                               /* For time functions      */
#include <string.h>                             /* For string functions    */
#include <stdlib.h>                             /* Required for exit()     */
#include <sqlutil.h>                            /* for reorg api           */
#include <sqlenv.h>                             /* includes sqlsystm.h,    */
                                                /* sql.h, sqlca.h, sqlda.h */

/* Define constants ********************************************************/

#define DEFAULT_OUTFILE       "reorgit.out"     /* output file             */
#define OPEN_MODE             "w"               /* write mode              */
#define RC_OK                 0                 /* good rc                 */
#define RC_FILE_ERROR         2                 /* error opening file      */
#define RC_DB2_ERROR          4                 /* db2 error               */
#define RC_INVALID_PARM       6                 /* invalid no of parm.     */
#define BLANK                 ' '               /* blank                   */
#define DOT                   "."               /* dot                     */
#define NULL_TERM             '\0'              /* null terminator         */
#define SYSTEM                "SYSIBM"          /* system                  */
#define TABLE                 'T'               /* table                   */
#define LINE_LEN              80                /* line length             */
#define ERR_BUFFER            512               /* err msg buffer          */
#define MAXTABLES             200               /* maximum no. of table    */


/* Global variables ********************************************************/

struct sqlca sqlca;          /*---------- declare sqlca structure -------------*/

/* Main function ***********************************************************/

int main(int argc, char *argv[])

{
  /* Program variables ****************************************************/

  FILE *outfileptr;                             /* output file pointer     */
  char outfilename[25];                         /* output file name        */
  short rc;                                     /* return code             */
  char * blankptr;                              /* ptr to 1st blank        */
  time_t countime;                              /* time stamp              */
  char qualindexname[26];                       /* qualified index name    */
  char qualtablename[26];                       /* qualified table name    */
  short ind1;                                   /* index offset for array  */
  short tabcount=-1;                            /* number of tables        */

  struct {                                      /* structure to hold       */
     char qualindexname[26];                    /* table & index names     */
     char qualtablename[26];                    /* used in reorg           */
     } tables[MAXTABLES];                       /* table name to reorg     */

/****************************************************************************/
/* Section 1 - Declaring Host variables                                   */
/****************************************************************************/

  EXEC SQL BEGIN DECLARE SECTION;

    /***** host variables used in connect ********************************/
    char dbname[9];
    char userid[9];
    char password[9];
```

```
      /***** host variables used in selecting SYSCAT.TABLES *****************/
      char tabqualifier[9];                          /* table qualifier      */
      struct {
         short len;
         char data[19];
         } tbname;                                    /* table name (VARCHAR) */
      char tabdefiner[9];                             /* table definer        */
      short indexid;                                  /* index id             */

      /***** host variables used in selecting SYSCAT.INDEXES *****************/
      char indqualifier[8];                           /* index qualifier      */
      struct {
         short len;
         char data[18];
         } indexname;                                 /* index name (VARCHAR) */
      char tablename[18];                             /* table name           */

   EXEC SQL END DECLARE SECTION;

   /* Function prototypes *************************************************/
   void check_error(void);

/*************************************************************************/
/* Section 2 - SQL Error handling                                        */
/*************************************************************************/

   EXEC SQL WHENEVER SQLERROR CONTINUE;
   EXEC SQL WHENEVER SQLWARNING CONTINUE;
   EXEC SQL WHENEVER NOT FOUND CONTINUE;

   /* Set stdout buffering off *******************************************/
   setbuf(stdout,NULL);
/*************************************************************************/
/* Section 3 - Install DB2 Signal Handler                                */
/*************************************************************************/

   rc = sqleisig(&sqlca);
   if (SQLCODE != 0) check_error();


/*************************************************************************/
/* Section 4 - Connecting to the database                                */
/*************************************************************************/

   printf("\n\n*** The REORGIT tool will reorg all user-created tables. ***\n");
   printf("*** Output will be displayed on screen and also    ***\n");
   printf("*** written into a file.                            ***\n");
   if (argc <4) {
      printf("\n\n*** INVALID number of parameters!\n");
      printf("*** Usage: \"REORGIT dbname userid password reportfile\"\n");
      printf("***         - reportfile is optional.  If not entered,\n");
      printf("***           default (REORGIT.OUT) will be used.    \n");
      exit(RC_INVALID_PARM);
   }
   else {
      strcpy(dbname,argv[1]);                  /*Setup the input host variables*/
      strcpy(userid,argv[2]);
      strcpy(password,argv[3]);
      if (argc == 5) {
        strcpy(outfilename,argv [4]);
        }
      else {
        strcpy(outfilename,DEFAULT_OUTFILE);
        }
   } /* endif */

   printf("\nConnecting to database %s ...", strupr(dbname));
   EXEC SQL CONNECT TO :dbname USER :userid USING :password;
   if (SQLCODE != 0) {
     check_error();
     }
   else {
     printf (" successful!\n");
     }
```

```
/* open output file and write timestamp ************************************/
  if ((outfileptr=fopen(outfilename,OPEN_MODE))==NULL) {
     printf("\n\nError opening output file.  Terminating ...");
     exit(RC_FILE_ERROR);
  }
  time(&countime);
  fprintf(outfileptr,"\nREORGIT timestamp: %s", ctime(&countime));

/***************************************************************************/
/* Section 5 - Unit of Work (Transaction)                                  */
/***************************************************************************/

/* Cursor declaration - FOR FETCH ONLY *************************************/

   EXEC SQL DECLARE c1 CURSOR FOR
            SELECT TABSCHEMA, TABNAME, DEFINER, KEYINDEXID
            FROM SYSCAT.TABLES
            WHERE TABSCHEMA NOT IN ('SYSCAT','SYSSTAT','SYSIBM')
            AND TYPE = 'T'
            FOR READ ONLY;

   if (SQLCODE != 0) check_error();

/* Open cursor ************************************************************/

   EXEC SQL OPEN c1;
   if (SQLCODE != 0) check_error();

/* Fetch first row using cursor (4 output host variables) ****************/

   EXEC SQL FETCH c1
            INTO :tabqualifier, :tbname, :tabdefiner,:indexid;

   if ((SQLCODE != 0)&&(SQLCODE != 100)) check_error();
   while (SQLCODE==0) {

/* set null terminators in host variables *******************************/

      blankptr = strchr(tabqualifier,BLANK);
      tabqualifier[strlen(tabqualifier)-strlen(blankptr)]=NULL_TERM;
      tbname.data[tbname.len]=NULL_TERM;
      blankptr = strchr(tabdefiner,BLANK);
      tabdefiner[strlen(tabdefiner)-strlen(blankptr)]=NULL_TERM;

      /* get qualified table name to be used in reorg API ****************/
      strcpy(qualtablename,tabqualifier);
      strcat(qualtablename,DOT);
      strcat(qualtablename,tbname.data);

      /* get table name to be used in selecting SYSCAT.INDEXES **********/
      strcpy(tablename, tbname.data);

      tabcount++;
      tables[tabcount].qualindexname[0]=NULL_TERM;
      strcpy (tables[tabcount].qualtablename ,qualtablename);

      /* get qualified INDEX name to be used in reorg API ***************/
      if ((indexid!=0)&&(indexid!=NULL)) {

/***************************************************************************/
/* Section 6 - SELECT INTO                                                 */
/* Single-Row SELECT statement (3 input host vars and 2 output host vars ***/
/* - No cursor declaration was required as the output was a single row   ***/
/***************************************************************************/

            EXEC SQL SELECT INDSCHEMA, INDNAME
                     INTO :indqualifier, :indexname
                     FROM SYSCAT.INDEXES
                     WHERE TABNAME = :tablename AND TABSCHEMA = :tabqualifier
                     AND IID=:indexid;

            if (SQLCODE != 0) check_error();
```

```
        /* Remove blanks ****************************************************/
        blankptr = strchr(indqualifier,BLANK);
        indqualifier[strlen(indqualifier)-strlen(blankptr)]=NULL_TERM;

        /* Copy qualified index name ***************************************/
        strcpy(qualindexname,indqualifier);
        strcat(qualindexname,DOT);
        strncat(qualindexname,indexname.data,indexname.len);

        strcpy (tables[tabcount].qualindexname ,qualindexname);
        strcpy (tables[tabcount].qualtablename ,qualtablename);

     } /* endif */

/* FETCH next row from SYSCAT.TABLES *************************************/

    EXEC SQL FETCH c1
           INTO :tabqualifier, :tbname, :tabdefiner, :indexid;
    if ((SQLCODE != 0)&&(SQLCODE != 100)) check_error();

  } /* end while SQLCODE = 0 */

/*************************************************************************/
/* Section 7 - Closing the cursor (no longer accessible)               */
/*************************************************************************/
   EXEC SQL CLOSE c1;
   if (SQLCODE != 0) check_error();

     for (ind1=0;ind1<tabcount ;ind1++ ) {
     if (strlen(tables[ind1].qualindexname)>1) {

/*************************************************************************/
/*  Section 8 - REORG the table on the primary index                   */
/*************************************************************************/
        rc = sqlureot(tables[ind1].qualtablename,
                     tables[ind1].qualindexname, NULL, &sqlca);

         if (SQLCODE != 0) {
           check_error();
           }
         else {
         printf("\nTable %-12s REORG was successful on key index %s",
                 tables[ind1].qualtablename, tables[ind1].qualindexname);
         fprintf(outfileptr,"\nTable %-12s REORG was successful on key index %s",
                 tables[ind1].qualtablename, tables[ind1].qualindexname);
         } /* endif */
       } else {

          /*************************************************************/
          /*   REORG the table in no particular order                 */
          /*************************************************************/

          rc = sqlureot(tables[ind1].qualtablename, NULL, NULL, &sqlca);

          if (SQLCODE != 0) {
            check_error();
            }
          else {
            printf("\nTable %-12s REORG was successful",
                    tables[ind1].qualtablename);
            fprintf(outfileptr,"\nTable %-12s REORG was successful",
                    tables[ind1].qualtablename);
          } /* endif */
          } /* endif */
      } /* endfor */


/*************************************************************************/
/* Section 9: Clean up and end program                                 */
/*************************************************************************/

  printf("\n\nDisconnecting from database ...");
```

```
/**************************************************************************/
/* Section 9: Clean up and end program                                    */
/**************************************************************************/

   printf("\n\nDisconnecting from database ...");

   EXEC SQL CONNECT RESET;
   if (SQLCODE != 0) {
     check_error();
     }
   else {
     printf(" successful!\n");
     }

   fclose(outfileptr);
   printf("\n\n");

return RC_OK;
}

/**************************************************************************/
/* Section 10 - Get the SQL error message text                            */
/**************************************************************************/

void check_error(void)

{
   char errmsg_buffer[ERR_BUFFER];
   short buffer_size = sizeof(errmsg_buffer);
   short line_length = LINE_LEN;

   if (SQLCODE<0)
     {
      printf("\n%s %i\n", "SQL Error!  SQLCODE is ", SQLCODE);
      sqlaintp(errmsg_buffer, buffer_size, line_length, &sqlca);
      printf(errmsg_buffer);
      exit(RC_DB2_ERROR);
     }
   else
     {
      printf("\n%s %i\n", "SQL Warning!  SQLCODE is ", SQLCODE);
      sqlaintp(errmsg_buffer, buffer_size, line_length, &sqlca);
      printf(errmsg_buffer);
     } /* endif */
return;
}
```

Fig. 9–18 Sample Program to **REORG** all User Tables

Summary

The process of creating static embedded SQL program modules was thoroughly discussed in this chapter. By embedding SQL statements into a programming language we can manipulate the data contained in a DB2 database. The program modules containing the SQL statements must be converted from SQL statements to DB2 library APIs. This step is known as the precompilation step, as it is always performed before the program module is compiled and linked.

The programming language variables used as input or output for SQL statements are known as **host variables**. These host variables must be declared to the precompiler and used properly within the embedded SQL statements. An input host variable can be used to define the conditions for the query (predicate) or data values in an **INSERT/UPDATE** statement. An output host variable can be used to receive the results of a **SELECT** or **VALUES** statement.

SQL statements can result in a single or multiple rows of data. A single row result can be retreived using the **INTO** clause to specify the output host variables. A multiple row result set must be manipulated using one or more cursors. A **cursor** is defined using the **DECLARE** statement. Once the cursor has been declared, the cursor must be opened using the **OPEN** statement. An open cursor can populate output host variables corresponding to the current data row. The **FETCH** statement is used to populate the host variables. Multiple cursors can be declared on the same result set.

Data can be deleted or updated using a condition (predicate) or using cursor manipulation. If a data record is to be modified using cursors, it is known as a positioned modification, using the **WHERE CURRENT CURSOR** phrase.

There are two types of database connection. The default database connection type is known as a **TYPE 1** connect. This connection only allows a single database to be involved in a transaction or unit of work. A **TYPE 2** connection allows establishing connections to multiple databases within the same unit of work.

In this chapter, we also examined the usage of an **ALIAS** with respect to accessing database objects from a program. Some of the most common DB2 APIs are also discussed, including the message retrieval API called **sqaintp**().

Questions

1. Given the statement:
    ```
    CREATE TABLE calene.test (
                date_taken          DATE NOT NULL,
                number              SMALLINT NOT NULL,
                PRIMARY KEY (number))
    ```
    What is the schema name for the table?

    ○   A. date_taken

    ○   B. number

    ○   C. test

    ○   D. calene

2. There are two tables defined in a database called:
    ```
    db2.staff
    payroll.staff
    ```

    An application issues a dynamic SQL statement "**SELECT * FROM staff**".
    What determines which table will be accessed?

    ○   A. the userid of the binder of the package

    ○   B. the userid connected to the database

    ○   C. the userid of the precompiler of the package

    ○   D. the userid specified in the db2cli.ini file

    ○   E. the userid of the creator of the staff table

3. The following tasks have been performed successfully:
    A user called Calene issues the command **PREP connect.sqx PACKAGE**.
    A user called Frank issues the command **PREP connect.sqx BINDFILE**.
    A user called Frank again issues the command:
    PREP connect.sqx PACKAGE USING connect.

    How many packages would exist in the database?

    ○   A. 0

    ○   B. 1

    ○   C. 2

    ○   D. 3

4. An application contains the dynamic SQL statement "**SELECT * FROM
    test**". There is a table defined as *db2.test* in the database. There are two
    users named Bob and Mary who need to execute the query. Which aliases
    should be defined so both users can access the *db2.test* regardless of the user
    id? (choose 2 answers)

    ○   A. CREATE ALIAS db2.test FOR bob

    ○   B. CREATE ALIAS db2.test FOR mary

    ○   C. CREATE ALIAS mary.test ON db2.test

    ○   D. CREATE ALIAS bob.test ON db2.test

    ○   E. CREATE ALIAS FOR mary.test AS db2.test

    ○   F. CREATE ALIAS FOR bob.test AS db2.test

5. What is the purpose of the **COLLECTION** precompile/bind option?

    ○   A. define the name of the package

    ○   B. provide an alias for the package

    ○   C. define the schema of the package

    ○   D. define the database of the package

6. If an application consists of four separate program modules where:
   2 modules contain embedded static SQL statements
   1 module contains embedded dynamic SQL statements
   1 module contains embedded dynamic SQL statements
   How many application packages will be created?

   ○   A. 1

   ○   B. 2

   ○   C. 3

   ○   D. 4

7. In which system catalog view would you find the timestamp corresponding to
   a precompile and subsequent bind operation?

   ○   A. SYSCAT.PRECOMPILE

   ○   B. SYSCAT.PACKAGES

   ○   C. SYSCAT.BIND

   ○   D. SYSCAT.TIMESTAMPS

   ○   E. SYSCAT.ACCESSPLAN

8. Which of the following programming methods will store an access plan in the
   system catalogs?

   ○   A. embedded dynamic SQL

   ○   B. embedded static SQL

   ○   C. Call Level Interface (CLI)

9. What authority or privilege is required to successfully issue the **BIND** command for a new application bind file?

   ○   A. **EXECUTE** privilege on the package

   ○   B. **SYSADM** authority for the DB2 instance

   ○   C. **BIND** privilege on the package

   ○   D. **BINDADD** authority for the database

10. Which system catalog view would contain locking information for an embedded static SQL application?

  ○   A. SYSCAT.TABLES

  ○   B. SYSCAT.PACKAGES

  ○   C. SYSCAT.ISOLATION

  ○   D. SYSCAT.LOCKS

11. Which DB2 programming method would you use if you want to allow end users the ability to update only a portion of a table?

  ○   A. embedded dynamic SQL

  ○   B. embedded static SQL

  ○   C. Call Level Interface

12. Your application query returns the following message:

  `SQL0803N One or more values in the INSERT or UPDATE state-ment are not valid because they would produce duplicate rows for a table with a unique index.`

  What could have caused this error to occur?

  ○   A. A foreign key constraint was defined on the table.

  ○   B. A table-check constraint was defined on the table.

  ○   C. A non-unique constraint was defined on the table.

  ○   D. A primary key constraint was defined on the table.

13. Given the following information from the **SYSCAT.PACKAGES** system catalog table:

```
pkgschema  pkgname    isolation        blocking
DB2        CONNECT    RR               N
```

Which **BIND** command, executed by a user named *db2*, created this entry in the system catalog table?

○   A.   **BIND** db2.bnd **BLOCKING UNAMBIG**

○   B.   **BIND** connect.bnd **COLLECTION RS**

○   C.   **BIND** connect.bnd **COLLECTION** db2 **ISOLATION RR**

○   D.   **BIND** connect.bnd **ISOLATION RR BLOCKING NO**

14. A table contains employee numbers and all employee numbers are between 1,000 and 5,000. What would be the easiest method using DB2 of ensuring the values are always within this defined range?

○   A.   Define a primary key using employee number.

○   B.   Define a foreign key using employee number.

○   C.   Define a table-check constraint.

○   D.   Define an insert constraint.

15. Given the tables:

TEST		TEST_TAKEN	
number	name	number	candidate_id
500	Fundamentals	500	111111111
501	Administration	501	111111111
502	Programming	500	222222222

```
EXEC SQL
DECLARE CURSOR c1 FOR
SELECT b.number, name
FROM test a, test_taken b
        WHERE a.number = b.number
        ORDER BY 1,2;
EXEC SQL OPEN c1;
EXEC SQL FETCH c1 INTO :v1, :v2;
EXEC SQL FETCH c1 INTO :v3, :v4;
EXEC SQL FETCH c1 INTO :v1, :v2;
```

What is the value of the host variable v2 after the third fetch?

○   A. 111111111

○   B. 222222222

○   C. Fundamentals

○   D. Administration

○   E. Programming

16. Given the table:

```
TEST
number     name                             cut_score
500        Fundamentals                     65
501        Administration                   69
502        Programming                      NULL

EXEC SQL
           UPDATE test SET score=64
           WHERE score = :hv1 :hvind;
```

To set a score for the Programming exam, what should the value of the host variable hvind be set to?

○   A. 0

○   B. 64

○   C. -1

○   D. 65

○   E. NULL

17. Given the tables:

```
TEST
number     name                          cut_score
500        Fundamentals                  NULL
501        Administration                69
502        Programming                   NULL
503        Adv. Admin                    0
```

and the code:

```
EXEC SQL UPDATE test SET cut_score = :sc1
         WHERE cut_score = :sc2 :scind;
```

The value of the host variables are:

```
sc1 = -1;
sc2 = 0;
scind = -1;
```

How many rows will have a positive value for the cut score?

○   A. 0

○   B. 1

○   C. 2

○   D. 3

○   E. 4

18. Which SQL function could be used to retrieve the first 2 characters from a column which is defined as a **CHAR(10)** column?

○   A. **STRING**

○   B. **TRANSLATE**

○   C. **POSSTR**

○   D. **LTRIM**

○   E. **SUBSTR**

19. Given the table:

```
TEST
number    name                      cut_score
500       Fundamentals              NULL
501       Administration            69
502       Programming               NULL
503       Adv. Admin                0
```

Which SQL function could be used to return the test name in uppercase characters?

○   A. **TOUPPER**

○   B. **UPPER**

○   C. **SUBSTR**

○   D. **TRANSLATE**

20. Given the SQL statements:

```
EXEC SQL
WITH best_scores AS
(     SELECT MAX(score) AS max_score, cid
      FROM test_taken
      GROUP BY max_score, cid
)
SELECT max_score, cid
FROM best_scores
WHERE max_score IS NOT NULL
```

What kind of table is the best_score table?

○   A. system catalog table

○   B. base table

○   C. permanent user table

○   D. temporary

21. How many rows can be retreived using a **SELECT INTO** statement in an application?

   ○   A. none

   ○   B. 1

   ○   C. 2

   ○   D. unlimited

22. Which statement uses dynamic embedded SQL?

   ○   A. **SELECT number INTO :hv FROM t1**

   ○   B. **DECLARE c1 CURSOR FOR s1**

   ○   C. **DECLARE c1 CURSOR FOR**
          SELECT number INTO :hv FROM t1

   ○   D. **IMMEDIATE SELECT number INTO :hv FROM t1**

23. What type of cursor should be used to maintain the position of the cursor between transactions?

   ○   A. **FOR HOLD**

   ○   B. **FOR UPDATE**

   ○   C. **FOR FETCH**

   ○   D. **WITH HOLD**

24. When can cursors start accessing data from the database?

   ○   A. After the cursor has been declared.

   ○   B. After the cursor host variable has been initialized.

   ○   C. After the cursor has been opened.

   ○   D. After the first fetch has occurred.

25. Why might you define a cursor to be **FOR READ ONLY** or **FOR FETCH ONLY**?

○   A. Change the locking semantics.

○   B. Ensure that the buffer pool is used.

○   C. Define that the cursor is a **SELECT** statement.

○   D. Make the cursor unambiguous to enable record blocking.

26. How would you determine that you are at the end of a result set?

○   A. Check the null indicator host variable after each fetch.

○   B. Check the SQLCA after closing the cursor.

○   C. Check the SQLCA after each fetch.

○   D. Check the SQLDA after each fetch.

27. What occurs when a cursor is closed?

○   A. the cursor can be used in a subsequent fetch

○   B. the transaction is committed

○   C. the transaction is rolled back

○   D. the cursor must be opened again to be used

28. You have been given a new application and its bind file. What must you do before using the application?

○   A. perform a rebind of the package

○   B. define the application in the db2cli.ini file

○   C. precompile the application

○   D. bind the bind files to the database

29. How should a host variable be defined to contain DB2 TIMESTAMP values?

○ A. decimal

○ B. float

○ C. binary large object

○ D. character string

30. How should a host variable be defined to determine nullability?

○ A. boolean

○ B. integer

○ C. character

○ D. binary large object

31. Given the table definition:

```
CREATE TABLE t1 (    c1 INTEGER NOT NULL,
                     c2 INTEGER,
                     c3 INTEGER NOT NULL)
```

How many host variables are required to select all of the columns for the table t1?

○ A. 1

○ B. 2

○ C. 3

○ D. 4

○ E. 5

32. Which is a correct embedded SQL statement in a C program?

   ○   A. SELECT c1 FROM t1

   ○   B. EXEC SELECT c1 FROM t1

   ○   C. EXEC SELECT c1 FROM t1;

   ○   D. EXEC SQL SELECT c1 FROM t1;

   ○   E. EXEC SQL, SELECT c1 FROM t1.

33. Which element of the **SQLCA** should be a positive value if the SQL statement was completed successfully?

   ○   A. sqlerrd

   ○   B. sqlerrmc

   ○   C. sqlstate

   ○   D. sqlwarn

   ○   E. sqlcode

34. What authority/privilege is required to use the **REBIND** command?

   ○   A. BINDADD authority for the database

   ○   B. EXECUTE privilege on the package

   ○   C. BIND privilege on the package

   ○   D. UPDATE privilege on the package

35. Why might you use the **REBIND** command?

   ○   A. To change the isolation level for a package.

   ○   B. To change the query optimization level for a package.

   ○   C. To take advantage of more recent statistics.

   ○   D. To bind a new application.

36. Where are index definitions stored?

○   A. in the DB configuration file

○   B. in the DBM configuration file

○   C. in the system catalog tables

○   D. in the database directory

Answers

1. (D)

    The schema name is the first part of the two part database object name.
    Most database objects are named using a two-part name which is in the
    format `<schema-name>.<object-name>`.

2. (B)

    For dynamic SQL statements the currently connected or active user id of the
    database will be used to as an implicit qualifier for any unqualified table ref-
    erences.

3. (C)

    There would be 2 packages created as the first precompile specified the
    BINDFILE option. This option will prevent a package from being created in
    the database. It would create the package in a separate file, known as a bind
    file.

4. (C,D)

    The **CREATE ALIAS** statement is used to specify an alternative name for a
    database object.

5. (C)

    The **PRECOMPILE** option called **COLLECTION** is used to specify a collection or
    schema for the package in the database.

6. (D)

    Each program module precompiled is a separate package.

7. (B)

    The timestamp generated during precompile is associated with the database
    package and stored in the **SYSCAT.PACKAGES** system catalog table.

8. (B)

    The only DB2 programming method which stores the access plan for a given
    SQL statement in the system catalog tables is embedded static SQL. Embed-
    ded dynamic SQL programs create the access plan in memory and discard
    the plan after it is no longer required.

9. (D)

    To create a new package in a database the binder must have **BINDADD**
    authority on the database (or a higher level authority).

10. (B)

    The isolation level of a package will influence the locking strategies and the
    isolation level information is stored in the **SYSCAT.PACKAGES**.

11. (B)

    Static SQL will allow access to a table indirectly through the **EXECUTE** privi-
    lege for a given package. If a user has **EXECUTE** privilege they do not require
    explicit privileges on the database objects being accessed.

12. (D)

    A primary key constraint will create a system generated primary index. A
    primary index is a unique index and if a new data value is not unique the
    SQL0803N error will be encountered.

13. (D)

The isolation level for the example repeatable read (RR), the record blocking was set to NO and the package schema name is DB2 as the binder's user id is DB2.

14. (C)

A table-check constraint can be used to restrict the valid data values for a column within a table.

15. (D)

The value of the host variable would be Administration as each **FETCH** replaces the current value of the host variables.

16. (C)

The host indicator variable should be set to -1 to represent a **NULL** value.

17. (C)

Two rows would be updated as two rows had a **NULL** representation for cut_score.

18. (E)

The **SUBSTR** function can be used to extract a number of characters from a character data value.

19. (D)

The **TRANSLATE** function can be used to convert lowercase characters to their uppercase representation.

20. (D)

The SQL statement is known as a common table expression. Such tables exist only during the processing of the statement and are therefore temporary in nature.

21. (B)

The **SELECT INTO** statement is used to retreive a single-row result into a number of host variables or an SQLDA data structure.

22. (B)

The **DECLARE CURSOR** statement can be used in static or dynamic embedded SQL applications. The correct syntax for the statement to declare a cursor for a dynamically prepared SQL statement is shown as option B.

23. (D)

To maintain the cursor position in a result set from transaction to transaction, the cursor needs to be declared using the **WITH HOLD** phrase.

24. (C)

Cursors cannot be used in a **FETCH** statement until the cursor has been successfully opened.

25. (D)

By declaring a cursor as a **READ ONLY** cursor, the cursor is no longer ambiguous in nature and therefore record blocking is more likely to occur.

26. (C)

To determine the end of a result, set simply check the SQLCA data structure for an SQLCODE of +100.

27. (D)

When a cursor is closed the only valid statement using the cursor is the **OPEN** statement. This would reopen the cursor for usage and a new result set is obtained (if the cursor is not declared as **WITH HOLD**).

28. (D)

When a new application has been provided, the application bind files need to be bound to the database.

29. (D)

A **TIMESTAMP** data value is externalized as a character string.

30. (B)

A null indicator host variable should be declared as an numeric (short in the C language).

31. (D)

A total of 4 host variables should be used: 3 variables for the column data and 1 for the null indicator for column c2.

32. (D)

The valid syntax for an embedded SQL statement in a C program is:
SQL EXEC <SQL statement>;

33. (E)

If an SQL statement completed successfully, a positive value for the SQL-CODE should be returned to the application.

34. (C)

To issue the **REBIND** command a user requires BIND privilege on the existing package.

35. (C)

The index definitions are stored in the system catalog table called **SYSCAT.INDEXES**.

Exercises

Part A — PRECOMPILE and Packages

1. From the \exercise\chapter9\parta directory, issue the following (CLP):
   CONNECT TO db2cert USER db2 USING db2

2. Precompile the connect program connect.sqc:
   PREP connect.sqc COLLECTION test
             PACKAGE USING new
             MESSAGES prep.err

   View the prep.err file for any precompile errors.
3. Issue the statement:
   SELECT pkgschema, pkgname, isolation
         FROM SYSCAT.PACKAGES
         WHERE pkgschema ='TEST'
                      AND pkgname = 'NEW'

   The name of the package does not correspond to the source file name connect.sqc. This can cause problems later as you can not remember the source program name for this package. To help remember, you could use the **COMMENT ON** statement to provide the name of the source program module in the entry for the package. Also note that the default isolation level is CS or Cursor Stability for this package. This can be changed using the **ISOLATION BIND** parameter.

Part B — DB2CERT Application

1. From the \exercise\chapter9\partb\src directory, examine the driver.sqc source file. This is the main driver for the DB2CERT application.

2. Let's build the application, assuming that your C compiler environment has been set up properly. The source code modules are in the partb\src directory and the executables are available in OS/2 format in the partb\bin directory.

3. Execute the application by typing (The instance DB2 should have already been started): **DB2CERT2**
   Many programming techniques have been used in this application. Most all of the application is static embedded SQL.
   The DB2CERT database should be recreated to ensure that correct data is being used.
   To populate the db2cert database, issue the command from the directory

\exercise\chapter9\partb\data:
```
db2 create db db2cert on <path/drive>
db2 connect to db2cert
db2 -tvf db2cert.ddl
db2 -tvf data.imp
db2 -tvf test1.ddl
```

4. If you examine the statements in the db2cert.ddl input file, you may notice that a number of triggers have been defined. These triggers reduced the amount of validation code that was required for the DB2CERT application.

5. Any errors encountered by the program are logged in a file called db2cert.err. This is a reliable technique of providing the end user with the information they require to understand why they might be encountering a problem.

6. Let's start the application, change to the \exercise\chapter9\partb\<platform>in directory and **BIND** the bind files (CONNECT.BND, SCHEDULE.BND, CHECKID.BND, DRIVER.BND).
Once the bind files have been successfully bound to the database execute the program: **DB2CERT2**

7. Try various options from the menus. You should be able to determine how triggers, table-check constraints, and user-defined data types were used throughout.

   Triggers were used to help schedule test candidates into proper time slots. Triggers were also used to identify the Certified candidates.

8. After starting the db2cert application select 4 from the main menu (schedule a candidate for a test). Select 1. For City type North York. Confirm with Y. The date to schedule, enter 01-01-1996 (USA format).

   A formatted schedule for the test center on that day should be displayed. On the left side are the seats and the asterisks (*) indicate an scheduled test. Enter s to schedule a test. Enter the candidate 444444444 for test 500 at 9:00. This entry should be successful. Any time slot that cannot be schedule is verified using triggers (not application code).

DB2 Advanced Application Programming

*T*here are many application programming languages and development tools available to develop database applications. There also are many database programming interfaces available. We will discuss some of the more advanced database programming techniques in this chapter.

We have already examined how to implement embedded static SQL applications, and in this chapter we will examine how to dynamically prepare SQL statements in a program module. Coding embedded dynamic SQL statements can be complex as a special data structure, known as an SQLDA, must be used to interpret the SQL statement. In this chapter, we will examine how to dynamically prepare any SQL statement.

A relatively recent DB2 programming method known as a callable SQL interface is also available. Many application developers today code using the C programming language. One of the key features of the C language is its portability from operating system to operating system. The callable SQL interface is also a portable language, but it is used to access relational databases.

There exist many callable SQL standards to encourage portable application development. These standards include X/Open Call Level Interface (CLI), ISO Call Level Interface, and Microsoft's Open Database Connectivity (ODBC) standard. All three of the standards are based on a similar access method. Callable SQL programs involve coding SQL statements as function or API calls. For the most part, these functions do not change between database vendors. This results in a highly portable database application. There are unique features which are available using callable SQL.

DB2 provides the necessary environment to develop callable SQL applications. There is a DB2 CLI (Call Level Interface) provided which contains all of the ODBC level 1 functions and most of the level 2 functions. The DB2 CLI interface also provides DB2 specific functions which are not part of any of the callable SQL standards. We will examine the basics of a DB2 CLI application.

There exist many powerful new application extensions with DB2 Version 2 and we will discuss why you would utilize these programming extensions.

Writing Dynamic Programs

If every possible SQL statement for the application is known during the development phase of a software project, then static embedded SQL statements could be used for the entire application. This is usually not the case as the end-user requirements will change **before**, **during**, and **after** the development cycle. The application may also require that an undetermined number of columns are being returned. If the columns (select list) being returned are unknown during application development, the developer must dynamically prepare the SQL statement, and initialize the appropriate number of return variables.

When a fully defined SQL statement are embedded into an application it is said to be *statically prepared*. The access plan for a static embedded SQL statement is generated during the **bind** process. If *deferred binding* is used during the precompile phase (**BINDFILE** option used), the access plan is generated when the **BIND** command is used to bind the packages to the database.

During the static preparation phase, all aspects of the SQL statement are known by DB2. Input host variables are treated as placeholders for portions of the following SQL statements. Output host variables are used as placeholders for return arguments for the results of the SQL statements **SELECT INTO**, **VALUES INTO**, or **FETCH INTO**.

Let's examine the basic components of an SQL statement to more easily understand the benefits and requirements for dynamic and static SQL statements.

```
SELECT <col1>, <col2>,...
FROM <tab1>, <tab2>,....
WHERE <condition1> <expression1> <condition2>....
```

Fig. 10–1 Simple SQL SELECT Statement

In Fig. 10–1, the basic parts of a **SELECT** statement are shown. If there are unknown elements at the time of statement preparation, they can either be satisfied using host variables, or the statement requires dynamic preparation. Table 10–1 provides a checklist of conditions when the statement would require dynamic preparation:

There is no requirement to dynamically prepare **INSERT** statements. assuming that the target of the **INSERT** and the source of the data are well defined. **INSERT** statements operate on all columns of a row and therefore, the column names/types and the number of columns are predefined within the table definition.

If the table or view name was **not** known during application development then the SQL statement would require dynamic preparation. Using dynamic SQL statements will also allow you the flexibility of controlling the compilation environment for each SQL statement by using *special registers*, such as, **CURRENT QUERY OPTIMIZATION**.

Table 10–1 Dynamic vs. Static Preparation Checklist

Condition	Requires Dynamic Preparation
The column names/types in the SELECT list are unknown.	✓
The number of columns in the SELECT list are unknown.	✓
The table/view names in the FROM section are unknown.	✓

Consequently, if you are planning to provide the end user with a very flexible interface to the database, some of the program modules will likely be coded using dynamic SQL statements, either embedded or using a callable SQL interface like CLI.

First Look at Dynamic SQL

Generally speaking, coding a dynamic SQL application requires more complex programming techniques as special data structures must be manipulated. The effort to incorporate dynamic SQL statements may be required to provide the end user with the flexible query interface which they require. A good example of a dynamic embedded SQL interface is the DB2 Command Line Processor (CLP) utility. This utility dynamically prepares each SQL statement, and if a DB2 command is issued from the CLP interface an appropriate DB2 API is invoked. All of the DB2 APIs are documented in the manual, *DB2 API Reference.*

Every dynamically prepared SQL statement is optimized and compiled during query processing. This is an important consideration, as it can directly affect the end-user response time for an SQL query. The more complicated the SQL statement the more time required to optimize and compile the query. If the same query were embedded into an application and statically prepared, the query compilation time would have occurred when the **BIND** command was issued.

Query compilation (optimization) for static embedded SQL statements will occur during application development, using **BIND**.
Query compilation (optimization) for dynamic SQL statements
(embedded or callable SQL) will occur during query processing.

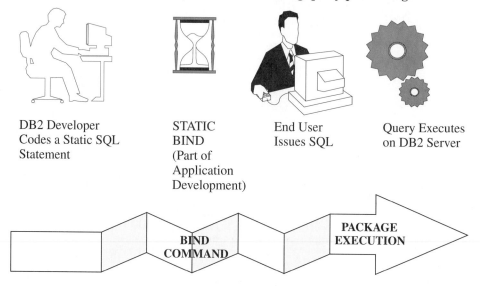

DB2 Developer	STATIC	End User	Query Executes
Codes a Static SQL	BIND	Issues SQL	on DB2 Server
Statement	(Part of		
	Application		
	Development)		

Fig. 10–2 Static Embedded SQL — Query Compilation Occurs during Bind

In Fig. 10–2 the static embedded SQL application development environment and program execution are shown. The end user is simply executing SQL
statements, known as *sections*, within a *package* stored in the database during
the bind phase. The section contains a fully optimized version of the SQL statement known as an *access plan*.

During the execution of the application in Fig. 10–2, host variables may
need to be resolved but the *access plan* or data access strategy has already been
determined.

 Since the access plan is chosen at bind time, ensure that the database statistics are updated prior to issuing the **BIND** command. The
RUNSTATS command will gather database statistics.

The **bind** process performs the following two major function:

- The SQL statement syntax will be verified and the privileges will be verified according to the user id of the individual *binding the package*.
- There will be an access plan chosen for the each SQL statement. This
access plan will include index usage and other data access techniques, such
as locking strategies. The access plan will be stored as a **section** within the
package, and it is considered a compiled representation of the SQL state-

ment. The term *compiled* means that there is no further processing by DB2 required for the statement.

We will now examine the development and execution of an application containing dynamic embedded SQL statements.

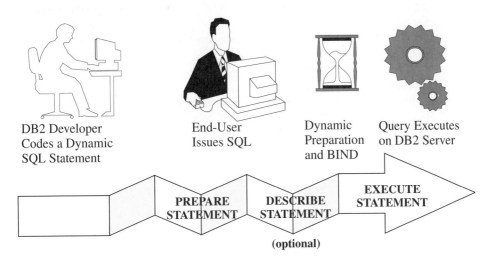

DB2 Developer   End-User   Dynamic   Query Executes
Codes a Dynamic   Issues SQL   Preparation   on DB2 Server
SQL Statement   and BIND

| | PREPARE STATEMENT | DESCRIBE STATEMENT | EXECUTE STATEMENT |

(optional)

Fig. 10–3 Dynamic Embedded SQL — Query Compilation during Query Execution

In Fig. 10–3 the preparation (parsing of the SQL statement) and the binding (determining the optimal access plan) are both performed after the query has been issued by the end user. Let's look at how the DB2 developer codes an application using dynamically prepared SQL statements.

Dynamic SQL Phases

PREPARE

If an SQL statement is dynamically prepared, the **syntax** of the statement must be checked during program execution. The **access plan** must also be generated during program execution. These two tasks are performed using the **PRE-PARE** SQL statement. The **PREPARE** statement will transform the string representation of an SQL statement into a form which can be executed by an application. The **PREPARE** statement will create a temporary executable module which is **not** stored in the database system catalog tables. By contrast, static SQL statements had their access plans stored in the system catalog tables.

The current authorization id is used to validate the privileges on the data objects that are referenced when the **PREPARE** of the statement occurs.

The **PREPARE** statement can **optionally** populate a structure known as the **SQLDA**.

DESCRIBE
The **DESCRIBE** statement can be used to provide the application developer with information about the SQL statement which has been previously prepared. For example, a **DESCRIBE** of the previously prepared **SELECT** statement would allow the application developer to determine the amount of storage required to store the query results.

EXECUTE
The **EXECUTE** statement is used to issue a previously prepared SQL statement. Therefore, it is possible for the developer to prepare and describe the statement and never actually execute the statement. This technique can be useful in determining information about the SQL statement without actually executing the statement.

FETCH
The **FETCH** statement is used to retrieve a single row of data from a result set. It is very similar to the **FETCH** statement used in embedded static SQL statements. The main difference is that this type of **FETCH** statement uses a cursor which represents a dynamically prepared SQL statement. The cursors must have been opened prior to the **FETCH** statement. Data can be retrieved into host variables or a properly allocated SQLDA structure.

EXECUTE IMMEDIATE (optional)
The **EXECUTE IMMEDIATE** SQL statement is a shortcut to issuing a dynamic SQL statement. An SQL statement which does not require any host variables and does not return a multi-row result set can be executed using the **EXECUTE IMMEDIATE** statement. The statement will be dynamically prepared and executed in a single embedded SQL statement.

Package Caching
As you might have already guessed, dynamically preparing SQL statements can negatively impact the query execution time. The access plan chosen for an SQL statement (dynamic or static) will be stored in a special cache, called the **package cache**. This cache is searched prior to query compilation. If the statement is found in the cache then the store access plan is used for the statement. This can dramatically increase the query execution time of dynamically prepared SQL statements if they are issued more than once by the same application. The execution time of static SQL statements will also be improved as the access plan will not have to be retrieved from the system catalog tables if it is found in the package cache.

The statement cache is a configured amount of memory on the database server which will be examined. If a matching access plan is **not** found in the statement cache, the SQL statement will be either:

- Retrieved from the system catalog tables for static SQL statements.
- Prepared and a temporary access plan created for dynamic SQL statements.

The size of the package cache is specified within the database configuration using the **pckcachesz** parameter. A separate cache is used for each database agent or application. By caching packages, DB2 can avoid the overhead involved in loading static SQL sections from system tables, and the overhead involved in determining an access plan for dynamic SQL statements. The access plan will remain in the cache until the application terminates, the cache becomes full and space is required, or the package becomes invalid.

✍️ SQL statements prepared and executed dynamically using the **EXECUTE IMMEDIATE** statement are stored in the same location within the package cache. Therefore, each **EXECUTE IMMEDIATE** statement will either find an exact match in the cache, or it will create a new access plan and replace the·previous **EXECUTE IMMEDIATE** SQL statement.

Types of Dynamic SQL Statements

There are two major types of dynamic SQL statements:

- Dynamic statements not requiring parameter markers
- Dynamic statements requiring parameter markers.

Parameter Markers

A dynamic SQL statement cannot contain host variables. Any missing information for a dynamic SQL statement should contain a **parameter marker**. A parameter marker is represented in an SQL statement using the question mark (?) character. In static SQL statements host variables can only be used as placeholders for certain parts of the statement. Host variables are usually used in the **WHERE** clause for static SQL statements. Parameter markers are more flexible than host variables. For example, a parameter marker can be used in the **FROM** clause or the **SELECT** list, as well as any place static host variables can used.

A parameter marker is defined in the SQL statement before the statement is prepared. The missing information is supplied in the **EXECUTE**, **FETCH**, or **CALL** statement using a host variable or an SQLDA data structure.

The **CALL** statement is used to invoke DB2 stored procedures. Data can be passed to stored procedures using host variables, or by using an SQLDA structure (see "Stored Procedures" on page 524).

Dynamic Statements without Parameter Markers

If the entire SQL statement is known at runtime, then the statement can be dynamically prepared and parameter markers are not required. These statements are fully optimized during the dynamic prepare as there is no missing information. This is the most common type of dynamic SQL statements.

Dynamic Statements With Parameter Markers

Parameter markers are used in dynamic SQL statement processing in a manner similar to how host variables are used in static SQL processing. The statement would contain a question mark (?) for each missing element. When the statement is processed, the missing data will be substituted using a host variable, or using an SQLDA data structure.

SQLDA Data Structure

The **SQLDA** data structure is a two-way communications data structure. The SQLDA is used to transfer data between the application and DB2. This structure actually contains a number of other structures named **SQLVAR**. Each SQLVAR data structure corresponds to a single column of data.

✍ When the select list includes user-defined data types (UDTs) and or
   a large object data type (LOB) then the SQLDA needs to be **twice**
   as large as the number of columns.

The SQLDA can be used as input to SQL statements and output from SQL statements. The SQLDA data structure is defined for C, REXX, FORTRAN, and COBOL.

✍ The SQLDA is defined in the **sqlda.h** file for C programs.
   The SQLDA is defined in the **sqlda.cbl** file for Cobol programs.
   The SQLDA is defined in the files **sqlda_cs.for** and **sqlda_cn.for**
   for Fortran programs.

Before we continue much further on the subject of embedded dynamic SQL statement processing we need to examine the SQLDA data structure. This data structure is used as output from DB2 in the following cases:

- During the PREPARE INTO or DESCRIBE statement as it will contain the required number of SQLVAR elements for the query or it will populate the SQLDA with the column data type information
- During the FETCH INTO statements as the SQLDA can be used as the location for the retrieved rows of data.
- During the EXECUTE USING statement as the SQLDA can be used to provide data for the parameter markers for the prepared SQL statement.

In **OPEN**, **FETCH**, **EXECUTE**, and **CALL** statements, the SQLDA is used to contain input and output host variables. In **DESCRIBE** and **PREPARE INTO** statements, the SQLDA is used to describe a column of a result table, including its length and data type.

Table 10–2 SQLDA Header Information

Name of Element	SQL Data Type	Purpose in DESCRIBE and PREPARE	Purpose in FETCH, EXECUTE, and CALL
sqldaid	CHAR(8)	The seventh byte is set to 2 if the SQLDA has been doubled, otherwise it is set to blank.	The seventh byte is set to 2 if the SQLDA is doubled.
sqldabc	INTEGER	The size of the SQLDA structure.	The size of the SQLDA structure.
sqln	SMALLINT	Must be set by the application to equal the number of SQL-VARs,	Total number of SQL-VARs in the SQLDA structure.
sqld	SMALLINT	Set by DB2 to the number of columns in the select list. If the statement is not a select, the value is zero.	The number of host variables described.

SQLVAR Elements

There are two types of SQLVAR structures in the SQLDA. There are base SQLVARS which contain information regarding the data type, column name, its length, host variable, and indicator variable for each column in the result set. The secondary SQLVARs are only present if the SQLDA has been doubled. As noted previously, an SQLDA is doubled if the select list includes LOB columns or user-defined data types (UDTs).

The SQLDA header information in Table 10–2 contains information regarding the size of the SQLDA, the number of SQLVARs allocated (**sqln**), and the number of SQLVARs required for the statement (**sqld**). Note that some of the elements of the SQLDA header are initialized by DB2 and others are initialized by the application. The sqln element is set by the application and the sqld element is set by DB2.

✍ A **DESCRIBE** or a **PREPARE INTO** statement will always populate the sqld element with the required number of SQLVARs for an SQL statement.

The value of **sqln** needs to be greater than or equal to the value of **sqld** before the SQLDA may be used in a **FETCH**, **EXECUTE**, or **CALL** statement. The **DESCRIBE** will not be successful until the application developer has allocated the proper number (**sqld**) of SQLVAR entries. If there are UDTs or LOB data types, then the twice as many (2*sqld) SQLVAR entries are required.

Table 10–3 SQLVAR Elements (Basic SQLVAR)

Name of Element	DATA TYPE	Purpose in DESCRIBE and PREPARE INTO statements	Purpose in FETCH, EXECUTE, and CALL statements
sqltype	SMALLINT	Contains a number which represents the data type defined for the column in the select list (set by DB2)	Contains a number representing the data type (set by application)
sqllen	SMALLINT	Contains the length of the column (set by DB2)	Contains the length of the host variable. (set by application)
sqldata	pointer (*)	Usually contains the code page. (set by DB2)	Contains the address of the host variable. (set by application)
sqlind	pointer	May contain the code page or the value of 0. (set by DB2)	Contains the address of an indicator variable. Not required for NOT NULL columns. (set by application)
sqlname	VARCHAR(30)	The column name. (set by DB2)	Not usually used.

Output SQLDA

If the number of columns defined in an SQL statement is unknown by the application developer, then they must be ready to accept any number of columns. The **maximum number of columns** in a **SELECT** statement is 255. Not only does the application developer need to know the number of columns, they must also know the data type of each column.

In Table 10–3 the SQLVAR structure is shown. The first element, **sqltype**, is used to indicate the data type. If the SQLDA is being used as input using the **FETCH**, **EXECUTE**, or **CALL** statements, the **sqltype** and a compatible **host variable** must be initialized. The possible values for **sqltype** are defined in the *DB2 SQL Reference*.

The end-user may supply the entire SQL statement or a portion of the SQL statement. Often there is only a portion of the SQL statement which is not known. Once the entire SQL statement text has been determined the developer must dynamically prepare the statement for execution using the **PREPARE** statement.

The first example will not contain any parameter markers as the entire statement text is known.

```
szSQLText='SELECT fname,lname FROM candidate'
PREPARE stat1 INTO :minsqlda FROM :szSQLText
```

Fig. 10–4 Preparing an SQL Statement into an SQLDA Structure

Let's example the example in Fig. 10–4 starting from the far right. A host variable called *szSQLText* is referenced. This host variable must contain a valid SQL statement. The host variable should simply be a string data type and contain the entire SQL statement (no parameter markers in this example).

If the SQL statement has any missing parts, they should be represented in the statement text using the (?) character and supplied during statement execution as host variables. The SQL statement is checked for syntax and information is provided about the number and data types of the columns referenced.

The **PREPARE** statement in Fig. 10–4 contains two other user-supplied (lowercase) components. A statement identifier of *stat1* is used to reference the prepared statement during query execution. The *stat1* identifier is **not** a host variable. It will be used during query execution and row fetching. Another host variable called *minsqlda* is also shown in Fig. 10–4. This data structure is used to contain information about the SQL statement. The SQL statement in Fig. 10–4 contains two columns of type varying length (**VARCHAR**).

The SQLDA structure, called *minsqlda*, will contain information about the query being prepared. Like all other host variables, the SQLDA data structure must be initialized prior to its usage in an SQL statement. An SQLDA contains a number of SQLVAR data structures. Each SQLVAR data structure corresponds to a single column for each row being processed. Since the nature of the query is unknown by the application developer, the required size of the SQLDA is also unknown.

There are two methods of initializing the SQLDA data structure:

- Allocate an SQLDA with the maximum number of SQLVAR elements.
- Allocate an SQLDA with the minimum number of SQLVAR elements and re-initialize the SQLDA with the proper number of SQLVAR elements following a **DESCRIBE** or a **PREPARE INTO** statement.

The statement being prepared in Fig. 10–4 contains a two-column select list. Therefore, an SQLDA structure with two SQLVAR elements is required. If the SQLDA does not contain enough SQLVAR elements for the query, the statement cannot be executed. If we decided to declare the maximum SQLDA size, then we would have been wasting memory, but we would avoid having to reallocate the SQLDA to a larger size. Remember, if any of the columns are defined as user-defined data types (UDTs), or large object data types (LOBs), the number of SQLVAR elements needs to be **doubled**.

If the SQLDA was not large enough, then additional SQLVAR elements must be allocated and the statement needs to be prepared again.

✍ A **PREPARE INTO** statement is functionally equivalent to a **PREPARE** followed by a **DESCRIBE** of the statement.

```
PREPARE stat2 FROM :szSQLText2
```

Fig. 10–5 Preparing an SQL statement

In Fig. 10–5 the SQL statement defined in the string szSQLText2 is being dynamically prepared. This will not populate an SQLDA structure. It is not mandatory that every dynamically prepared SQL statement needs to be described using the **PREPARE INTO** or the **DESCRIBE** statement. Remember that the proper SQLDA structure needs to be provided when the statement is executed.

The example dynamic SQL program in Fig. 10–6 demonstrates many of the dynamic embedded SQL programming techniques. The program retrieves the current user id using the **VALUES INTO** statement. The program then retrieves all of the currently defined tables within the user's schema. Until this point in the application there is no need for dynamically prepare SQL statements.

The end-user provides the name of the table about which they wish to obtain more information. Since the table is unknown at application development time, we need to dynamically prepare the statement and use the SQLDA data structure to handle the multiple number of columns in the **SELECT** list.

Once the statement (**SELECT * FROM tabname**) has been prepared, it is executed and fetched into an SQLDA data structure. The **DESCRIBE** statement was used to provide detailed information regarding the column name, length, null constraints, and data type.

```
/***************************************************************************
** Dynamic Embedded SQL program - DYNA1.SQC
****************************************************************************/

#include <stdio.h>
#include <stdlib.h>
#include <time.h>
#include <sql.h>
#include <sqlcodes.h>
#include <sqlda.h>
#include "cert.h"
#define sLine_Width 80

EXEC SQL BEGIN DECLARE SECTION;
  char szTabName[19];
  char szTabSchema[19];
  char szUser[20];
  char szStatement[3000];
EXEC SQL END DECLARE SECTION;

short i;
FILE *fp;

int main(int argc, char *argv[]) {

    struct sqlda *myda;
    char msg[255];
    char szUserid[9];
    char szPassword[19];
    char szTestNumber[7];
    short retcode;
    strcpy (szUserid,"db2");
    strcpy (szPassword,"db2");

    fp = fopen ( "db2dyn.err", "a+");
    if (fp == NULL) {
      printf ("Could not open the DB2 error file!\n");
        return 1;
    } /* endif */

    if ((Start_Instance() ) < 0 ) {
        Record_SQL_Error ();
    } /* endif */

    if (Establish_Connection(szUserid,szPassword) < 0) {
        Record_SQL_Error ();
    } /* endif */
        fflush (stdin);
        printf ("Dynamic embedded SQL Example\n");
        printf ("The following is a list of tables within your schema.\n");
        EXEC SQL VALUES(USER) INTO :szUser;
        printf ("Your user id is:%s\n\n",szUser);
        printf ("        Table Name\t Table Schema\n");

    EXEC SQL DECLARE c1 CURSOR FOR
            SELECT tabname, tabschema
                FROM SYSCAT.TABLES
                WHERE tabschema = USER
                FOR FETCH ONLY;

    EXEC SQL OPEN c1;
    EXEC SQL FETCH c1 INTO :szTabName, :szTabSchema;
                Record_SQL_Error();
            } /* endif */
            } /* endif */
    EXEC SQL CLOSE c1;
```

```
if (SQLCODE < 0) {
        Record_SQL_Error();
        }
   else {
        if (SQLCODE != 100) {
        printf ("%18s\t%18s\n",szTabName,szTabSchema);
          do {
              EXEC SQL FETCH c1 INTO :szTabName, :szTabSchema;
              printf ("%18s\t%18s\n",szTabName,szTabSchema);
          } while (SQLCODE==0); /* enddo */
        } else {
   do {
     printf ("\nWhich Table would you like to examine?\n");
     printf ("Table Schema\t:");
     fflush (stdout);
     scanf ("%19s",szTabSchema);
     fflush (stdin);
     printf ("Table Name\t:");
     fflush (stdout);
     scanf ("%19s",szTabName);
     fflush (stdin);

     strcpy (szStatement,"SELECT * FROM ");
     strcat (szStatement,szTabSchema);
     strcat (szStatement,".");
     strcat (szStatement,szTabName);

       EXEC SQL PREPARE stmt FROM :szStatement;
       if (SQLCODE < 0) {
          Record_SQL_Error();
          if (SQLCODE == -204) {
             printf ("Table is undefined, try again.\n");
          } /* endif */
       } /* endif */
   } while ((SQLCODE !=0)); /* enddo */
   EXEC SQL PREPARE stmt FROM :szStatement;
   if (SQLCODE < 0) {
       Record_SQL_Error();
   } /* endif */

   /* Allocate an SQLDA with 255 SQLVAR element */

   myda=(struct sqlda*) malloc(SQLDASIZE(255));
   myda->sqln=255;
   EXEC SQL DESCRIBE stmt INTO :*myda;

   if (SQLCODE < 0) {
       Record_SQL_Error();
   } /* endif */
   if GETSQLDOUBLED(myda) {
      printf ("\nThe SQLDA has been DOUBLED, either UDTs or LOBs are used.\n");
   } /* endif */
   printf ("\nThe number of columns is the table was %d.\n",myda->sqld);
   printf ("The number of SQLVARs provided was %d.\n\n",myda->sqln);
/* IF the SQLTYPE is ODD then the host variable requires a NULL indicator*/
   for (i=0;i< myda->sqld; i++ ) {
       printf ("Column Name %18s\tSQLTYPE = %d",
               myda->sqlvar[i].sqlname.data,myda->sqlvar[i].sqltype);
       if ( (myda->sqlvar[i].sqltype) % 2) {
          printf ("\tNULLABLE\n");
       } else {
          printf ("\tNOT NULL\n");
       } /* endif */
   } /* endfor */
/* IF the SQLTYPE is ODD then the host variable requires a NULL indicator*/
 fclose (fp);
 return 0;
}
```

Fig. 10–6 DYN1.SQC Example Program

Dynamic SQL — Call Level Interface

Callable SQL Interfaces

We have been discussing static and dynamic SQL statement processing by embedding the SQL statements in an application module. A precompile stage was required to map these SQL statements to API calls to the database itself. We were required to manipulate SQLDA data structures to handle dynamic SQL and it became quite complex and more importantly it was prone to error and not easily ported to various database vendors. A major alternative method of developing database applications has been developed and has become a popular technique of creating powerful yet highly portable applications. The method is known as a *callable SQL interface*.

A callable SQL interface involves invoking APIs which allow the developer to access database information directly; therefore there is no need for precompiling the application and there is no database-specific language to learn. There are slightly different callable SQL interface standards known as Call Level Interface (CLI) as defined by groups such as X/Open and ISO. One of the main callable SQL interface standards was developed by Microsoft and it is known as Open Database Connectivity or ODBC.

All of the SQL statements are dynamically prepared and executed using a callable SQL interface such as CLI. The programming techniques and the run-time environment are quite different. We will discuss many of these differences.

ODBC vs. CLI

The ODBC and CLI standards overlap in many areas as they are both based on a set of APIs which access data sources using the C/C++ programming language. The initial ODBC standard was based on an early version of the X/Open CLI standard and the two have evolved over the years.

The ODBC standard is based on levels of conformance based on the APIs that have been implemented. The DB2 product provides both a CLI driver and an ODBC driver. The ODBC driver is optionally installed with the DB2 product. The ODBC driver can be installed using the ODBC administrator as shown in Fig. 10–7.

Fig. 10-7 DB2 ODBC Administrator

✍️   The ODBC driver is **only** required to be installed if ODBC applications are being executed. The driver is not required for DB2 CLI
applications, only the DB2 CAE layer would be required.

There must be an ODBC driver manager installed on the computer where
the ODBC application has been installed. For all Microsoft operating systems
the ODBC driver manager is provided by Microsoft; for other operating system
an ODBC driver manager must be obtained. The DB2 ODBC driver, or another
ODBC driver, must be installed and configured. The data source or database
must be identified to the ODBC driver manager.

A DB2 CLI application does not require the ODBC driver or the ODBC
driver manager to operate properly. The advantage of coding an ODBC applications the ease of portability and the application can access more than one database source. Therefore, you could develop an application which accesses data
from multiple data sources quite simply with the ODBC interface where it would
be impossible with the DB2 CLI driver. The DB2 CLI driver can only access DB2
Family data sources.

The ODBC standard continues to evolve. The DB2 ODBC driver currently
supports all of the level 1 functions and most of the level 2 functions and Version
3 of the ODBC standard is on its way. If you are developing ODBC-compliant
applications, you should refer the *ODBC 2.0 Programmer's Reference and SDK
Guide* published by Microsoft as the main reference for conformance. The *DB2
Call Level Interface Guide and Reference* will contain the DB2-specific APIs and
the support ODBC APIs only.

Embedded Dynamic vs. Call Level Interface

Developing an application using CLI is quite different than using embedded SQL
techniques, so before we examine how to code CLI applications, let's examine
some of the key differences.

The DB2 Call Level Interface (CLI) environment is different from embedded SQL in the following ways:

- No explicit cursors are used
- No precompile stage is required
- No application level packages are created — there is a single CLI package which is only bound once for all CLI applications.
- No **COMMIT/ROLLBACK** statement is used to control transaction processing. An API called **SQLTransact()** is used to commit or rollback a transaction.
- No SQLDA data structure is required
- No SQLCA data structure is used as the errors are analyzed using SQL-STATES, return codes and special error handling APIs.
- No host variables are used in SQL statements; parameter markers are used instead.

Not only are the above differences important to understand before attempting to develop CLI applications, but there are some unique features provided with CLI that are not available in an embedded SQL environment including:

- Multiple database concurrent database connections
- Manipulation of multiple rows of data at a time (array fetch/insert)
- Easier to query the system catalog tables as there are predefined APIs to query system catalog table resources

Setting Up a CLI Development Environment

We have already discussed the steps necessary to set up an ODBC environment. Fortunately there are fewer steps involved in setting up a DB2 CLI environment. All of the CLI APIs are contained in a static library. These are the names of the libraries on various DB2 development operating systems:

- The DB2 CLI library on OS/2 is called db2cli.lib.
- The DB2 CLI library on AIX is called libdb2.a.
- The DB2 CLI library on Windows is db2cliw.lib.

Before we can attempt to develop an application we must ensure the following steps have been performed successfully:

- Database being accessed has been cataloged properly. If the database is remote, a node must also be cataloged.
- DB2 CLI bind files must have been bound to the database. Configure the CLI environment using the Client Setup tool or edit the **db2cli.ini** file directly. It is important to remember to examine the CLI environment settings in the **db2cli.ini** file. These settings will affect the execution behavior of all CLI applications executing on the workstation.

CLI Bind Files

The bind files required for CLI applications will be automatically bound when the first CLI application executes, but the bind may not be successful if the user does not have **BINDADD** authority on the database. Therefore, the database administrator may be required to bind the necessary bind files. Each of the supported DB2 servers different bind files which need to be bound.

These bind files are slightly different for the various DB2 database servers as shown in Table 10–4.

Table 10–4 CLI Bind Files

Bind File	DB2 Server
db2cli.lst	DB2 Common Server (AIX, OS/2, NT, Other UNIX)
ddcsvm.lst	DB2 for VM (SQL/DS)
ddcvse.lst	DB2 for VSE (SQL/DS)
ddcsmvs.lst	DB2 for MVS/ESA
ddcs400.lst	DB2 for OS/400

Configuring CLI

It is usually not necessary to modify the DB2 CLI configuration file (db2cli.ini) but, it is important to understand that it exists and it may require small modifications. Some of the reasons for modifying the CLI configuration file include:

- increase CLI application performance
- enable workarounds for specific applications

The **db2cli.ini** file is located in the **sqllib/cfg** directory of the instance owner in UNIX environments, or in the **sqllib** directory for OS/2, or the **sqllib/win** directory for Windows environments.

```
; Comment Goes Here
[DB2CERT]
AUTOCOMMIT=0
CURSORHOLD=0
MULTICONNECT=0
PATCH1=2
TNXISOLATION=4
```

Fig. 10–8 Example db2cli.ini Configuration File

An example db2cli.ini file is shown in Fig. 10–8. There are many more options which can be specified in the CLI configuration file but these options were chosen for a reason. They can all drastically affect an application's execution environment.

The first line is simply a comment about this section of the file, multiple databases can be configured in this single file. The second line contains the database alias name in brackets [DB2CERT]. The db2cert database could still be accessed from a DB2 CLI application without an entry in the db2cli.ini file but, if there is no section for the db2cert database all of the default values for the parameters will be used (this may not be desirable).

The five lines below the database name contains keywords and corresponding values. Each of these keywords are defined in the manual but let's examine the keywords defined in Fig. 10–8.

Table 10–5 Configuring a DB2 CLI Environment

Keyword	Meaning
AUTOCOMMIT	0 = OFF / 1 = ON The default value of this keyword is 1. This means that every successful SQL statement will be automatically committed and therefore no need to issue the SQLTransact() API to commit the unit-of-work. Many CLI/ODBC applications have been designed assuming this behavior so be careful if you decide to change this parameter. In our example we decided to turn auto-commit off so that we could control the commit scope of our transactions.
CURSORHOLD	0 = CURSOR NO HOLD / 1 = CURSOR HOLD The default value of this keyword is 1. This means that the cursors are maintained across units of work. This is quite different from embedded SQL as all cursors exhibit the cursor without hold behavior unless the DECLARE CURSOR statement includes the phrase WITH HOLD. In our example we decided to turn of the cursor hold default behavior as we do not need to maintain cursor position across transactions.
MULTICONNECT	0 = false (default) 1 = true The default value of this keyword is false (0). The parameter is used to identify if the SQLConnect() API will establish a new physical connection (like CONNECT TO in embedded). If the value is set to 1 or true, then all SQL statements are mapped to a single database connection.
TXISOLATION	1 - Uncommitted Read 2 - Cursor Stability (default) 8 - Repeatable Read 16 - Repeatable Stability 32 - No Commit (DB2 for OS/400 only) This keyword identifies the isolation level used for concurrency.

Stored Procedures

A DB2 stored procedure is application code which may or may not access DB2 resources. The procedure is built as a dynamically loadable library and stored on the DB2 server. A DB2 application can invoke the stored procedure from a remote client.

The data is exchanged between the client application and the stored procedure using the SQLDA data structure or host variables. An SQLCA data structure is also passed to communicate the success or failure of any SQL statements. The stored procedure is called using the SQL **CALL** statement. The **CALL** statement can pass input and output arguments. Usually an SQLDA data structure is used.

The stored procedure is developed and compiled/linked into a DLL or export library and physically stored on the DB2 server. The return code of the this function is not passed back to the calling application (the SQLDA is used to pass information to the calling application). The return code is used to determine the behavior of the stored procedure. For example, the return code **SQLZ_DISCONNECT_PROC** is used to ensure that the library is released on the DB2 server.

As previously discussed (Chapter 8), a DB2 stored procedure can be executed as a **fenced** or a **not fenced** resource.

User Defined Functions

Creating a user-defined function is similar to creating a stored procedure as a UDF is also a function within a dynamically loadable library located on the server. However, there are many differences in their usage and the method of exchanging data.

A UDF is invoked from any SQL statement which references the function. The data values are passed from the SQL function call to the UDF using special DB2 data structures. We have included an example UDF to understand the data exchange methods. In Fig. 10–9 the function called *id_format* is shown. There is a single input argument and single output argument.

✍ Don't forget that NULL values must be passed also.

The output variable called *output* in Fig. 10–9 is set before the function has exited. The value is then passed back to the calling application.

✍ User-defined functions form the basis of **OBJECT RELATIONAL** extensions to the SQL language.

COMPOUND SQL

Compound SQL can be used to perform a number of SQL statements in a single block on the DB2 server. There are no special coding techniques required as compound SQL is a single SQL statement.

```
/****************************************************************
/* User Defined Function Example Program (idformat.c)          *
/*                                                             *
/* Purpose: Convert the UNIQUE_ID value associated with a      *
/*          database package into a string representation      *
/*                                                             *
/* (C) COPYRIGHT International Business Machines Corp. 1996     *
/****************************************************************/

#include <stdio.h>
#include <string.h>
#include <sqludf.h>

short convert(char val)
{
  if ((val >= 'A') && (val <= 'Z'))
    return (val - 'A');
  if ((val >= 'a') && (val <= 'z'))
    return (val - 'a' + 26);
  if ((val >= '1') && (val <= '9'))
    return (val - '1' + 52);
  if (val == '0')
    return (61);
  return (-1);
}

/****************************************************************
/* INPUT: The arg structure is used to pass data into the UDF. *
/*        The innull will indicate if the data value is null.  *
/*                                                             *
/* OUTPUT: The output structure used to return the time string.*
/*         The return value is not used in this UDF.           *
/****************************************************************/

void SQL_API_FN id_format(
         SQLUDF_CHAR    *arg,          /* input argument       */
         SQLUDF_CHAR    *output,       /* output result        */
         SQLUDF_NULLIND *innull,       /* input NULL indicator */
         SQLUDF_NULLIND *outnull,      /* output NULL indicator */
         SQLUDF_TRAIL_ARGS)            /* trailing arguments   */
{

  short yy,mm,dd,hh,mn,ss,hs;
  *outnull = 0;

  yy = convert(arg[7]) + 84;
  mm = convert(arg[6]);
  dd = convert(arg[5]);
  hh = convert(arg[4]);
  mn = convert(arg[3]);
  ss = convert(arg[2]);
  hs = convert(arg[1]) * 62 + convert(arg[0]);

  sprintf (output, "%d/%d/%d %d:%d:%d:%03d",yy,mm,dd,hh,mn,ss,hs);

  if ((yy<84) || (mm<0)  || (dd<0)  || (hh<0)  || (mn<0)  || (ss<0)  || (hs<0) ||
      (yy>99) || (mm>12) || (dd>31) || (hh>23) || (mn>59) || (ss>60) || (hs>99)) {
    strcpy(sqludf_sqlstate, "38999");
    sprintf(sqludf_msgtext, "Invalid UNIQUE_ID: %s",arg);
  }
  return;
}
```

Fig. 10–9 User-Defined Function — idformat.c

Summary

DB2 provides many advanced programming techniques. This chapter provided dynamic SQL programming techniques including dynamic embedded SQL and Call Level Interface (CLI) programming techniques.

This chapter is an introduction to many of these advanced techniques including: stored procedures and user-defined functions. We discussed the steps required to **PREPARE**, **DESCRIBE**, and **FETCH** using dynamically prepared SQL statements in an embedded SQL application.

An example user-defined function was provided. The *id_format* function is useful to determine the actual date and time that a DB2 package was precompiled (unique timestamp).

A complete DB2 application using embedded static and dynamic SQL statements is provided in Appendix E. This application is also on the CD-ROM in the chapter9 directory.

For more detailed analysis of advanced programming techniques, see the following references:

1. DB2 Application Programming Guide for common servers Version 2, IBM, 1995.
2. Using the New DB2: IBM's Object-Relational Database System by Don Chamberlin published by Morgan Kaufmann Publishers, San Francisco, 1996.

Questions

1. Which command would gather detailed information regarding the access plans of all static SQL statements?

   ○   A. **BIND a.bnd BLOCKING ALL**

   ○   B. **BIND a.bnd EXPLSNAP ALL**

   ○   C. **BIND a.bnd ACCESS PLANS ALL**

   ○   D. **BIND a.bnd PLANS ALL**

2. Which sample code fragment could be used to retreive all of the columns for any table using dynamic embedded SQL?
   Note: The host varible :da1 is defined to be a maximum sized **SQLDA** structure.

   ○   A. text = "SELECT * FROM t1"
            EXEC SQL PREPARE stmt FROM :text;
            EXEC SQL FETCH INTO :da1;

   ○   B. text = "SELECT * FROM t1"
            EXEC SQL PREPARE stmt FROM :text;
            EXEC SQL DECLARE c1 CURSOR FOR stmt;
            EXEC SQL OPEN c1;
            EXEC SQL FETCH c1;
            EXEC SQL CLOSE c1;

   ○   C. text = "SELECT * FROM t1"
            EXEC SQL PREPARE stmt INTO :da1 FROM :text;
            EXEC SQL DECLARE c1 CURSOR;
            EXEC SQL OPEN c1;
            EXEC SQL FETCH c1 INTO :da1;
            EXEC SQL CLOSE c1;

   ○   D. text = "SELECT * FROM t1"
            EXEC SQL PREPARE stmt INTO :da1 FROM :text;
            EXEC SQL DECLARE c1 CURSOR FOR stmt;
            EXEC SQL OPEN c1;
            EXEC SQL FETCH c1 INTO :da1;
            EXEC SQL CLOSE c1;

3. Which embedded dynamic SQL statement may be used to replace the DESCRIBE statement?

    ○   A. **OPEN USING**

    ○   B. **DECLARE INTO**

    ○   C. **PREPARE INTO**

    ○   D. **SELECT INTO**

4. Given the code segment (psuedo-code):
```
if salary less than 8000 then
EXEC SQL UPDATE employee SET salary = 8000
WHERE id = :hv1;
end if
```

What DB2 object could be defined to avoid checking that the salary is always less than 8000?

    ○   A. table check constraint

    ○   B. a primary key constraint

    ○   C. a foreign key constraint

    ○   D. a user defined data type

5. Which element in the **SQLDA** should be examine to determine the nullability of a data value?

    ○   A. SQLDABC

    ○   B. SQLVAR

    ○   C. SQLIND

    ○   D. SQLDAID

6. Given the table:
    CREATE TABLE t1 (c1 CHAR(3), c2 INTEGER)

    and the SQL STATEMENT:

    SELECT c1 FROM t1

    How many additional **SQLVAR** elements are required in the **SQLDA** data structure to fetch data using the **SELECT** statement?

    ○   A. none

    ○   B. one

    ○   C. two

    ○   D. three

7. What type of function is required to compare a user-defined data type and its base data type?

    ○   A. converting function

    ○   B. column function

    ○   C. table function

    ○   D. casting function

8. Assume telephone numbers were stored using a fixed character string data type and the first three characters represented the area code. What type of function would you create to provide the area code for any given telephone number?

    ○   A. column function

    ○   B. table function

    ○   C. user defined sourced function

    ○   D. user defined external function

9. How are stored procedures executed from an application?

○   A. Using the **INVOKE** API.

○   B. Using the **CALL** API.

○   C. Using the SQL **CALL** statement.

○   D. Using the SQL **VALUES** statement.

10. A transaction involves a number of SQL statements. What option could be used in a static embedded SQL program to optimize the execution of the transaction without creating application code on the DB2 server?

○   A. stored procedures

○   B. triggers

○   C. user defined functions

○   D. compound SQL

11. How many databases can be involved in a transaction if you are using a type 1 connection?

○   A. none

○   B. one

○   C. two

○   D. unlimited

12. Which command is only allowed when using a type 2 connection?

○   A. **CONNECT**

○   B. **DISCONNECT**

○   C. **TERMINATE**

○   D. **CONNECT RESET**

13. Application app1 has updated a value and has not committed the update. Another application app2 attempts to read the value and the updated value has been returned. What is the isolation level being used by application app2?

  ○   A. cursor stability

  ○   B. read stability

  ○   C. uncommitted read

  ○   D. repeatable read

14. What type of record lock is obtained when a value is being updated?

  ○   A. update

  ○   B. share

  ○   C. intent exclusive

  ○   D. exclusive

15. If an application receives an error code indicating a deadlock condition, what should the application do next?

  ○   A. Free all of its current locks using the RELEASE command.

  ○   B. Lock the table in exclusive mode.

  ○   C. Reissue the unit-of-work.

  ○   D. Terminate and restart the program.

16. If application 1 has a share lock on a record, which type of lock could another application obtain on the same record?

  ○   A. read

  ○   B. exclusive

  ○   C. update

  ○   D. share

  ○   E. super exclusive

17. How are data records returned from a stored procedure?

  ○   A. as a result table

  ○   B. as a return code

  ○   C. as a SQLDA structure

  ○   D. as a SQLCA structure

18. How is data returned from a user-defined function?

  ○   A. as a SQLDA structure

  ○   B. as a SQLCA structure

  ○   C. as a scalar value

  ○   D. as a result table

19. Where is explain information stored?

  ○   A. In the bind file.

  ○   B. In the application.

  ○   C. In the system catalog tables.

  ○   D. In user tables.

20. Which are charcteristics of a common table expression?

  ○   A. they are permanent user tables

  ○   B. they are defined within the system catalog tables

  ○   C. they are defined within applications

21. Which SQL statement is only valid in dynamic embedded SQL programs?

○   A. **PREPARE**

○   B. **OPEN**

○   C. **DECLARE**

○   D. **FETCH**

○   E. **CONNECT**

22. An application developed using the DB2 Call Level Interface (CLI) is to be provided to a new user. What step does the user have to perform before the application can be used?

○   A. the application bind files need to be bound to the database

○   B. the CLI bind files need to be bound to the database

○   C. the db2cli.ini file needs to be updated to include the application name

○   D. the DB2 ODBC driver needs to be installed and configured

23. When are database object privileges checked when using CLI applications?

○   A. when the application is bound to the database

○   B. when the application is being developed (created)

○   C. when the application is being used by the end-user

○   D. when the db2cli.ini file is refreshed

24. Where is the isolation level defined for a DB2 CLI application?

○   A. in the system catalog tables

○   B. in the db2cli.ini file

○   C. in the application code

○   D. in the database configuration file

25. What must be installed to use an application, such as, Lotus Approach, to access a DB2 database?

    ○   A. an ODBC driver

    ○   B. the DB2 Software Developer's Kit (SDK)

    ○   C. the bind files for the application

    ○   D. the bind files for the Command Line Processor (CLP)

26. DB2 CLI applications may be written in which programming language?

    ○   A. COBOL

    ○   B. C

    ○   C. PL/1

    ○   D. Basic

27. Which SQL data structure is used to pass data arguments?

    ○   A. SQLCA

    ○   B. SQLOPT

    ○   C. SQLDATA

    ○   D. SQLDA

28. What is a valid file name extension for a C program module containing embedded dynamic SQL statments?

    ○   A. c

    ○   B. cpp

    ○   C. sql

    ○   D. sqc

Answers

1. (A)

   The **BIND** option **EXPLSNAP** is used to determine if the access plans for static SQL statements will gathered.

2. (D)

   Dynamic embedded SQL statements are issued using the **PREPARE**, **DECLARE**, **OPEN**, **FETCH**, **CLOSE** sequence. The statement is prepared into a statement identifier, a cursor is declared using the prepared statement and then the cursor is manipulated using the **OPEN**, **FETCH**, and **CLOSE** statements.

3. (C)

   The **PREPARE INTO** statement will describe the SQL statement and store the description of the statement in the provided SQLDA data strucutre

4. (A)

   A table check constraint may be defined to ensure that a data value always meets certain conditions.

5. (C)

   The **SQLIND** element of the SQLDA data structure is used to indicate that the data value is null or not null.

6. (A)

   There would be no extra SQLVAR elements for a single column **SELECT** statement.

7. (D)

   Casting functions are used to convert user defined types with their base data type.

8. (C)

   A user defined sourced function could be used to return the first 3 characters of a fixed character string data type (use the **SUBSTR** or **VALUES** SQL function).

9. (C)

   The **CALL** statement is used to invoked stored procedures (also known as DARI programs).

10. (D)

    Compound SQL may be used to execute a number of SQL statements as a group on the server. This would optimze the execution of the statements as less data would flow from the DB2 client and the server.

11. (B)

    A type 1 connection (default) only allows a single databaase connection within a unit of work.

12. (B)

    The **DISCONNECT** command is only used for type 2 connections. The command is used to release a connection to a database. The equivalent command in a type 1 connection environment is **CONNECT RESET**.

13. (C)

The uncommitted read (UR) isolation level allows an application to retrieve modified data which has not yet been committed.

14. (D)

When a data record is being modified an exclusive lock is required. An exclusive table lock or an exclusive row lock is required.

15. (C)

If a deadlock condition was detected the unit of work which was rolled back should be reissued by the application.

16. (D)

A share lock is compatible with another share lock. This allows multiple applications the ability to read data, but not modify the data, or allow the data to be modified.

17. (C)

A DB2 stored procedure may return data values in an SQLDA data structure.

18. (C)

A user-defined function may return data as a scalar value, an SQLDA data structure is not used.

19. (D)

Explain information is stored in special user tables, created using the DDL file called EXPLAIN.DDL.

20. (C)

A common table is a temporary table which is defined within a application. The temporary table definition is stored in the application and not in the system catalog tables. By contrast, VIEW definitions are stored in the system catalog tables.

21. (A)

The PREPARE statement is only used in dynamic embedded SQL applications. It is used to check the syntax and privileges for a given SQL statement.

22. (B)

The CLI bind files need to be bound to the database in order to use a DB2 CLI application. The CLI bind files are automatically bound to the database when a CLI application establishes a database connection.

23. (C)

Database object privileges are checked when they are issued by the end-user if the application is using the DB2 CLI interface.

24. ((B)

The isolation level used for CLI applications is established in the DB2CLI.INI file (located on the DB2 client).

25. (A)

To use an ODBC enabled application, such as Lotus Approach, an DB2 ODBC driver must be installed and configured.

26. (B)

   DB2 CLI applications are coded using the C/C++ programming language.

27. (D)

   The SQLDA data structure is used to store and retreive data arguments between the application and the database.

28. (D)

   A C program module containing embedded SQL statements needs to have the extension SQC during the **PRECOMPILE**.

Exercises

Part A — Dynamic Embedded SQL

1. Go to the Chapter 10/parta directory.Compile, link and execute the
    DYN1.SQC program.

    Examine the packages generated for DYN1. Examining the
    SYSCAT.PACKAGES tables for the DYN1 package. Also, use the **db2bfd**
    tool in the sqllib/misc directory.
    db2bfd dyn1.bnd -s
    Note: there are 4 sections.
    Section 0 is declaring host variables.
    Section 1 is a single row SELECT, acutally a VALUES statement.
    Section 2 is a dynamically prepare statement involving cursor c1.
    Section 3 is a DESCRIBE of another statement.

2. Examine the DYN2.SQC program.
    This program will finish a partially completed SQL statement (specifically, it
    will determine the **FROM** clause). The table or view in a FROM clause must be
    defined for static embedded SQL, but for dynamic SQL we can dynamically
    prepare the statement and return the results.

    The DYN2 program also demonstrates the usage of the SQLDA data struc-
    ture. To fully understand a dynamic SQL programming environment it is
    important to understand the use of this structure. Even CLI applications uti-
    lize the SQLDA data structure internally.

3. Examine the DYN3.SQC program.
    This program demonstrates the **EXECUTE IMMEDIATE** statement. In this pro-
    gram the statement being executed cannot be returning data. If a SELECT
    statement is attempted using this program an error would occur as there are
    no output variables defined.

    To allow any SELECT statement the application required would be much
    larger than DYN3.SQC.

Test Objectives
DB2 Fundamentals (500)

*T*his appendix includes the test objectives for exam number 500 — DB2 Fundamentals. To prepare for this exam, Chapter 1 through Chapter 5 should be completed. There are sample questions for this test located at the end of each of the chapters. Where appropriate, there are exercises provided at the end of each of the chapters. The test objectives are provided here to assist you in you in preparing for the DB2 Certification Exam.

DB2 Fundamentals (500) — Test Objectives

Installation and Planning

1.1 Given a situation, identify when to use DB2 Single-User or DB2 Server.
1.2 Identify characteristics of DB2 Single-User and DB2 Server.
1.3 Identify characteristics of DB2 Client Application Enabler (CAE).
1.4 Identify characteristics of DB2 Software Developer's Kit (SDK).
1.5 Given a situation, identify when to use Distributed Database Connection Services (DDCS).
1.6 Identify and explain the factors contributing to the size of a DB2 database.
1.7 Identify the software requirements for DB2.
1.8 Identify and explain the hardware requirements for DB2.
1.9 Identify base licensing for Server/SDK/DDCS.
1.10 Given a situation, identify the license requirements for Server/SDK/DDCS.
1.11 List communications protocols supported by DB2.
1.12 Identify required software for DB2 client/server scenarios.
1.13 Install DB2 Server or Single-User.
1.14 Install DB2 CAE/SDK.
1.15 Configure DB2 clients and servers using APPC/NETBIOS/TCPIP/IPXSPX

Security and Instances

2.1 Invoke the Command Line Processor.
2.2 Describe the functionality of the Database Director.
2.3 Create groups.
2.4 Create user ids.
2.5 Create DB2 instances using db2icrt.
2.6 Given a situation, identify required DB2 instances.
2.7 Identify characteristics of an instance.
2.8 Identify the active instance.
2.9 Identify database security groups.
2.10 Provide users with authority on database objects.

Creating and Accessing DB2 Databases

3.1 Create a DB2 database.
3.2 Interpret the contents of the system database directory.
3.3 Interpret the contents of the node directory.
3.4 Interpret the contents of the local database directory.
3.5 Catalog a node.
3.6 Catalog a remote database.
3.7 Catalog a local database.

SQL Usage

4.1 Given a DDL SQL statement, identify the results.
4.2 Given a DML SQL statement, identify the results.
4.3 Given a DCL SQL statement, identify the results.
4.4 Use SQL to SELECT data from a single table.
4.5 Use SQL to SELECT data from multiple tables.
4.6 Use SQL to SORT data.
4.7 Use SQL to UPDATE data.
4.8 Use SQL to DELETE data.
4.9 Use SQL to INSERT data.
4.10 Identify the effect of a COMMIT statement.
4.11 Identify the effect of a ROLLBACK statement.

Database Objects

5.1 Demonstrate usage of DB2 data types.
5.2 Given a situation, show how table spaces are used.
5.3 Identify default DB2 table spaces.
5.4 Identify the location of database objects.
5.5 Given a situation, create tables.
5.6 Given a situation, identify when referential constraints can be used.
5.7 Identify methods of data validation.
5.8 Identify and explain how DB2 logs are used.
5.9 Identify and explain how system catalogs are used.
5.10 Identify the characteristics of a view.
5.11 Identify the characteristics of an index.
5.12 Identify the characteristics of a database package.

Database Concurrency

6.1 Identify factors that influence locking.
6.2 List the objects that locks can be obtained on.
6.3 Identify the scope of different types of DB2 locks.
6.4 Identify factors affecting the types of locks that are used.
6.5 Differentiate the isolation level locking semantics.
6.6 Given a situation, identify the isolation level.

Test Objectives
DB2 Database Administration (501)

*T*his appendix includes the test objectives for exam number 501 — DB2 Database Administration. To prepare for this exam, Chapter 6 through Chapter 8 should be completed. There are sample questions for this test located at the end of each of the chapters. Where appropriate, there are exercises provided at the end of each of the chapters. The test objectives are provided here to assist you in you in preparing for the DB2 Certification Exam.

DB2 Database Administration (501) — Test Objectives

DB2 Server Management

1.1 Managing DB2 instances (authentication, scope).
1.2 Managing DB2 groups and users.
1.3 Differentiate database security levels.
1.4 Describe the use of the SYSADM, SYSCTRL, SYSMAINT authority levels.
1.5 Set user/group access to database objects using **GRANT/REVOKE**.
1.6 Force users/applications off of DB2.
1.7 Distinguishing between fenced and not fenced resources.
1.8 Explain how to set up a server to support various client protocols.

Data Placement

2.1 Create a database.
2.2 Differentiate between DMS and SMS table spaces.
2.3 Alter table space characteristics.
2.4 Explain how to determine table space pending states.

Database access

3.1 Bind applications to the database.
3.2 Create indexes on tables.
3.3 Create views on tables.
3.4 Set table check constraints.
3.5 Set referential constraints.
3.6 Examining the contents of the system catalog tables.

Monitoring DB2 Activity

4.1 Obtain/modify database manager configuration information.
4.2 Obtain/modify database configuration information.
4.3 Explain how the BUFFERPOOL is used.
4.4 Capture EXPLAIN information.
4.5 Analyze EXPLAIN information. (sortheap, buffpage)
4.6 Capture database monitor snapshots.
4.7 Analyze database monitor snapshot information.
4.8 Explain the aslheapsz parameter.
4.9 Explain how sorting is performed.
4.10 Explain/modify the caching parameters.
4.11 Explain the differences between monitor types.
4.12 Identify factors influencing network activity for DB2.

DB2 Utilities

5.1 Use **EXPORT** utility to extract data from a table.

5.2 Use **IMPORT** utility to insert data into a table.

5.3 Identify when to use different export file formats.

5.4 Use the **LOAD** utility to insert data into a table.

5.5 Identify when to use **IMPORT** vs. **LOAD**.

5.6 Using the **REORG** and **RUNSTATS** utilities.

Database Recovery

6.1 Perform a database-level **BACKUP**.

6.2 Perform a database-level **RESTORE**.

6.3 Set up linear logging.

6.4 Set up circular logging.

6.5 Perform a **ROLLFORWARD** recovery.

6.6 Examine contents of recovery history file.

6.7 Tablespace-level recovery.

Problem Determination

7.1 Analyze the contents of the SQLCA data structure.

7.2 Modify deadlock checking interval.

7.3 Determine applications which are causing concurrency problems.

7.4 Interpret basic information in the DB2DIAG.LOG file.

Test Objectives
DB2 Application Development (502)

This appendix includes the test objectives for exam number 502 — DB2 Application Development. To prepare for this exam, Chapter 9 through Chapter 10 should be completed. There are sample questions for this test located at the end of each of the chapters. Where appropriate, there are exercises provided at the end of each of the chapters. The test objectives are provided here to assist you in you in preparing for the DB2 Certification Exam.

DB2 Application Development (502) — Test Objectives

Database Objects

1.1 Understanding naming conventions of DB2 objects (aliases, views).
1.2 Examining packages.
1.3 Understanding authorities needed to access data in an application.
1.4 Locating database objects from the system tables

Data Manipulation (with host variables)

2.1 Querying data across multiple tables.
2.2 Changing data.
2.3 Utilize DB2 SQL functions.
2.4 Utilize common table expressions.
2.5 Identify when to use cursors in an SQL program.
2.6 Identify types of cursors.
2.7 Identify scope of cursors.
2.8 Manipulating cursors.
2.9 Managing a unit-of-work.

DB2 Programming Methods

3.1 Identify differences between dynamic and static embedded SQL.
3.2 Determine when to use CLI/ODBC.

Programming Basics — Embedded SQL

4.1 Identify steps involved in creating a static embedded SQL program.
4.2 Identify the output of the precompile phase of development.
4.3 Identify the output of the bind phase of development.
4.4 Identify when host variables are used (begin-declare).
4.5 Declaring host variables.
4.6 Utilizing host variables in queries.
4.7 Identify characteristics of DB2 programs written in C.
4.8 Identify characteristics of DB2 programs written in COBOL.
4.9 Explain/analyze content of SQLCA.
4.10 Precompile database programs (.sqc, .c, etc)
4.11 **BIND** database programs (common errors, tables exist).
4.12 Modify isolation levels at the program level.

Advanced Programming

5.1 Utilize dynamic SQL within programs.

5.2 Use the **PREPARE** statement within dynamic SQL.

5.3 Use the **DESCRIBE** statement within dynamic SQL.

5.4 How signal handlers are used with DB2.

5.5 Utilize RI within a program.

5.6 Explain/analyze content of SQLDA.

5.7 Embedding application logic in DB2 (constraints, triggers, views).

5.8 Casting UDTs within a program.

5.9 Identify usage of UDFs.

5.10 Identify when to use stored procedures.

5.11 Identify when to use compound SQL.

5.12 Connecting to databases within an application.

5.13 Concurrency considerations within an application.

Application Tuning

6.1 Obtain database configuration information.

6.2 Use Explain Facility to modify statements.

6.3 Analyze Visual Explain output.

DB2 Tools and Utilities

Tools are provided with DB2 to help the database administor. Many of these tools are provided on an "as-is" basis which means that they are not a necessary part of performing the tasks required of a database administrator, but they may be used to save time and better understand the DB2 environment.

DB2 Sample Tools and Utilties

These tools are locted in the **misc** sub-directory under the sqllib directory of the DB2 instance.

Performance Aids

db2batch — Benchmark Tool

The **db2batch** utility is a benchmark tool. A benchmark is usually a series of SQL statements which are used to examine the effects of configuration modifications. The db2batch utility is similar to the CLP, but it provides better performance and more information regarding the details of query execution. Usually the input for the db2batch utility would be placed in a file and the output would include detailed information regarding the execution of the query. To obtain more information about this utility issue **db2batch -h**.

db2evmon — Event Monitor Formating Tool

The **db2evmon** utility is an event monitor formating tool. If the DBA creates an event monitor and turns the monitor on to capture event records to disk, the output event records are in a binary format. The **db2evmon** tool can be used to analyze the captured event records. A graphical alternative to this tool is known as the event analyzer.

db2exfmt — Explain Table Extracting Tool

The **db2exfmt** utility simply gathers the important information for a group of explained SQL statements. The explain tables can be queried by any user with the proper access privileges, but the tool simplifies the process of analyzing the information in these tables. To obtain more information about this utility, issue **db2exfmt -h**.

db2expln — DB2 Explain Tool

The **db2expln** utility is similar to the Visual Explain facility as they both provide an access plan representation of SQL statements. It is highly recommended to use the Explain Facility and Visual Explain to interpret the explain information. The output of the db2expln utility is an ASCII report. It is an easy alternative method to obtain SQL access plans. To obtain more information about this utility, issue **db2expln -h**. (The dynexpln tool is a variation of the db2expln tool to explain a single SQL statement.)

DB2CERT Application Source Code

*T*he DB2CERT application is provided as a complete application which utilizes many of the features of DB2. The source code and the executables can be found on the companion CD-ROM.

```
/****************************************************************************
**
** Application = DB2CERT Application
**
** PURPOSE: This is the DB2 Certification application. Most of the modules
**          are not included here. To try out this application execute
**          the db2cert executable from the /exercise/chapter9/app/bin
**          directory on the CD-ROM for your platform.
**
**          The complete source code and build scripts for the application
**          are in the /exercise/chapter9/app/src directory for your
**          platform.
**
**          The program contains a complete text-based application including
**          input forms, modification forms, and various reports.
**
****************************************************************************/
#include <stdio.h>
#include <stdlib.h>
#include <string.h>
#include <time.h>
#include <sql.h>
#include <sqlcodes.h>
#include "cert.h"
#define sLine_Width 80

FILE *fp;

EXEC SQL BEGIN DECLARE SECTION;
char szCandidateID[10];
char szLName[31];
char szFName[31];
char cInitial;
char szHPhone[11];
char szWPhone[11];
char szStreetNo[9];
char szStreetName[21];
char szCity[31];
char szProvState[31];
char szCode[7];
char szCountry[21];
char cCertDBA;
char cCertAPP;
char szTestNumber[7];
char szTestName[51];
char cType;
short iCutScore;
short iCutScoreind;
short iLength;
char szCitySearch[31];
char szCitySearch2[50];
char szTCID[7];
char szTCName[41];
char cTCType;
char szPhone[11];
short iNoSeats;
char szDateTaken[14];
char szSeatNo[3];
char szStartTime[14];
char szFinishTime[14];
short iStartHour;
short iSMinutes;
short iFinishHour;
short iFMinutes;
short iSeatNo;
char szCurrentDate[14];
char szID[10];
char szDummy[31];
short iCnt500;
short iCnt501;
short iCnt502;
double dAvg500;
double dAvg501;
double dAvg502;
EXEC SQL END DECLARE SECTION;
```

```c
int main(int argc, char *argv[]) {

    char msg[255];
    char szUserid[9];
    char szPassword[19];
    char szTestNumber[7];
    char cMenu;
    char cSubMenu;
    short sTestLength;
    short retcode;

    setbuf(stdin,NULL);
    setbuf(stdout,NULL);
    strcpy (szUserid,"db2");
    strcpy (szPassword,"db2");

    fp = fopen ( "db2cert.err", "a+");
    if (fp == NULL) {
        return 1;
    } /* endif */

    if ((Start_Instance() ) < 0 ) {
        Record_SQL_Error ();
    } /* endif */

    if (Establish_Connection(szUserid,szPassword) < 0) {
        Record_SQL_Error ();
        goto finish;
    } /* endif */
    do {
      main_menu(&cMenu);
      switch (cMenu) {
      case '1' : do {
                  candidate_menu(&cSubMenu);

                  switch (cSubMenu) {
                    case '1' : Add_Candidate();
                               break;
                    case '2' : Delete_Candidate();
                               break;
                    case '3' : Modify_Candidate();
                               break;
                    case 'x' : break;
                    default  : break;
                    }
                 } while ( cSubMenu != 'x');
                 break;
        case '2' : do {
                  test_menu (&cSubMenu);
                  switch (cSubMenu) {
                    case '1' : Add_Test();
                               break;
                    case '2' : Modify_Test();
                               break;
                    case 'x' : break;
                    default  : break;
                    }
                 } while ( cSubMenu != 'x');
                 break;
        case '3' : do {
                  center_menu (&cSubMenu);
                  switch (cSubMenu) {
                    case '1' : Add_Center();
                               break;
                    case '2' : Modify_Center();
                               break;
                    case 'x' : break;
                    default  : break;
                    }
                 } while ( cSubMenu != 'x');
                 break;
        case '4' : do {
                  schedule_menu (&cSubMenu);
                  switch (cSubMenu) {
                    case '1' : List_Schedule();
                               break;
                    case 'x' : break;
                    default  : break;
```

```
                        }
                      } while ( cSubMenu != 'x');
                      break;
            case '5' : do {
                        score_menu (&cSubMenu);
                        switch (cSubMenu) {
                         case '1' : Update_Score_ID();
                                    break;
                         case '2' : Update_Score_Name();
                                    break;
                         case 'x' : break;
                         default  : break;
                         }
                      } while ( cSubMenu != 'x');
                      break;
            case '6' : Print_Test_Schedule();
                      break;
            case '7' : Print_Test_Summary();
                      break;
            default  : break;
            }
          } while (cMenu != 'x');
finish:

    printf ("Thank-you for using the DB2 Certification Application!!\n");
    fclose (fp);
    return 0;

}

void Record_SQL_Error ( )
{

 char szMessageBuffer[1024];
 short sBufferSize;
 short rc;
 struct tm tp;
 time_t ltime;

 sBufferSize = sizeof(szMessageBuffer);
 rc = sqlaintp ( szMessageBuffer, sBufferSize, sLine_Width, &sqlca);
 if (rc > 0) {      /* The length of the message is returned. */
     if (time (&ltime) != NULL){
        fprintf (fp, "%s", ctime(&ltime));
        fprintf (fp, "%s\n",szMessageBuffer );
        fflush (fp);
        }
 } /* endif */
 printf ("A database error has occurred. Please check db2cert.err file for details.\n");
 return;

}

void clr_screen(void)
{
short i;

    printf ("\n");
    fflush (stdout);
return;

}

void main_menu(char *cMenu)
{
    clr_screen();
    printf ("DB2 Certification Main Menu\n");
    printf ("============================\n\n");
    printf ("1 - Add/Remove/Modify a candidate\n");
    printf ("2 - Add/Remove/Modify a test\n");
    printf ("3 - Add/Remove/Modify a testing center\n");
    printf ("-------------------------------------\n");
    printf ("4 - Schedule a candidate for a test\n");
    printf ("5 - Enter a candidate's test score\n");
    printf ("--------------------------------\n");
    printf ("6 - Print a test schedule for a test center\n");
    printf ("7 - Print a summary of tests taken\n");
    printf ("--------------------------------\n");
```

```c
      printf ("x - Exit the DB2 Certification Application\n");
      *cMenu = getchar();
      if (*cMenu == 0x0a) {
         *cMenu =getchar();
      } /* endif */
      return;
}
void test_menu(char *cSubMenu)
{
   clr_screen();
   printf ("DB2 Certification Test Menu\n");
   printf ("===========================\n\n");
   printf ("1 - Add a new test\n");
   printf ("2 - Modify a test\n");
   printf ("--------------------------\n");
   printf ("x - Exit to Main Menu\n");
      *cSubMenu = getchar();
      if (*cSubMenu == 0x0a) {
         *cSubMenu =getchar();
      } /* endif */
      return;
}

void center_menu(char *cSubMenu)
{
   clr_screen();
   printf ("Testing Center Menu\n");
   printf ("==================\n\n");
   printf ("1 - Add a new test center\n");
   printf ("2 - Modify the number of seats\n");
   printf ("--------------------------\n");
   printf ("x - Exit to Main Menu\n");
      *cSubMenu = getchar();
      if (*cSubMenu == 0x0a) {
         *cSubMenu =getchar();
      } /* endif */
      return;
}
void schedule_menu(char *cSubMenu)
{
   clr_screen();
   printf ("DB2 Test Scheduling Menu\n");
   printf ("=========================\n\n");
   printf ("1 - List Exams at Test Center for a given Day\n");
   printf ("--------------------------\n");
   printf ("x - Exit to Main Menu\n");
      *cSubMenu = getchar();
      if (*cSubMenu == 0x0a) {
         *cSubMenu =getchar();
      } /* endif */
      return;
}
void score_menu(char *cSubMenu)
{
   clr_screen();
   printf ("Test Score Menu\n");
   printf ("===========================\n\n");
   printf ("1 - Find Candidate by ID number and update score\n");
   printf ("2 - Find Candidate by Name and update score\n");
   printf ("--------------------------\n");
   printf ("x - Exit to Main Menu\n");
      *cSubMenu = getchar();
      if (*cSubMenu == 0x0a) {
         *cSubMenu =getchar();
      } /* endif */
      return;
}
void candidate_menu(char *cSubMenu)
{
   printf ("DB2 Certification Test Candidate Menu\n");
   printf ("=====================================\n\n");
   printf ("1 - Add a test candidate\n");
   printf ("2 - Remove a test candidate\n");
   printf ("3 - Modify a test candidate\n");
   printf ("--------------------------\n");
   printf ("x - Exit to Main Menu\n");

      *cSubMenu = getchar();
```

```
        if (*cSubMenu == 0x0a) {
           *cSubMenu =getchar();
        } /* endif */
     return;
}
void Add_Candidate ()
{
char szInput[13];

   clr_screen();
   printf("Add Candidate Form\n");
   printf("==================\n\n");
   printf("Candidate ID \t:");
   scanf ("%9s",szCandidateID);
   if (!(Check_Candidate (szCandidateID))) {
      printf ("Surname \t:");
      scanf ("%30s",szLName);
      printf ("First Name\t:");
      scanf ("%30s",szFName);
      printf ("Initial\t\t:");
      cInitial = getchar();
      if (cInitial == 0x0a) {
         cInitial = getchar(stdin);
      } /* endif */

      do {
         printf ("Home Phone (999-999-9999)\t:");
         scanf ("%12s",szInput);
           } while ( (szInput[3] !='-') || (szInput [7] != '-'));
         strncpy (szHPhone,szInput,3);
         szHPhone[3] = '\0';
         strncat (szHPhone,szInput+4,3);
         szHPhone[6] = '\0';
         strncat (szHPhone,szInput+8,4);
         szHPhone[10] = '\0';
      do {
         printf ("Work Phone (999-999-9999)\t:");
         scanf ("%12s",szInput);
           } while ( (szInput[3] !='-') || (szInput [7] != '-'));
         strncpy (szWPhone,szInput,3);
         szHPhone[3] = '\0';
         strncat (szWPhone,szInput+4,3);
         szHPhone[6] = '\0';
         strncat (szWPhone,szInput+8,4);
         szHPhone[10] = '\0';
      printf ("Street Number \t:");
      scanf ("%7s",szStreetNo);
      printf ("Street Name \t:");
      scanf("%30s",szStreetName);
      printf ("City  \t\t:");
      scanf ("%30s",szCity);
      printf ("Province/State \t:");
      scanf ("%30s",szProvState);
      printf ("Code (Zip/Post)\t:");
      scanf ("%6s",szCode);
      printf ("Country \t\t:");
      scanf ("%20s",szCountry);

      EXEC SQL INSERT INTO candidate VALUES
                                  ( :szCandidateID,
                                    :szLName,
                                    :szFName,
                                    :cInitial,
                                    :szHPhone,
                                    :szWPhone,
                                    :szStreetNo,
                                    :szStreetName,
                                    :szCity,
                                    :szProvState,
                                    :szCode,
                                    :szCountry,
                                    'N',
                                    'N',
                                    NULL);

      if (SQLCODE != SQL_RC_OK)
         Record_SQL_Error();
```

```
    }
    else {
      printf ("Invalid Candidate ID. Candidate was not added to the database.\n");
      fflush (stdout);
    }

return;
}

void Add_Center ()
{
char szInput[13];

  clr_screen();
  printf("Add a Test Center\n");
  printf("=================\n\n");
  printf("Test Center ID \t:");
  scanf ("%7s",szTCID);
  if (!(Check_Center (szTCID))) {
    printf ("Center Name \t:");
    fflush(stdin);
    gets(szTCName);
    printf ("Type of Center (T)emporary (P)ermanent\t:");
    cTCType = getchar();
    if (cTCType == 0x0a) {
      cTCType = getchar();
    } /* endif */
    do {
      printf ("Phone (999-999-9999)\t:");
      scanf ("%12s",szInput);
        } while ( (szInput[3] !='-') || (szInput [7] != '-'));
      strncpy (szPhone,szInput,3);
      szHPhone[3] = '\0';
      strncat (szPhone,szInput+4,3);
      szHPhone[6] = '\0';
      strncat (szPhone,szInput+8,4);
      szHPhone[10] = '\0';
    printf ("Street Number \t:");
    scanf ("%7s",szStreetNo);
    printf ("Street Name \t:");
    scanf("%30s",szStreetName);
    printf ("City  \t\t:");
    scanf ("%30s",szCity);
    printf ("Province/State \t:");
    scanf ("%30s",szProvState);
    printf ("Code (Zip/Post)\t:");
    scanf ("%6s",szCode);
    printf ("Country \t:");
    scanf ("%20s",szCountry);
    printf ("Number of Seats \t:");
    scanf ("%i",&iNoSeats);

        EXEC SQL INSERT INTO test_center VALUES
                                    ( :szTCID,
                                      :szTCName,
                                      :szStreetNo,
                                      :szStreetName,
                                      :szCity,
                                      :szProvState,
                                      :szCountry,
                                      :szCode,
                                      :cTCType,
                                      :szPhone,
                                      :iNoSeats);

      if (SQLCODE != SQL_RC_OK)
         Record_SQL_Error();

         EXEC SQL COMMIT;

         if (SQLCODE != SQL_RC_OK) {
            Record_SQL_Error();
         }

  }
  else {
    printf ("Invalid Test Center ID. Test Center was not added to the database.\n");
  }
```

```
return;
}

void Modify_Candidate ()
{

char szInput[13];
char cChoice;

    clr_screen();
    printf("Modify Candidate Form\n");
    printf("====================\n\n");

    printf("Candidate ID \t:");
    scanf ("%9s",szCandidateID);


    if (Check_Candidate (szCandidateID)) {

    EXEC SQL SELECT CID,LNAME,FNAME,INITIAL,HPHONE,WPHONE,STREETNO,
                    STREETNAME,CITY,PROV_STATE,CODE,COUNTRY,CERT_DBA,CERT_APP
                    INTO
                        :szCandidateID,
                        :szLName,
                        :szFName,
                        :cInitial,
                        :szHPhone,
                        :szWPhone,
                        :szStreetNo,
                        :szStreetName,
                        :szCity,
                        :szProvState,
                        :szCode,
                        :szCountry,
                        :cCertDBA,
                        :cCertAPP
                    FROM candidate
                    WHERE CHAR(CID) = :szCandidateID;

        Display_Candidate_Record();

        printf ("Which field would you like to modify? (a..k) (x-exit)\t:");
        do {
         cChoice = getchar();
         if (cChoice == 0x0a) {
           cChoice = getchar();
         } /* endif */
        } while (cChoice < 'a' || (cChoice > 'k' && cChoice != 'x'));
        switch (cChoice) {
          case 'a' : printf ("New Last Name\t:");
                     scanf("%31s",szLName);
                     break;
          case 'b' : printf ("New First Name\t:");
                     scanf("%31s",szFName);
                     break;
          case 'c' : printf ("New Initial\t:");
                     cInitial = getchar();
                     if (cInitial == 0x0a) {
                       cInitial = getchar();
                     } /* endif */
                     break;

          case 'd' :
                   do {
                       printf ("Home Phone (999-999-9999)\t:");
                       scanf ("%12s",szInput);
                       } while ( (szInput[3] !='-') || (szInput [7] != '-'));
                   strncpy (szHPhone,szInput,3);
                   szHPhone[3] = '\0';
                   strncat (szHPhone,szInput+4,3);
                   szHPhone[6] = '\0';
                   strncat (szHPhone,szInput+8,4);
                   szHPhone[11] = '\0';
                   break;
          case 'e' :
                   do {
                       printf ("Work Phone (999-999-9999)\t:");
```

```
                          scanf ("%12s",szInput);
                       } while ( (szInput[3] !='-') || (szInput [7] != '-'));
                    strncpy (szWPhone,szInput,3);
                    szWPhone[3] = '\0';
                    strncat (szWPhone,szInput+4,3);
                    szWPhone[6] = '\0';
                    strncat (szWPhone,szInput+8,4);
                    szWPhone[11] ='\0';
                    break;
         case 'f' : printf ("New Street No \t:");
                     scanf ("%6s",szStreetNo);
                     break;
         case 'g' : printf ("New Street Name\t:");
                     scanf ("%30s",szStreetName);
                     break;
         case 'h' : printf ("New City\t:");
                     scanf ("%30s",szCity);
                     break;
         case 'i' : printf ("New Province/State \t:");
                     scanf ("%30s",szProvState);
                     break;
         case 'j' : printf ("New Code (Zip/Post)\t:");
                     scanf ("%7s",szCode);
                     break;
         case 'k' : printf ("New Country \t:");
                     scanf ("%30s",szCountry);
                     break;
         case 'x' : break;
         default  : break;
         } /* end of the switch statement */
            if ((cChoice >= 'a') && (cChoice <= 'k')){

            EXEC SQL UPDATE candidate
                        SET CID        = :szCandidateID,
                            LNAME      = :szLName,
                            FNAME      = :szFName,
                            INITIAL    = :cInitial,
                            HPHONE     = :szHPhone,
                            WPHONE     = :szWPhone,
                            STREETNO   = :szStreetNo,
                            STREETNAME = :szStreetName,
                            CITY       = :szCity,
                            PROV_STATE = :szProvState,
                            CODE       = :szCode,
                            COUNTRY    = :szCountry
                            WHERE CHAR(CID) = :szCandidateID;
            if (SQLCODE != SQL_RC_OK) {
                Record_SQL_Error();
            }
            EXEC SQL COMMIT;

            if (SQLCODE != SQL_RC_OK) {
                Record_SQL_Error();
            }
            } /* end if something was to be modified */
      }            /* end of the if Candidate exists clause */
   else {
     printf ("Invalid Candidate ID\n");
   }
return;
}

void Modify_Center ()
{

char szInput[13];
char cChoice;

   clr_screen();
   printf("Modify Center\n");
   printf("=============\n\n");

   printf("Center ID \t:");
   fflush (stdin);
   scanf ("%7s",szTCID);
   fflush (stdin);

   if (Check_Center (szTCID)) {
```

```
    EXEC SQL SELECT NOSEATS INTO :iNoSeats FROM test_center
                   WHERE TCID = CENTER_ID (:szTCID);

    printf("The only value that can be modified is the Number of Seats\n");
    printf("\nCurrently there are %d seats at this center.\n",iNoSeats);
    printf("New number of seats is: ");
    scanf ("%3d",&iNoSeats);

    EXEC SQL UPDATE test_center SET NOSEATS = :iNoSeats
         WHERE TCID = CENTER_ID (:szTCID);

    if (SQLCODE != SQL_RC_OK)
       Record_SQL_Error();

    EXEC SQL COMMIT;

    if (SQLCODE != SQL_RC_OK)
       Record_SQL_Error();
  }
  else
  {
    printf ("Not a valid test center ID\n");
  } /* endif */
  return;
}

void Delete_Candidate ()
{

char cChoice;

  clr_screen();
  printf("Delete Candidate Form\n");
  printf("====================\n\n");

  printf("Candidate ID \t:");
  scanf ("%9s",szCandidateID);


  if (Check_Candidate (szCandidateID)) {

    EXEC SQL SELECT CID,LNAME,FNAME,INITIAL,HPHONE,WPHONE,STREETNO,
                    STREETNAME,CITY,PROV_STATE,CODE,COUNTRY,CERT_DBA,CERT_APP
                    INTO
                      :szCandidateID,
                      :szLName,
                      :szFName,
                      :cInitial,
                      :szHPhone,
                      :szWPhone,
                      :szStreetNo,
                      :szStreetName,
                      :szCity,
                      :szProvState,
                      :szCode,
                      :szCountry,
                      :cCertDBA,
                      :cCertAPP
                    FROM candidate
                    WHERE CHAR(CID) = :szCandidateID;
    Display_Candidate_Record();

    printf ("Are you sure you would like to delete this candidate? (y/n)\t:");
    do {
      cChoice = getchar ();
      if (cChoice == 0x0a) {
        cChoice = getchar();
      } /* endif */
    } while (!(cChoice == 'y' || (cChoice == 'n')));
    if (cChoice == 'y'){
       EXEC SQL DELETE FROM candidate
                 WHERE CHAR(CID) = :szCandidateID;

       if (SQLCODE != SQL_RC_OK) {
          Record_SQL_Error();
       }
       EXEC SQL COMMIT;
```

```
      if (SQLCODE != SQL_RC_OK) {
          Record_SQL_Error ();
      }
   }   /* end of the if candidate is to be deleted */

}          /* end of the if Candidate exists clause */
else {
   printf ("Invalid Candidate ID\n");
}
return;
}

void Display_Test_Record()
{

  printf ("a-Test Name\t:%s\n",szTestName);
  printf ("b-Test Length\t:%d Minutes\n",iLength);
  if (cType == 'P') {
    printf ("c-(P) Production\n");
    if (iCutScoreind == 0) {
      printf ("d-Cut-Score \t:%d\n",iCutScore);
    } else {
      printf ("d-Cut-Score \t:NULL (not defined)\n");
    } /* endif */
  } else if (cType == 'B') {
    printf ("c-(B) Beta\n");
    printf ("Cut-score has not been established\n");
  }
  else
  {
    printf ("Invalid Test Type\n");
  } /* endif */

return;
}
void Display_Candidate_Record()
{

    printf ("a-Surname \t:%s\n",szLName);
    printf ("b-First Name\t:%s\n",szFName);
    printf ("c-Initial\t:%c\n",cInitial);
    printf ("d-Home Phone (999-999-9999)\t: %s\n",szHPhone);
    printf ("e-Work Phone (999-999-9999)\t: %s\n",szWPhone);
    printf ("f-Street Number \t:%s\n",szStreetNo);
    printf ("g-Street Name \t\t:%s\n",szStreetName);
    printf ("h-City  \t\t:%s\n",szCity);
    printf ("i-Province/State \t:%s\n",szProvState);
    printf ("j-Code (Zip/Post)\t:%s\n",szCode);
    printf ("k-Country \t\t:%s\n\n",szCountry);
    if (cCertDBA == 'Y') {
      printf ("This candidate is a Certified DB2 Database Administrator.\n");
    }
    if (cCertAPP == 'Y') {
      printf ("This candidate is a Certified DB2 Application Developer.\n\n");
    }

return;
}
void Add_Test ()
{

  clr_screen();
  printf("Add Test Form\n");
  printf("=============\n\n");
  printf("Test Number\t:");
  scanf ("%7s",szTestNumber);
  if (!(Check_Test (szTestNumber))) {
    printf ("Test Name\t:");
    fflush (stdin);
    gets (szTestName);
    printf ("Type (P-Production / B-Beta) \t:");
    scanf ("%1c",&cType);
    if (cType == 'P') {
      printf ("Cut Score \t:");
      scanf ("%d",&iCutScore);
    }
    else {
```

```
            iCutScoreind = -1;
          }
        printf ("Length (minutes)\t:");
        scanf ("%d",&iLength);

        EXEC SQL INSERT INTO test VALUES
                                ( :szTestNumber,
                                  :szTestName,
                                  :cType,
                                  :iCutScore:iCutScoreind,
                                  :iLength,
                                  0,
                                  0);

        if (SQLCODE != SQL_RC_OK)
           Record_SQL_Error();

        EXEC SQL COMMIT;

           if (SQLCODE != SQL_RC_OK) {
              Record_SQL_Error();
           }
    }
    else {
      printf ("Invalid Test Number\n");
    }

return;
}

void Modify_Test()
{

char cChoice;

    clr_screen();
    printf("Modify Test Form\n");
    printf("================\n\n");

    printf("Test ID \t:");
    scanf ("%7s",szTestNumber);

    if (Check_Test (szTestNumber)) {

       EXEC SQL SELECT NUMBER,NAME,TYPE,CUT_SCORE,LENGTH
                INTO :szTestNumber,
                     :szTestName,
                     :cType,
                     :iCutScore:iCutScoreind,
                     :iLength
                FROM
                     test
                WHERE
                     CHAR(NUMBER) = :szTestNumber;

       Display_Test_Record();

       printf ("Which field would you like to modify? (a-d, x-exit)\t:");
       do {
         cChoice = getchar ();
         if (cChoice == 0x0a) {
           cChoice = getchar();
         } /* endif */
       } while (cChoice < 'a' || (cChoice > 'e' && cChoice != 'x'));

       switch (cChoice) {
         case 'a' : printf ("New Test Name\t:");
                    scanf("%31s",szTestName);
                    break;
         case 'b' : printf ("New Test Length\t:");
                    scanf("%d",&iLength);
                    break;
         case 'c' : do {
                       printf ("New Test Type (P/B)\t:");
                       cType = getchar();
                       if (cType == 0x0a) {
                         cType = getchar();
                       } /* endif */
```

```
                         }
                      while (!(cType == 'P') && !(cType == 'B'));
                      break;
            case 'd' : printf ("New Cut-Score\t:");
                      scanf ("%d",&iCutScore);
                      break;
            default  : break;
              } /* end switch */

            if ((cChoice >= 'a') && (cChoice <= 'd')){

            EXEC SQL UPDATE test
                         SET NAME        = :szTestName,
                             LENGTH      = :iLength,
                             TYPE        = :cType,
                             CUT_SCORE   = :iCutScore
                         WHERE
                             CHAR(NUMBER) = :szTestNumber;

            if (SQLCODE != SQL_RC_OK) {
               Record_SQL_Error();
            }
            EXEC SQL COMMIT;

            if (SQLCODE != SQL_RC_OK) {
               Record_SQL_Error();
            }
      }  /* end of the if test is to be modified*/
   }       /* end of the if test exists clause */
  else {
    printf ("Invalid Test Number\n");
  }
return;
}

void List_Schedule ()
{

char cChoice;
short getoutnow=0;

  clr_screen();
  getchar();
  printf ("Which City would you like to take the test?\t:");
  fflush(stdin);
  gets(szCitySearch);
  strcpy (szCitySearch2,"%");
  strcat (szCitySearch2,szCitySearch);
  strcat (szCitySearch2,"%");

  EXEC SQL DECLARE c1 CURSOR FOR
          SELECT TCID, NAME,STREETNO,STREETNAME,CITY,PROV_STATE,
                 COUNTRY, CODE, TYPE, PHONE,NOSEATS
          FROM
                 test_center
          WHERE CHAR(city) LIKE :szCitySearch2
          FOR FETCH ONLY;

  EXEC SQL OPEN c1;
  do {
     EXEC SQL FETCH c1 INTO :szTCID,
                            :szTCName,
                            :szStreetNo,
                            :szStreetName,
                            :szCity,
                            :szProvState,
                            :szCountry,
                            :szCode,
                            :cTCType,
                            :szPhone,
                            :iNoSeats;
     if (SQLCODE == SQL_RC_OK) {
        printf ("Center Number\t:%s\n",szTCID);
        printf ("Center Name\t:%s\n",szTCName);
        printf ("City\t\t:%s\n",szCity);
        printf ("Number of Seats\t:%d\n\n",iNoSeats);

        printf ("Schedule at this Test Center (Y/N)?\t:");
```

```
        do {
          cChoice =getchar();
          if (cChoice == 0x0a) {
            cChoice = getchar();
          } /* endif */
        } while (!(cChoice =='Y') && !(cChoice =='N')); /* enddo */

        if (cChoice == 'Y') {
          getoutnow = 1;
        } /* endif */
      } /* endif */

    } while ((SQLCODE == SQL_RC_OK) && !(getoutnow));

    if (SQLCODE < SQL_RC_OK) {
        Record_SQL_Error();
        }
    else if (SQLCODE == 100) {
        printf ("No more Test Centers found for %s.\n",szCitySearch);
        printf ("Press <Enter> to Return to Menu\n");
        getchar();
        }
  EXEC SQL CLOSE c1;
  EXEC SQL COMMIT;
  if (getoutnow) {
    Sched_Test ();
  } /* endif */
  return;
}

void Sched_Test()
{

short sched[40][32];
char szTempHour[4];
char szTempHour2[4];
short iOffset;
short iOffset2;
short iSeatNumber;
short i,j;
char cChoice;
short ijunk;
short getout = 0;

    for (i=0;i<=39;++i ) {
    for (j=0;j<=31;++j ) {
      sched[i][j] = (short) 0x20;
    } /* endfor */
    } /* endfor */
  do {
      printf ("\nWhich date would you like to Schedule the Test? (MM/DD/YYYY)\t:");
      scanf ("%s",szDateTaken);

  EXEC SQL DECLARE c2 CURSOR FOR
          SELECT SEAT_NO, CID,
                 HOUR(START_TIME),MINUTE(START_TIME),
                 HOUR(FINISH_TIME),MINUTE(FINISH_TIME),
                 START_TIME,FINISH_TIME
          FROM
                 test_taken
          WHERE
                 CHAR(TCID) = :szTCID AND
                 DATE_TAKEN = :szDateTaken
          ORDER BY SEAT_NO, START_TIME;

    if (SQLCODE < SQL_RC_OK) {
        Record_SQL_Error();
        }

  EXEC SQL OPEN c2;
    if (SQLCODE < SQL_RC_OK) {
        Record_SQL_Error();
        }
  do {
    EXEC SQL FETCH c2 INTO :szSeatNo,
                           :szCandidateID,
                           :iStartHour,
                           :iSMinutes,
```

```
                                       :iFinishHour,
                                       :iFMinutes,
                                       :szStartTime,
                                       :szFinishTime;

        if (SQLCODE == SQL_RC_OK) {
           iSeatNumber = atoi(szSeatNo);
           iStartHour = iStartHour - 9;
           iFinishHour = iFinishHour - 9;

           for (i=(iStartHour*4+iSMinutes/15)  ;
                    i<(iFinishHour*4+iFMinutes/15) ;i++ ) {
             sched[iSeatNumber-1][i] = (short) 0x2A;
           } /* endfor */
           }
        } while (SQLCODE == SQL_RC_OK);

        printf ("Current Testing Schedule on %s for Test Center %s\n",
                  szDateTaken,szTCID);
        printf ("      \t          Test Times\n");
        printf ("Seat\t   9  10  11  12   1   2   3   4   5\n");

        for (i=0;i<iNoSeats;i++) {
          printf ("%d\t    ",i+1);
          for (j=0;j<=31 ;j++ ) {
          if (sched[i][j] == (short) 0x2A) {
            putchar(0x2A);
          } else {
            putchar(0x20);
          } /* endif */
          } /* endfor */
          printf ("\n");
        } /* endfor */

      EXEC SQL CLOSE c2;

       if (SQLCODE < SQL_RC_OK) {
          Record_SQL_Error();
          }
      EXEC SQL COMMIT;

       if (SQLCODE < SQL_RC_OK) {
          Record_SQL_Error();
          }

/* We will reopen the same cursor to reposition it to the first row. */

      EXEC SQL OPEN c2;
         if (SQLCODE < SQL_RC_OK) {
            Record_SQL_Error();
            }
         else if (SQLCODE != 100)
         {
         printf ("\n");
         printf ("Seat Number\tCandidate\tStart Time\tFinish Time\n");
         printf ("===========\t=========\t==========\t===========\n");
      do {
         EXEC SQL FETCH c2 INTO :szSeatNo,
                                :szCandidateID,
                                :iStartHour,
                                :iSMinutes,
                                :iFinishHour,
                                :iFMinutes,
                                :szStartTime,
                                :szFinishTime;
         if (SQLCODE == SQL_RC_OK) {
           printf ("%s         \t%s      \t%s         \t%s\n",szSeatNo,szCandidateID,szStart-
Time,szFinishTime);
         } /* endif */
         } while (SQLCODE == SQL_RC_OK);

      EXEC SQL CLOSE c2;

       if (SQLCODE < SQL_RC_OK) {
          Record_SQL_Error();
          }
      EXEC SQL COMMIT;
```

```
  if (SQLCODE < SQL_RC_OK) {
    Record_SQL_Error();
    }

  }  /* end if */
    do {
      printf("<x> to Exit to Main Menu or <s> to Schedule a test\n");
      cChoice = getchar();
      if (cChoice == 0x0a) {
        cChoice = getchar();
      } /* endif */
    } while (!(cChoice == 'x') && !(cChoice =='s')); /* enddo */

  if (cChoice == 's') {
      printf ("What is your Candidate ID?\t");
      scanf ("%s",szCandidateID);
      printf ("Which Test would you like to take?\t");
      scanf ("%s",szTestNumber);
      printf ("What time would you like to take the test?\t");
      scanf ("%s",szStartTime);

EXEC SQL SELECT LENGTH INTO :iLength FROM test
      WHERE CHAR (NUMBER) = :szTestNumber;

  if (SQLCODE < SQL_RC_OK) {
    Record_SQL_Error();
    }

EXEC SQL COMMIT;

  if (SQLCODE < SQL_RC_OK) {
    Record_SQL_Error();
    }

iSeatNo = 1;
do {

EXEC SQL INSERT INTO test_taken VALUES
                  ( :szCandidateID,
                    :szTCID,
                    :szTestNumber,
                    :szDateTaken,
                    :szStartTime,
                    NULL,
                    NULL,
                    NULL,
                    CHAR(:iSeatNo));

iSeatNo = iSeatNo +1;
ijunk = sqlca.sqlcode;
} while ( (SQLCODE < SQL_RC_OK) && (iSeatNo <= iNoSeats)); /* enddo */

iSeatNo--; /* Reset the seat number */

if (SQLCODE == SQL_RC_OK) {
  printf ("Your seat was assigned.\n");
  printf ("Seat Number \t:%d\n",iSeatNo);
  printf ("Start Time \t:%s\n",szStartTime);
  printf ("Finish Time \t:%s\n",szFinishTime);
} else
  if (SQLCODE == -438) {
      printf ("DB2 triggers identified that a seat could not be assigned.\n");
      printf ("Error Message: (%d) ",SQLCODE);
      getchar();
      for (i=0;i<sqlca.sqlerrml ;i++ ) {
          putchar( *((sqlca.sqlerrmc)+i));
      } /* endfor */
      printf("\n"); /* New Line */
  } else
    if ( SQLCODE == -503) {
        printf ("Error Message : Candidate ID is invalid!\n");
      } else {
        printf ("SQLCODE : %d\n",SQLCODE);
        getchar();
      } /* endif */
} /* endif */
EXEC SQL COMMIT;
```

```
    if (SQLCODE < SQL_RC_OK) {
       Record_SQL_Error();
       }

         printf("(x) to exit to Menu\n");
         printf("(s) to schedule another\n");
         do {
           cChoice = getchar();
           if (cChoice == 0x0a) {
             cChoice = getchar();
           } /* endif */

           if (cChoice == 'x') {
             getout = 1;
           } else if (cChoice == 's') {
             getout = 0;
           } /* endif */
         } while (!(cChoice == 'x') && !(cChoice == 's')); /* enddo */
    } while (!getout); /* enddo */
return;
}

void Print_Test_Summary()
{
char cChoice;
FILE *p;
char szFileOut[255];

printf("Print Test summary to (s)creen or (f)ile\t:");
do {
  cChoice = getchar();
  if (cChoice == 0x0a) {
    cChoice = getchar();
  }  /* endif */
} while (!((cChoice == 's') || (cChoice =='f')) );

if (cChoice == 'f') {
   printf ("Provide filename of Test Summary Report \t:");
   scanf ("%s",szFileOut);
   p = fopen ( szFileOut, "a+");
} else {
   p = stdout;
} /* endif */

EXEC SQL VALUES (CURRENT DATE) INTO :szCurrentDate;

if (SQLCODE < SQL_RC_OK) {
       Record_SQL_Error();
       }
fprintf (p,"Exam Summary Report as of %s\n",szCurrentDate);
fprintf (p,"=================================\n\n");

EXEC SQL
    SELECT COUNT(*) INTO :iCnt500
          FROM TEST_TAKEN WHERE SCORE IS NOT NULL AND
                   char(number) = '500';
EXEC SQL
    SELECT COUNT(*) INTO :iCnt501
          FROM TEST_TAKEN WHERE SCORE IS NOT NULL AND
                   char(number) = '501';
EXEC SQL
    SELECT COUNT(*) INTO :iCnt502
          FROM TEST_TAKEN WHERE SCORE IS NOT NULL AND
                   char(number) = '502';


fprintf (p,"Total 500 tests taken      : %d\n",iCnt500);
fprintf (p,"Total 501 tests taken      : %d\n",iCnt501);
fprintf (p,"Total 502 tests taken      : %d\n",iCnt502);
fprintf (p,"Total Number of tests taken : %d\n\n",iCnt500+iCnt501+iCnt502);

EXEC SQL
    SELECT COUNT(*) INTO :iCnt500
          FROM TEST_TAKEN WHERE SCORE IS NULL AND
                   number = test_id ('500');
EXEC SQL
    SELECT COUNT(*) INTO :iCnt501
```

```
                FROM TEST_TAKEN WHERE SCORE IS NULL AND
                        number = test_id ('501');
     EXEC SQL
        SELECT COUNT(*) INTO :iCnt502
                FROM TEST_TAKEN WHERE SCORE IS NULL AND
                        number = test_id ('502');

     fprintf (p,"Total 500 tests scheduled        : %d\n",iCnt500);
     fprintf (p,"Total 501 tests scheduled        : %d\n",iCnt501);
     fprintf (p,"Total 502 tests scheduled        : %d\n",iCnt502);
     fprintf (p,"Total Number of tests scheduled : %d\n\n",iCnt500+iCnt501+iCnt502);

     EXEC SQL
        SELECT AVG(SCORE) INTO :dAvg500
                FROM TEST_TAKEN WHERE SCORE IS NOT NULL AND
                        number = test_id ('500');
     EXEC SQL
        SELECT AVG(SCORE) INTO :dAvg501
                FROM TEST_TAKEN WHERE SCORE IS NOT NULL AND
                        number = test_id ('501');
     EXEC SQL
        SELECT AVG(SCORE) INTO :dAvg502
                FROM TEST_TAKEN WHERE SCORE IS NOT NULL AND
                        number = test_id ('502');

     fprintf (p,"Average for test 500 : %6.2f\n",dAvg500);
     fprintf (p,"Average for test 501 : %6.2f\n",dAvg501);
     fprintf (p,"Average for test 502 : %6.2f\n",dAvg502);


     return;
     }


     void Update_Score_ID()
     {
     char cChoice;
     char szID[11];
     unsigned long sID;

       clr_screen();

     printf ("Update test score\n");
     printf ("-----------------\n");
     printf ("Enter the candidate ID \t:");
        scanf ("%9s",szID);
        printf ("\nID was :%s\n",szID);

     EXEC SQL SELECT cid INTO :szDummy FROM candidate where CHAR(cid) = :szID;

     if (SQLCODE < 0 ) {
       printf ("The test candidate (%s) does not exist, please register the candi-
     date\n",szID);

     } else {
     } /* endif */
     EXEC SQL COMMIT;


        return;


     }
     void Update_Score_Name()
     {
     char cChoice;
     char szLName[50];

       clr_screen();

     printf ("Update test score\n");
     printf ("-----------------\n");
     printf ("Enter the candidate's Last Name (Surname) \t:");
        scanf ("%50s",szLName);
        printf ("\nName was :%s\n",szLName);

        return;
```

```
}
void Print_Test_Schedule()

{
char cChoice;
short getoutnow=0;
short sched[40][32];
char szTempHour[4];
char szTempHour2[4];
short iOffset;
short iOffset2;
short iSeatNumber;
short i,j;
short ijunk;

FILE *p;
char szFileOut[255];

clr_screen();
printf("Print Test Schedule to (s)creen or (f)ile\t:");
do {
  cChoice = getchar();
  if (cChoice == 0x0a) {
    cChoice = getchar();
  } /* endif */
} while (!((cChoice == 's') || (cChoice =='f')) );

if (cChoice == 'f') {
  printf ("Provide filename of Test Summary Report \t:");
  scanf ("%s",szFileOut);
  p = fopen ( szFileOut, "a+");
} else {
  p = stdout;
} /* endif */

/* Initialize the array for the test center schedule */
    for (i=0;i<=39;++i ) {
      for (j=0;j<=31;++j ) {
        sched[i][j] = (short) 0x20;
      } /* endfor */
    } /* endfor */

  getchar();
  printf ("Which City would you like to print a schedule?\t:");
  fflush(stdin);
  gets(szCitySearch);
  strcpy (szCitySearch2,"%");
  strcat (szCitySearch2,szCitySearch);
  strcat (szCitySearch2,"%");

      EXEC SQL DECLARE c4 CURSOR FOR
              SELECT TCID, NAME,STREETNO,STREETNAME,CITY,PROV_STATE,
                     COUNTRY, CODE, TYPE, PHONE,NOSEATS
              FROM
                    test_center
              WHERE CHAR(city) LIKE :szCitySearch2
              FOR FETCH ONLY;

      EXEC SQL OPEN c4;
      do {
          EXEC SQL FETCH c4 INTO :szTCID,
                                 :szTCName,
                                 :szStreetNo,
                                 :szStreetName,
                                 :szCity,
                                 :szProvState,
                                 :szCountry,
                                 :szCode,
                                 :cTCType,
                                 :szPhone,
                                 :iNoSeats;
          if (SQLCODE == SQL_RC_OK) {
             printf("Center Number\t:%s\n",szTCID);
             printf("Center Name\t:%s\n",szTCName);
             printf("City\t\t:%s\n",szCity);
             printf("Number of Seats\t:%d\n\n",iNoSeats);
```

```
        printf("Schedule at this Test Center (Y/N)?\t:");
        do {
          cChoice =getchar();
          if (cChoice == 0x0a) {
            cChoice = getchar();
          } /* endif */
        } while (!(cChoice =='Y') && !(cChoice =='N')); /* enddo */

        if (cChoice == 'Y') {
          getoutnow = 1;
        } /* endif */
        } /* endif */

     } while ((SQLCODE == SQL_RC_OK) && !(getoutnow));

     if (SQLCODE < SQL_RC_OK) {
        Record_SQL_Error();
        }
     else if (SQLCODE == 100) {
        printf ("No more Test Centers found for %s.\n",szCitySearch);
        printf ("Press <Enter> to Return to Menu\n");
        getchar();
        }
  EXEC SQL CLOSE c4;
  EXEC SQL COMMIT;
  if (getoutnow) {
     printf ("\nWhich schedule date? (MM/DD/YYYY)\t:");
     scanf ("%s",szDateTaken);

  EXEC SQL DECLARE c3 CURSOR FOR
          SELECT SEAT_NO, CID,
                         HOUR(START_TIME),MINUTE(START_TIME),
                         HOUR(FINISH_TIME),MINUTE(FINISH_TIME),
                         START_TIME,FINISH_TIME
          FROM
                  test_taken
          WHERE
                  CHAR(TCID) = :szTCID AND
                  DATE_TAKEN = :szDateTaken
          ORDER BY SEAT_NO, START_TIME;
     if (SQLCODE < SQL_RC_OK) {
        Record_SQL_Error();
        }

  EXEC SQL OPEN c3;
     if (SQLCODE < SQL_RC_OK) {
        Record_SQL_Error();
        }
  do {
      EXEC SQL FETCH c3 INTO :szSeatNo,
                             :szCandidateID,
                             :iStartHour,
                             :iSMinutes,
                             :iFinishHour,
                             :iFMinutes,
                             :szStartTime,
                             :szFinishTime;

     if (SQLCODE == SQL_RC_OK) {

        iSeatNumber = atoi(szSeatNo);
        iStartHour = iStartHour - 9;
        iFinishHour = iFinishHour - 9;


        for (i=(iStartHour*4+iSMinutes/15)  ;
               i<(iFinishHour*4+iFMinutes/15) ;i++ ) {
          sched[iSeatNumber-1][i] = (short) 0x2A;
        } /* endfor */
        }
     } while (SQLCODE == SQL_RC_OK);
     fprintf(p,"Current Testing Schedule on %s for Test Center %s\n",
              szDateTaken,szTCID);
     fprintf(p," \t       Test Times\n");
     fprintf(p,"Seat\t   9  10  11  12   1   2   3   4   5\n");

     for (i=0;i<iNoSeats;i++) {
```

```
           fprintf(p,"%d\t    ",i+1);
           for (j=0;j<=31 ;j++ ) {
           if (sched[i][j] == (short) 0x2A) {
             putc(0x2A,p);
           } else {
           } /* endif */
           } /* endfor */
           fprintf(p,"\n");
         } /* endfor */

      EXEC SQL CLOSE c3;

       if (SQLCODE < SQL_RC_OK) {
          Record_SQL_Error();
          }
      EXEC SQL COMMIT;

       if (SQLCODE < SQL_RC_OK) {
          Record_SQL_Error();
          }

/* We will reopen the same cursor to reposition it to the first row. */

      EXEC SQL OPEN c3;
         if (SQLCODE < SQL_RC_OK) {
            Record_SQL_Error();
            }
         else if (SQLCODE != 100)
         {
         fprintf(p,"\n");
         fprintf(p,"Seat Number\tCandidate\tStart Time\tFinish Time\n");
         fprintf(p,"===========\t=========\t==========\t===========\n");
      do {
         EXEC SQL FETCH c3 INTO :szSeatNo,
                                :szCandidateID,
                                :iStartHour,
                                :iSMinutes,
                                :iFinishHour,
                                :iFMinutes,
                                :szStartTime,
                                :szFinishTime;
         if (SQLCODE == SQL_RC_OK) {
         fprintf(p,"%s        \t%s       \t%s        \t%s\n",szSeatNo,szCandidateID,szStart-
Time,szFinishTime);
         } /* endif */
         } while (SQLCODE == SQL_RC_OK);
         } /* endif */

      EXEC SQL CLOSE c3;

       if (SQLCODE < SQL_RC_OK) {
          Record_SQL_Error();
          }
      EXEC SQL COMMIT;

       if (SQLCODE < SQL_RC_OK) {
          Record_SQL_Error();
          }
      } /* endif */
      return;
   }
```

Index

CD-ROM Installation

*T*he accompanying CD-ROM contains a complete set of DB2 products for Windows NT, Windows 95 and OS/2. These products are provided in "Try and Buy" mode. Once the product has been installed, it will continue to operate for 60 days. To use this software past the 60 day period requires a DB2 licence which is not provided. It is recommended to select **DB2 Single-User** during installation. The version of DB2 provided is Version 2.1.1 (English only). Remember, select "Try and Buy" mode during installation.

Windows NT and Windows 95 Installation
To install DB2 for Windows NT, perform the following steps:
Instructions are for an Intel processor, if you are using a Power PC-based system substitute I386 with PPC.

- Insert CD-ROM.
- From File Manager,
  Execute X:\I386\EN\DISK1\SETUP.EXE
  (where X is the drive letter of your CD drive).

To install DB2 for Windows 95, perform the same steps as Windows NT. The install should be performed using the Add/Remove program option from the Windows 95 Control Panel.

OS/2 Installation
To install OS/2 for Windows NT, perform the following steps:

- Insert CD-ROM.
- From an OS/2 Window,
  Execute X:\EN\INSTALL (where X is the drive letter of your CD drive).

✍ All DB2 commands must be issued from the DB2 CLP Window in Windows 95 and Windows NT. Also, ensure that the **DB2PATH** and the **DB2INSTANCE** environment variables are set properly.

End of Chapter Exercises

All of the end of chapter exercises are contained within the X:\EXERCISE directory on the CD-ROM. It is recommended to copy all of the exercise files to a local drive. Use operating system file copy commands to perform this task.

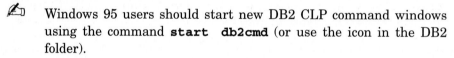   UNIX users will need to read the CD-ROM from a Windows or OS/2 workstation. It is recommended to copy all of the exercise files to the DB2 (UNIX) workstation using a network file transfer.

Performing the Exercises

The exercises can be completed individually for the most part. Most of the source code and executables are located in the x:\exercise\chapter9 directory. The **DB2CERT2** application (see Appendix E for source code) can be found in the partb directory. The sample UDF, *idformat* and the **REORGIT** application can be found in the parta directory.

To use the **DB2CERT2** application the **DB2CERT** database should be recreated and populated with new table data. The **DB2CERT** database can be recreated using the CLP files in the x:\exercise\chapter9\data directory.

     Windows 95 users should start new DB2 CLP command windows using the command **start db2cmd** (or use the icon in the DB2 folder).

LICENSE AGREEMENT AND LIMITED WARRANTY

READ THE FOLLOWING TERMS AND CONDITIONS CAREFULLY BEFORE OPENING THIS CD PACKAGE. THIS LEGAL DOCUMENT IS AN AGREEMENT BETWEEN YOU AND PRENTICE-HALL, INC. (THE "COMPANY"). BY OPENING THIS SEALED CD PACKAGE, YOU ARE AGREEING TO BE BOUND BY THESE TERMS AND CONDITIONS. IF YOU DO NOT AGREE WITH THESE TERMS AND CONDITIONS, DO NOT OPEN THE CD PACKAGE. PROMPTLY RETURN THE UNOPENED CD PACKAGE AND ALL ACCOMPANYING ITEMS TO THE PLACE YOU OBTAINED THEM FOR A FULL REFUND OF ANY SUMS YOU HAVE PAID.

1.   **GRANT OF LICENSE:** In consideration of your purchase of this book, and your agreement to abide by the terms and conditions of this Agreement, the Company grants to you a nonexclusive right to use and display the copy of the enclosed software program (hereinafter the "SOFTWARE") on a single computer (i.e., with a single CPU) at a single location so long as you comply with the terms of this Agreement. The Company reserves all rights not expressly granted to you under this Agreement.

2.   **OWNERSHIP OF SOFTWARE:** You own only the magnetic or physical media (the enclosed CD) on which the SOFTWARE is recorded or fixed, but the Company and the software developers retain all the rights, title, and ownership to the SOFTWARE recorded on the original CD copy(ies) and all subsequent copies of the SOFTWARE, regardless of the form or media on which the original or other copies may exist. This license is not a sale of the original SOFTWARE or any copy to you.

3.   **COPY RESTRICTIONS:** This SOFTWARE and the accompanying printed materials and user manual (the "Documentation") are the subject of copyright. The individual programs on the CD are copyrighted by the authors of each program. Some of the programs on the CD include separate licensing agreements. If you intend to use one of these programs, you must read and follow its accompanying license agreement. If you intend to use the trial version of Internet Chameleon, you must read and agree to the terms of the notice regarding fees on the back cover of this book. You may not copy the Documentation or the SOFTWARE, except that you may make a single copy of the SOFTWARE for backup or archival purposes only. You may be held legally responsible for any copying or copyright infringement which is caused or encouraged by your failure to abide by the terms of this restriction.

4.   **USE RESTRICTIONS:** You may not network the SOFTWARE or otherwise use it on more than one computer or computer terminal at the same time. You may physically transfer the SOFTWARE from one computer to another provided that the SOFTWARE is used on only one computer at a time. You may not distribute copies of the SOFTWARE or Documentation to others. You may not reverse engineer, disassemble, decompile, modify, adapt, translate, or create derivative works based on the SOFTWARE or the Documentation without the prior written consent of the Company.

5.   **TRANSFER RESTRICTIONS:** The enclosed SOFTWARE is licensed only to you and may not be transferred to any one else without the prior written consent of the Company. Any unauthorized transfer of the SOFTWARE shall result in the immediate termination of this Agreement.

6.   **TERMINATION:** This license is effective until terminated. This license will terminate automatically without notice from the Company and become null and void if you fail to comply with any provisions or limitations of this license. Upon termination, you shall destroy the Documentation and all copies of the SOFTWARE. All provisions of this Agreement as to warranties, limitation of liability, remedies or damages, and our ownership rights shall survive termination.

7.   **MISCELLANEOUS:** This Agreement shall be construed in accordance with the laws of the United States of America and the State of New York and shall benefit the Company, its affiliates, and assignees.

8.   **LIMITED WARRANTY AND DISCLAIMER OF WARRANTY:** The Company warrants that the SOFTWARE, when properly used in accordance with the Documentation, will operate

in substantial conformity with the description of the SOFTWARE set forth in the Documentation. The Company does not warrant that the SOFTWARE will meet your requirements or that the operation of the SOFTWARE will be uninterrupted or error-free. The Company warrants that the media on which the SOFTWARE is delivered shall be free from defects in materials and workmanship under normal use for a period of thirty (30) days from the date of your purchase. Your only remedy and the Company's only obligation under these limited warranties is, at the Company's option, return of the warranted item for a refund of any amounts paid by you or replacement of the item. Any replacement of SOFTWARE or media under the warranties shall not extend the original warranty period. The limited warranty set forth above shall not apply to any SOFTWARE which the Company determines in good faith has been subject to misuse, neglect, improper installation, repair, alteration, or damage by you. EXCEPT FOR THE EXPRESSED WARRANTIES SET FORTH ABOVE, THE COMPANY DISCLAIMS ALL WARRANTIES, EXPRESS OR IMPLIED, INCLUDING WITHOUT LIMITATION, THE IMPLIED WARRANTIES OF MERCHANTABILITY AND FITNESS FOR A PARTICULAR PURPOSE. EXCEPT FOR THE EXPRESS WARRANTY SET FORTH ABOVE, THE COMPANY DOES NOT WARRANT, GUARANTEE, OR MAKE ANY REPRESENTATION REGARDING THE USE OR THE RESULTS OF THE USE OF THE SOFTWARE IN TERMS OF ITS CORRECTNESS, ACCURACY, RELIABILITY, CURRENTNESS, OR OTHERWISE.

IN NO EVENT, SHALL THE COMPANY OR ITS EMPLOYEES, AGENTS, SUPPLIERS, OR CONTRACTORS BE LIABLE FOR ANY INCIDENTAL, INDIRECT, SPECIAL, OR CONSEQUENTIAL DAMAGES ARISING OUT OF OR IN CONNECTION WITH THE LICENSE GRANTED UNDER THIS AGREEMENT, OR FOR LOSS OF USE, LOSS OF DATA, LOSS OF INCOME OR PROFIT, OR OTHER LOSSES, SUSTAINED AS A RESULT OF INJURY TO ANY PERSON, OR LOSS OF OR DAMAGE TO PROPERTY, OR CLAIMS OF THIRD PARTIES, EVEN IF THE COMPANY OR AN AUTHORIZED REPRESENTATIVE OF THE COMPANY HAS BEEN ADVISED OF THE POSSIBILITY OF SUCH DAMAGES. IN NO EVENT SHALL LIABILITY OF THE COMPANY FOR DAMAGES WITH RESPECT TO THE SOFTWARE EXCEED THE AMOUNTS ACTUALLY PAID BY YOU, IF ANY, FOR THE SOFTWARE.

SOME JURISDICTIONS DO NOT ALLOW THE LIMITATION OF IMPLIED WARRANTIES OR LIABILITY FOR INCIDENTAL, INDIRECT, SPECIAL, OR CONSEQUENTIAL DAMAGES, SO THE ABOVE LIMITATIONS MAY NOT ALWAYS APPLY. THE WARRANTIES IN THIS AGREEMENT GIVE YOU SPECIFIC LEGAL RIGHTS AND YOU MAY ALSO HAVE OTHER RIGHTS WHICH VARY IN ACCORDANCE WITH LOCAL LAW.

ACKNOWLEDGMENT

YOU ACKNOWLEDGE THAT YOU HAVE READ THIS AGREEMENT, UNDERSTAND IT, AND AGREE TO BE BOUND BY ITS TERMS AND CONDITIONS. YOU ALSO AGREE THAT THIS AGREEMENT IS THE COMPLETE AND EXCLUSIVE STATEMENT OF THE AGREEMENT BETWEEN YOU AND THE COMPANY AND SUPERSEDES ALL PROPOSALS OR PRIOR AGREEMENTS, ORAL, OR WRITTEN, AND ANY OTHER COMMUNICATIONS BETWEEN YOU AND THE COMPANY OR ANY REPRESENTATIVE OF THE COMPANY RELATING TO THE SUBJECT MATTER OF THIS AGREEMENT.

Should you have any questions concerning this Agreement or if you wish to contact the Company for any reason, please contact in writing at the address below.

Robin Short
Prentice Hall PTR
One Lake Street
Upper Saddle River, New Jersey 07458